The Sports Funding Guide

Second Edition

Nicola Eastwood

With contributions from:

Richard Baldwin, Deloitte & Touche
Martin Cannon, Cannon Communications
Lindsay Driscoll, Sinclair Taylor & Martin Solicitors
Public Affairs Unit, Sport England Lottery Unit

DIRECTORY OF SOCIAL CHANGE

in association with

SPORT ENGLAND

Published by:
The Directory of Social Change
24 Stephenson Way
London NW1 2DP
Tel: 0171 209 5151, Fax: 0171 209 5049
E-mail: info@d-s-c.demon.co.uk
from whom further copies and a full publications list are available

Loughborough
COLLEGE est 1909

The Directory of Social Change is a Registered Charity no. 800517

First published 1995
Second edition 1999
Copyright © The Directory of Social Change 1995 and 1999

ISBN 1 900360 49 7

British Library Cataloguing in Publication Data
A catalogue record for this book is available from the British Library

Cover design by Kate Bass
Designed and typeset by Midlands Book Typesetting Company
Printed and bound by Page Bros., Norwich

Directory of Social Change London Office:
Courses and Conferences tel: 0171 209 4949
Charityfair tel: 0171 209 1015
Research tel: 0171 209 4422
Finance and Administration tel: 0171 209 0902

Directory of Social Change Northern Office:
3rd Floor, Federation House, Hope Street, Liverpool L1 9BW
Research tel: 0151 708 0136
Courses and Conferences tel: 0151 708 0117

Contents

Introduction

The second edition

The first edition of the *Sports Funding Guide* was published in 1995. It was very successful and found its place quickly on the bookshelves of those looking for money to develop their sport. Although it is already difficult to remember a funding climate without the National Lottery, the first edition of the Guide coincided with the first year of lottery sports grants. It is now firmly established as a central funder of sport. The dash for cash has quickened as television rights and the growing professionalism of formerly amateur games make sport a bigger economic concern than ever. The second edition of the Guide is written in a time when there has never been more money in sport, but also where there has never been as great a need for a variety of funders.

Sport and its economic place

Sport and physical recreation are an integral part of British life. Around 65% of the adult British population participate in sport and physical recreation each month. Sport provides jobs for nearly 500,000 people, contributes £3.6 billion in taxation and attracts £10.4 billion in consumer spending in the UK. Worldwide, sport is thought to account for 2.5% of world trade or 1% of European Community Gross National Product. More and more people are participating in a wider and wider variety of sports.

The scope of this book

This book is about raising money for sport. It is written in the belief that sport can be an important force for positive change, both in society and in individual people. It is concerned as much with participation as with excellence. It does not cover how to run sports clubs or how to train future world champions. Rather, it deals with the different range of fundraising possibilities and how best to exploit them.

Some of those involved in sport stress the importance of sport for the sake of sport, whilst others highlight the place of sport in the economic and social life of the country. Throughout this Guide there are pointers to the part sport plays in the wider scheme of things, especially in helping bring new heart to disadvantaged communities. It becomes clearer that the government is looking to sport as never before to earn its place and to provide new solutions to social and economic challenges.

Since the previous edition there have been fundamental changes in the way that sport is run nationally. A new government department that names sport in its letterhead – The Department for Media, Culture and Sport – has replaced the Department of National Heritage. Two new Sports Councils have emerged – Sport England and the UK Sports Council – to cover participation and excellence. (Even at the time of writing the English Sports Council evolved into Sport England.) The UK Sports Institute has arrived to produce champions.

Alongside these structural changes has been a change of government and with it new priorities that will have a significant impact upon the way sport is administered and funded. The growing regionalisation of government for example will alter how sport is represented regionally. The New Opportunities Fund will decrease the amount of money available to sport through the National Lottery. Furthermore, changing EU directives have affected the amounts available directly for sport.

Winners and nearly winners

It was obvious from the first Guide that some sports are, and have always been, successful in attracting money. It remains the case in this Guide where cricket, golf, rugby union, football, sailing, tennis and rowing for example have well established social, professional and sporting networks that harness public, charitable and sponsorship support. Other sports do less well, and will have to work harder at developing contacts and making their case, particularly to funders where there is no background of giving to sport.

Be creative

It is clear that some of the old ways of fundraising are still some of the best. For example, at the local level a really good sponsored activity can raise cash, increase membership, generate good publicity and still give people a really good time. Indeed, this kind of smaller-scale fundraising will remain at the heart of many clubs' income generation plans. Also, the most successful fundraising is about maximising available support from existing supporters rather than constantly scouting around for new funding sources.

However, as in many areas of public life, 'partnership' is now the key word. The Cricket Foundation's 1998 annual report stresses the need for cricket clubs to cast their net widely for future funders: 'As cricket faces up to the realities of life in a world of fierce market place competition and intense demand for limited resources so the ECB and County Boards alike must be alert to, and embrace, the benefits that can be realised by partnership arrangements... Cricket must think laterally and take responsibility for its own future. This can only be done in partnership with other agencies that can provide a resource or service to the sport...'

Partnerships are now a reality. For example, to obtain money from the National Lottery, the Single Regeneration Budget or from Europe – to name but three – clubs have to show either that they can raise some of the money from elsewhere or that they are working with other organisations.

It is increasingly hard to raise money for your whole club or organisation. Most donors want to achieve something particular with their money. So, it may well be that as a fundraiser you stop seeing your club as one organisation, rather you see it as a series of separate but related projects. It may require you to divide your work into different elements and raise money from a range of funders. It may even mean that you will have to begin to do new things or work with new people in new ways. It may not simply be a question of 'this is what we do and this is what we need'; applicants may have to be more sophisticated than that. For example, to raise money from grant-making trusts, applicants have to show that their work is charitable in law. This may restrict the application to the youth section or a club's work with disabled or disadvantaged people.

Depending upon your perspective, having insufficient funds can be a problem or an opportunity. It is a problem because your club needs the cash. It is also an opportunity for the club to think creatively and imaginatively about what it is doing. It may encourage those working in sports clubs and societies to meet influential people, to recruit celebrities, to negotiate exciting sponsorship deals, to run high class events. In fact, it can be the spur to make you do what you've always wanted to do, but have never had the impetus. It can be the project that revitalises your club and fires your members' enthusiasm. Thinking through some of these possibilities and making them happen is the purpose of this book.

Acknowledgements

I am very grateful to all those who have helped the research for the Guide in any way. To name everyone would be impossible. However, in addition to those contributors credited on the title page, I would also like to thank David Carpenter, Roger Coombes, Susan Forrester, Chris Goldie, Sean Lee, Jonathan O'Neil, Bethany Rawles, Geoff Thompson, Joe Waterton and Rachel Wilson for their invaluable help, and John Smyth who helped start the whole thing with his work on the first Guide. Mike Eastwood remains the best coach.

As always, I am appreciative of all those who corrected entries and drafts, sometimes at short notice. However, the text and any errors within it remain ours alone.

Conclusion

The research was done as fully and carefully as possible, but there may be funding sources that have been missed and some information may be incomplete or will become out of date. If any reader comes across omissions or mistakes in the book, please let us know so that they can be rectified in future editions. A telephone call to the Research Department of the Directory of Social Change (0151-708 0136) is all that is needed.

And finally ...

It is often said that fundraising is simple but never easy. This Guide explains the rules of the game as we see them, but it still requires persistence and hard work. However, a successful outcome usually makes it all worthwhile. Good luck!

Nicola Eastwood
December 1998

How to use this guide

This book is organised into three sections as follows:

The first four chapters form section 1. They give you the basic tools to start fundraising and to increase your chances of success. Anyone new to fundraising should read them before they move onto the fundraising sources in section 2.

Section 2, chapters 5 to 15 details the main areas of funding available to sports organisations. You need to think about what you want support for in order to decide who to apply to.

The main sources of support are:

The Sports Councils

For further information, see chapter 6.

The National Lottery

This is the largest single giver to sport with about £200 million available a year. It is administered by the Sports Councils. Grants are given for capital projects (that is buildings, equipment etc.), as well as élite performers.

For further information see chapter 7 for capital grants and chapter 14 for grants to individuals.

Governing bodies

All major sports have their own governing body. Their role is mainly to develop their sport. However, some give grants to organisations and individuals. They are also useful sources of advice and endorsement.

For further information, see chapter 15.

Companies

Company sponsorship for sport is a big money area. However, it is not all for test match cricket or premier league football. A great deal of sponsorship takes place at the local level and involves sums of a couple of hundred pounds.

For further information, see chapter 9.

Sportsmatch

This is a pool of money which can be used to match some sponsorship payments made by companies. This means that you can double your sponsorship income at no extra cost to you. It has recently been widened to allow for smaller projects.

For further information, see chapter 9.

Grant-making trusts

These are charities which give money to other charities. Some are for specific sports; most are for wider community benefit either locally or nationally. Most support salaries and project costs for up to three years; others give small one-off grants for equipment or to individuals.

For further information, see chapter 12 for grants to organisations and chapters 12 and 14 for grants to individuals.

The Foundation for Sport and the Arts

The largest sports specific grant–making trust and one of the largest of all funders of sport.

For further information, see chapter 8.

Central and regional government

Most government money for sport is directed through the Sports Councils and the National Lottery. However, there are other support programmes which are not aimed specifically at sports organisations but which sports groups can apply to for certain activities.

For further information, see chapter 10.

Local authorities

Central government support for sports is also directed to local authority departments responsible for sport and leisure in their area. Support for project costs, programme development, equipment, salaries and so on can still be raised from your local authority. As with central government, sports organisations can also apply to programmes not aimed specifically at sports activities. Each will be different and there are guidelines for making your approach.

For further information, see chapter 11.

European money

There is a variety of support programmes within the European Union. Where sports projects have been successful, they have often been involved with large scale developments, employment training initiatives or part of a targeted economic and geographical area. There is also a dedicated sports programme of funding.

For further information, see chapter 13.

Members, friends, the local community

These represent possibly the largest of all funders of sport as donors, event organisers, sponsors, fundraisers, collectors, buyers of raffle tickets etc. Ignore them at your peril!

For further information, see chapter 5.

Section 3 of the book contains two chapters on financial and legal administration for your organisation. Both are essential to efficient fundraising.

There is a list of useful addresses and contacts and an index of the funding sources at the back of the book.

Chapter 1

Getting started in fundraising

■■

Raising money is a challenge. Sometimes it is frustrating, sometimes it is immensely enjoyable; sometimes you win, sometimes you don't. It is often rewarding; it is always hard work. Like any game, fundraising has its own rules. This section explains the basic rules and gives you strategies for success.

The fundraiser

In theory, anyone can be a fundraiser. You don't have to belong to a particular professional body; you don't have to take exams; you don't even have to have done it before. However, it is important that you get the right person to do it. The fundraiser will be saying all kinds of things about your organisation and making all kinds of promises on your behalf; if he or she says or does the wrong thing, it will reflect badly on you. So what do you need to be a good fundraiser?

Time
There are few quick fundraising fixes. Getting serious money takes serious time. It may be a year before you get your first big grant. Be realistic from the start both about how much time you all have and how much time it will all take.

Commitment
This is one of the most important qualities in any fundraiser. It soon becomes clear to the outsider if people are just going through the motions. Some people can raise fortunes through sheer force of personality, even if they break all the fundraising rules.

Stamina and persistence
Fundraising can be a hard and dispiriting business. People who quit easily will not succeed. Those who keep their eyes on the prize are usually successful.

Truthfulness and realism
There can be a temptation to promise the earth in order to get money, or to say what you know the donor wants to hear. This is a recipe for fundraising disaster. Raise money for what you want and for what you know you can deliver. What's the point in having a state-of-the-art facility if you have no money to run it?

Knowledge

When talking to potential donors, you must be able to answer their questions. The fundraiser who says: 'I'm never allowed to see the books so I don't know how much money we've got' is on a loser from the start.

Equipment

You will need at least a telephone (and maybe an answering machine) and a typewriter or word processor and printer. You don't necessarily have to buy them; you may well be able to borrow or scrounge them from members, supporters, local companies or whoever.

Willingness to ask

One major charity commissioned a piece of research about why people were not supporting them. Was it the charity's image? Was it the cause? Was it donor fatigue? No, it was simply that the people had never been asked. We often assume that just because people know we are there and that we need the money then they will dig into their pockets. They may well give, but only if we ask them to.

Opportunism

The good fundraiser makes things happen. For example, the difference between an OK event and a successful one could be the fact that a major sporting celebrity turns up. This always gives an event a high profile and prestige. Often such people come because somebody knows somebody who knows them. The alert fundraiser breaks into these networks. Or perhaps a local company is having a really good (or really bad) time, so is ripe to sponsor an event to celebrate their success (or restore their image and profile). The opportunist gets in there, and first.

Luck

You may just happen to say the right thing at the right time, or bump into someone who could be a really useful contact. For example, a colleague was recently doing a radio interview about a new community sports project. After the broadcast a major funder who happened to be listening rang the radio station to find out more and the funder and project were put into contact with each other. You cannot plan for this. However, you must be ready to make the most of any opportunities.

To say thank you

Remember, getting money is only the start of the process. Once people have given once, they are more likely to give again, but only if you treat them properly. At the very least say thank you. You should also aim to keep them informed of what is going on.

Six golden rules of fundraising

Fundraising is a people business

People do not give to organisations; they do not give to abstract concepts. They give to help people or to do something to create a better world. The fundraiser is the person who shows them how to achieve this. Always stress the human aspect of your work – how you give people a new chance in sport and/or life, or enable them to experience things they otherwise wouldn't, or whatever.

Fundraising is about the donor

Too many fundraisers concentrate on what they want to tell the donor ('we do this' or 'we need that'). However, you need to scratch each donor where he or she itches. Always ask yourself: 'Why would this donor want to support us? What are their particular concerns and interests?' For example, a parent who simply wants their child to learn to play badminton will give on a totally different basis to a company thinking of its future workforce. Try and get into the minds of the different donors and show that you understand their specific interests and concerns and are doing something about them.

The more personal the better

Donors like to be treated and appreciated as individuals. So the more personal you can make your approach the better. A face-to-face meeting is far better than a personalised letter which is far better than a circular letter which is far better than a poster.

Fundraising is selling

Fundraising is a two-stage process. The first thing you need to do is show people there is an important need and that you can do something useful about it. If they agree that the need is important and that something should be done; if they agree that your organisation is doing something significant to make a difference; and if you can show them how some extra support will help you do something even better – then the second stage of asking for money becomes easy. Fundraising is more about selling an idea that the donor can make a difference than it is about asking for money. Once people have been sold the idea, they will normally want to give.

Giving is a matter of trust

People give money to you on the understanding that you will do certain good things. You need to show that you are capable of doing the work, that the money will actually achieve something, that they can trust you to use their money well. This generally boils down to your credibility. In other words, can you show the donor that you have done things like this really successfully before; that you have really good people to do the work; that you are well-liked and respected throughout the community; that lots of other people trust you to do this work?

It's not all about cash now

Donors also tend to give money to organisations and causes they have heard of. This means that it is not always a case of trying to raise money now. You actually may need to spend time building your relationships, becoming better known, getting on local radio or in the press, obtaining endorsements about the quality of your work from experts or prominent people. All this will help strengthen any fundraising case that you eventually make.

Basically, in the words of the old cliché, fundraising is friend-raising. Try to build and keep your fundraising relationships with the same care as you do your friendships. Get to know your donors personally if at all possible; make them feel a valuable part of things; and try to show that you are as keen to listen to what they have to say as to tell them what you want from them.

Also, you need to think and plan ahead. If you want to approach a local company for support, can you spend time getting to know them and them getting to know you before you actually ask for money? If so, where are you going to meet them? Who is going to introduce you? What are you going to say?

The strategy

When people start talking about developing fundraising strategies, you immediately assume they are talking about a sophisticated plan that could only be drawn up by a fundraising professional. Nothing could be further from the truth. All a fundraising strategy looks to do is answer four basic questions:

- What do you want?
- Why do you want it?
- When do you need it by?
- How are you going to get it?

This section looks at how to draw up a basic plan that will make your fundraising easier.

Why do we need a strategy?

Why bother having a fundraising strategy? Why don't we just get on with the fundraising? If all you need to do is raise £250 for some equipment, you don't need a strategy other than to get 10 members of the club to do a sponsored event and raise £25 each. However, if you need £100,000 to modernise and re-equip your gym, you will almost certainly be looking at raising large chunks of money from different sources. If you fail in one area (e.g. the Lottery Board turns your application down) the whole project may fail.

So how do you develop a basic fundraising strategy? Here's a six-stage plan.

Step 1 – What do we need money for?

You are going to be asking people for money. Therefore you need to be absolutely clear what you are asking for. 'Equipment' isn't much use as an answer. Exactly what equipment? You need to provide a list. If you didn't get all the money, which pieces would you buy? Similarly, 'salary costs' doesn't tell the donor much. Whose salary? What work will they be doing? Why is employing someone the best way of meeting this need?

Step 2 – Why is it important?

It's not enough to say to possible donors, 'This is what we want'. You have to show them why it is important. 'We need a five-a-side pitch,' doesn't get you very far. 'We need a five-a-side pitch because lots of kids hang around on street corners and get into trouble. We want to organise a league to give them something good to do with their time,' is starting to get somewhere.

Step 3 – How much will it cost?

There are basically two kinds of costs:

- Capital costs – these are the costs of physical items, e.g. buildings, equipment, furniture.
- Revenue costs – these are the costs of running your activity, e.g. salaries, rent, rates, telephone bills.

You need to be realistic about both these costs. For example, you may want a new athletics track (capital expenditure). Fine. The National Lottery gives capital grants. So you apply to the Lottery and get your grant. Then what? Who is there to look after it? How will you meet the higher insurance costs? Who will handle the extra membership applications as a result of the new facility? How much will the new high-tech floodlighting cost to run?

You need to think all this through before you write for money. There is no point getting your wonderful new facility only to find that you haven't got the money to run it and so the club has to close. You will also need to explain how you came up with the figures you arrived at. (See chapter 2 on drawing up a budget for more information.)

You may need two lists:

(a) One-off capital costs

This will include all the costs associated with the building or renovation work e.g.:

Building work	£50,000
Furniture	£10,000
Equipment	£25,000
Architect's fees	£5,000
Quantity surveyor	£2,500
Legal fees	£2,500
Non-reclaimable VAT	£2,500
Fundraising expenses	£2,500
TOTAL	**£100,000**

Or it could simply be the cost of the minibus i.e.:

Minibus (second-hand)	£10,000

(b) Ongoing revenue costs

These apply once the capital work is finished. So, the organisation undertaking the above building work may find itself with increased costs e.g.:

	1998 (before the building work)	1999 (after the building work)
Rent/rates	£1,000	£3,000
Building repair	£5,000	£1,000
Heat/light	£1,000	£3,000
Salaries	£25,000	£35,000
Insurance	£500	£1,500
Postage & telephone	£750	£1,500
Maintenance of equipment	£1,000	£3,000
Computer costs	Nil	£1,000
Events/competitions	£100	£2,000
Publicity	Nil	£500
Audit costs	£1,000	£4,000
Bank charges	£200	£750
Other ... (this list is not supposed to be comprehensive)		

Similarly, with the minibus, you will need to cover petrol, insurance, repairs, road tax etc.

Once you know how much you need you can then decide where the extra money is coming from.

Step 4 – How much have we got?

You need to ask yourselves:

- Can we contribute to the capital part of the project?
- Have we got enough revenue funding once it is built?

Again, you need to be honest and realistic about this. Things almost always end up costing more rather than less than you think and plan for. If you stake every penny you have on getting the thing done, you may run out of money before the project is completed. However, if you play too safe and look as if you are hoarding money, donors may think you are not committed and not give you support.

Have you got the money for all your day-to-day costs once the fundraising is over? Will you need to employ a caretaker or coach or physio or whoever? Will you need to double your membership to pay for this? Do you need an increased local authority grant? Will you get it? Will you need to get your members to run the London Marathon to raise the £10,000 extra a year? Will they do it? Will there be any loss of income while building work is being done (e.g. will you need to close the swimming pool for two weeks)? Are there any tax or VAT implications?

If you have money that you can put into the project it is an important sign of commitment and is very attractive to other funders. However, don't commit what you haven't got and make sure you allow for contingencies and overspends.

Step 5 – Where is the money coming from?

You need to know where you expect the money to come from *before* you start fundraising. Obviously this can only be an educated guess. You may well end up with something like this:

Management committee donations	£1,000
Management committee fundraising	£5,000
Members' donations	£2,500
Members' fundraising	£12,500
National Lottery	£25,000
Foundation for Sport & the Arts	£5,000
Company support	£1,000
English Partnerships	£8,000

You now know who you expect to give what. If they don't, then you need to make plans accordingly. In any case, the different funders will want to know how you expect to raise the money.

The different chapters in this Guide will help you decide where to expect to get your money from.

Step 6 – Who is going to do the fundraising?

It is all very well writing lots of plans; unfortunately this doesn't actually get the money raised! The final part of this planning stage is the hardest. This is where your arm-twisting skills will come into their own.

You may be thinking of organising the whole fundraising appeal yourself. This has the major advantage of being absolutely clear about who is doing what because you are doing everything. However, be honest!

(a) Do you have the time?
(b) Do you have the expertise?
(c) Do you have the contacts?
(d) Do you have active support from the rest of the organisation?
(e) Do you have the necessary financial information?
(f) In general, are you the best person to be doing it?

If you are convinced that you can and should organise it all, you may well still need help with administrative detail. For example, if you are organising an event, you cannot be in more than one place at once. You will need to delegate. Equally importantly, you may well need people with contacts.

The most effective way of raising money is through personal contacts. You are much more likely to get money from a friend than from someone who hardly knows you. For example, if you were about to do a sponsored abseil, who would you ask to sponsor you? Well, the same principles apply to other kinds of fundraising.

Therefore, if you want to get sponsorship from local companies, why not try to get a prominent local business person onto your fundraising committee? This means that any requests for their support will come from someone they know and respect (i.e. a fellow company chairman) rather from a sports club whom they have never heard of and have no incentive to support.

Ask around your club. Try the youth section. Whose parent is famous or well-off or well-connected? Ask your staff, management committee, coaches, volunteers. Is anyone married to the president of the chamber of commerce or the president of the local Rotary club? Who plays golf with whom? Produce a 'shopping list' for the ideal fundraising committee and try to recruit it. For example, you may want:

1 lawyer (to provide services free of charge)
1 accountant (ditto)
1 prominent local businessman (to raise money from colleagues in local businesses)
1 local councillor (to lobby the local authority)
1 prominent sportsperson, active or retired (to make lots of fundraising speeches and appearances)

1 events organiser
2 – 3 members of the club
1 person to chair the committee

Alternatively, you could ask famous people if they want to be presidents or vice-presidents of the appeal. Presidents are usually 'figureheads' who add credibility to the appeal and feature on the letterhead. However, they would only usually expect to make three or four appearances at key points in the appeal (e.g. to open an event, present some awards, receive a significant cheque).

The trick with getting outside people in is to make sure you get what you want from them. There is no point asking the local Olympic champion to make six appearances in aid of the appeal only to find out that (a) he/she keeps letting you down at the last moment, or (b) he/she charges you a fortune for each appearance. The first case severely annoys your sponsors and those attending the event; the second case lands you with costs that you didn't expect, and which may even wipe out the event's surplus. When formally inviting people onto the committee, make it clear in the letter what you expect from them.

Also, avoid the temptation to go for too large a committee. It may be that the committee as a whole never or only rarely meets. If you have busy people they do not have much time; get the best from them.

Once you have done all this basic planning, you are ready to begin to raise money.

Chapter 2

How much do we need?

A guide to basic budgeting

■■■

Success in raising money depends upon focus, planning and presentation. All of these are involved in drawing up a budget for a project. You want to be confident that what you are asking for is realistic in terms of what the funder can give, but also that you have asked for enough. Surprisingly often, funders say that projects have been under-costed and applicants should have asked for more.

A budget will help your organisation with:

- planning
- accountability
- setting objectives
- directing funders
- raising money for core costs.

Who should draw up the budget?

There is no magic formula or sorcerer's skill in formulating a budget. There are undoubtedly people who cope with figures more confidently than others and hopefully there is at least one person in your organisation who has this expertise. However, the process of budgeting should also involve those who will actually carry out the work as they are likely to have an idea of what will be involved. They will also carry the burden of an under-funded project if the costing is not realistic.

Consultation also encourages accountability. Where people have been involved in drawing up targets for income and expenditure they will have more idea of what resources are really available and why they should keep to their forecasts.

What to include in the budget

How much a project really costs

Before looking at any income that will come to the project you need to look first at how much the project will cost to run. There are obvious costs and other costs that are hidden. Some items such as equipment may seem easier to fund than others. Do not leave less attractive elements out as these are part of the real cost of running a project. This is an opportunity to apportion core costs to a project and raise money for salaries, running costs, depreciation for instance. (See chapter 3 on Fundraising for projects.)

Some organisations are nervous about this approach, worrying that funders may be scared off by large amounts that seemed to have been 'smuggled in'. Do not be. Funders who have a feel for the business of sifting applications will recognise a realistic project costing when they see one. (If you are applying to funders who you suspect may not appreciate this approach you can explain your figures more fully, or simply present a shopping list of items for them to choose from.) If you ask for too little you may not be able to run the project at all, or if you do, only run it half as well as if you had allocated costs properly.

Having a realistic grasp of how much a project will cost means allowing for:

- capital costs (that is machinery, equipment, buildings etc.)
- running costs (that is salaries, rent, heating, depreciation, decoration etc.)

Whether you are budgeting for a capital item, or the running costs of the project, the processes will be the same.

> The Foundation for Sport and the Arts, the largest trust giver to sport and arts projects says:
> 'Applicants sometimes seem to lack confidence to ask for the full sum that they need; this does not help their case. If your proposal is well thought out and it requires £20,000 rather than £10,000 to see it through you should apply for the full amount.'

Drawing up a budget – Estimating your costs

Capital costs
If you are planning a capital project (an extension to your existing facilities, or a new changing room area for example) you need firstly to list all your costs. These may include some or all of the following.

Land and buildings
How much will it cost to buy the land?
How much will it cost to rent office/play space?

Professional charges
Accountant
Architect
Feasibility studies
Quantity surveyor
Solicitor
Structural engineer

Building costs
Site works before construction
Construction cost (as on contractor's estimate)
Furniture and fittings
Security system
Decoration
Equipment

You should add to this list as necessary. However, these are only the costs of *building* your extension or new changing rooms. They do not show how you will pay for the long-term costs (such as maintenance, heating, lighting, security, insurance and so on). These ongoing costs should be included in your revenue budget as below.

The above list also assumes that you will be paying for everything. In fact, a friendly architect may reduce their fees as a donation; you may be able to get your members to paint the changing rooms with donated paint from a local factory, and your fixtures and fittings may be given by a firm that has recently been refurbished. All this should be taken into account and your budget adjusted as necessary. In some cases when applying to funders it helps your case to show how much you have raised from your own resources. Gifts in kind (such as donated furniture, reduced solicitor's services etc.) should be costed and their financial value recorded.

Revenue costs
These are your main running costs and will include all or some of the following.

Premises
Rent
Rates
Maintenance of the building, inside and outside
Heating
Lighting
Health and safety measures
Security
Insurance
Depreciation of equipment

Administration
Salaries (including National Insurance)
Telephone
Postage
Stationery/printing
Cleaning/caretaking

Book-keeping, audit and bank charges
Training courses
Child care
Miscellaneous (e.g. travel, tea, coffee)

Project costs

These are the costs of running individual activities or pieces of work which take place in the building or as part of your remit as a sports organisation. Where you can, split your work up into separate units that can be costed individually. You can then look at what a project costs, which includes capital items and revenue costs such as those listed above. By costing projects separately you can keep track of individual project costs; allocate some of your general running costs to projects; and prepare funding applications. (For further information on how to cost a project see chapter 3 on Fundraising for projects.)

No budget will be 100% accurate. It is your best guess at the time you are planning the project of how much money you will need. You may wish to put in a contingency for unforeseen costs, if you feel this is a sensible precaution. And if at a later stage it appears that your figures are no longer accurate, you can always revise your budget so that it reflects the financial situation as you then know it. Remember though, that you may not be able to get any extra money from existing funders to cover this.

Drawing up a budget – Estimating your income

Your budgeted costs set out what you need to spend. However, you can only spend money you have earned, raised or borrowed. The other side of a budget needs to show where you intend the money to come from and sets your fundraising targets.

Look at each source of income you can expect (local authority, company sponsorship, membership subs, fundraising events etc.) and list them as you did your expenditure. You will need to look at where this year's income came from and make a reasonable guess about what will happen next year.

Most of this is common sense rather than crystal ball gazing. You can look at opportunities as well as threats to your funding. Is there a new source of trust support that has opened up? Do you have more members this year than you did last year? Has your funding been affected by local government reorganisation? Is your three-year grant from the Bootstrap Trust finishing this year?

It is much easier to predict expenditure than income. You obviously need to keep a close eye on both. There is a tendency for expenditure to be higher and income to be lower than budgeted! Monitor your income frequently and carefully. Allow for any shortfall in your expected income quickly. For example, if you had expected to raise £30,000 from the National Lottery to upgrade your premises, but your application fails, you then have to make some decisions. Have you got reserves, and do you want to use them for this? Can you borrow the money? Can you raise money through cutting expenditure in other areas? Do you have time to find another funder? Should you abandon the scheme?

It helps to list both definite and hoped for income.

Source of income	Budget	Certain	Probable	Possible
National Lottery	£25,000	£25,000	–	–
Memberships subs (i)	£1,700	£1,000	£500	£250
Trusts (ii)	£5,000	–	£3,000	£2,000
Local companies (iii)	£250	£250	£250	–

Notes

(i) **Membership subs:** Imagine you have 100 members paying £10 each. You can enter £1,000 in the definite column for next year. You estimate you can accommodate more (although you will have to work out any significant increases in expenditure that this will cause). You have a waiting list of around 50, and you predict that they are all likely to join, so enter £500 in the probable column. You also hope that some publicity will bring in an extra 25, but you are not sure, so put £250 in the possible column.

(ii) **Trusts:** Your budgeted £5,000 can be entered in the probable column if you are confident of the trust (e.g. the grant is recurrent). You would put the figure in the possible column if you know less about the trust(s).

(iii) **Local companies:** Similarly with companies, if you have a warm relationship with local businesses, they are represented on your management committee, or if you play golf with the chairman of the board, the £250 can go under probable. Otherwise enter under possible.

Income vs. expenditure

Having listed your projected spending and income you will now have an idea of where you stand. This process can give an overview for the whole organisation but can also give the picture for individual projects. You may predict that the money coming in is greater than your anticipated spending. In your understandable euphoria you should check the budget carefully. Have you been too optimistic on your sources of income, or have you missed some areas of expenditure or under costed them?

If your income is below your projected spending you will need to look carefully at the reasons for this. Is the snapshot year you are looking at exceptional in some way? Do you have a large number of one-off start-up costs related to a big project (such as building work, feasibility studies, equipment costs etc.) which will not be repeated in following years, or does the deficit come as a result of regular income failing to match routine expenditure? Wherever there is a shortfall you will have to do some planning immediately. At this point, people often make one or more of the following mistakes:

- To assume the figures must be wrong and carry on regardless. This is a recipe for disaster.
- To assume that you are going to be 100% successful in all your fundraising activities (a bit unrealistic) and that costs will also all be down, so somehow things will be all right.
- To hope that you are actually going to be more successful in your fundraising and so add a couple of noughts to some categories of income. If you are going to do this, you may as well have not bothered doing the budgets in the first place.
- To plan for some fundraising event or money making scheme which will cover the deficit, but have no idea what the event is. Alternatively, to say 'we will have an appeal to members' when you have no idea what that will bring in.

What you need to do is look very carefully at the figures, satisfy yourself that they are all reasonable and then decide what you can afford to do. You may need to scale certain things down or wait a bit longer. Whatever you decide, make sure that it is reasonable and that it is clearly understood within the organisation.

By now, you should have a chart (see page 16).

Cash flow forecasts

The final part of this phase of the planning process is looking at your cash flow. This is where you try to predict when money will come in and when money will go out. This is particularly important if you are doing a large building project where some big bills will have to be paid. Will you have enough money to meet them when they are due?

Take all the different areas of expenditure that you have listed. Try to work out in which month each will be paid. For example, salaries are paid evenly throughout the year; rent may be paid quarterly; the bill for the summer cricket festival comes at the end of September. Once you have done this, total up each month's expenditure.

You should now do the same with your expected income. Again, this may be erratic and difficult to predict. If you have a local authority grant, this may be paid in April; membership subs may be collected throughout the year; National Lottery money may be paid in September; and your second year's funding from the Fair Dues Trust is sent after their February trustees' meeting. These are the

Income/expenditure budget

Date of budget:

Expenditure:

Item	Cost	Notes*
....	....	....
....	....	....
....	....	....
....	....	....
....	....	....
....	....	....
....	....	....
....	....	....
....	....	....
....	....	....

TOTAL COSTS £ ....

* How reliable is this figure? What is it based on?

Income:

Source	Total	Certain	Probable	Possible
....	....	☐	☐	☐
....	....	☐	☐	☐
....	....	☐	☐	☐
....	....	☐	☐	☐
....	....	☐	☐	☐
....	....	☐	☐	☐
....	....	☐	☐	☐
....	....	☐	☐	☐
....	....	☐	☐	☐

TOTAL INCOME £ ....

PROJECTED SURPLUS/DEFICIT £ ....

Notes:

....
....
....
....

sources you can predict. There may be others such as the various award schemes that change each year and make planning difficult. If you have a source of money such as a grant from the European Social Fund, which is new to your organisation, you will have to spend time becoming familiar with the timing of payments.

By matching the expected monthly spending with the expected monthly income you will spot any gaps where there is little or no money to meet expected bills. You need to plan and take action for this. You may be able to renegotiate your payment terms for some items. You may need to arrange an overdraft facility. If you are hiring equipment you will want to schedule payments in months that have less expenditure.

This kind of forecasting is vital if you are planning a major capital project. Some funders will only pay once the work has been completed, so you may have to pay the contractors before you get the money from your funder. Some funders will not pay if the work has been started already, and you may have to find money for feasibility studies and surveys before any grant is awarded. How will this affect your finances?

Having done your income and expenditure forecasts and worked out your likely cash flow, you now know what you need and when you need it by. You are in a position to go to funders.

Chapter 3
Fundraising for projects
■■■

Fundraising is about getting hold of enough money to meet the day-to-day or capital costs of your organisation, plus the resources required for future development. However, it is far easier to raise money for something specific than to appeal for administrative costs or general funds. This is because donors can then match the support they give to a particular piece of work that they are really interested in. They will feel that their money is actually doing something and that they have made a real contribution.

For example, a Save the Children Fund appeal asking for money for rent and rates would not get very far; appeals asking for help with work in Somalia (or wherever) have been really successful.

The same principle applies to your fundraising. Asking for money towards the upkeep of the local sports centre may work with applications to local authority; it won't get you very far if you are writing to the Foundation for Sport and the Arts. They will only want to fund a particular 'project' or part of your work (e.g. the new all-weather pitch). Your members will also respond much better to an appeal for one thing (e.g. a new climbing wall) than a request for 'a generous contribution to the organisation's expenses'.

Thinking of your work in project terms and designing projects which will attract support is the basis of successful fundraising.

Make your project sound exciting

One of the great advantages with project fundraising is that you can highlight special areas of your work that will interest the particular person you are writing to. However, make sure you do everything that you can to show that the work is lively, worthwhile and worth funding. The donor's first response should be 'Gosh, that sounds good; we ought to be backing that', rather than 'I've had ten applications like that in the last month, and none of them are likely to achieve very much'.

A fundable project should be:

■ Specific – an identifiable piece of expenditure or aspect of the organisation's work.
■ Important – both to the organisation and to the cause or need it is meeting.
■ Effective – there should be a clear and positive outcome.
■ Realistic – the work proposed must be achievable.

- Good value – the work should be a good use of the donor's money.
- Relevant – it should meet the donor's interests and funding concerns.
- Bite-sized – it should not be too large or too small for a donor to support, although the cost might be shared through several smaller grants. If it is too large, it might be broken down further into sub-projects.
- Topical – it should be looking at current needs and concerns.

How to identify a project

Case study: Anytown Basketball Club

Anytown Basketball Club currently has three teams: a men's team, a women's team and a youth team. The hall is used four nights and three afternoons a week. The club needs to generate another £1,000 a year to cover its costs. It also wants to relay the floor which (a) is totally unsuitable for wheelchair users and (b) is getting unsafe anyway. This will cost £10,000. The club has just £500 in the bank. What can it do?

- Put the **membership fees up** to cover the £1,000 a year deficit. However, many members struggle to afford the current fee and would probably leave if it went any higher.
- Have a **one-off appeal to members**. OK, but what about next year?
- Apply to the **local authority** for a grant. Possible, but unlikely.
- Organise an **annual tournament** to raise the money. Fine, but who is going to do it?
- Write round to **local trusts and companies** to ask for help with the deficit. They wouldn't fund it. Nor would the Foundation for Sport and the Arts.

Clearly there are problems with all the above strategies. Also, none of them has begun to tackle the floor problem. So, the club could try to divide its needs into more attractive projects:

1. They could write to local companies to sponsor the different teams, rather than give a donation to general expenses. Try to write to appropriate companies. For example, which companies are interested in women's health? Try to get them to sponsor the women's team.
2. They could get funding to recruit new members. For example, they could aim to set up a league run by and for unemployed people. This could be paid for by a trust with an interest in helping unemployed people.
3. They could set up an after-schools club two nights a week so that children whose parents are working can go somewhere safe after school, play basketball and/or do a bit of homework before their parents come to collect them. This would attract funding from various groups interested in the welfare of children. It would also be run on a fee-paying basis.
4. They could set up a team or league for wheelchair users. Again, this would broaden their funding base.

There are plenty of other options as well. However, the advantage of breaking things down into projects is:

- You can appeal to a wider range of funders. You are no longer restricted to people just interested in sport. You can apply to people interested in the health and welfare of women and/or children and/or disabled people.
- Having done this, the replacement of the floor is a much easier prospect because (i) the building is clearly being used for the benefit of the wider community, and (ii) the kinds of target groups for the National Lottery (e.g. disabled people) stand to benefit.
- You can hive off some of your central costs into the applications for funding (see below).

By breaking things down into projects, you can focus on activities (e.g. women's and children's teams) rather than your own needs (money for bills), widen the range of possible funders (because you are no longer just a sports club) and force yourselves to be a bit more creative in your fundraising.

How to cost a project

To cost a project properly, you need to include all the direct and all the indirect costs which can reasonably be said to be necessary to the running of the project. This means you should allocate a proportion of your central (or core) costs to the project. The process of costing a project has several stages.

Stage 1 – describe the project
Be clear about what the project is. By this, you should identify what the project will do for its users rather than how it will solve your funding problems. For example: 'We will run an after-school club (as in the case study above) which will ...'

Stage 2 – the direct costs
Write down a list of all the direct costs. For the after-school club these could include:
Leaders' costs
Tables and chairs (for the children to do homework)
Pens, paper and exercise books
Drinks and biscuits
Advertising and publicity

Stage 3 – the indirect costs
Write down a list of all the relevant indirect costs. These indirect costs (sometimes called support costs or hidden costs) can be harder to pinpoint. They generally include items such as staff time for those not involved on a day-to-day basis in the project (e.g. manager, admin staff, finance manager), depreciation,

use and maintenance of the building (including rent, rates, heat and light), insurance, post, telephone, stationery and other office costs.

These indirect costs are all part and parcel of running the project so you need to cost them in. The after-school club cannot run without a building; the building needs heat, light and insurance; the leaders of the club will need the use of a telephone and photocopier; they need supervision and support, and so on. Please note, you shouldn't be trying to fiddle any figures or pretend that you have costs you really don't. You are simply recognising that the work you do requires a wide range of expenditure.

So your list of indirect costs may include:

- rent and rates
- heat and light
- post and telephone
- management and supervision of the project
- admin support
- book-keeping
- health & safety
- insurance
- caretaking/cleaning

Stage 4 – costing the costs

Put a figure against all the areas of expenditure you have identified. This is pretty straightforward for the direct costs, although make sure you get more than one quote on each cost.

A more difficult area is how to calculate the central or office costs. Obviously, you cannot work out in advance exactly how many telephone calls you will make, stamps you will need or paperclips you will buy. The best way to come to a reasonable estimate is to try and work out how much of your organisation's time and facilities will be taken up by the project.

So, say the Basketball Club is currently used 30 hours a week and you intend to run the After-School Club for a further 15 hours a week. This means the After-School Club is in the building 33% of the time. You could apportion 33% of the rent, rates etc. to the After-School Club.

Say the building has a Centre Manager who has responsibility for all the activities in the building. You will need to work out how much time this person will spend supervising the after-school project and allocate the salary and national insurance costs accordingly. So, for example, if the manager works a 35-hour week and will spend on average six hours per week on the after-school project, allocate 17% of the salary and national insurance to that.

You can work out your postage, stationery and photocopying costs on a similar basis.

You will also need to work out an allocation for the caretaker, cleaner, administrator or any other salary costs associated with the Centre and the project.

Sample budget

Project name: After-School Club

Timing: The club will run every week-day evening from 3.30 pm to 6.30 pm.

Number of attendees: 20 children per night

Number of staff: Four leaders per night

Costs:

(a) Equipment/materials

Tables/chairs	£
Pens/paper/books	£
Drinks/biscuits	£
etc.	

(b) Staff

Leaders (i)	£
Project manager (ii)	£
Admin support (iii)	£
etc.	

(c) Building use (iv)

Heat/light	£
Rent/rates	£
Telephone/stationery	£
Photocopier	£
Caretaking/cleaning	£
etc.	

(d) Promotion & publicity

Leaflet print & design	£
Poster print & design	£
Leaflet distribution	£
etc.	

(e) General overheads

Insurance	£
Depreciation (v)	£
Health & safety	£
Finance	£
etc.	

(i) Requires 4 leaders for 3 hours a night @ £7.00 per hour for 40 weeks (5 days a week) i.e. 4 x 3 x 7.00 x 200.

(ii) A part-time post @ £ ... per year. This may or may not represent an allocation of someone's current salary depending on whether you need to appoint someone from outside the organisation to manage this project.

(iii) You could calculate this as a proportion of the administrator's salary in the same way you calculated the proportion of the project manager's salary.

(iv) Includes office space for the project manager and administrator during the day and the space used by the after school club each afternoon.

(v) Equipment is usually depreciated over three years so you would need to allow 33% of the purchase price of the equipment each year – this is so that you can build into the budget the cost of replacing out-of-date or broken equipment.

Stage 5 – is it reasonable?

Ask yourself: 'Does the total figure look reasonable?' Is it too high or too low? Does it look real value for money? Many of the costs you will put down (e.g. premises) are effectively impossible to put a precise figure on, so the budget is flexible. You may need to juggle the final total a bit. The key thing is that you can justify how you have arrived at those figures if a funder pushed you on it.

Who will pay for central (core) costs?

Your membership fees
Income from fundraising events
The local authority
Other general income

Who prefers to pay for project costs?

The Foundation for Sport and the Arts
The National Lottery
Grant-making trusts
Companies
Members (when it is a special appeal)

Remember, the trick is to include the relevant core costs in your project budget. Use the 'glamour' of the project to get the 'unattractive' administrative costs paid for.

And finally ...

You now have to decide who will pay for what. Are you going to ask one funder for the whole amount for the project? Are you going to ask various funders? Are you going to allocate some of your own money to the project (e.g. 20% of subscriptions)? Remember:

- Apply to a funder who is interested in this kind of work.
- Ask for an amount they can conveniently give.
- Stress the benefits of the project and show how it is real value for money.

Chapter 4

Preparing and writing a good fundraising application

∎∎

Fundraising is about selling an idea to someone who has the means to make it happen. The fundraising application is the point of contact between you who needs the support and those who can give it. The more you can help funders do a difficult job, the more they may be inclined to help you. This help may be a cash donation, sponsorship of an event, gifts for a raffle, time and expertise from a member of staff, equipment or whatever. Your task is to make them interested enough in your ideas to want to support you.

There are many ways of asking. You can ask face to face; you may make a presentation to a group or meeting of supporters; you may use the telephone. The most likely approach, however, is by writing a letter. This chapter will look at what to include in a letter, and also how to improve your presentation.

Some cautionary words

Writing applications is not a science. You may write the clearest, brightest, most engaging application that fits all the funder's criteria, and yet still not be successful. You may not even get a photocopied rejection slip, let alone an explanation of why you did not get a grant. On the other hand you may know of people who break all the 'rules' and yet their spidery illegible scrawl and rambling prose brings in thousands regularly. There is no easy explanation for this and you should not take it personally. Don't give up; keep trying.

Most of the effort of application writing goes into condensing a full account of the project and organisation into one to two sides of A4 or, at worst, a 3cm x 14cm box on an application form. This makes good sense from the funder's point of view. They have many applications to look through and cannot spend time reading and interpreting vast amounts of information, however interesting and worthwhile. If looked at positively, application writing can be an opportunity to hone your strategic thinking as well as your style.

Some key points

1. You cannot tell funders everything; there is not enough time and they would not listen. Many application letters are far too long. Put yourself in your reader's place. Would you persevere through long pages of information about an organisation you knew little or nothing about? A general rule would be one and a half sides of A4 maximum for a letter to a grant-making trust, and one side maximum to a company. Proposals to local authorities and central government departments may give you more space – on the whole, officials will be more used to reading long project descriptions. This should not be an excuse for wasted waffle. You should still keep to a clear, positive and succinct style.

2. In your letter, select and concentrate on your main selling points, emphasising those which will be of most interest to the particular person/supporter you are writing to.

3. Generally, it is best if you are not asking funders to support your organisation. Instead, ask them to support the people you help, the work you do, and preferably, a specific project.

4. Believe in what you are doing. Be upbeat. Positive messages are more inviting than negative ones. Have faith in your project. If you do not believe in what you are doing why should potential supporters? Too many applications strike a defensive note and end up apologising for their work. Do not focus on the gloomy consequences of not getting the money. Paint an exciting picture of all the things that will happen when you do get the money. You want to enthuse people, not resort to emotional blackmail.

Ingredients of a good application

Most funders (including members of the public) receive thousands of requests each year. You have to think carefully about how you can make your application stand out from the crowd by making a number of key points which will catch the reader's attention, arouse interest in the work, and 'sell' your proposal. Ask yourself:

- Why on earth should anyone want to support us?
- What is so important about what we are doing?

Try to tell people why your work is important, not just what you do.

In other words what is unique about your work? What is different? Why is it necessary? What will it achieve? And why should this particular donor want to support it? You should try your answers and application out on a friend who does not work in the same field and has no knowledge of your work. Their view can tell you whether you are assuming too much of your reader, whether you need more or less information to make your case, and when you have got it about right.

Six essential elements of an application

- Who you are
- The need you meet
- The solution you offer
- Why you should do it
- The amount you need
- The future you have.

1. Who you are

The funder wants to know what kind of organisation they are dealing with. How long have you been going? What are your key activities? What have you done that has been especially brilliant? What have been some of your major successes? In other words, can you show the funder that you are reliable, respectable and someone they would want to be associated with?

2. The need you meet

Fundraising is about persuading the donor that there is a problem to be solved and that you can do that. You need to show that you will help certain people or will make society better in some way. Sport will be the means, but what is the end you have in mind? So you need to:

- Describe the problem (e.g. 'More and more young people are developing long-term health problems through lack of exercise'.)
- Support this by evidence (e.g. 'Over 50% of children aged 11–16 watch more than 3 hours of television each night. Only 5% regularly do more than 2 hours physical exercise each week.')
- Say why this is important (e.g. 'Already health specialists are saying ...')

Can you add to the above? For example, how widespread is the problem? Is it local or does it have regional, national or international implications? If it is local, what special features of the community make it special or interesting to support? Point to who will be helped by your work, which can be a wider group than just the young people involved in the project. Emphasise any elements that are special or unique in the need you are trying to meet.

3. The solution you offer

Once you have established the need and said how important it is to do something about it, you need to show that you can offer a plausible solution. It is not enough to say 'here's a real need and something must be done'. The reader must get a clear idea of how you will achieve it, e.g. 'Coaches will go into every secondary school and youth club in the area to talk to children about the health risks they run without proper physical exercise. They will hand out basic training programmes for everyone. This will be followed up both by repeat visits to the schools and clubs and by "come and try it" days at the club.'

You need to point to the actual or expected results of your work, and how these will be measured. This may be, for instance, how many young people will take part; how teachers and parents will be involved; how many do you expect to attend the 'come and try it' days.

Make sure that what you want to do is workable, that it can be done in a reasonable time, by you, and that it gives value for money. In short, the donor should now be saying: 'I can see there is a real problem and the project would certainly make things better'.

4. Why you should do it

You need to establish your credibility. Why should you be the group to run the project? Why should the funder trust you? This can be done by showing:

- **Your ability/professionalism:** show you are a well-run outfit which helps people fulfil their potential, that you have grown over the years, that you are soundly financed, that you have a wide support base, that you produce 25 world junior champions a year, or whatever.
- **Your reputation:** show how you have support and goodwill throughout the community. Get quotes from a wide range of people, from members to parents to local councillors to business leaders to famous people to whoever makes the application sound more convincing. This shows you have across-the-board support. You may want to attach a quotes sheet to your application in any case.
- **Your track record:** show how you have very successfully done similar work in the past, or that you have set up other projects which have gone really well. Try to show that you can be relied on to turn plans into action.
- **Value for money**: show that your work is good value for money and that you are more cost-effective than alternatives. Or is your approach an example of good practice that could be copied and applied elsewhere?

You should be able to come up with a number of good reasons why you should be supported, why you are the right people to be meeting this need. The more you can do this, the more credibility you have. The more credibility you have, the more likely the donor is to trust you with their money. Success breeds success and funders will be attracted to a confident upbeat approach. Your plus points will all help to sell your case, so make them clearly and confidently in your application.

5. The amount you need

Funders are keen to know first of all about the project and the value of the work being done. But you also need to tell them very clearly what it costs and how much you expect them to give. Some applications tail off when it comes to asking for money. There is no need, because you should have made a good case for someone to support you and proved that you can be trusted with their money. This is the point of the letter after all, and if you're too embarrassed to ask for the money there is little point in sending it off.

6. The future you have

Make sure that you emphasise your long-term viability. This underlines your credibility and why funders should support you. If your future is not at all sure, funders may think their money would be better used elsewhere. Show how the project will be funded once the grant has been spent. Where you are applying for money for a new facility, who will pay for its running costs once it is opened? How will you continue a project when the three-year grant has finished?

What to say in the application letter

Now that you have done your research and pulled all your selling points together you need to put them into some kind of order. There are no golden rules for writing proposals, no perfect letters of application. What works for the club down the road will not necessarily work for you. Inject your own personality and approach as far as possible. The following is a structure that many have used successfully, and this can be a starting point for your own letter.

A basic structure for an application

Project title
Summary sentence
Introduction: who you are
The problem: why something needs to be done now
Your proposals: what you intend to do about the problem
Why you should do it
The budget: how much you need
The request: how much to ask for
Funding plan: how you will get the money
The rationale: why the funder might be interested and what their role is

1. Project title

This can be really effective, especially if it is catchy and quickly describes what you want to do.

2. Summary sentence

This is the first bit of the application to be read. It may be the last! It tells the reader what the application is about and whether it is likely to be relevant to them. 'I am writing to you to ask for a donation towards the cost of...' is a reasonable start. Keep it short and to the point.

Selling points: an example

A local athletics club for young people will highlight different selling points when appealing to different donors. For example:

1. **To the National Lottery**
   You have won the county championships for the last three years.
   Your membership is the largest in the city, is drawn from a cross section of the community and you have a long waiting list.
   Your membership doubled in five years and includes people who have never played sport before.
   All this has been achieved with below average facilities.

2. **To the local authority – all the points above, plus:**
   You provide a good 'containment' service because you take people off the streets and keep them out of harm's way.
   You are about prevention as well as cure and can prevent people from drifting into anti-social behaviour patterns.
   You give them skills (e.g. motivation, discipline and organisational ability) which will help them in a non-sporting context.
   You do all this at very low cost – only a few pounds per young person.

3. **To a grant-making trust**
   There is a real need – as above.
   Your work is well thought of by community leaders and you have got all the funding possible from statutory sources.
   Your approach to the problem is innovative and exciting, and has every chance of success.
   You are trying to reach out to people and offer them something new.
   Other trusts are or have been supporting you.

4. **To local companies**
   You are well-known locally and always appearing in local papers because of your success.
   You hold major meetings every year where X number of people attend.
   Your young people are highly successful in getting and holding down jobs because they understand the need for discipline and perseverance.
   Members of company staff are volunteer coaches.
   The company will get lots of good local publicity (give examples of where you have got good publicity before).

These are only examples. You will be able to think of lots more under each heading. But it shows how you have to think who you are writing to and what do they want to hear.

Your selling points: an example

Try to write down at least three selling points under each of the following headings. Ask other people in the club what they would say:

We meet the following need(s) ....

The needs we meet are particularly important because ....

Our solution is new and ground-breaking because ....

We are effective because ....

We can prove this by ....

We are different/unique because ....

Our other strengths are ....

If we did not exist then...

Funders usually prefer to support successes rather than failures. Therefore you need to be able to show a track record of successes. List your five greatest successes in the past five years:

1.   ....
2.   ....
3.   ....
4.   ....
5.   ....

We are the best because ....
....
....
....
....
....
....
....
....
....
....
....

3. The introduction: who you are

Many applications say little or nothing about who the organisation is; they just go on about what they want. Assume that the reader knows nothing about you. What would they need to know to trust you with their money? You need to show you are good, reliable, well-used and well-liked – in three or four sentences.

4. The problem: why something needs to be done now

Now you move onto the problem you want to solve. This is where you explain the needs of your users, the problems they face in life, the opportunities you can provide, the better society you can help create, or whatever. Remember, successful fundraising isn't about asking people to support your organisation; rather it's about asking support for the work you do and the people you help.

5. Your proposals: what you intend to do about the problem

You now need to show what you intend to do and how you intend to do it. You should set yourself targets (e.g. how many young people will you attract to your activities? How many disabled people will become members or leaders? How many leaders will you train?) If you are having problems with this part, maybe you could try predicting what the club will be like in two years' time and how things will have changed.

The reader must gain a clear idea of how you will achieve your targets. Many grant-makers are moving towards 'output' funding, where they judge the success of the project on the measurable things it achieves. They will certainly want to see that you have an idea of what the money will buy and how you can keep track of the success or otherwise of your plans.

6. Why you should do it

By now you have stated who you are, the need you want to meet and how you are going to do it. Now you need to show why you are the best people to do it. Assume your reader is saying: 'This is all very well but how can I trust this group to deliver on this?' This question will partly be answered by how good and clear your solutions to the problem are. However, you should also establish the credibility of your club.

> Remember to ask first if the funder has an application form to fill out. There is no point sweating blood to get the perfect letter of application written only to find out that you have to redo the whole thing on an application form. If you are unsure about the information required on the form, contact the funder for clarification if you can. With an application form there will be more scope for this than with a letter. Sort out all the problem areas on the form before you ring, and go through each in one phone call. This will save time for you and the funder.

Start making sense – A guide to writing simply

- Keep sentences short and to the point.
- Explain complicated ideas simply.
- Keep paragraphs short. Look at the layout critically. Would it entice you to read further. Are you put off by long sections of text? If you are, your reader will be as well.
- Avoid jargon. You may understand what you are talking about; outsiders generally will not.
- Be direct; do not waffle. Use as few words as possible. It adds to the 'readability' of your application, and keeps the length down.
- Use personal pronouns such as 'we', 'our', 'you' and 'your' rather than 'the organisation/association', 'the users' etc.
- Use strong verbs and tenses, rather than weaker ones like the passive. 'Our coaches work closely with local schools' reads better than 'Local schools have become involved with the activities organised by our coaching staff.'
- Weed out waffle and waste. Say something sincerely, simply and succinctly.
- Re-read and rewrite.

7. The budget: how much you need

This is how much you intend to spend on the project. It includes direct costs and overhead costs. (See chapter 2 on drawing up a budget and chapter 3 on Fundraising for projects for further details.)

When asking for money, make sure you propose an amount the donor can give. Local companies tend to give around £100 to £200 (unless it is a proper sponsorship). Grant-making trusts with an income of over £1 million do not want to be giving less than £500 or £1,000 because it would make the whole thing an administrative nightmare. Most of your members may be prepared to give £10, but with a shopping list some will be persuaded to give considerably more.

8. The request: how much to ask for

This is where most applications tail off into a murmur that 'any help you can give would be gratefully received'. This is partly because people are embarrassed to ask for money. But remember, you have made a really good case and persuaded the donor (i) of the need for support, and (ii) that it will be a really good use of their money. So, don't be afraid to put the final piece into the jigsaw.

You can ask for money in a number of ways:

- Name a specific sum of money (i.e. 'We are writing to ask you for a donation of £1,000 towards the cost of this work').
- Give a range of amounts (e.g. 'We are aiming to get 1 donation of £5,000; 3 donations of £2,000 and 9 donations of £1,000').
- Mention the total sum required and how you intend to get it (e.g. 'We are writing to you and 10 other grant-making trusts asking for a total of £20,000'). This shows that you are hoping for at least £2,000 from each trust, but give the option of much more.
- Quote other grants already awarded (e.g. 'Company x has already agreed a payment of £500, and we are asking for similar amounts from six other local companies').
- Produce a 'shopping list' and highlight one you think the donor would like to pay for. A shopping list is where you give a range of options as follows:

New all-weather pitch – shopping list

Surface	£50,000
Lighting	£30,000
Fencing	£10,000
Hockey nets	£2,000
Line markings	£2,000
Football nets	£1,000
Basketball nets	£1,000
Balls	£500
etc.	

The idea is that you give a range of prices starting at a level that all those you are writing to can afford but by listing more expensive items you hopefully persuade them to give more. Also, you are giving them something specific to pay for which many donors like. It can work particularly well with companies and individuals; it is generally less successful with trusts, the lottery and statutory funders.

9. Funding plan: how you will get the money

You need to show the funder where you intend to get the money from. It may be that you are asking this funder for the whole amount, or you may be getting it from a variety of sources. Therefore, you need to say something like: 'The total cost of this project is £50,000. Sport England have agreed to give us £10,000 if we can raise the rest by September 1st. We aim to raise £10,000 from our members, £20,000 from the National Lottery, £5,000 from our annual summer games and £5,000 from grant-making trusts.'

You may also need to show how you intend to meet the longer-term costs if you want money for a new building or for work which will carry on after this funder's grant has expired.

How to ask for money

Fraser Falconer, Regional Coordinator, Scotland BBC Children in Need Appeal

- State clearly how much the overall project will cost (e.g. 'We are looking to raise a total of £30,000').
- Give the funder a clear idea of how much you expect them to contribute. You can do this in one of three ways:
  (i) Ask for a specific amount (i.e. 'I am therefore writing to ask you for £2,000').
  (ii) Show how much other trusts have given (e.g. 'BBC Children-in-Need have already given us £2,000'). This will indicate that you expect a similar amount from the trust you are currently writing to.
  (iii) Show how many trusts you are writing to (e.g. 'I am therefore writing to you and eight other major trusts to ask for a total of £10,000'). This gives the trust a pretty good idea of how much you expect them to give (i.e. around £2,000), but gives them flexibility to give more or less than this.
- Show where the rest of the money is coming from (i.e. 'The overall project will cost £30,000. We expect to raise £15,000 from our members and supporters; £5,000 from other fundraising events and £10,000 from grant-making trusts. I am therefore writing to you and eight other major trusts to ask for a total of £10,000'). This will give the trust more confidence that you know what you are doing and you can raise the necessary money.

10. The rationale: why the funder might be interested and what their role is

It can help to have a final rallying call before you sign off to leave the reader feeling positive and enthusiastic. There are many reasons why the donor may be interested:

- you are running a good project which is right at the heart of their stated policies and priorities;
- you have already received support from them and this further grant will allow you to build on that success;
- there is a personal contact which it will pay to highlight;
- there is a particular benefit to the donor which you want to stress. (This is particularly the case with companies who will want to see a business or public relations return on their money.)

Sometimes, people sum up on a negative note: 'Wouldn't it be a tragedy if all this good work came to an end' or, 'If we don't raise £30,000, the project will have to close'. Avoid this kind of thing at all costs. You've made a good, convincing case with positive reasons for supporting your work. There is no reason to assume you will not get the money.

The Bare Bones Application Letter

Note, there is no such thing as a model application letter. Write your letter in the way that best suits you and the work you are doing. Be yourself and let your work be seen in its best light. However, here is one skeleton outline that will help you put fundraising muscle on in the right places.

Dear ... *(wherever possible use the name of the correspondent. If you do not know it, make every effort to find out, and get the spelling right)*

I am writing on behalf of ... seeking funding towards the cost of ...

... was set up in ... by ... to do ... Major initiatives have included ...

I am writing about our ... project. The need we are meeting is particularly important because ...

We know the project will be effective because ...

We know we are the best people to do this work because ...

The project will cost £ ... We intend to raise the money as follows: ...

As you are interested in ... *(location, funding criteria etc.)* I am therefore writing to you for ...

At the end of the grant we expect the project will be funded by ...

If you require further information, or you wish to discuss the application, or you would like to visit and see the work, please contact me on ...

Yours sincerely,

Don't forget: Use headed notepaper, include your charity number (if you have one) and sign the letter.

11. The signatory: who puts their name to the application

This could be anybody e.g. the project leader, the director, the fundraiser, the chairman of the management committee, an appeal patron. Whoever signs it must:

- **Appear sufficiently senior**. This shows you are treating the application seriously.
- **Be knowledgeable**. The funder may well ask for more information. The person who signs the letter should be able to tell them what they need to know, including the overall financial position of the organisation. If the name

on the letter cannot give this information it appears that the application has not been well organised, and the project not well thought through. If you have a patron who signs the letters but does not know about the day-to-day running of the project, you should include the contact details of someone who will be able to answer more detailed questions.

- **Be available**. Again, if the funder wants more information they don't want to have to leave a whole series of messages before they get the details they need to make a decision.
- **Be open**. Leave your potential supporter with plenty of opportunity to talk to you, find out more, or visit. Many will decline your invitations to come and look at the work or meet the members, but people like to be asked.

What do you send with the application letter?

If the funder has an application form you must fill it out following its instructions. However, if you are writing an application letter, you should send the following supporting materials:

- a set of your most recent accounts, or a budget for the year if you are a new organisation;
- a budget for the particular project you are wanting support for, including estimated income and expenditure;
- an annual report (if you have one). If you have not done so before, think about your annual report as a fundraising tool. It does not have to be a dry as dust account of the last year with minimal information on what you do. It can say as much about your activities and success stories as you want it to.

You can also enclose anything else that will support the application (e.g. newsletters, press cuttings, quotes sheets, videos, photos, drawings, letters of support from famous people). However, do not rely on these extra bits to get you the money. They will not compensate for a hopeless letter. Assume that the trust will only read your letter and the financial information (budget and accounts). They should be able to get the complete picture from these. If in doubt, ask yourself:

- Is this relevant to the application? Is it absolutely essential or a nice extra?
- Will it help the funder to make a decision in our favour?
- Can I afford to send all this?
- Does it present the right image? Is the additional material so glossy that it implies you are a rich organisation, or is it a tatty photocopy which suggests that you can't really be bothered?

Remember, everything is for a fundraising purpose. If the accompanying information does not help the application, do not include it. It is definitely not a case of never mind the quality, feel the width.

Your application letter

Your application letter should tell any reader everything they need to know about your appeal in a short space of time. Assume they will not read anything else you send, and then answer the following:

- Will they have a clear idea of who you are, what you want, why you want it?
- Will they see what good it will do, what you expect from them, where else the money will come from, and what happens when their support has finished?

Before you send the letter, give it to a friend who knows little or nothing about your project. After reading the letter quite quickly, if your friend cannot answer the above questions, nor will your potential supporter be able to.

What do you do with the letter?

There are two main strategies.

1. Send it out to all relevant funders all at once. This is the most common technique. It has the advantage of getting the appeal up and running and you will know reasonably quickly where you stand.
2. You may wish to send the application out in stages. Write to a few of your key supporters first and see if they will lead the appeal (i.e. give you a grant which then encourages others to do the same). When some of these have committed themselves to supporting you, then write to the rest saying that firstly, you have already raised £10,000 of the £20,000 needed, and secondly, that X, Y and Z funders gave it to you.

Money tends to follow money. The more you raise, the easier it is to raise more. Highlight any money that has already been raised or pledged. Sending applications out in stages usually improves your chances because you concentrate initially on those most likely to support you. Then you widen the net to include those who don't know you as well but will take their cue from other funders' confidence in you. However, this approach is more time consuming and needs more planning. It may not be the remedy for crisis funding where you are desperate to get money in as soon as possible.

What to do after the letters have been sent

You should keep a simple record of what you have sent where. It will help you keep track of applications and to know how supportive each funder is. Note also the supporting materials you have sent, or the events you have invited funders to.

Apart from this, mostly you can do nothing except wait for a yes or no. You can ring to check that the application has arrived, but you do not want to seem to be hassling or pressurising people. Different types of funders will have different expectations of this.

If you get a positive response, write to say thank you immediately and put these people on your mailing list for the future. Keep them informed of your progress. Note any conditions on the grant that have to be met (e.g. sending a written report to the funder each year) and make sure you keep to them. You will want to go back to those that have supported you for help in the future. Keep them interested in your progress and how the money has been spent. Stories from individual beneficiaries and general progress reports can be an easy and friendly way of keeping the funder interested and enthusiastic about what their money has helped to achieve.

It is perfectly possible to send those funders still considering your appeal a further letter to update them on progress. The letter can be quite short, saying: 'We understand you are still considering our application about ... However, you may be interested to know that we have so far raised £10,000 of the £20,000 we need. This has come from ... Please contact me if you need any further information.'

If at first you don't succeed ...

Don't be afraid to go back to people who turned you down, unless they have said that they would never support your kind of work. There are many reasons why you might not have got money; they may have funded something similar the previous week; they may have run out of money; they may have had a deluge of brilliant applications and yours was next on the list; they may have never heard of you before. Go back next year with a different proposal, and the next year and the next year.

Think about different supporters

In following chapters there are details on who might support you and their reasons. You will have to take into account what each funder will be looking for and why. A company, for instance, will be looking at the commercial possibilities of linking up with you; what is good for their business. They may look for more tangible benefits in the short term than say, a trust or local authority. Read each of the chapters that cover the funders you are hoping to approach for tips on how to apply.

And finally ...

A major grant-making trust states in its guidelines: 'A thoughtful and honest application always stands out in the crowd! Tell us clearly what the problem is, and how your project will do something about it. Give us relevant facts and figures, please don't use jargon, and don't be vague. You don't need to promise the moon just tell us what you can realistically achieve. Your budget should show that you've done your homework and know what things cost.

'A thoughtful and honest application isn't a hurried and last minute dash to meet our deadlines with something dreamed up overnight. It is a serious and sincere attempt by your organisation to use its experience and skill to make a positive difference where it is needed.'

Applications checklist

- Does it have a personal address? (If it's the 'Dear Sir/Madam' variety, don't bother until you have more information on the supporter.)
- Does the first paragraph catch the reader's attention?
- Are you clear about what you want and why you want it?
- Is your work likely to be interesting to the donor?
- Is it clear how much the donor is expected to give? Is this reasonable?
- Is the application nicely presented? Does it attract the eye with short paragraphs and no spelling mistakes?
- Does it back up what it says with good supporting evidence?
- Is it positive or upbeat? (If it's gloomy and negative, think again.)
- Does it take account of guidelines published by the donor? Does it make a connection with the supporter's interests?
- Is it written in clear, plain English, or does it use lots of long sentences full of qualifying clauses and jargon?
- How long is the application? Two sides of A4 is plenty for a trust; one side for a company. Remember it does not have to say everything, but it has to say enough.
- Crucially, is the application appropriate? A brilliant letter to the wrong people will not get support.

Chapter 5
Raising money from the public

▪▪▪

When you are thinking of raising money, the first people you think of are the big funders (e.g. the National Lottery and the Foundation for Sport and the Arts). However, if you need to raise £10,000 and you have 1,000 members, it may well be much easier to raise £10 from each. It also helps to make your case to other funders if you have a well-established track record of successful fundraising from the public.

Members of the public are probably the most dependable and generous supporters of voluntary and sporting activity. There are no reliable figures for how much individuals give for sport. In terms of charitable giving, they give about 10 times as much as companies and five times as much as grant-making trusts. They give about 20 times as much as the Lottery Sports Fund. This chapter looks in outline at a few of the most effective ways of getting support from the general public.

Why would an individual support your appeal?

The first thing to do is work out what an individual stands to gain from giving you money. There are many possible motivations.

- *Because they support your cause.* For example, Cliff Richard has put a lot of money into tennis in schools. Similarly, people have supported appeals to enable young children to take part in overseas competitions.
- *Because they have been involved in the past.* Former members, old boys' and girls' networks, and people who have benefited from the club. Former members/former junior members will still have some affection for the club, and hopefully, fond memories. They will want to support the present activities and reunions, particularly if combined with an anniversary, which can be a way of focusing their financial support. But this is likely to be occasional rather than regular, so plan your fundraising accordingly.
- *Because they like the fundraising idea.* They may have no interest in your club, but really want to take part in the fundraising activity (e.g. you are running a sponsored abseil and they have always wanted to abseil). Often, people will attend concerts or other events because they like the event or because someone famous is turning up. They don't really care who stands to benefit from the event; they just want to have a good time.

- *Because a friend asked them to.* Much of the most effective fundraising is done between friends. I am doing a sponsored event and so ask my friends to sponsor me. They're not necessarily interested in who will benefit; they may even not agree with it. However, as friends they will still sponsor.
- *Because they stand to get something in return.* People often buy raffle tickets or take part in lotteries because they hope to win them. Again, it doesn't necessarily matter where the money goes.

However, the most important factor is the personal contact between the donor and the person/organisation asking for money. How do you build these relationships?

1. Through those involved in the club

There are various people involved in the club, from coaches and administrative people to the management committee, members and parents. All these are to be nurtured and cherished as key elements in your fundraising strategy. They have a stake in the club and its future success. They have access to a wide range of people, as do their families. Obviously you don't want to take advantage of them, but they may well be prepared to put in extra effort every now and again.

2. Through your publicity

You may need to put a bit of effort into improving your local publicity. The local press can be a good way of doing this if you have a good story about a league success, county champion, overseas tour or famous person coming. You can use this kind of publicity to raise awareness of your fundraising events or other activities.

3. Through fundraising activities themselves

Fundraising activities themselves can be very attractive and fun. This section looks at two of the most popular: events and sponsored activities. It also looks at how to find and use celebrities to help with your fundraising.

Useful books
Two useful books are *Tried and Tested Ideas for Raising Money Locally* and *Good Ideas for Raising Serious Money* by Sarah Passingham, published by the Directory of Social Change (0171-209 5151) at £9.95 each + £2.50 p&p.

Organising fundraising events

Sports clubs are in a strong position when it comes to organising events. They have activities and access to facilities. They can often attract famous people, which always gives things more of a buzz. You can run sports specific events (e.g. five-a-side tournaments) or more general events – the principles are the same.

Before organising your event you need to be sure of why you are asking people for money. It will help to decide which event and the way it will be run if you have considered why people will want to give. As mentioned above, people give for a number of reasons which can be simplified to four:

- they like the **organisation**
- they like the **people**
- they like the **cause**
- they like the **event**.

You need to be sure which interest you are appealing to and plan your events and coverage in this light.

> The history of event fundraising is littered with grand failures where groups organised too much too soon, and assumed that initial enthusiasm would become sustained commitment. Be ruthlessly realistic about the numbers involved, possible disasters and public apathy before you give something the go ahead.

The key thing is not just to look at the event's fundraising potential; evaluate the risk as well. What happens if it rains? Are you sure enough people will come? Is everyone else doing the same thing? Is it a tired formula?

Before you begin planning, ask yourself the following questions:

- What is the main purpose of the event? Is it to raise money, or a PR exercise, a thank you to volunteers and supporters, a way of channelling the enthusiasms of members or what?
- Who is going to attend the event? How can you reach them? If you intend to sell tickets door to door, who is going to do this?
- What is the main focus of the event (e.g. a football competition)? Can you guarantee to organise it successfully?
- Do you want a celebrity presence? If so, who will it be and how can you guarantee they will be there?
- Who is going to organise the event? What help do they need? Is it the best use of their time, i.e. could they be raising more money elsewhere if they were not stuck with this event to do?
- Have you the capacity to manage the event both beforehand and on the day?
- Can you get it sponsored to minimise the financial risk and maximise the potential benefit?
- Is there a clear budget for all of this? Does the budget make sense?

Once you have a satisfactory answer to these questions, you can start planning in earnest. The key is to start early and be clear about what you are doing.

If you have never run an event before, it is best to start off small. You will grow in confidence once you have had two or three success stories.

> There are basically two types of fundraising event:
>
> - ticket events where money is raised through ticket sales
> - participation events where money is raised through sponsorship of those taking part.

There isn't the space in this book to look at how to plan an event. If you want ideas or help with this, we suggest you read *Organising Local Events* by Sarah Passingham, available from the Directory of Social Change (0171-209 5151) 1995 edition priced £9.95 + £2.50 p&p.

Organising sponsored events

These are one of the most effective ways of raising money. They are really popular amongst participants and you can pretty much have a sponsored anything. All you need is an attractive idea and people willing to do it. Those taking part in the sponsored event are the ones who do the fundraising. The great advantages are that you may not necessarily need to organise anything, and that people are giving money to friends that they know and like rather than to an organisation they have never heard of promoting an activity they have no intention of doing.

There are three kinds of people who tend to take part in sponsored events:

- Those people who want to support your organisation.
- Those people who have taken part in previous sponsored events and enjoyed them.
- Those people who enjoy the chosen activity.

The aim is to get a core group (or charismatic individual) to do something they like and get a wider group of people to sponsor them. You need to find something sufficiently popular and trouble free, and something that you can build on and repeat year by year to achieve greater returns. The best sponsored events have been built on small beginnings, and now have the organised expertise and a band of loyal helpers to generate a substantial annual income.

The first thing to do is think about who you will be able to attract and design the activity accordingly. Young children are not the most obvious people to take part in a sponsored weight lift; older people are unlikely to want to do a sponsored bounce. Also, you don't have to restrict it to sport. Just because you are a boxing club doesn't mean to say that all your sponsored activities centre on boxing. You could just as easily do a sponsored walk as anyone.

43

Secondly, you don't necessarily need to organise the event yourself. It may well be much easier to raise £2,000 by persuading 20 club members to do the Great North Run than to organise your own (risky) mass participation event.

Either way, the sponsor forms require thought. They must say exactly what is being done, but they also provide an opportunity to state what money is needed. Then they have to allow the sponsors to commit themselves to a generous level of sponsorship. Most sponsors do not know what is expected and are guided by what has been written before. Therefore, you need to keep three things in mind:

- If sponsors go by what is written above, try to start each sheet off with people you know will be generous. This may encourage people to follow this lead.
- Try and break the sponsorship down into units which will encourage people to give more. For example, to sponsor 10p per kilometre will generate more money than 10p per mile.
- Maybe you could offer a prize to the person bringing in the most sponsorship money or the most sponsors. This will encourage people to generate as much income as possible. (However, make sure the prize goes to the one who delivers rather than promises the most!)

Sponsored event checklist

1. Choose a good activity: one that people will want to do and will enable them to get sponsorship. Make sure it is safe and appropriate.
2. Set a date and venue: make sure you give people lots of warning to allow for preparation.
3. Get necessary permission: from the police or local authority, and parents/guardians.
4. If it's a sponsored walk/run/bike ride make sure the route goes from A to A, that it starts and finishes in the same place – otherwise your participants will find themselves with complicated transport arrangements.
5. Organise local publicity: get any celebrities and media people signed on if possible.
6. Seek local commercial sponsorship: for costs and any prizes needed.
7. Produce sponsor forms: give examples of what amounts you expect and get good amounts first.
8. Prepare for the day: ensure you have all the stewards, equipment and information for the event.
9. Tidy up afterwards.
10. Thank all participants. Give prizes if necessary.
11. Chase all uncollected pledges.
12. Publicise the amount of money collected and tell those who gave what the money bought.

You need to think through how you are going to publicise the event well in advance; you must make sure that you are well-organised on the day, that you thank participants properly, and that you chase payments. You should also try to maximise the benefit to your organisation. Can you sign all those taking part up as members? Can you keep them involved so they support you again in the future? At least let them know how much was raised and what it helped the club to do. Make them feel part of the achievement.

There are many key elements about events which are not covered here. For example, for each event or activity you may need to think about the following:

- Budgeting
- Car parking
- Celebrities
- Fire regulations
- First aid
- Food hygiene
- Insurance
- Keeping money safe
- Licences

- Loos and litter
- Media coverage
- Police notification
- Publicity
- Safety
- Security
- Sponsoring the event

Do the Right Thing – do you need a licence?

The regulatory hurdles you will have to clear will depend upon the event you are running. Here are some you may have to consider.

- Public Entertainment Licence – Chief Executive's Department of your local authority.
- Liquor Licence – Magistrates Court.
- Lotteries – small, one-off events may not need a licence, but door-to-door ticket selling will.
- Bye-laws – check with the Leisure and Recreation Department, or other authorities such as rivers, waterways, footpath, coastal, heritage and so on.
- Health and Safety – check all aspects of your activity with the local Health and Safety Office.
- Safety Certificates – particularly if you are organising fairground rides, steam fairs, motorised tours or the like. The National Association for Leisure Industry Certificates can send an inspector to check the site.
- Public Liability Insurance.
- First Aid.

(From: *Organising Local Events* and *Tried and Tested Ideas for Raising Money Locally* by Sarah Passingham)

Planning events

Checklist – how to organise an event

The Community Council of Lancashire has produced a list to cover planning, preparation and running a village event. You can adapt the following to your own activity, but remember this cannot cover all eventualities and you should use this as the start for your planning, rather than the last word.

If you are thinking of holding an event, a logical approach to the planning process will always produce a better organised, safer and more enjoyable event.

This list has been designed to be a step-by-step guide and checklist, taking an organising committee through all the stages necessary in planning a wide range of community events.

> The event has to be appropriate. A group of keen schoolboys had their heads shaved to raise money for a new school rugby kit. Their efforts were rewarded by suspension from school by a not-too-pleased headteacher.

The list follows the logical order of event planning, starting with:

1. The following points should be considered to assess the feasibility of your event before planning starts.

- What type of event are you planning?
- Why are you holding it?
- When will you hold it? Will it clash?
- Where will you stage it, safely?

2. Once you are satisfied that the event is feasible, the next stage is to PLAN IT.

3. After deciding that your idea is sound, and getting committee approval, the final task is to **appoint an overall event coordinator** – who has overall control – and **an organising committee**.

Planning

Agree the date of the event, and set realistic timetables for preparation. Consider the main areas of planning. The Outline Plan for your event should cover the areas listed below:

Safety

	Assigned	Finalised
Insurance	☐	☐
Risk Assessment	☐	☐
Health & Safety	☐	☐
Safe Site	☐	☐
Occupier's	☐	☐
Liability Act	☐	☐
Health & Safety at Work Act	☐	☐
Other...	☐	☐

Budget

	Assigned	Finalised
Draft Budget & Contingency	☐	☐
Break Even Point	☐	☐
Sponsorship/Grant Aid	☐	☐
Costs/Sales	☐	☐
Trade/Concessionaires	☐	☐
Re-instatement Deposit	☐	☐
Other...	☐	☐

Publicity

	Assigned	Finalised
Sponsors' Requirements	☐	☐
Trade Adverts	☐	☐
Advertising Costs	☐	☐
Publicity Material Costs	☐	☐
Other...	☐	☐

Programme

	Assigned	Finalised
Time/Date – Other Local Events	☐	☐
National Events	☐	☐
Holidays	☐	☐
Legal Considerations		
– Food Hygiene	☐	☐
Planning Permission	☐	☐
Licences – Alcoholic Drinks	☐	☐
Music/Dance	☐	☐
Personalities/Guests	☐	☐
Other...	☐	☐

Site

	Assigned	Finalised
Mains Services	☐	☐
Car Parking	☐	☐
Access To/From	☐	☐
Marquee Hire	☐	☐
Reinstatement	☐	☐
Other...	☐	☐

Staffing

	Assigned	Finalised
Numbers Required	☐	☐
Paid	☐	☐
Volunteers	☐	☐
Other...	☐	☐

Preparation

Having planned the event and agreed the timetable for preparation. You must assign tasks to members or sub-groups, and arrange dates for their completion. For larger events, sub-committees for each area of preparation e.g. safety or publicity, should be set up. The event committee must meet regularly to make sure everything is going to plan – or to iron out any problems. Members of the organising committee should take responsibility for individual areas. Completion dates should be set.

	Assigned	Completed
Safety		
Signs	☐	☐
Barrier Hire	☐	☐
First Aid Personnel	☐	☐
PA Systems/Radio	☐	☐
Public Liability	☐	☐
Other...	☐	☐
Budget		
Costs – services	☐	☐
staff	☐	☐
site	☐	☐
equipment	☐	☐
supplies	☐	☐
Income – Sponsorship	☐	☐
Admission Charge	☐	☐
Trade Stands	☐	☐
Advertising		
On Site/Programme	☐	☐
Tickets/Programme Sales	☐	☐
Insurance	☐	☐
Other...	☐	☐
Publicity		
Radio/TV What's On	☐	☐
Programmes	☐	☐
Press Release	☐	☐
Sponsors' Requirements	☐	☐
Handbills	☐	☐
Posters	☐	☐
Photographer	☐	☐
Other...	☐	☐

	Assigned	Completed
Programme		
Start/Finish Times	☐	☐
Food Hygiene	☐	☐
Planning Permission	☐	☐
Insurance – High Risk Activities	☐	☐
Specific Items	☐	☐
Third Party Claims	☐	☐
Consequential Loss	☐	☐
Cancelled Event	☐	☐
Damage to Site	☐	☐
Weather Insurance	☐	☐
Catering Bars	☐	☐
Other...	☐	☐
Site		
Sign Posting	☐	☐
Site Plan	☐	☐
Electricity/Water	☐	☐
Toilets – Disabled Access	☐	☐
First Aid Post	☐	☐
Lost Children Area	☐	☐
Seating – Fire/Safety Regulations	☐	☐
Car park – Disabled Vehicle Recovery	☐	☐
Other...	☐	☐
Staffing		
Recruitment – Parking, Tickets, Officials, Catering	☐	☐
Security	☐	☐
Uniforms/Bibs	☐	☐
Expenses/Meal Tickets	☐	☐
Troubleshooters	☐	☐
Other...	☐	☐

On the Day

Arrive early – earlier than you think you'll need. Ensure individual members know their delegated tasks. Check all tasks have been completed. Run through the event and the volunteer jobs. The event coordinator should not be tied to one job, but should be free to assist and troubleshoot where necessary.

Safety	Assigned	Checked	Site	Assigned	Checked
PA/Radios & Coded Messages	☐	☐	Car Park – Security Disclaimer	☐	☐
Marshals – Bibs	☐	☐	Toilets – Clean/Check Regularly/		
Barriers – Secured	☐	☐	Well Positioned/Accessible	☐	☐
Signs – Keep Out, Exit etc.	☐	☐	Lost Children Area		
First Aid Post – Signposted	☐	☐	– Staffed/Signposted	☐	☐
Experienced Personnel	☐	☐	Seating – Set Out/ Checked/		
Fire Fighting Equipment	☐	☐	Anchored	☐	☐
Police	☐	☐	Electrical Supply/Generator	☐	☐
Electrician	☐	☐	Water/Drainage	☐	☐
Other...	☐	☐	Catering Outlets		
Money			– Clean & Priced	☐	☐
Float	☐	☐	Bars – Plastic Glasses		
Prize Money/Cheques	☐	☐	– Clean & Priced	☐	☐
Secure Cash Boxes	☐	☐	Other...	☐	☐
Tickets – Start No.	☐	☐	**Staffing**		
End no.	☐	☐	Easily Identified	☐	☐
Other...	☐	☐	Briefed/Specific Duties	☐	☐
Publicity			Given Meal Tickets/Expenses	☐	☐
To the Event Signs	☐	☐	Other...	☐	☐
Programmes on Sale	☐	☐			
Radio/TV on the day	☐	☐	*REMEMBER – This list cannot cover all*		
Banners/Flags	☐	☐	*eventualities. Space has been left for*		
Reporters/Photographers	☐	☐	*you to fill in the individual*		
Other...	☐	☐	*requirements specific to your event.*		

After the Event

Thank your team but try to maintain momentum to ensure that all post event jobs are completed. Discuss problems and how the event could be improved next year. Start planning now!

	Assigned	Checked		Assigned	Checked
Return Site to Original State	☐	☐	De-briefing	☐	☐
Extra Litter Collection	☐	☐	Press Release/Photos	☐	☐
Thank You Letters	☐	☐	Bank Money		
			– Prepare Accounts	☐	☐

49

Working with celebrities

Sports clubs have a natural affinity with sporting celebrities. Such associations can be converted into major fundraising opportunities. Well-known people can be used in a variety of ways, from being your patron to joining your board of trustees, from signing appeal letters to appearing in photo calls. They can help propel you from obscurity to high profile.

However, they can be more trouble than they are worth. They may not turn up. Their after-dinner speech may be a complete disaster. They may be found guilty of drug-taking the day before your event. They may be used to a certain level of attention and not be overly flexible in how they are prepared to do things. They may charge you a fortune which means the whole thing loses money.

By and large, working with celebrities is a tremendous experience and is highly beneficial to both the celebrity and the club. What advantages do celebrities bring?

- They give the event a higher profile. This can bring much more press coverage.
- It makes obtaining sponsorship, or increasing the value of the current deal, much easier.
- Their presence at the event will draw in more people.
- You can charge a higher entrance fee or ticket price.
- People will feel they have had a better time.
- Celebrities have access to celebrities, so you could build up your network of contacts.
- Celebrities often have access to funders and those with influence. You can use this to your advantage.
- An appeal letter signed by a celebrity often has greater success than one signed by an unknown fundraiser.

This list could go on and on. However, you need to remember two things:

- You have to work as hard with a celebrity as anyone else to make sure you get what you want from them.
- It is up to you to make sure that all the benefits associated with having a celebrity actually come off.

Finding celebrities

Some people just strike lucky. They write speculative letters to famous people and one or two come off. However, most of the time getting to a celebrity takes time and an awful lot of persistence.

As with everything else, it's a question of who you know, or at least who you can get to know. Start off within the club and your supporters. The most obvious people to look out for are those who used to be in the club but have now moved onto bigger and better things. They will still probably look back on their 'early days' with affection and you should be able to tap into this.

Alternatively, the members and supporters in the club may not know Chris Boardman personally, but they may know someone who knows Chris Boardman. Or is there anyone you can recruit into the organisation with these contacts? Can you get to parties or functions that celebrities are at and introduce yourself? Can you get a ticket to hear their after-dinner speech? Do you know their agent? Can you get to them through this route?

> You should always try to keep in touch with former members; you never know what may become of them. You only need one to make it big and you could be looking at fundraising gold.

Managing celebrities

As with any area of fundraising, you should be highly professional in how you manage your celebrities. You must control access to them. If they think you have opened a floodgate of requests from other people that they cannot meet, they will not be impressed. Also, they have their own reputations to consider and will not want to be associated with bad publicity or something controversial.

You must give the celebrity a very clear idea of what they are expected to do and when they can discreetly slip away. Are they just going to cut a ribbon to open the event, have one picture taken and disappear? Are they expected to shake hands with the managing director of the sponsoring company and receive a cheque from them? If so, are they happy to be photographed with this sponsor? It is disastrous when you say that person x will be presenting the prizes when they have no intention of doing so. It annoys the celebrity and it greatly upsets your supporters.

You should also be clear about fees and expenses. If the celebrity wants a fee, find out how much. It may be more than the value of their support. Will a car be provided? By being open and professional you not only get the most out of this event but give yourself every chance of persuading the celebrity to help you again.

In general

Raising money from your members and other individuals can be really effective. The amount you can raise is limited only by your time, energy, resources and creativity. The important things are:

- Make sure that each event is carefully and realistically budgeted. Raising money from the public is one of the least predictable areas of fundraising. Do not let it get out of control.

- Start small and build up. Don't go for a really big event unless you know you can do it. So many organisations have lost so much money by being too ambitious too early on.
- Sports clubs have a natural advantage in that they have facilities and activities that are already popular. You may be able to raise enough money through a series of open days which are far less risky.
- It is not all about sport. You should be able to organise a sponsored silence by your young members as easily as any other youth club. You could organise a raffle or small lottery just like any local society.
- You don't have to organise anything yourselves. You can simply take part in other people's events.
- Be aware of the law. For example, it is illegal for children under 16 to undertake a public collection.
- Use the local press. Get yourself known.
- Get as much help and advice as possible.

Chapter 6
The Sports Councils

■■■

The role of the Sports Councils

Since the first edition of this Guide published in 1995 there has been a wholescale reorganisation of the Sports Councils. In the previous edition there was one Sports Council responsible for developing and improving the knowledge and practice of sport and physical recreation throughout the UK. There were separate autonomous Councils for Scotland, Wales and Northern Ireland.

Important note

Just before this Guide went to print the English Sports Council was rebranded as Sport England. This is the title of the Sports Council responsible for England used throughout the Guide.

There are now five separate Sports Councils within the United Kingdom with distinct responsibilities for the development of sport in their home countries. These are:

- the United Kingdom Sports Council
- Sport England (previously the English Sports Council)
- the Scottish Sports Council
- the Sports Council for Northern Ireland
- the Sports Council for Wales.

These bodies are responsible for:

- funding programmes related to developing sport within the UK through their own exchequer grant-in-aid budgets;
- the distribution of Lottery money.

This chapter outlines the missions and functions of all five Sports Councils. The UK Sports Council mainly focuses on high performance sport so we have outlined its role here in order to clarify how it relates to all the Home Country Sports Councils.

The UK Sports Council

The United Kingdom Sports Council (UKSC) focuses directly on high performance sport at the UK level, with the express aim of achieving sporting excellence on the world stage. The UKSC also has a brief to take a lead among the family of Sports Councils (England, Northern Ireland, Scotland and Wales) in all aspects of sport that require strategic planning, administration, coordination or representation for the benefit of the UK as a whole.

The UKSC has a budget of £11.8 million from the Department for Culture, Media and Sport which is used to fund sporting projects of UK significance. The UKSC was established by Royal Charter and its broad remit covers a range of objectives:

- to encourage and develop higher standards of sporting excellence in the UK;
- to identify sporting policies that should have a UK-wide application;
- to identify areas of unnecessary duplication, overlap and waste in the way that sport is administered in the UK;
- to develop and deliver appropriate grant programmes developed by the governing bodies with a UK or Great Britain remit in conjunction with the Home Country Sports Councils;
- to oversee policy on sports science, sports medicine, drug control, coaching and other areas where there may be a need for the Home Country Sports Councils to deliver a consistent UK-wide policy;
- to coordinate policy for bringing major international sporting events to the UK;
- to represent the UK internationally and increase the influence of the UK at an international level.

How the UKSC works

The UKSC is centred on the needs of UK athletes: 'The UK's sportsmen and women are the UKSC's sole purpose for existence and the athlete's needs are placed at the heart of all Council strategies.'

There are four Directorates to support this central aim.

Performance Development

This Directorate is responsible for developing and delivering strategies to significantly improve the performance of UK teams and athletes on the world stage. The UKSC's Performance Development Team works with sports governing bodies to provide funding for performance related programmes, so that élite athletes receive the highest standards of coaching and other vital support services.

UK Sports Institute

Following the Government's announcement in December 1997, that Sheffield would be the HQ site of the UK Sports Institute (UKSI), the UKSI's Project Team is now responsible for providing support to top sportsmen and women to enable them to compete and win at the highest level. By setting national standards and giving support locally, the UKSI aims to give athletes the help they want, where and when they want it.

International Relations and Major Events

The International Relations Directorate is responsible for raising the UK's international sporting profile. It supports British representatives on International Sports' Federations and works with development agencies such as the British Council, Department for International Development and Voluntary Service Overseas.

The Directorate will also enable the UKSC to spearhead campaigns to bring major events, such as the Olympic Games and the World Cup to the United Kingdom.

Ethics & Anti-Doping

The Directorate aims to ensure a fair and ethical sporting environment for all and to protect athletes' rights to participate in drug free sport. Domestically, the UKSC uses education as an essential preventative measure, combined with a comprehensive testing programme. It also contributes to the worldwide fight against drugs and sport through involvement in various international projects.

What the UKSC does not do

The UKSC operates at a UK level only. The Home Country Sports Councils for England, Scotland, Northern Ireland and Wales have responsibility for developing sport in their own home countries. This includes supporting the development of sport and physical recreation generally, the development of excellence, and the provision of facilities.

The United Kingdom Sports Council
10 Melton Street
London
NW1 2EB
0171-380 8021; Fax: 0171-380 8025

Sport England (previously the English Sports Council)

The English Sports Council (Sport England) is an independent body, established in 1997 by Royal Charter. The Sports Council for England was created, along with the UK Sports Council, when the former GB Sports Council, originally established in 1972, was split. Sport England has a remit for English matters similar to that for the previously existing separate autonomous Councils for Scotland, Wales and Northern Ireland.

Sport England plays a leading strategic role in the development of sport and physical recreation. Under the terms of its Royal Charter Sport England is committed to 'fostering, supporting and encouraging the development of sport and physical recreation and the achievement of excellence therein among the public at large in England and the provision of facilities therefore'.

55

Sport England is funded from Exchequer grant-in-aid from the Department for Culture, Media and Sport. (For further information see page 165.) In 1997/98, grant-in-aid totalled £33.27 million. This grant is supplemented by income from Sport England's own commercial activities, such as the sale of publications. Sport England is also the designated distributing body for the Lottery Sports Fund, the sports element of the proceeds earmarked for good causes from the National Lottery. (See chapter 7.)

The actual Sports Council, as distinct from the organisation, currently has 15 members, all appointed by the Secretary of State. Current Council members are:

Trevor Brooking MBE, Acting Chairman	Tim Marshall MBE
Gerald Dennis, Vice Chairman	Jim Munn MBE
Phyllis Avery	Keith Oates
Peter Blake OBE	David Oxley OBE
Chris Boardman MBE	Jeff Probyn
Julia Bracewell	Sam Stoker
Garth Crooks	Geoff Thompson MBE
Carol Gustafson	

Sport England's objectives

Sport England aims to lead the development of sport in England by influencing and serving the public, private and voluntary sectors. Simply put, it wants *more people* involved in sport, *more places* to play sport, and *more medals* through higher standards of performance in sport.

There are three main programmes administered by Sport England.

More people

- This programme introduces sport to young people. It gives opportunities to acquire basic sports skills at an early age at school and through physical education instruction develop the interest in sport that will see them continue participating as adults. This also involves ensuring that teachers and coaches of young people are properly trained and supported and links between schools and clubs are developed.
- Increasing participation in the community is encouraged by including everyone in sport and ensuring that nobody is excluded from the opportunity to take part. Specific action is taken in disadvantaged areas and for women, people with disabilities and black, Asian and other ethnic minorities. Helping the people who run sport, especially volunteers, is vital.
- It is important to ensure that everyone with interest and ability has the opportunity to improve personal standards of performance in sport and fulfil

their potential. Sport England works closely with local authorities in building and coordinating an infrastructure for sports development at a local and regional level and with the governing bodies of sport in providing education and training programmes for coaches, officials and administrators.

More places

- This programme aims to ensure that the right facilities for sport are built in the right place. Social requirements and developments are taken into account.
- Sport England supports the optimum quality of design of sporting facilities so that there are better places for sport which are suited to local needs. All projects, from small local community facilities to large schemes of national and international importance need to be successfully developed.
- Where facilities are available they have to be run efficiently and effectively. Improved facility management is achieved by accreditation schemes to ensure that standards are maintained.

More medals

- Sport England aims to help teams and individuals to perform better and win medals. It ensures that everyone with the interest and ability has the opportunity to reach the highest standards of sporting excellence through the World Class Programme. This is done with effective talent identification and development, support for specialist training and competition facilities and subsistence funding for top athletes. (See chapter 14 on grants for individuals.)
- Sport England is supporting the development of the UK Sports Institute. It works with partners to develop an English network to help the country's élite sportsmen and women, including those with disabilities, to have the best facilities and services.
- Sport England provides services to athletes and coaches through the National Sports Centres and supports the delivery of sports science and medicine services.

Sport England provides information and maintains a network of sports organisations to ensure that all are working towards the same goals for English sport. It assesses and evaluates supported schemes to ensure they are effective, and carries out or commissions research into sport and recreation. Sport England also encourages and supports the adoption of the highest ethical standards among people or teams participating in sport and physical recreation.

Sport England and governing bodies

Sport England works closely with over 100 governing bodies giving revenue grants totalling nearly £5 million in 1997/98. These grants go directly to governing bodies rather than their member organisations and clubs and are intended to support the infrastructure development of the governing body. Not all governing bodies receive Sport England funding. It initially depends on whether Sport England (a) recognises the sport, and (b) recognises the individual governing body. When deciding on grants, the Council pays particular attention to the governing body's plans for delivery of the Council's primary objectives to expand and enhance opportunities for all and the improvement of performance standards. The governing body must demonstrate sound administrative practice and outline its development proposals in a comprehensive plan for the future. (See chapter 15 for further information on Sports governing bodies.)

In addition to funding specific sports governing bodies Sport England also grant aids national sporting organisations such as the Central Council of Physical Recreation, National Coaching Foundation, Commonwealth Games Council for England, SportsAid and national disability organisations.

Sport England Regional Offices

Although its role is changing, the regional offices of Sport England remain an important resource for local organisations and clubs. There are 10 regions of Sport England in England. The major role of a region is to translate Sport England's aim at a regional level to develop sport in England by encouraging more people, more places and more medals.

The focus at regional level is to support key partners in local authority leisure and education departments, governing bodies of sport and clubs to achieve and sustain comprehensive sports development programmes. This involves working closely with these partners to identify how Sport England can help, which of its products and services are appropriate, where and when these can be used to best effect and how they fit into the wider national picture of sports development. Once partnerships have been created, the regional offices will work to ensure that they are maintained.

The regional office provides information and advice on likely sources of funding and provides an information pack containing general advice on funding sources and contacts.

A proportion of Sport England's exchequer grant from central government is used to implement programmes in the regions which contribute towards the More People, More Places, More Medals aims. This support is given in the regions alongside Lottery funding.

> 'Whilst much of the ESC's work may be delivered at regional level, it is aimed at meeting the objectives set out in the Council's Operational Plan. For that reason, investment of the exchequer funds is targeted at those projects which will assist the Council to meet its objectives and is not available for unsolicited applications.'
> Sport England

The regional office is not a source of funding as it once was. Rather, funding will follow defined objectives which have been decided at a regional level following national plans. Organisations looking for support should consider the following questions:

- Does the regional office publish a local strategy document or other guidelines?
- How do we fit in with their policy objectives?
- Have we got up-to-date information?
- Who is the first point of contact?
- Have we contacted them for advice or other support?
- Are there regional contacts with a specialism in our sport?
- Is help given with equipment costs; revenue or running costs or with capital projects such as building or site development?
- Is in kind support available such as advice and help with coaching or the loan of equipment?

> The regional grants programme that once supported sports projects is now being wound down. In many ways working with the regional offices is similar to developing relationships with the local authority. Increasingly, local sports organisations will have to fit in with a regional strategy for sports development to be part of the support network. Support will be directed to those organisations that the regional office knows and trusts and where regular communication and confidence has been built up. Local sports organisations should also ensure they are linked in with any regional initiatives promoted by their governing body.

Examples of initiatives in which investment was made in and up to 1997/98 include:

More people
- Provision of training and resources for 10,600 primary schools through the TOPs programme.
- Support for 135 local authorities undertaking community delivery of TOPs with 2,250 equipment bags supplied.
- Projects to bridge the gap for young people between schools and clubs involving over 1,000 schools.
- Sports specific courses for over 10,000 teachers in the Coaching for Teachers programme.
- Over 80 local education authorities employing sports development officers.
- Volunteer management training delivered to over 2,800 people.
- The establishment of a Regional Training Unit in each region.
- The establishment and maintenance of a Regional Disability Forum in each region.

More places
■ Production of District Sport and Recreation Strategies.

More medals
■ Over 80 sports specific development officers working in the regions.
■ Training and establishment of networks of sports science and medicine practitioners.

'Whilst the above list illustrates those areas for which exchequer funding has been used to stimulate development, it must be recognised that funding is but one 'tool' available to the ESC. The expertise of its staff, its advisory services and its information service all contribute to effective sports development. Equally, the significant contribution made by the Lottery Sports Fund, particularly in the More Places and More Medals programmes, is complementary, and contributes to delivery of what is probably the world's most comprehensive sports development programme.'

Sport England
16 Upper Woburn Place
London WC1H 0QP
Information Centre: 0171-273 1500;
Fax: 0171-3835740
Publications: 0990-210255;
Fax: 0990-210266

Regional offices
Sport England East Region
Crescent House
The Crescent
Bedford MK40 2QP
01234-345222; Fax: 01234-359046

Sport England East Midlands Region
Grove House
Bridgford Road
West Bridgford,
Nottingham NG2 6AP
0115-982 1887; Fax: 0115-945 5236

Sport England Greater
    London Region
PO Box 480
Crystal Palace National Sport Centre
Ledrington Road
London SE19 2BQ
0181-778 8600; Fax: 0181-676 9812

Sport England North Region
Aykley Heads,
Durham DH1 5UU
0191-384 9595; Fax: 0191-384 5807

Sport England North West Region
Astley House
Quay Street
Manchester M3 4AE
0161-834 0338; Fax: 0161-835 3678

Sport England South Region
51a Church Street
Caversham
Reading RG4 8AX
0118-948 3311; Fax: 0118-947 5935

Sport England South East Region
PO Box 480
Crystal Palace National Sports Centre
Ledrington Road
London SE19 2BQ
0181-778 8600; Fax: 0181-676 9812

Sport England South West Region
Ashlands House
Ashlands
Crewkerne
Somerset TA18 7LQ
01460-73491; Fax: 01460-77263

Sport England West Midlands Region
Metropolitan House
1 Hagley Road
Five Ways
Edgbaston
Birmingham B16 8TT
0121-456 3444; Fax: 0121-456 1583

Sport England Yorkshire Region
Coronet House
Queen Street
Leeds LS1 4PW
0113-243 6443; Fax: 0113-242 2189

Sports Council for Northern Ireland

As a lead facilitator in the development of sport the Council will work with partners to:

- increase and sustain committed participation, especially amongst young people;
- raise the standards of sporting excellence; and
- promote the good reputation and efficient administration of sport.

These aims translate into three focus areas: starting well; staying involved; striving for excellence. Under these headings, there are the following objectives:

Starting well

- *Objective 1:* to create locally available high quality sporting opportunities
- *Objective 2:* to equip volunteers, especially those working with young people, for the challenges they face in the development of sport

Staying involved

- *Objective 3:* to provide structured opportunities for participants to continue their involvement by fostering cooperation between sports organisations, education services, district councils and community groups
- *Objective 4:* to train and support volunteers to deliver sport so that as many people as possible are encouraged to sustain their interest

Striving for excellence

- *Objective 5:* to establish an organisation focused on the development of excellence
- *Objective 6:* to identify talented performers and to offer the support they need
- *Objective 7:* to raise the standard of coaching for high level performers.

Information about grants is available by contacting the Council at the following address:

The Sports Council for Northern Ireland
House of Sport
Upper Malone Road
Belfast BT9 5LA
01232-381222; Fax: 01232-682757

For more information on the Lottery Sports Fund please call 01232-382222; Fax: 01232-383822.

Scottish Sports Council

The Scottish Sports Council's mission is to lead the development of sport and physical recreation in Scotland, with the aim of increasing participation and improving standards of performance. The Council has three visions which form the cornerstone of Sport 21, a national strategy for sport in Scotland:

- a country where sport is more widely available to all
- a country where talent is recognised and nurtured
- a country achieving and sustaining world class performances in sport.

In 1998/99, the Council received £9,809,000 grant-in-aid from the Scottish Office. A significant proportion of this money goes directly to programmes and projects run by governing bodies and local authorities.

The Council is also responsible for the distribution of the Lottery Sports Fund in Scotland.

For more information on the Scottish Sports Council contact:

The Scottish Sports Council
Caledonia House
South Gyle
Edinburgh EH12 9DQ
0131-317 7200; Fax: 0131-317 7202

For more information on the Lottery Sports Fund please call 0131-339 9000; Fax: 0131-339 5361.

Sports Council for Wales

'The Sports Council for Wales (SCW) provides a range of services to a variety of organisations, all geared to achieving the twin goals of increasing sports participation and improving standards of performance.'

In 1998/99, SCW received £6,596,000 from the Welsh Office. It gives over £1 million directly to governing bodies of sport in Wales each year. It also administers a range of other schemes to which other organisations can apply for financial assistance. The following gives a broad outline of each of these schemes, providing details of their purpose, who or what is eligible and how to obtain further information.

Local Sports Development Grant (LSDG)

The LSDG scheme is geared to helping fund sports development programmes and projects, including minor items of equipment. The level of assistance depends on the merits of the scheme and the amount of money necessary to ensure its success.

Eligible projects include those which are aimed at:
- increasing participation in sport
- improving standards of performance
- increasing the number and quality of sports leaders, coaches and officials
- creating school/club/community links
- establishing junior clubs and junior sections of adult clubs.

The above list is not meant to be all-encompassing. Priority is given to schemes which cater for children of school age.

Eligible items within the above projects include:
- the cost of hiring facilities
- expenses incurred by sports leaders/coaches/instructors and officials
- purchase/hire of initial equipment essential to establish the scheme
- the cost of attending coach education courses
- initial promotion/publicity costs.

Applications are accepted from one or a combination of the following:
- voluntary sports clubs
- appropriate voluntary organisations
- local authorities
- other local, regional or national agencies.

All clubs and organisations have to be properly constituted. Any organisation interested in applying should contact their nearest SCW regional office.

Sports safety grants

This is a scheme to help national organisations and clubs provide safety cover for the general public taking part in recreational activities in the natural environment. The level of assistance is up to 75% of the cost of eligible items. Difference ceilings apply for capital projects, revenue and vehicles.

What projects are eligible? Organisations and clubs can apply for support for equipment, capital buildings and specific schemes, such as establishing a new club. For organisations only, grants are also available for all aspects of training and publicity/promotion.

Who is eligible? Properly constituted organisations and clubs which are mainly involved in providing a sports safety service. Clubs must also be part of the appropriate national organisations.

How to apply: Application forms are available from the SCW's head office in Cardiff or from recognised sports safety organisations.

Élite Cymru scheme

Élite Cymru is aimed at providing the most highly promising athletes in Wales with the support they need to achieve their potential. It is a scheme which provides financial support as well as much more, including sports science testing and advice, psychological preparation, medical back-up, lifestyle management training and a counselling service.

Who is eligible? Only those athletes proposed by their relevant governing bodies of sport. No direct approaches by individuals to the SCW can be accepted.

How to apply: The stringent eligibility criteria are set out in an leaflet, available from the SCW's National Development Services section in Cardiff. Anyone who feels they meet the criteria should approach their sport's governing body.

Overseas Expeditions Development Support

This is a grant to help overseas expeditions which will enhance the development of a sport. The grant is limited to a contribution of up to 50% of the estimated costs of travel, safety equipment and other essential materials. The level of grant rarely exceeds £1,000.

What is eligible? Welsh-based expeditions with a majority of members from Wales (further details below) and which already have the support of their respective governing bodies of sport. Expeditions exclusively of an educational or scientific nature are not eligible.

Who is eligible? The expedition members who need to be in a majority qualify by birth, parentage or residence in Wales for at least 12 months in the past two years.

How to apply: Applications have to be lodged before December 31st prior to the financial year (April 1st – March 31st) in which the expedition is planned to take place. Further information is available from the SCW's National Development Services section in Cardiff.

Sports Council for Wales Offices

Head Office
Sophia Gardens, Cardiff CF1 9SW
01222-300500; Fax: 01222-300600
South West Regional Office
10 Quay Street, Carmarthen SA31 3JT
01267-233924; Fax: 01267-222388

North West Regional Office
Plas Menai, Llanfairisgaer,
Caernarfon LL55 1UE
01248-670964; Fax: 01248-671380

South East Regional Office
Sophia Gardens, Cardiff CF1 9SW
01222-300500; Fax: 01222-300600

North East Regional Office
Deeside Leisure Centre,
Chester Road West, Queensferry,
Deeside CH5 1SA
01244-822600/822625;
Fax: 01244-822662

For more information on the Lottery Sports Fund please call 01222-300500.

This chapter has been written by the Public Affairs Unit of Sport England Lottery Unit.

Chapter 7
The National Lottery
■■■

The National Lottery has rapidly established itself as one of the key funders of sports activity. Although sport's share of Lottery income has gone down (to pay for the extra money required by the government for the New Opportunities Fund), it will still receive over £200 million a year.

Sports Lottery grants are given to increase participation in sport, particularly amongst young people, and to assist the development of talented performers. Funding is divided into two broad categories:

- Capital – this is money for buildings, equipment and other physical items. All capital money is given to organisations and is covered in this chapter
- Revenue – recently Sport England has introduced a second programme of grant-giving. Grants are given to governing bodies to develop individual sportspeople under the World Class Performance Programme. For further details of this support, refer to chapter 14 on grants for individuals, page 265.

Capital grants are given to build, upgrade and extend facilities. They can also be given for major pieces of permanently-based equipment (e.g. gymnastics apparatus). However, no grants are given for renewals, repair and maintenance, transport, personal sports equipment and finishing off projects already started. Further details are given later in the chapter.

How the National Lottery was set up

The National Lottery was set up in 1993 through the National Lottery etc. Act. The Act set out how the Lottery would operate and established five areas to benefit from the Lottery: sport, the arts, heritage, charities and projects to mark the year 2000 and the beginning of the third millennium. In addition, the National Lottery Act 1998 created a sixth good cause of health, education and the environment (the New Opportunities Fund).

Lottery sales and payouts, 1998

Sales	£5.2 billion
Prizes (50%)	£2.6 billion
The 'good causes' (28%)	£1.5 billion
Lottery duty (12%)	£0.6 billion
Retailer commission (5%)	£260 million
Camelot costs & profit (5%)	£260 million

The responsibility for distributing these proceeds does not rest with the Government, but with a number of independent distributing bodies. These are the four national Arts Councils, the five national Sports Councils, the Heritage Lottery Fund, the National Lottery Charities Board, the Millennium Commission and the New Opportunities Fund. They make their funding decisions independently of government, although the policies of the New Opportunities Fund are a particular interest of the current government.

Lottery funds made available to the six good cause areas are allocated in the following way:

Arts	16.67%
Sport	16.67%
Heritage	16.67%
Charities	16.67%
Projects to mark the year 2000	20%
New Opportunities Fund	13.33%

The Millennium share of Lottery income will transfer to the New Opportunities Fund after 2001. The Millennium Commission is guaranteed an income of £2.017 billion over its lifetime. The Secretary of State for Culture, Media and Sport announced that the arts, sport, heritage and charities would continue to receive a 16.67% share of Lottery income after 2001.

Income to sport

Sport, as one of the six 'good causes' receives 4.6p for every £1 spent on a National Lottery ticket. This means that, on current forecasts, sport should receive over £1.8 billion by the end of 2001.

The bodies responsible for distributing lottery funds for sport are the Sports Councils for England, Scotland, Wales and Northern Ireland. The total income is subdivided on the basis of population as follows:

Sport England	83.3%
Scottish Sports Council	8.9%
Sports Council for Wales	5.0%
Sports Council for Northern Ireland	2.8%

Recently, the Government designated the UK Sports Council as a Lottery distributor too. Discussions are underway as to how much Lottery money they will distribute. They currently play a role in allocating a portion of each of the home country Sports Councils' share to élite athletes and governing bodies which represent the UK or Britain instead of one particular home country. This role is carried out under the World Class Performance Programme (see chapter 14 on grants to individuals).

Funding policies

The underlying aim of the policies adopted by all four home country Sports Councils for the use for lottery funding is to increase participation in sport, particularly amongst young people, and to assist the development of talented performers. Each of the four Sports Councils has slightly different policies that reflect the local environment but a number of key criteria are constant.

> The success of the National Lottery is having a direct impact on the profitability of the football pools. This in turn reduces the income of the Foundation for Sport and the Arts which receives all its income from pools companies. For further information about this, please see chapter 8.

Government framework

The government issued a series of guidelines to all lottery distribution bodies. These guidelines (or Policy Directions) set out the operation framework and are summarised overleaf.

The first nine points relate primarily to the use of Lottery money for capital projects and represent a summary of the original directions issued by the then Secretary of State for National Heritage in 1994. The final two relate to the use of Lottery funds for major international sporting events and support for individuals in this country i.e. revenue funding. The last directions were added two years later on.

In the light of the National Lottery Act 1998, new Policy Directions for the existing good causes were published, after consultation, by the Secretary of State on 1 June 1998. They

- shift the focus away from big spending on bricks and buildings and concentrate on making sure more Lottery money goes on people and activities;
- acknowledge the particular developmental and creative needs of children and young people;
- remove the requirement for significant levels of partnership funding, making it easier for less wealthy organisations and areas to benefit;
- for the first time encourage distributors to consider how their strategies will contribute to sustainable development;
- invite them to look at the contribution they can make, through the good causes, to reducing economic and social deprivation;
- ensure that all regions and parts of society can benefit from the lottery.

Policy Directions issued by the Secretary of State for Culture, Media and Sport

The bodies responsible for distributing the National Lottery proceeds to good causes should take the following matters into account:

1   They should not solicit particular applications from individual organisations.
2   They must consider applications relating to the complete range of activities falling within their particular remit.
3   They must ensure that money is only distributed to projects which are of benefit to the general public or which are charitable. Any project seeking funding must not have private gain as a primary purpose.
4   Funds should be concentrated on projects which involve capital expenditure on new and improved facilities. Money should only be used for revenue grants or for setting up endowments where these costs are connected with capital projects which have already received lottery funding and would not otherwise be completed because of a lack of other sources of finance.
5   The viability of projects must be taken into account, and in particular there should be available resources to pay for future running and maintenance costs.
6   Projects must be supported by a significant element of partnership funding from non-lottery sources, which may include gifts in kind.
7   Distributing bodies should obtain such information they consider necessary to make decisions, and may wish to consult with independent expert advisers.
8   Distributors must not give money to any organisation over which they have material influence or control (this repeats a condition laid down in the National Lottery Act).
9   Distributing bodies should look for the highest standards of architectural quality and building design, with particular reference to general accessibility and the needs of people with disabilities.
10 The home country Sports Councils shall look to support the development of sporting talents and skills, particularly of young people.
11 Sport England shall take into account the funding of major international sporting events.

Eligible sports

The National Lottery Act 1993 refers to funding being applied to projects 'on or connected with sport', and the four home country Sports Councils have agreed on a common interpretation of this principle in terms of eligibility for Lottery funding.

Activities which are starred (*) in the box opposite are those where safety is particularly important and affiliation to the recognised governing body/bodies

Aikido*	Handball	Roller skating
American football	Hang/paragliding*	Rounders
Angling	Highland games	Rowing
Archery*	Hockey	Rugby league
Arm wrestling	Horse racing	Rugby union
Association football	Hovering	Sailing/yachting*
Athletics	Hurling	Sand and land
Australian rules football	Ice hockey	yachting
Badminton	Ice skating	Shinty
Ballooning*	Jet skiing*	Shooting*
Baseball	Ju jitsu*	Skateboarding
Basketball	Judo*	Skiing*
Baton twirling	Kabaddi	Skipping
Bicycle polo	Karate*	Snowboarding*
Billiards & Snooker	Kendo*	Softball
Bobsleigh*	Korfball	Sombo wresting*
Boccia	Lacrosse	Squash
Bowls	Lawn tennis	Street & Skater hockey
Boxing*	Life saving*	Sub-aqua*
Camogie	Luge *	Surf life saving*
Canoeing*	Modern pentathlon*	Surfing*
Caving*	Motor cycling*	Swimming & Diving
Chinese martial arts*	Motor sports*	Table tennis
Cricket	Mountaineering*	Taekwondo*
Croquet	Movement & Dance*	Tang soo do*
Crossbow*	Netball	Tenpin bowling
Curling	Orienteering	Trampolining*
Cycling	Parachuting*	Triathlon
Disability sports	Pétanque	Tug of war
Dragon boat racing	Polo*	Unihoc
Equestrian*	Pony trekking	Volleyball
Exercise & Fitness*	Pool	Water skiing*
Fencing*	Quoits	Weightlifting*
Fives	Racketball	Wrestling*
Flying*	Rackets	Yoga
Gaelic football	Racquetball	
Gliding*	Rambling	
Golf	Real tennis	
Gymnastics*	Roller hockey	

of the sport is a condition of grant for lottery funding. Any of the home country Sports Councils can assist if this information is not readily available.

National Lottery Grants – England
Sport, to September 1998

Region	Grant total	%	Population	Grant per head (000s)
North East	£54,684,940	6.8	2,605.1	£20.99
North West	£121,102,024	15.1	6,899.9	£17.55
Greater London	£117,677,220	14.7	7,007.1	£16.79
East Midlands	£66,545,407	8.3	4,123.9	£16.14
South West	£74,573,974	9.3	4,826.9	£15.45
Yorks/Humber	£66,330,084	8.3	5,029.5	£13.19
South East	£96,577,440	12.0	7,847.2	£12.31
Eastern	£60,019,622	7.5	5,257.4	£11.42
West Midlands	£55,402,008	6.9	5,306.4	£10.44
England	£89,315,556	11.1	48,903	£1.83
United Kingdom	£134,500	0	57,806	£0.23

Later in this chapter there are more details of what each of the Sports Councils is looking for in an application for National Lottery funding under their capital funding programmes. However, the following is a summary of what is generally looked favourably upon, what is a lesser priority and what is definitely not considered.

Examples of schemes that could be eligible for Lottery funding

New, upgraded or extended facilities, such as:

- Artificial turf pitches with floodlighting
- Athletics tracks, indoor and outdoor
- Bowling greens, indoor and outdoor
- Bridleways, cycle routes, etc. – where they are of strategic importance and will lead to a measurable increase in participation
- Climbing walls
- Golf courses
- Gymnastics centres, purpose-built
- Ice rinks
- Jetties and slipways
- Multi use games areas with floodlighting
- Natural turf pitches
- Riding centres

- Sports halls
- Squash courts
- Swimming pools, indoor only
- Tennis courts, indoor and outdoor

Essential support facilities, such as:

- Changing rooms, showers, toilets etc. for participants, including people with disabilities
- Changing for officials
- Equipment stores, such as boat houses, drying rooms etc.
- Improvements to facilities to make them accessible to, and usable by, people with disabilities
- Safety equipment and safety boats
- Social and activity areas, but ONLY if an integral but not the most significant part of a larger application
- Sports medicine and science at centres recognised and accredited by governing bodies

Purchase of land and water facilities, such as:

- Fishing rights
- Freeholds and long leases – 99 years or more of existing facilities, or of sites with concurrent development

Purchase of major, permanently based equipment, such as:

- Club boats, gliders etc.
- Gymnastics apparatus
- Pools of equipment bought for a single sport by governing bodies – where part of structured development programme

Examples of schemes not eligible for Lottery funding under the capital funding programmes – and why

All renewals, repairs and maintenance

This is not capital expenditure. Moreover, any work necessary as a result of past neglect is ineligible. A possible exception might be major items of equipment that you require for essential maintenance – for example, the purchase of a roller to provide good quality pitches.

Transport – team and mini-buses, vans etc.

Minibuses and other road vehicles are not eligible. Sport England believes that the life expectancy of the vehicles is too short and it is difficult to monitor use. Rescue vehicles or those specially adapted for use by disabled people might be eligible in exceptional circumstances.

Support facilities
When they are not essential and integral to the current application.

Personal sports equipment
This is not a lasting asset, nor is it of wide enough community benefit. Exceptions are:

- equipment that is a necessary part of a capital project being supported by Lottery funding
- substantial equipment that will be used for at least five years and be permanently based on site. We will also consider applications for 'pools' of equipment for use by, for example, a governing body of sport or a network of youth groups as part of a structured development programme.

Buying land or facilities for future use or development
This does not constitute the development of a specific or immediate project.

Finishing off projects that have already been started Lottery regulations do not permit funding to be applied retrospectively for whatever reason.

Examples of schemes which are eligible for Lottery funding under the capital funding programmes but which are given low priority

The Sports Councils want to support schemes that demonstrate a quantifiable sporting gain and which result in a direct increase in participation in the sport, particularly by sections of the community that are under-represented. In this context they consider that some types of project are a low priority. As a result, they are unlikely to be granted an award. If your project is primarily for any of the elements listed below, the Sports Councils may well deem it to be a low priority. You may be well advised to reconsider submission of your application.

Low priority projects – reason for low priority

- Artificial Turf Pitches (ATPs) without floodlights: they would not be able to be used intensively enough
- Floodlighting for main grass (match) pitches in order to meet league requirements: the justification for projects must be for sound sporting reasons – not to satisfy regulations alone
- Outdoor swimming pools: indoor pools are a far better investment as they provide year-round use and can be timetabled with confidence, ignoring climatic factors
- Second-hand equipment (unless re-conditioned and providing value for money): would not provide value for money or ensure quality

- Spectator stands or other provision for spectators/non-participants: they do not increase active participation in sport and recreation
- Stand-alone social facilities (or projects solely concerned with social provision): not sufficiently related to increasing active participation
- Car parks: not sufficiently related to increasing participation
- Perimeter fencing (except for compelling reasons of security): not sufficiently related to increasing participation
- Informal recreation projects unless of strategic significance leading to a demonstrable change in access/participation: more to do with informal recreation than to providing an introduction to organised sport.

In addition, we consider the following to be low priority unless they are an integral, but not the most significant, part of a larger project.

- Artificial turf banking and ditches for bowling greens: not sufficiently related to increasing participation
- Automatic watering systems for bowling greens: they relate more to saving on maintenance than to increasing participation or improving performance
- Automatic watering systems for golf tees (greens may be funded if sporting benefit can be demonstrated): they relate more to saving on maintenance than to increasing participation or improving performance
- Cricket pitch covers, score boards and boxes (except where a relatively small part of a larger scheme): not sufficiently related to increasing participation
- Kitchens and bars (except where an integral part of a larger scheme): not sufficiently related to increasing active participation
- Office/administrative accommodation or office equipment: not sufficiently related to increasing active participation
- Finishing off projects which have already started (especially where the reason for the shortfall in funds is a lack of financial planning for the project): Lottery funding cannot be applied retrospectively and compliance with Sport England technical standards could not be ensured
- Maintenance projects, including equipment (unless essential initial provision or major refurbishment): these are revenue rather than capital items.

National Lottery Capital Awards

By 1st September 1998 over £868 million had been given in Lottery awards to sport as follows:

England	£732,746,878 (2,673 awards) of which £45,011,632 was awarded to national, England-wide schemes (12 awards)
Wales	£44,873,115 (353 awards)
Scotland	£65,508,193 (463 awards)
Northern Ireland	£25,010,428 (366 awards)

Sport England Lottery Sports Fund Awards

Awards distributed to individual sports since 1995

Sport	Number of awards	Total project cost	Total amount awarded	Average award
Angling	28	£2,293,100	£1,444,400	£51,600
Archery	5	£173,500	£112,600	£22,500
Association Football	392	£111,758,400	£80,258,000	£204,700
Athletics	41	£49,521,200	£31,843,100	£776,700
Badminton	33	£30,088,000	£17,884,700	£542,000
Basketball	36	£45,908,000	£27,693,100	£769,300
Billiards & Snooker	5	£393,700	£183,500	£36,700
Bobsleigh	1	£100,400	£62,600	£62,600
Bowls	278	£39,576,700	£24,108,400	£86,700
Canoeing	29	£5,909,600	£4,050,200	£139,700
Caving	2	£32,100	£19,000	£9,500
Cricket	454	£98,137,000	£54,560,100	£120,200
Croquet	4	£146,100	£91,000	£22,800
Cycling	10	£1,494,000	£869,100	£87,000
Disability Sports	20	£7,355,500	£4,757,100	£237,900
Dragon Boat Racing	2	£20,000	£12,600	£6,300
Equestrian	20	£7,272,700	£4,300,800	£215,000
Exercise & Fitness	31	£7,769,100	£4,641,000	£149,700
Gaelic Football	1	£99,600	£51,600	£51,600
Gliding	18	£1,231,700	£707,200	£39,300
Golf	33	£20,165,300	£7,683,300	£232,800
Gymnastics	40	£15,499,500	£10,596,000	£264,900
Hang-gliding & paragliding	3	£54,500	£34,700	£11,600
Hockey	106	£59,066,700	£40,238,000	£379,600
Ice Skating	2	£55,491,500	£34,996,600	£17,498,300
Judo	6	£1,392,500	£923,100	£153,900
Lacrosse	2	£215,500	£111,100	£55,600
Lawn Tennis	407	£73,205,500	£45,944,900	£112,900
Motor Sports	3	£168,300	£69,200	£23,100
Mountaineering	36	£7,705,000	£4,350,200	£120,800
Movement & Dance	2	£1,065,200	£691,200	£345,600
Multi Sports	134	£157,580,800	£104,323,400	£778,500
Netball	32	£22,117,200	£16,267,500	£508,400
Orienteering	2	£18,900	£12,600	£6,300
Pétanque	2	£29,000	£18,600	£9,300
Pony Trekking	1	£87,300	£62,000	£62,000
Rambling	4	£660,600	£307,400	£76,900
Real Tennis	2	£962,100	£594,800	£297,400

Sport	Number of awards	Total project cost	Total amount awarded	Average award
Roller Hockey	2	£152,000	£82,000	£41,000
Roller Skating	3	£86,800	£53,900	£18,000
Rowing	49	£26,060,000	£14,979,000	£305,700
Rugby League	21	£5,627,300	£4,355,200	£207,400
Rugby Union	97	£33,042,700	£20,801,700	£214,500
Sailing & Yachting	111	£40,635,500	£22,192,100	£199,900
Sand & Land Yachting	1	£73,300	£47,700	£47,700
Shooting	11	£648,900	£409,700	£37,200
Skateboarding	3	£261,900	£173,500	£57,800
Skiing	6	£1,204,400	£671,000	£111,800
Softball	1	£14,600	£9,100	£9,100
Squash	16	£5,023,129	£2,463,518	£154,000
Sub-aqua	70	£1,570,200	£1,030,500	£14,700
Surf Life Saving	4	£110,300	£73,700	£18,400
Swimming & Diving	97	£296,850,800	£175,921,500	£1,813,600
Table Tennis	23	£6,969,300	£4,214,600	£183,240
Trampolining	7	£1,413,500	£874,400	£124,900
Tug of War	1	£15,300	£10,000	£10,000
Volleyball	2	£10,431,000	£8,768,800	£4,384,400
Water Skiing	3	£2,595,400	£1,138,400	£379,500
Weightlifting	9	£432,900	£272,500	£30,300
Wrestling	1	£27,600	£24,100	£24,100

Awards by County

Sport	Number of awards	Total project cost	Total amount awarded	Average award
Avon	51	£24,760,400	£14,533,300	£285,000
Bedfordshire	27	£3,019,900	£2,109,000	£78,100
Berkshire	43	£16,991,800	£9,746,000	£226,700
Buckinghamshire	44	£17,459,800	£7,099,600	£161,400
Cambridgeshire	47	£22,320,800	£12,668,500	£269,500
Cheshire	68	£17,216,900	£12,067,000	£177,500
Cleveland	27	£29,943,100	£18,152,100	£672,300
Cornwall	56	£15,126,400	£7,120,000	£127,100
Cumbria	63	£13,686,800	£8,915,400	£141,500
Derbyshire	51	£13,885,900	£9,005,900	£176,600
Derbyshire/Yorkshire	1	£3,683,800	£1,841,900	£1,841,900
Devon	95	£25,215,500	£15,362,500	£161,700
Dorset	50	£15,235,500	£8,091,100	£161,800
Durham	28	£10,823,200	£7,104,000	£253,700
East Sussex	58	£15,673,000	£9,927,200	£171,200

Awards by County cont.

Sport	Number of awards	Total project cost	Total amount awarded	Average award
East Yorkshire	1	£93,800	£37,000	£37,000
Essex	81	£15,051,000	£9,789,400	£120,900
Gloucestershire	62	£24,586,400	£16.698,300	£269,300
Greater London	173	£174,631,146	£121,339,000	£701,400
Greater Manchester	97	£85,717,900	£59,815,800	£616,700
Hampshire	113	£84,350,134	£45,665,200	£404,100
Hereford & Worcestershire	36	£16,920,100	£10,389,800	£288,600
Hertfordshire	82	£37,146,300	£20,708,700	£252,500
Humberside	39	£7,887,700	£4,400,900	£112,800
Isle Of Wight	18	£5,324,400	£3,894,000	£216,333
Kent	96	£25,563,000	£13,453,200	£140,100
Lancashire	93	£45,621,600	£26,884,400	£289,100
Leicestershire	70	£21,913,700	£16,616,600	£237,400
Lincolnshire	38	£22,167,900	£7,241,600	£195,500
Merseyside	36	£30,669,700	£21,583,200	£599,500
Norfolk	48	£26,581,000	£19,674,200	£409,900
North Yorkshire	85	£21,508,900	£9,639,200	£113,400
Northamptonshire	45	£20,236,200	£10,643,000	£236,500
Northumberland	27	£5,410,600	£3,020,800	£111,900
Nottinghamshire	61	£57,165,400	£34,000,000	£557,400
Oxfordshire	65	£12,305,500	£6,402,100	£98,500
Scilly Isles	1	£70,900	£56,400	£56,400
Shropshire	34	£10,773,800	£6,541,000	£192,400
Somerset	61	£14,253,700	£9,515,300	£156,000
South Yorkshire	42	£32,473,700	£24,528,400	£584,000
Staffordshire	45	£13,219,500	£10,174,700	£226,100
Suffolk	73	£11,882,100	£7,302,200	£100,000
Surrey	89	£20,921,000	£12,314,000	£138,400
Tyne and Wear	37	£36,281,300	£24,554,900	£663,600
Warwickshire	29	£4,400,900	£2,687,000	£92,700
West Midlands	86	£45,022,600	£29,567,900	£343,800
West Sussex	46	£12,687,900	£7,405,000	£161,000
West Yorkshire	108	£61,071,200	£37,452,600	£346,800
Wiltshire	45	£8,789,400	£5,527,000	£122,800
Yorkshire	1	£417,600	£268,800	£268,800

To give a flavour of the range of grants given, we have listed all the grants given which are England-wide. We have also listed the largest and smallest award made within each successful local authority of three counties in England.

England-wide   12 awards   Grant total: £45,011,632

All England Netball Assn	Portable floors	£32,500
British Canoe Union	Equipment for junior sports development	£192,383
British Federation of Sand and Land Yacht Clubs	Purchase of a national fleet of 60 land yachts	£47,660
England and Wales Cricket Board Ltd	50 non-turf wickets	£134,500
English Cricket Board	50 non-turf pitches	£137,500
English Golf Union	National Golfing Centre	£650,000
English National Stadium Trust	English National Stadium, Wembley	£21,500,000
EOBI Ltd England	Outdoor Basketball Initiative	£6,173,916
National Cricket Association	50 non-turf pitches	£125,720
National Sports Medicine Institute	Development of centres of excellence	£3,012,452
Nottinghamshire County Cricket Club	Redevelopment of stands at Trent Bridge	£5,250,001
Youth Sports Trust	Equipment for TOP Play & TOP Sport Community Programmes	£7,755,000

Cumbria   62 awards   Total awarded: £8,463,629

Allendale   *12 awards*   *Total awarded:*   *£2,305,509*

Keswick School (Grant Maintained)   £671,000
New four court community sports hall

Baggrow And Blennerhasset Cricket Club   £3,742
Purchase land, re-align football pitch, construct two artificial practice wickets, purchase portable nets and erect perimeter fencing

Barrow   *14 awards*   *Total awarded:*   *£1,501,930*

Barrow Community Trust   £1,115,337
Basketball centre

Furness Falcons Wheelchair Basketball Club   £7,800
Wheelchairs for basketball team

Carlisle   *9 awards*   *Total awarded:*   *£1,509,650*

St Aidans County High School   £522,346
Installation of 100m x 63m floodlit artificial turf pitch on the site of an existing all-weather pitch

Carlisle Cricket Club   £7,909
4 lane practice pitch; artificial match pitch and scarifying machine

Copeland   *9 awards*   *Total awarded:*   *£767,291*

Adams Recreation Ground   £175,000
New Pavilion Wasdale Mountain Rescue Team   £8,603
Extension and refurbishment of existing building

Eden	*9 awards*	*Total awarded:*	*£1,749,004*

Eden District Council £457,329
   New training pool and changing rooms at Penrith
   swimming pool
Upper Eden Rugby Union Football Club £9,100
   Purchase the freehold of a second pitch

Penwith	*1 award*	*Total awarded:*	*£25,506*

Eden Hall And Langwathby Sports And Recreation Field £25,506
   Extension to pavilion and creation of new junior
   football pitch

South Lakeland	*8 awards*	*Total awarded:*	*£604,739*

Kendal Ski Club £195,437
   Replacement of a dry ski slope with an all year artificial
   slope and extension of the slope
Corinthians F C £7,120
   Upgrading of changing facilities

Kent   92 awards   Total awarded: £13,146,852

Ashford	*10 awards*	*Total awarded:*	*£2,207,245*

Ashford Borough Council £1,807,583
   Athletics track with indoor training and warm-up area
Woodchurch Memorial Hall/Woodchurch Short Mat
   Bowls Club £3,400
   New levelled floor

Bexley	*3 awards*	*Total awarded:*	*£312,414*

Bexley Lawn Tennis And Squash Rackets Club £298,534
   To build a new clubhouse and two new glass-backed
   squash courts; to resurface two tennis courts with an
   all-weather surface; to enlarge the car park
Crayford Dartfordians Cricket Club £3,322
   Cricket Practice Nets

Bromley	*3 awards*	*Total awarded:*	*£156,583*

Westcombe Park & Orpington Sports Club £97,264
   Land purchase element of major club development
   including clubhouse refurbishment, stand and floodlights
West Wickham Playing Fields Trust Ltd £3,124
   Replacement of wire fencing for three tennis courts,
   including two gates, at Corkscrew Hill Tennis Club

Canterbury	*3 awards*	*Total awarded:*	*£292,545*

Whitstable R F C £246,497
   Construction of building, ball court and associated
   facilities including changing
Herne Bay Amateur Rowing Club £8,310
   Safety boat and boat house

Dartford	*2 awards*	*Total awarded:*	*£248,867*
Dartford Harriers			£167,906
New pavilion			
Hayden Football Club			£80,961
New clubhouse and multi-use games area			
Dover	*4 awards*	*Total awarded:*	*£128,220*
Ash Bowling Club			£43,826
New pavilion			
Dover District Council			£22,326
Conversion of two tennis courts to floodlit MUGA			
Gillingham	*3 awards*	*Total awarded:*	*£1,079,283*
Gillingham Jumpers Trampoline Club Ltd.			£742,763
To build a rebound centre – first of its type in the UK			
Medway Badminton Association Ltd			£5,280
Upgrade sports hall electrics and lighting			
Gravesham	*5 awards*	*Total awarded:*	*£524,887*
Meapa Gym Club			£281,098
Construction of an international standard gymnastics centre at the Southfields School site			
Harvel Cricket Club			£4,289
Installation of two bay cricket practice nets			
Maidstone	*13 awards*	*Total awarded:*	*£906,146*
Maidstone Hockey Club Ltd.			£239,812
Floodlit artificial turf pitch			
Maidstone Sailing Club			£3,205
Clubhouse alterations: conversion of store room into training room and provision of disabled access			
Rochester-Upon-Medway	*2 awards*	*Total awarded:*	*£1,038,141*
Shaftesbury Homes And Arethusa			£867,513
New indoor climbing wall, badminton-size gymnasium, changing rooms and ancillary facilities			
Holcombeians Sports Club			£170,628
Full size floodlit ATP			
Sevenoaks	*3 awards*	*Total awarded:*	*£121,996*
Edenbridge Angling Society			£98,696
Purchase of land and construction of lake			
Otford Sports Association			£7,000
Floodlighting for football pitch			
Shepway	*6 awards*	*Total awarded:*	*£365,133*
Lydd Town F C			£128,315
New pavilion; football pitch and MUGA			
Kent County Council/Dymchurch Cricket Club			£3,487
All-weather practice pitch and net			

Swale	6 awards	*Total awarded:*	*£345,805*
Dawes Community Association			£124,555

    Pavilion extension including changing rooms and MUGA
    (1-court size)

Woodstock Divers	£7,700

    Purchase of a 5.8m rigid inflatable boat

Thanet	7 awards	*Total awarded:*	*£243,343*
Thanet Wanderers R U F C			£74,300

    New clubhouse

Quarterdeck Youth & Training Centre	£13,500

    Upgrading outdoor multi-sport area

Tonbridge And Malling	11 awards	*Total awarded:*	*£2,101,998*
Buckmore Park Scout Centre			£1,520,442

    Sports centre

Bewl Bridge Rowing Club	£9,755

    Purchase of 2 rowing VIII boats

Tunbridge Wells	10 awards	*Total awarded:*	*£2,970,377*
Tunbridge Wells Borough Council			£2,563,090

    Weald Sports Centre comprising a 25m x 10.5m swimming
    pool, four-court sports hall, fitness gym, exercise studio and
    ancillary facilities

Horsmonden Cricket Club	£3,885

    Artificial match pitch

Wealden	1 award	*Total awarded:*	*£103,869*
Bowles Rocks Trust Ltd			£103,869

    Extension to residential accommodation

West Midlands 82 awards Total awarded: £23,028,888

Birmingham	30 awards	*Total awarded:*	*£7,905,732*
Birmingham City Council For Moseley School			£1,792,649

    Health and fitness centre

Nantmor Mountain Centre Association	£5,960

    Upgrade kitchen/catering facilities

Bromsgrove	2 awards	*Total awarded:*	*£872,915*
Hereford And Worcester County Council (Haybridge High School)			£866,526

    Four court sports hall with 2 squash courts, fitness suite

Wake Green Amateur Football Club	£6,389

    Drainage for Sports Fields

Coventry	8 awards	*Total awarded:*	*£2,600,382*
Coventry & Warwickshire Award Trust			£1,630,880

    Extension to indoor facilities (gym, exercise/ fitness/ martial
    arts studio, table tennis, bowls, cricket) and outdoor areas

Coventry British Sub Aqua Club	£10,410

    Boat Purchase

Dudley	13 awards	Total awarded:	£2,293,930

Dudley Metropolitan Borough Council (The Dormston School) £1,000,000
    Sports and arts centre
Coseley Cricket Club   £4,550
    All-weather practice pitch with cage.

Sandwell	8 awards	Total awarded:	£3,523,612

Sandwell Metropolitan Council   £3,312,561
    Tipton Sports Academy
Alpha Divers (Warley)   £8,995
    Purchase of a diving boat and safety equipment

Solihull	5 awards	Total awarded:	£655,570

Solihull Indoor Bowls Club Ltd.   £447,100
    Eight rink indoor bowling facility
    Nauctius Divers   £14,275
    6m Osprey RIB

South Staffordshire	3 awards	Total awarded:	£105,619

Wollaston Lawn Tennis Club   £71,414
    Conversion of four shale courts to floodlit artificial grass courts
Prima Sub-Aqua Club   £16,955
    Dive boat and training equipment

Walsall	7 awards	Total awarded:	£679,820

Walsall Lea (Alumwell School Community Association)   £466,029
    Construction of eight floodlit tennis courts and one
    floodlit artificial turf pitch
Pelsall Cricket Club   £3,287
    Mobile nets and bowling machine

Wolverhampton	7 awards	Total awarded:	£4,307,510

Wolverhampton Borough Council   £3,185,500
    Aldersley Leisure Village
Linden Lea Tennis Club   £8,000
    Floodlighting for two all-weather courts

Worcester	1 award	Total awarded:	£162,148

Worcester City Council   £162,148
    Extension of golf course from 9 holes to 18 holes

England

The portion of Lottery proceeds which benefits sport in England is distributed by Sport England. Recommendations on applications are made by Sport England's Lottery Awards Panel. The recommendations are then ratified by Sport England members. Administrative back-up is supplied by Sport England Lottery Unit.

Eligible organisations

Under Sport England's Capital Facilities Award Programme, Lottery funding is only available to sports which are recognised by Sport England. If your organisation's activities are not included in the list on page 69 you will not be able to apply. And for those which are starred (★) you must be affiliated to your sport's national governing body for safety reasons.

With this provision in mind, the following types of organisation are eligible to apply for funding from the Lottery Sports Fund, as long as they are based in and operate in England:

Voluntary sports clubs – if membership is open to all and no application for membership or access is refused other than on reasonable grounds. Also their constitution must clearly state that a recognised sport is a primary purpose of their organisation.

Area sports associations – if composed of local sports clubs involved in recognised activities.

National governing bodies – but only those which are recognised by Sport England.

Local authorities and other public bodies.

Charitable trusts, playing fields associations, youth clubs and **community associations** – but only if a recognised sport is part of the constitution and public access will be provided to the facility.

Schools, colleges, and universities can only apply if their proposals are not just for curricular activities, and if the proposals will help resolve a real shortage of facilities. There must be guaranteed public access of more than 40 hours a week backed up by a Community Use Agreement. (Guidelines for schools and colleges are set out under Sport England's School Community Sport Initiative [SCSI] – see page 89 for more information on this initiative).

Commercial organisations and **professional sports clubs** are only eligible if their proposals will provide a benefit to the community which cannot be met otherwise. Any such facility should not be primarily for personal gain or shareholders' dividends, should help resolve a real shortage of facilities and show that their project delivers significant guaranteed public access.

Excluded organisations

Sports not recognised by Sport England are not eligible for funding, and individuals cannot apply for money for their own benefit. Commercial bodies and professional sports clubs are generally excluded unless their projects are for the public benefit and not their commercial gain. Children's play activities will not be considered initially, although 'mini' versions of recognised sports are eligible. Organisations not based in England or not providing benefit in England will normally be excluded – those based in the other home countries should apply to their relevant Sports Council.

Eligible projects

For a list of example projects which are eligible under Sport England's Capital Facilities Awards Programme, please see list above under the heading 'Examples of schemes that could be eligible for Lottery funding'.

Capital funding

Under this programme, money is only available for capital projects. Lottery money will not normally be available to support ongoing revenue costs associated with salaries, maintenance, heating, cleaning etc. In exceptional cases, however, an application for revenue funding may be considered if connected with a capital project already supported by the Lottery Sports Fund, and needed for specific start-up costs which cannot be met from other sources. The project will have to be judged a high priority by Sport England, and even so will only provide revenue funding for no more than three years. Revenue funding is available from the Lottery Sports Fund, but for other purposes. The World Class Performance and World Class Events programmes provide revenue funding for élite sporting individuals and the staging of major events in England. (See chapter 14 on Raising money for individuals.)

Minimum total project size: £5,000
Sport England will not normally consider applications involving projects with a total cost of less than £5,000. (See page 94 for details of the Awards for All programme for projects of less than £5,000.)

Backers of projects with a total cost of more than £5 million should discuss their application as soon as possible with officers based in Sport England's Facilities Development Unit.

Partnership funding

The Lottery Sports Fund will only provide a maximum of 65% of the total costs of any project, and would prefer at least half the costs to come from other sources. It expects your organisation to supply some of this funding, normally a minimum of 10% if you are a voluntary organisation. Your contribution does not have to be in cash, and it could take the form of donated land and materials, or the equivalent value of volunteer work. Sport England states that if you manage to increase the proportion of money from non-lottery sources above the minimum level this is 'bound to help your application'.

In certain circumstances Sport England will provide up to 90% of the project cost – see Initiatives under the Capital Facilities Award Programme below.

Financial Priorities

There are five financial priorities which the applicant must demonstrate clearly in their application:

- financial need
- financial support
- financial viability
- value for money
- Lottery Sports Fund investment

1. Financial need

The primary consideration for all Lottery funding is financial need.

- Do you really require the Lottery Sports Fund's financial assistance?
- Can you afford to pay for the project yourselves without putting undue strain on your organisation's viability?

If your organisation has uncommitted, readily accessible, reserve funds that you are not intending to contribute to the project you will need to explain why. This does not mean that an organisation should be expected to commit its entire reserves to a project, and the applicant could reasonably be expected to retain up to one year's running costs in hand after the project has been completed (to hedge against an unavoidable but temporary slump in turnover).

A less obvious consideration on the question of need is whether the project is extravagant, for example in the provision of lavish social accommodation. In overall terms the cost figure may substantiate a case for financial need, but it is nevertheless necessary to consider whether the facility could be provided on a more modest but adequate scale without (or with less) Lottery funding. This is a value for money judgment, though the Lottery Sports Fund has a commitment to quality and not just economy. The former should not be compromised by the latter.

2. Financial support

The higher your partnership contribution and the greater the number of partners, the better (see heading 'Partnership funding' above). Although it will not be the most critical aspect of the assessment, it is a concrete demonstration of support. It increases the number of people that have a stake in the project and proves that they intend to make use of it. This will be useful in years to come, when you have to find money for maintenance and repair.

3. Financial viability

Once it has been established that there is genuine financial need and the shortfall level of assistance has been confirmed, the financial viability of the project will be examined and must be satisfied on two counts:

- Capital – sufficient capital finance should be assured or in reasonable prospect to enable the project to be started within six months and satisfactorily completed within a reasonable time;

- Running costs – the organisation should be assured of sufficient income when the facility is completed to meet all running costs, including adequate maintenance, repairs and renewals (sinking fund), together with the cost of any loan repayments.

If the information in the application form and accounts is not sufficient to satisfy these points, the applicant will be asked (in preliminary correspondence) to supply the necessary financial information.

In considering capital viability, it is important that contributions shown from other agencies are reasonably certain and not just hopefully expected; if necessary the applicant will be asked to supply some supporting evidence. The proportion of the capital cost to be financed from loans is a relevant consideration in financial appraisal.

Justify your fundraising strategy!

Funds from the organisation's own resources should be consistent with the position shown in the accounts and balance sheet. Organisations frequently show part of the capital cost as coming from 'fundraising'. If this is a relatively small proportion of the total cost it will probably be acceptable, since most organisations can usually raise some funds by special effort. But if 'fundraising' accounts for a substantial share of the cost, or if it already constitutes a significant proportion of their regular income upon which their current operational viability depends, then the organisation will be asked to provide more specific details (i.e. type of events, time-scale, expected income) together with some supporting evidence to demonstrate that their estimated receipts from this source are realistic.

With running costs, the nature of the project and the organisation may make it unnecessary to investigate in any detail; for example, an existing viable tennis club could reasonably be expected to undertake two additional courts. This aspect will therefore be more significant in the case of a new organisation starting from scratch, or in the case of facilities which are expensive to run (e.g. swimming pools, indoor bowls) and in these circumstances it will be necessary to examine carefully the financial projections (which must be) submitted.

4. Cost effectiveness and value for money

Cost effectiveness is a measure of cost related to the outcomes of your project. For example, putting down an all-weather pitch which then allows the facility to be used all year can be a very cost-effective way of increasing the capacity of a club.

Value for money is a measure of cost related to the long-term benefits of your project. For example, if you can show that the development of your facility will increase participation in sport in your area by 10% (or 250 people a week) over the next 10 years, this would represent terrific value for money.

So, Sport England will want to know:

- Is your project over-elaborate or costly?
- Have you gone 'over the top' because you expect the majority of the funding to come from the Lottery Sports Fund?

A high cost project benefiting a relatively small number of people has to make a stronger case that one with a high participation, built to a good standard.

Sport England certainly want to see quality facilities being built but over-provision or over-lavish social facilities will probably not be cost effective or provide value for money.

5. Lottery Sports Fund investment

A judgment will also be made about the potential sporting gain and community gain of your project in relation to the amount of money you're requesting.

Project quality

Your proposals should:

- be of high quality and able to withstand many years of use;
- meet the appropriate sporting standards imposed by Sport England and other national sports governing bodies;
- meet statutory requirements and any appropriate specifications for lighting, ventilation and heating.

Any facility must:

- provide full access for people with disabilities;
- be designed and built to a high standard.

The capital application pack contains a core set of Guidance Notes produced by Sport England and designed to assist the applicant in meeting Sport England technical requirements.

Preparations in place

Your project should be ready to start as soon as possible after a Lottery grant has been awarded. You should not be too hasty, however, as the Sports Council will not consider your proposal if any contracts for building works have already been signed.

Breadth of appeal and support

You should obtain support for your proposals from as many different communities and organisations as possible, and in particular local, regional, and national sports bodies. Openness and equality of access for the whole community are essential principles of Lottery Sports Fund funding. All new and improved facilities must be open to all sectors of the community regardless of gender, sexuality, race, religion and disability.

Increasing participation

Your project should address the needs of the widest possible cross-section of the community – the more people who stand to benefit from your proposal, the greater its chance of lottery funding. Preference will also be given to projects which will increase the participation of people who are at present denied access to sport and recreation.

However, in certain cases you will also be required to demonstrate how the need for community access can be appropriately balanced with use by élite performers for training.

Relevance to other plans and facilities

Wherever possible, your application should be in line with sports strategies drawn up by local authorities, regional and national sports governing bodies (including the Sports Council). Sport England does recognise, however, that applications may arise which challenge existing priorities or come from sports or areas where there are no existing strategies. Your proposals should also take full account of the relationship with similar facilities which already exist in your area or sport.

Improving standards in performance

The fund also wants to support capital projects which offer talented performers the opportunity to develop their skills. Such projects might provide:

- world-class facilities for training competitions
- world-class coaching support
- access to other specialist support such as sports science

These facilities are likely to be centres of excellence and designed as such by a governing body of sport. Your capital project may be solely to provide these facilities. It may provide them as part of a larger project catering for a wider range of needs. Not every project will do this.

However, even a modest, local project can achieve improvement in sporting performance by:

- providing better surfaces on which a higher standard of play is possible
- conforming to national and international governing body technical specifications.

Management and organisation

You need to show that your project has been properly researched and thought through. How can you show that there is a need or demand for the project being planned? For example, Sport England will examine:

- how the application conforms to the strategies of Sport England, governing bodies of sport and local authorities;

- the relationship between your project and other similar facilities;
- evidence of unsatisfied demand?

Sports development

Sports development records in a logical way what every organisation should be about – winning. Not just winning trophies and medals but helping people achieve their sporting and wider personal goals as well – better fitness, a healthier lifestyle, camaraderie, team work.

Probably all organisations involved in sport have a sports development plan already. In many cases it may be just one or two broad ideas in people's heads, for example, 'winning the league' or 'attracting more young players'. But how are you going to achieve your goals and when? A goal with no target date is unlikely to be reached. It can always be put off 'until tomorrow' or 'next season'.

An athlete who wants to win an Olympic gold medal sets that as a long-term goal. They also set milestone targets on the way to measure their progress. The first few steps will not be too difficult even if the ultimate goal may appear, at the outset, beyond reach. Athletes will also modify their short-, and sometimes longer-term goals in the light of actual events, such as injury. A sports development plan should be just like this.

The key to a good sports development plan is that it should be a living document, not just something that is written down to use in a Lottery application! All the members of the applicant organisation should be familiar with it so that the everyone works together for a common purpose. The applicant should also try to involve in their plan as many partners as possible. The partners may include nearby schools, other clubs, the local authority or county governing body. Once it is written, put it in a prominent place to remind all the organisation's members what their sporting goals are.

Sports Development Plan

A sports development plan explains how the applicant's organisation will achieve its sporting goals. The applicant should enclose the plan with their application. Local authority applicants should enclose a copy of their leisure and recreation strategy as well.

If you need guidance in writing a sports development plan, you should be able to get help from:

- your local authority
- governing body Development Officers

If you need assistance in contacting someone to help with your plan, please call your Sport England regional office.

Initiatives under the Capital Facilities Award Programme

Priority Areas Initiative (PAI) – Special provisions for urban and rural deprived areas is available through the PAI. Up to 90% of the cost of new capital schemes can be met from the fund for projects that meet the criteria. The PAI includes the 100 most deprived local authority areas and all rural development areas as well as 'pockets' of deprivation that exist outside these areas. You need to show that there is a lack of the particular facility you are applying for, and you will need a Sports Development Plan (or similar).

School Community Sport Initiative (SCSI) – Schools and other educational establishments are encouraged through the SCSI to make new and upgraded sports facilities available to the community. Awards of up to 80% of the capital cost are available. However, you will need a Sports Development, a Management Plan and a Community Use Agreement which ensures that the proposed facility will be used by the surrounding community (not just the school itself) for at least 40 hours per week.

Further details of the additional criteria which has to be met under these initiatives are available in leaflet form from the Lottery Line on 0345-649649.

Projects excluded under the Capital Facilities Awards Programme

Revenue funding
Sport England will not normally provide lottery finance for day-to-day running costs, except in the circumstances outlined above.

Equipment
Lottery funding will not normally be available for the purchase of small-scale items of equipment, including mini-buses and equipment for personal use.

Maintenance
Sport England will not provide lottery funds for maintenance, repairs, renewals, or any other work which is necessary as a result of past neglect. In certain cases it might, however, provide funding for major items of maintenance equipment.

Spectator facilities
As the Lottery Sports Fund has the aim of increasing active participation in sport, backing will not initially be given for projects solely concerned with spectator or social accommodation. These facilities may be funded, however, if they comprise a necessary part of a larger scheme, such as the development of strategically important venues.

Projects with a total cost of less than £5,000
As noted above, the Lottery Sports Fund will normally consider only those applications involving projects with a total cost of £5,000 or more.

Projects based outside England
Projects which are not based in England will not normally be funded by Sport England.

Applications procedure

1. Obtain application pack

If you think your organisation may wish to apply for lottery funds for a sports capital project, the first step is to obtain an application pack from Sport England by phoning their Lottery Line on 0345-649649 (charged at local rate for whole of the country). You will receive an application pack along with your unique reference number.

2. Send Consultation Forms to relevant bodies

If, having read the Essential Guide you consider your organisation and project to be eligible for funding, you can then start the application process properly. You should be 100% sure that your project will meet all Lottery Sports Fund funding criteria before continuing. You should then send the consultation forms contained in the application pack to all organisations relevant to your project: the national governing sports bodies (form A), other national organisations (form A), local authorities (form B), county playing fields association (form C), local sports council (form C). These consultation forms ask the organisations to state whether they are, or will be, giving your organisation any financial support, how your project fits into any strategic plans, and what priority they would place on the scheme.

These forms should be sent to the appropriate bodies a few weeks before you submit your application to Sport England. They will fill them in and direct them straight to Sport England (and not return them to you).

3. Complete and return application form

The next stage is to complete the application form provided by Sport England. All sections should be completed, and answers should either be typed or handwritten in black ink and preferably in block capitals. The application form is also available on computer disk, if you prefer to submit your proposal in that form. The headings of the sections contained in the application form are as follows:

- Applicant's details
- Type of organisation
- VAT registration
- Sports which will benefit from the proposal
- Project type (brief description of project must be made)
- Site of project
- Planning permission details
- Ownership of land upon which facility is to be built
- Total project cost
- Partnership funding for project (confirmed and unconfirmed)
- Amount of funding requested
- What existing facilities you have

- Sports development plans and past achievements
- Participation predictions
- Coaching programme
- Age group profile
- Ethnic profile
- People on low incomes profile
- Access for disabled people
- Running cost forecasts
- Technical advice received
- Other Lottery applications

Once the application form has been completed it should be sent along with one copy of any supporting documentation to the address shown at the end of this section. If at any stage of the application process you have any queries you should telephone the Lottery Line on 0345-649649.

Supporting documentation required

You need to enclose a copy of the following:

- constitution or Memorandum and Articles of Association for your organisation
- latest annual accounts and balance sheet
- project brief
- proposed site plan (where applicable)
- schedule of proposed equipment (where applicable)
- draft lease (where applicable) – for freehold ownership a copy of the Land Registry certificate or other evidence must be provided
- letters of confirmation for project finance
- detailed income and expenditure projections
- evidence relating to the breakdown of your project costs
- Priority Areas Initiative paperwork, if relevant

Additional documentation for building projects only:

- feasibility study (where applicable)
- building drawings and/or A4 size sketch drawings (whichever are available)
- copies of planning permission

Applications from ALL schools and other education institutions serving mainly 16–18 years olds must provide supporting information clearly indicating how your project meets the School Community Sport Initiative guidelines.

Further documentation is required if the project cost comes to more than £250,000 including a detailed project plan and a business plan.

Advice from Sport England on project development

Sport England provides the following advice on developing projects to help applicants maximise their chances of an award. It also gives information on Sport England's priorities when assessing applications. These are (although not in any priority order):

- applicants should: 'ensure that all qualifying criteria are met and the case is thoroughly argued;
- concentrate on ensuring that the project objectives are delivered within the project content and resist overscaling the size of the project (say, by determining the scale of the project by reference to the anticipated maximum funding available rather than the sporting need);
- secure the largest amount of partnership funding possible from the widest range of business and community financial partners, then provide a clear rationale and financial case for the level of award requested, after demonstrating that all other avenues of financial support for the project have been exhausted;
- establish a wide range of sporting and community partnerships, with an emphasis on securing commitment to use the facility and, where possible, providing financial revenue support towards the project;
- use available advice, including working closely with Sport England officers in London HQ and the regional offices;
- make contact with successful applicants to exchange ideas and experiences;
- ensure that care is taken on every part of the application, particularly that all legal requirements (including, where relevant, European Procurement Regulations) are fulfilled.'

Once you have applied

1. Acknowledgement of application

Once Sport England has received your application form it will send you a letter of acknowledgement within four working days of its receipt.

2. Consultation process

Your application will be evaluated by one of the Lottery Unit's Lottery case officers according to the criteria laid out in Sport England's documentation (summarised above). There will be a process of consultation with relevant national, regional and local bodies. The relevant Sport England regional office will also offer its comments.

3. Decision by the Sport England Lottery Awards Panel

Once the period of consultation and the application's appraisal has been completed, it will go before the Lottery Awards Panel with a recommendation.

The panel will then make its decision, and you will be informed of this outcome 'as soon as possible'. There are three possible outcomes:

- **Full award** – you will receive a formal offer of an award, along with the relevant conditions. Once the applicant has signed and returned the 'Award Acceptance form', together with any specific documentary requirements, applicants can proceed with the implementation of their projects and the signing of contracts with builders etc.

- **Support in principle** – in some cases, especially for very costly projects, Sport England may not be able to make a final decision until the applicant has carried out further project development work. If the Panel is convinced that the broad concept of the project is sound but insufficiently developed, say in terms of design, management or finance, they may indicate their support in principle.

  Sport England will then ask the applicant to undertake further developmental work, such as preparation of more detailed designs or management plans, together with a more accurate cost estimate. (Initially, the applicant will have to fund this developmental work from its own resources and 'at risk', though this may be recoverable in part if the project eventually receives an award). The Panel and Council will then make a decision, taking into account the additional information.

  'Support In Principle' does **not** constitute any commitment to assist a project from the Lottery Sports Fund and the final outcome could be either a Full Award or a Rejection.

- **Rejection** – if your application is not successful you will receive a letter with the reasons for rejection (where appropriate). You can ask for a review of this decision if you have suitable grounds. Any re-assessment is made on the grounds that Sport England have misunderstood, misinterpreted or failed to take account of information contained within the application. No new information can be added at the appeal stage.

Lottery Sports Fund contact address:

Lottery Unit
Sport England
PO Box 649
London WC1H 0QP
Lottery Line: 0345-649649 for enquiries and requests for application packs

Awards for All

Awards for All (A for A) – England is a joint scheme between the English Lottery distributors: Sport England, the Arts Council of England, the National Lottery Charities Board and the Heritage Lottery Fund with the Millennium Commission also being involved as part of the Millennium Festival for the year 2000 (see below). A similar scheme has been in operation in Scotland since the beginning of 1998. At present there are no plans to run A for A in Wales or Northern Ireland.

Guidelines for applicants
- A for A will provide grants of up to £5,000 mainly for smaller, voluntary sector groups. This will almost certainly mean that the lower limit for existing Sport England capital programme applicants will change from a *project cost* of £5,000 to a *grant sought* of £5,000.
- Although schools will be eligible to apply, most other statutory organisations (including local authorities) will not.
- Applicants must be properly constituted and have a written constitution and annual accounts, which must be included with the application. (Newly established organsiations will not need to provide accounts.)
- Applicants will not have to find any cash partrnership funding, although the grant may be used as part funding for a larger scheme.
- Priority will be given to organisations whose income is less than £15,000 a year.
- Initially the scheme will start in the East Midlands region only. (This includes the counties of Derbyshire, Leicestershire, Lincolnshire, Northamptonshire, Nottinghamshire and Rutland.) Aplications forms for East Midlands projects are available from December 1998 and awards will be decided in March 1999.
- For application packs for the East Midlands, call 0845 600 2040.
- Applications for the rest of the country will be available in June 1999 with the first awards in August. When the scheme is extended nationally in June 1999 and for applications up to June 2000 the scheme will come under the Millennium Festival.
- Application forms will be widely available (from distributing bodies, local authorities and so on). No Unique Reference Number (URN) will be issued at the time of issuing an application pack. URNs will be allocated following the receipt of applications.

Sport England's themes
Sport England's funding under the A for A scheme will concentrate on projects which come under the following two themes:

a) Sportslink
This will support projects with a practical link between a school and a sports club to benefit young people. The aim is to ensure that more young people have access to, and participate in, local sports clubs.

Areas to be supported include:
- attainment of professional coaching qualifications for teachers, students and club personnel
- newly structured activities for young people
- new competitive opportunities
- club recruitment
- start up equipment
- transport costs
- hire of facilities

Areas that will not be supported include:
- payment of teachers for extra curricular work
- personal equipment/clothing
- buying of minibuses or other transport

b) Sportsreach
This will support projects which extend the reach of sport and sporting organisations to New People, New Places/things, New Standards of Acheivement.

Sportsreach will be targeted at voluntary sports clubs and non-sporting community groups who wish to extend their activities to include sport. For those groups which are new to sport there will be help for youth clubs and associations, playcentres, community and special interest groups, to include an introductory level of sport in their programmes. Local or area school sports associations, local sports associations, local sports councils and county governing bodies of sport will also be able to apply.

Areas to be funded include:
- new activities for juniors, women, seniors, people with disabilities and diverse ethnic groups
- minor capital adaptations to buildings and playing areas, including access to new places to play
- new levels of competition, access to training venues, development of coaches and administrators etc.
- buying in coaching and leadership skills
- start up costs for new activities and teams
- team equipment
- education and training costs for new coaches, leaders and officials

Areas that will not be funded include:
- personal equipment/clothing
- buying of minibuses or other transport

Scotland

The Scottish Sports Council is responsible for distributing a percentage of National Lottery ticket sales to sport in Scotland. It has set up the Lottery Sports Fund Unit to deal with the administration of applications, headed by the director of the Lottery Sports Fund, Ivor Davies. Final decisions on awards are made by a meeting of the Scottish Sports Council. The following is information relating to the Scottish Sports Council's Capital Programme.

Eligible organisations

The Scottish Sports Council will only provide lottery funding to bodies involved with sports which are already recognised by the Sports Councils (see box on page 69). Your organisation should be Scottish based and involved with increasing sports participation in Scotland. Your organisation can be any of the following:

Local voluntary sports clubs – as long as your constitution states that a recognised sport is a primary purpose. User groups representing consortia of local recognised clubs are also eligible.

Area sports associations – but only those with a constitution and composed of local clubs of recognised sports.

National governing bodies of sports – but only those recognised by the Scottish Sports Council as the sole body for that activity in Scotland.

Charitable trusts, playing fields associations, youth and uniformed associations and **community associations** – but only if the playing of sport is an object in your constitution, your membership is open to all parts of the community, and significant public access will be provided to the project or facility.

Local authorities and other **public bodies**.

Quasi-commercial organisations which re-invest all surpluses back into the project or facility (rather than distributing profits to managers or shareholders).

Universities, colleges, schools and other educational establishments – but only if the proposed facility will be available to local sports clubs and the general public for a significant amount of time. This should normally be at least 50% of opening hours or available playing time.

Professional sports clubs and commercial organisations are only eligible if their projects will bring about significant benefits to the community whilst not providing commercial benefit to the organisation. In the case of commercial bodies, there should be no other public or voluntary organisation prepared to provide the facility.

Excluded organisations under the Capital Programme

- Professional sports clubs and commercial organisations are excluded from seeking funds for any project involving significant commercial gain.
- Bodies which are not based in Scotland, or which do not benefit the country, are also excluded.
- Individuals are not eligible to apply for funding on their own behalf.

Eligible projects

The Scottish Sports Council's Capital Programme focuses on capital projects which are for the public good and will provide a lasting benefit to the community. The Council also aims to spread its support over the entire range of sports, at all levels, and in all parts of Scotland.

Preference is given to projects which promote participation in sport, improve sporting performance, and fill the 'high priority deficiencies' identified by the Scottish Sports Council in terms of existing knowledge and strategies. The Council cites the following specific types of facility being given priority:

- sports halls
- upgraded turf pitches
- indoor tennis courts
- upgraded outdoor tennis courts
- synthetic grass pitches
- changing pavilions
- swimming pool upgrading
- pay-as-you-play golf courses
- various resource-based developments.

As well as trying to rectify these current deficiencies in Scottish sports provision, the Council will adopt a further priority ranking based on the type of project. This ranking is shown in the box overleaf, in order of stated preference.

In general, the following additional criteria will be used by the Scottish Sports Council when it is assessing applications:

Capital funding

The Scottish Sports Council will normally fund only those sports projects involving 'expenditure on the purchase, improvement, restoration, construction or creation of an asset', including any costs (such as professional advisers' fees) directly incurred in the process. In certain cases, money may be available for feasibility studies or design competitions necessary prior to the submission of a full application for a major capital project.

Revenue funding for day-to-day running costs will not normally be provided. However, in exceptional circumstances assistance may be given for a period of up to three years towards the cost of initiatives which add value to a project which has been granted a capital award.

HIGHEST PRIORITY

- Development (construction, extension or improvement) of playing facilities, including those for natural resource-based activities
- Acquisition or retention of playing facilities, such as purchase of land or rights of access
- Plant (water treatment, heating, lighting, ventilation, booking systems) for sports facilities
- Major sports equipment – usually large and/or expensive, but with a long life span (of at least seven years)
- Changing accommodation for participants
- Facilities and equipment for sports medicine and science
- Equipment storage in new developments
- Facilities for sports officials – which should be essential for performance and not just comfort
- Conditioning suites for participants, where they are an essential feature of sports facilities and consistent with applicable sports plans or strategies
- Crèches to enable greater sports participation
- Dual social and activity areas, dependent upon a clear benefit to sports
- Access facilities such as car parking which are in balance with, and essential to, sports facilities
- Boundary fences necessary for safety and security
- Spectator accommodation – but only at facilities of national and regional importance and where consistent with sports development strategies
- Landscaping – where it is as an essential part of new facilities
- Residential or overnight accommodation at key locations

LOWEST PRIORITY

Partnership funding

The Council will normally only provide a maximum of 50% of the total capital costs of any project with not less than 25% coming from your own organisation. The Council, however, has discretion to be flexible in the case of projects in areas of special needs or in respect of national or regional facilities provision.

Financial viability during project and after completion

You should be able to demonstrate that your project is financially viable, both during and after its completion.

Increase in sports participation and relationship with other strategies

Proposals should increase participation in sports and recreation, and/or provide anticipated improvements in performance. There should be a clear demand for the planned facilities, which should also relate to other community programmes and initiatives.

Fit for purpose
Any proposed facilities must be 'fit for purpose' in terms of their location, scale, content, design and construction, accessibility for people with disabilities, management and environmental impact.

Excluded projects
The main types of projects which are not eligible for lottery funding from the Scottish Sports Council are:

Revenue projects
In general, revenue funding will not be provided (although under exceptional circumstances it may be available, see above).

Repairs
Lottery funding will not be used to pay for repairs, renewals or maintenance brought about by prior neglect.

Small scale items of equipment
Only the purchase of major items of equipment will normally be funded – minor items, including items of equipment for personal use, mini buses, vans and other vehicles, will not receive support from lottery proceeds.

Social facilities
Dedicated social areas, dining rooms or bars not connected to participants' residential accommodation will not normally be funded. Neither will free-standing administration areas or committee rooms which do not comprise an essential part of large sports projects.

Spectators' facilities
Because lottery funds are being used to promote active participation in sport, funding will not be available for spectators' facilities unless part of a major capital project.

Projects outside Scotland
Projects located outside Scotland are not eligible, and should approach their relevant national Sports Council.

Minimum total project cost: £10,000
The Scottish Sports Council is initially concentrating its lottery funds on applications involving projects with a total project cost of £10,000 or more. It also has a maximum award level of £1 million which it will exceed only in very exceptional circumstances.

Applications procedure

1. Obtain application pack

The first stage is to request the guidelines and application pack from the Scottish Sports Council. If you expect your project to have a total cost of £1 million or more, you should contact the Lottery Sports Fund Unit to inform them about your project before applying.

2. Complete and return application form

Applications should be made on the official form supported by all relevant documentation. If the answers are not typewritten, the form should be completed in black ink using block capitals. The main sections of the form are as follows:

Details of your organisation and any previous lottery funding

The first section on the form asks for details about your organisation, such as its status (e.g. registered charity, voluntary body, company, local authority) and affiliation with any of the national governing bodies of sport. You must also state whether your organisation has previously applied for, or received, any lottery funding. If your organisation is a club with individual members you also have to provide information about the composition of your membership.

Project details

You then have to give details about your proposed project, including:

- a description, its location (and ownership of the site)
- the sport(s) it will benefit
- the existence of any similar facilities.

A further part asks for technical and safety information, and for the names of any professional advisers you have used in drawing up your project. It also expects you to show the extent to which your project will be accessible to people with various disabilities.

Supporting documentation required

You need to enclose a copy of the following:
- constitution or Memorandum and Articles of Association (not statutory authorities)
- latest annual accounts and balance sheet
- evidence of ownership of project site (not statutory authorities), and a copy of any lease, draft lease, rental or access agreement
- any feasibility study and/or design brief, along with drawings, site plans and/or location plans
- full or outline planning consent
- schedule of equipment (if any)
- project brief (projects costing over £100,000 only).

Project costs and funding

The next sections request information about the estimated project cost, and a breakdown of the costs and the sources of funding for the project, including the level of support needed from the Scottish Sports Council. You should also state the amount your own organisation is contributing from its own resources, and where the remainder of the money is expected to come from. The next section deals with project costs when it is up and running, and you have to give details of how day to day revenue funding will be provided.

Use of proposed facilities

This section requests information about the current users of any facilities you may operate and of the expected users of the proposed facilities. You also have to give details of the availability of the facilities to members and to the general public, how access will be granted, and the coaching opportunities which will be offered.

Project policy

The final section deals with the ways in which your proposals fit into national, regional or local sports development strategies. You also have to state why you believe your proposed facility is needed, what you hope to achieve, how you intend to do this, and how you will measure progress.

The completed application form and supporting documentation should be sent to the address below. If you need advice at any stage, you should contact the Lottery Sports Fund Unit on 0131-339 9000. Written guidance on technical matters is available in the form of a series of Technical Digests produced by the Scottish Sports Council.

Once you have applied

1. Receive letter of acknowledgement

You will be sent a letter of acknowledgement once the Scottish Sports Council has received your application.

2. Consultation process

The Scottish Sports Council will then assess your application, and consult with relevant bodies.

3. Decision

Decisions will be made by meetings of the Scottish Sports Council, which will take place monthly for projects with a total cost of less than £100,000 and quarterly for projects involving a larger total amount. The possible outcomes are:

- **Approval of award**, either full or conditional.

- **Carried forward to next meeting** – usually only for high quality projects which might have been successful but encountered strong competition.

- **Rejection of application**, after which you cannot re-submit an application relating to the same proposal for two years.

Contact address:
Lottery Sports Fund Unit
Scottish Sports Council
Caledonia House
South Gyle
Edinburgh EH12 9DQ
Tel: 0131-339 9000
Fax: 0131-339 5361

Wales

The Sports Council for Wales administers SPORTLOT – the Lottery Sports Fund for Wales – which receives 5% of the total lottery proceeds allocated to sport in the UK.

Eligible organisations

The Sports Council for Wales will only provide funding for bodies and projects which exist primarily for the benefit of a sport or group of sports recognised by the home country Sports Councils (see table on page 69). Applications can only be submitted by bona fide organisations, which should be based in Wales.

Your organisation will be eligible to apply if it is a:

- formally constituted club, association, voluntary body or trust.
- governing body of sport.
- local authority, district council or other public body.
- school, college, university or other educational establishment (but only if there is a local identified sports deficiency and there will be substantial public access).
- commercial organisation (but only if the project is primarily for the public good and not private profit).

Excluded bodies

The following are not eligible to apply for funding from SPORTLOT in Wales:

- Individuals seeking funds on their own behalf.
- Organisations based outside Wales.
- Bodies over which the Sports Council for Wales has material influence or control.
- Commercial organisations and professional sports clubs if their proposals are for commercial gain rather than the public good.

Eligible projects

Priority will be given by SPORTLOT for capital projects whose 'main purpose is to provide a facility which directly enables people to take part in sport or raises standards of performance'. Examples of such projects include:

- New, upgraded or extended playing facilities.
- Purchase of land, water or facilities.
- Changing accommodation for participants.
- Major sports equipment, but only if it has a permanent base and will remain in use for at least five years.
- Ancillary and support facilities which are essential for participation or performance.

The following criteria should be taken into account when considering whether your project is eligible to apply for funding from SPORTLOT:

Capital projects

Your project must involve either capital expenditure on building and construction, purchase of land or land rights, or the purchase of capital equipment. Revenue funding of day-to-day operational costs is unlikely to be provided.

Partnership funding

The Sports Council for Wales will not use lottery funds to support the entire costs of your project. Lottery funding will be provided up to the maximum limits shown below, with the remainder of project costs being met either by your own organisation (at least 10% if you are a voluntary body) or by other non-lottery funders.

Projects of local significance
>   Voluntary sector   70%
>   Private and public sectors   50%
>   Education (public and private) sectors   50%

Projects of regional and national significance
>   Proportion will be determined on merit

Minimum total project cost: £5,000

SPORTLOT funding will not normally be provided for projects with a total cost of less than £5,000.

Quality of project

Your project should be fit for its purpose, well-designed and of high quality. Any facility should also meet the minimum technical standards for the relevant sport(s).

Financial viability

Your project must be financially viable, with adequate capital and revenue funding to start, complete and sustain it.

Community benefit and support

Your project must benefit the local community and not be primarily for private gain.

Accessibility

Projects must be accessible to the general public for a substantial part of the time (particularly if your organisation has a restricted membership). No individual should be unreasonably denied access to your facility, and buildings must provide access for people with disabilities.

The X factor

In addition to the eligibility criteria listed above, the Sports Council for Wales cites the following additional factors which will give your project a greater chance of success:

- Your project should meet an **accepted sports need**, either in an area or for a particular sport.
- Your project should be **supported by the community** and should have **significant partnership funding**.
- Your project should show **links between schools and sports**, and offer the opportunity of greater use by the **wider community** of schools' sports facilities.
- Opportunities should be provided for **school-aged children**.
- Facilities should be **multi-purpose** or serve more than one sport.
- Your project should be part of, or contribute to, any wider schemes of development supported by your sport's **governing body**.
- **Existing facilities** should be safeguarded.
- **Coaching and training** – access to coaching should be demonstrated, and specialist training/playing facilities should be provided in line with wider strategies.

Excluded projects

Projects with a total cost of less than £5,000
Only projects with a total cost of more than £5,000 will normally be considered for funding.

Repairs
Funding will not be provided for the repair or maintenance of existing facilities.

Personal equipment
Only major capital equipment is eligible – smaller pieces of equipment for the use of single individuals will not be funded.

Non-essential ancillary facilities
Funding will not be provided for any ancillary facilities that are neither essential to the sporting use of a facility nor an integral part of the building.

Projects located outside Wales
Any project not based in Wales is not eligible for SPORTLOT funding, and instead should apply to the appropriate national Sports Council.

Revenue projects
Revenue funding to support everyday running costs will not normally be available.

Spectator accommodation
Funding for the construction of spectator accommodation will not normally be provided, as the aims of SPORTLOT are to increase active participation in sport.

Application process

1. *Request the information booklet* Does Your Sports Project Qualify for Lottery Funding?

   The first step is to request the information booklet. *How to Apply to the Sportlot Capital Grants Scheme* is also available from the Sports Council for Wales by contacting them on 01222-300500.

2. *Complete and return Application Pack Request Form*

   You should read the guidance contained in the information booklet. If you consider your project to be eligible for funding, you should then complete and return the Application Pack Request Form which is contained in the booklet. This consists of questions about your organisation and your proposed project (type, location, start/finish dates, total cost, description). This request form should be returned to whichever of the following Sports Council for Wales regional offices is nearest to your project location as detailed overleaf.

Powys; Rhonbla Cynon Taff; Torfaen; Blaenau Gwent; Bridgend; Caerphilly; Cardiff; Merthyr Tydfil; Monmounthshire; Newport; Vale of Glamorgan:
SPORTLOT Fund for Wales
Sports Council for Wales
Sophia Gardens
Cardiff CF1 9SW

Carmarthenshire; Ceredigion; Swansea; Neath and Port Talbot; Pembrokeshire:
SPORTLOT Fund for Wales
Sports Council for Wales
10 Quay Street
Carmarthen SA31 3JT

Conwy; Denbighshire, Flintshire; Gwynedd; Wrexham; Ynys Mon:
SPORTLOT Fund for Wales
Sports Council for Wales
Deeside Leisure Centre
Chester Road West
Queensferry
Deeside CH5 1SA

3. Complete and return the application form

When they have received your request form, the Sports Council for Wales will then send you an application form suitable for the type of project you are proposing. You should then complete and return this application form to the Sports Council for Wales. For applications where project costs exceed £50,000 there is a two-stage application and assessment process where case officers will work closely with applicants. Any applications under £50,000 will be subject to a one stage process.

4. Application assessment

Your application for funding will then be assessed by the Sports Council for Wales by checking it against their criteria and consulting with other bodies. A decision will then be made, and you will be informed about the outcome. Further details of the assessment process were not available at the time of writing.

Contact address:
SPORTLOT Fund for Wales
Sports Council for Wales
Sophia Gardens
Cardiff CF1 9SW
Tel: 01222-300500 ext. 418

Northern Ireland

Northern Ireland receives just under 3% of the sports portion of the National Lottery proceeds. This money is being distributed by the Sports Council for Northern Ireland, with operations headed by its lottery director, Danny O'Connor. Preliminary decisions are made by the Sports Council for Northern Ireland's Lottery Committee, which makes recommendations to the Council, which then makes the final accept/reject decisions. The following information relates to the Sports Council for Northern Ireland's capital funding programme.

Eligible bodies

The Sports Council for Northern Ireland will only provide funding for bodies and projects which exist primarily for the benefit of sports recognised by the UK Sports Councils (see table on page 69). Organisations should usually be based in Northern Ireland, and can be:

- Formally constituted clubs, associations, voluntary bodies or charitable trusts.
- Area sports associations or national governing bodies of sports.
- Local authorities, district councils or other public bodies.
- Schools, colleges, universities or other educational establishments (but only if there is a local identified sports deficiency and there will be substantial public access).
- Commercial organisations (but only if projects are primarily for the public good and not private profit).

Excluded bodies

The following are not eligible to apply for funding from the Northern Ireland lottery sports fund:

- Individuals seeking funds on their own behalf.
- Organisations based outside Northern Ireland.
- Bodies over which the Sports Council for Northern Ireland has material influence or control.
- Commercial organisations and professional sports clubs if their proposals are for commercial gain rather than the public good.

Eligible projects

The Sports Council for Northern Ireland will normally make lottery funding available for capital expenditure on the purchase, improvement, restoration, construction or creation of assets and facilities which promote participation in the sports in Northern Ireland. The money will be targeted on 'the development of high quality, safe, well designed and built facilities aimed at attracting the community to sport and holding their interest'.

Examples of eligible projects include:

- Construction, upgrading or extension of indoor or outdoor playing facilities. Any projects involving the improvement of facilities must be able to demonstrate a significant increase in: capacity; the level of existing users' performance; and/or the lifespan of the asset.
- Purchase of land, water or other playing facilities.
- Purchase of major, permanently-based equipment serving a single sport.
- Changing accommodation for participants, not spectators.
- Ancillary or support facilities where essential to safe participation or part of a larger project. These can include: safety equipment, equipment stores, sports officials' facilities, conditioning suites, childcare facilities, access facilities, boundary fences, landscaping, or overnight accommodation for participants.

The following basic criteria are being used by the Sports Council of Northern Ireland to assess applications:

Capital projects

As noted above, funding will normally only be available for capital projects and not to support day-to-day running costs. Revenue funding will only be provided in exceptional circumstances.

Partnership funding

You will not be able to obtain the entire costs of your project from the Council as it expects an element of funding from other sources. The higher the degree of partnership funding, the greater your likely chance of obtaining lottery funding, as this will be taken as demonstrating community support for your project. The proportion the Sports Council will provide depends upon the type and size of your project, as shown in the box.

Partnership funding

All voluntary sector projects	up to 70% of total project costs will be provided
Locally significant projects (i.e. costing under £200,000)	up to 70% will be provided
Projects of district significance (i.e. costing over £200,000)	up to 50% will be provided
Projects of national significance (such as facilities for high level competition and training)	the proportion will be set on merit

---

Minimum total project cost: £5,000

The Sports Council of Northern Ireland will normally only consider applications for projects with a total value of more than £5,000. Smaller projects may be considered in exceptional circumstances, however, where funding is not available from other sources and the projects are likely to be of sustained importance to the sporting community.

Financial viability

Projects must be financially viable, especially with respect to day-to-day operational costs and sources of partnership funding.

Quality of construction and design

Projects must be of high quality construction and design, be fit for their purpose, and should meet the minimum technical standards laid down by relevant sporting bodies.

Access

No person should unreasonably be denied access to any project in receipt of lottery funding.

Other criteria

The Sports Council for Northern Ireland also lists the following characteristics which a project should have if it is to be considered a priority for lottery funding. The relative importance of these criteria will vary according to the scale and type of sporting activity:

- The project should meet an accepted sports need (either in an area or for a particular sport) which has been recognised in the local/district/national strategies.
- The project should be supported by the community and should have significant partnership funding.
- The project should show links between schools and sports, and offer the opportunity of greater use by the wider community of sports facilities at schools.
- Young people should be catered for.
- More than one sport should be serviced.
- Existing facilities should be safeguarded.
- Access to coaching should be provided, and specialist training or playing facilities should be provided in line with wider strategies.

Excluded projects

Revenue funding
Funding for daily running and administration costs will only be provided for a maximum of three years, for projects which are considered a high priority, which have already received lottery funding for capital costs, and which cannot get revenue funding from elsewhere.

Spectator accommodation
The aims of the Lottery Sports Fund are to increase active participation in sports and recreation. As a result, funding of spectator accommodation will be restricted to agreed locations of regional or national importance in line with the sport's performance strategy.

Outside Northern Ireland
Funding will only be provided for projects located within Northern Ireland. Sports projects based in other home countries should apply to their appropriate Sports Council.

Maintenance
All renewals, repairs and maintenance are not considered as capital expenditure, rather as a sign of past neglect.

Personal equipment
Equipment for an individual's personal use will not be funded as projects should be for the wider public benefit.

Projects with a total cost of less than £5,000
The Sports Council for Northern Ireland will not normally consider applications for projects with a total cost of less than £5,000.

Applications procedure

1. Obtain Information and Guidance Pack

The first step in applying for lottery funding is to request an Information and Guidance Pack from the Sports Council for Northern Ireland by contacting them on 01232-382222.

2. Send Application Request Form at least 12 weeks before anticipated submission of application form

If, having read the Information and Guidance Pack, you consider yourself to be eligible for funding you should then complete the Application Request Form and return it to the Sports Council for Northern Ireland. This form asks for various details about your organisation, your proposed project and its funding sources. The Council will then send you a letter of acknowledgement, along with a customised pack including an application form containing your lottery application number (which should be quoted in all future correspondence).

3. Send Consultation Forms to relevant bodies

The application pack contains Consultation Forms which you should send to all organisations relevant to your project once you have decided to apply for lottery funding. There are separate forms to send to: national governing bodies; district council or education and library board; local sports council or other relevant body. These organisations will then forward their copies of the completed consultation forms to the Sports Council for Northern Ireland, along with their comments on your project.

4. Complete and return application form not sooner than 12 weeks after sending your request for the form

You should then fill in the application form, either by typing or by writing in black ink and block capitals. Your form should be complete in every regard, as incomplete forms will be returned to you. The main sections of the application form are summarised below.

Details of your organisation

The form starts with sections requesting details about your organisation, along with information about any lottery grants you have previously requested or received.

Project details

The next section asks for a description of the project, the sport it will benefit, the proposed site, its ownership and necessary planning permissions, and the proximity of similar facilities. You also have to calculate the resultant increase in sports participation, and give details of the usage of any current facilities.

Supporting documentation required

You will need to submit a copy of the following:

- constitution or Memorandum and Articles of Association (except statutory bodies)
- latest annual accounts and balance sheet (except statutory bodies)
- detailed income and expenditure projections (except statutory bodies)
- letters of confirmation of project finance
- site plan (where applicable)
- draft lease (where applicable)
- schedule of equipment (where applicable)
- project brief (projects with total cost over £100,000 only)
  Building projects only must also provide the following where appropriate:
- feasibility study
- building drawings or A4 size sketch drawings.

111

Project costs and funding

The form then asks for a breakdown of the estimated total project cost, how much you require from lottery funds, and the other anticipated sources of finance. You must show that you will be able to provide for the operational costs of the facility.

Technical details

This section requests information about your project's compliance with technical requirements, the degree of access for people with various disabilities, and provisions for use by either sex.

Project policy

The final section asks how your proposals fit in with other strategic plans for sport. You also have to state your aims, objectives and targets, how you will achieve these, and how progress will be assessed.

The completed application form and any supporting documentation should be returned, not sooner than 12 weeks after sending your request for the form itself, to the address shown at the end of this section. If at any stage of the application process you have any queries you should phone the Sports Council for Northern Ireland on 01232-382222 (Monday–Friday, 2pm–5pm only).

Once you have applied

1. Acknowledgment of application

You will receive a letter acknowledging your application, which will identify the Lottery Officer assigned to your case (who should be your first point of contact if you have any future enquiries about your application).

2. Consultation process

The Sports Council will then evaluate your application according to the criteria laid out above, and will consult with appropriate experts, governing bodies, sports organisations or district councils.

3. Decision by Sports Council for Northern Ireland's Lottery Committee

Your lottery officer will then present the findings of this consultation process to the Sports Council for Northern Ireland's Lottery Committee, who will make a recommendation to the Sports Council as to what its decision might be. The Council then makes the final decision, which can be:

- **Grant awarded**.

- **Grant awarded dependent** upon the provision of extra information for a more detailed appraisal.

- Proposal **carried forward** until next meeting, but not for more than two further distribution meetings.

- **Rejection** – you will receive a letter informing you, where appropriate, of the reasons for failure. Any project which is rejected cannot be resubmitted within 12 months of the date of rejection.

You will be informed of the decision as soon as possible, which should usually be within six months of your full application being received, but should be quicker if you are applying for less than £10,000.

Contact address:
Lottery Sports Fund
Sports Council for Northern Ireland
House of Sport
Upper Malone Road
Belfast BT9 5LA
Tel: 01232-382222
Fax: 01232-383822

Applying to other distribution boards

As mentioned above, there are five other 'good causes'. In certain circumstances, even though you are a sports organisation you may be able to apply to one of the other boards. For certain types of project it may be difficult to determine which of the distributing bodies to approach for funding. If you think that your project could be relevant to more than one distributor, you should decide which one has criteria covering the main aims of your project and apply to that body. If you are not sure, contact the relevant bodies for guidance and if necessary the distributors will discuss your case between them to determine who can best handle your application. If a distributing body receives a request which it considers to be more appropriate for a different body, it will be returned to the applicant with advice about the correct body to approach.

If you are proposing a major project which can be divided into distinct elements, each of which is relevant to different distributing bodies, you can approach different lottery distributors to fund each separate part. You should send a copy of the whole application to each distributor, making clear it is a joint application and specifying which elements each distributor is being asked to finance. You may, however, still have to obtain non-lottery sources of funding for part of the cost of your project.

The following examples cover some of the overlap situations which may arise, and how they would be resolved.

Historic Sporting Material

If you need funds for the storage, conservation or presentation of a collection of historic sporting material or equipment you should apply to the Heritage Lottery Fund, and not the Sports Councils, which aim to encourage active participation in sport.

Joint arts and sports buildings

If you want to develop a building for both arts and sports use, such as a sports hall with a stage and theatre facilities, you should submit your application to the distributor most relevant to the primary purpose of the facility, and send a copy to the other body. For example, if the project will be used more often for arts than sport you should apply to your relevant home country Arts Council and send a copy of your application to your relevant home country Sports Council.

Disadvantaged people

If your project is about people living in low income communities – for example by taking greater control over their own lives or playing a more active part in their community – you may be able to apply to the Charities Board. However, you will need to persuade them that the project is primarily about the welfare of disadvantaged people and that sport is simply a way of meeting their needs.

The telephone numbers for the other Distribution Boards are as follows:

Arts

England	0171-312 0123
Scotland	0131-226 6051
Wales	01222-388288
Northern Ireland	01232-667000

Charities

Application packs only   0345-919191
General enquiries:

England	0171-747 5300
Scotland	0131-221 7100
Wales	01686-621644
Northern Ireland	01232-551455

Heritage

0171-591 6000

Millennium
0171-880 2030

New Opportunities Fund
0171-222 3084

Project development and business plans

Large capital projects of the type generally eligible for lottery funding require careful planning and management to ensure their successful completion. If you are requesting more than £100,000 from any distributor of lottery funds (or £200,000 in the case of Sport England) you will normally be required to provide a detailed business plan and cashflow forecast. The following notes provide a brief outline of the stages through which you should progress as part of your project development and, although most relevant to building projects, can be applied with some alterations to other types of project. Some of the distributing bodies issue their own guidance about project development in their main application packs.

Project coordination

A fundamental part of the development process is setting up an effective way of managing and coordinating the project. It may be a good idea to establish a project committee which has responsibility for drawing up the project brief and supervising the entire project development process. The committee members with the most appropriate skills should be assigned to the role of project coordinator. The project coordinator should be given authority to make day-to-day decisions on behalf of the project committee, and should be the single point of contact between your organisation and all the outside bodies involved with your project (such as lottery distributing bodies, local authorities, professional advisers).

Think about what you are trying to achieve

Once an effective management structure is in place, the next step is to put together a business plan – an outline of what you want to achieve and how you plan to do it, along with estimates of how much it will cost. You should be able to do this by yourself, but you may wish to consult an accountant or other adviser. Your business plan should cover topics such as:

- What you want to achieve
- Why you want to do it
- When you will do it
- How you will do it
- How you will pay for it
- How you will measure your achievements

You will also need to address questions such as: Is your proposed facility really necessary? What is the market? Will the project be viable? How will the project affect your organisation's finances? How will the completed project be managed? You also should consider whether refurbishing or improving existing facilities is preferable to starting from scratch with a new building.

Development of project brief

A project brief is a clearly defined statement which sets out the nature of your project and its main purpose, so that your design team, professional advisers, and potential funders can interpret your plans. A project brief should normally address several key topics:

- Timescale – planned start and finish dates.
- Cost limit, if known, and running costs.
- The problems with your existing facilities (if any) which make your proposals necessary, or evidence of currently unfulfilled demand.
- A list of the facilities proposed, including main dimensions and estimated capacities.
- A description of how the proposed facilities will be used, and the degree to which they will be flexible in use and able to meet changing demands.
- General design issues including any planning constraints, and key design factors relating to structure, finishes and services.
- Any special requirements for particular activities.
- Access for people with a disability.
- Whether development needs to be staged or phased, and whether you need to keep existing facilities open during construction.
- Marketing of completed project.

You should also start thinking about sources of funding for your project's capital and revenue costs. You should try to keep key people up to date with how things are going.

Planning permission and other statutory consents

If your project involves changing the use of a piece of land or constructing or altering a building you will probably need planning permission and/or buildings regulations approval. If your project involves a building which is listed because of architectural or historic importance you will also need listed building consent for any alterations. You will need the advice of an architect or planner at this stage.

You should normally have at least outline planning permission (in principle) before making any full application for lottery funding. Remember, your local authority has the power to make you reverse any work undertaken without the necessary planning permission – this can even include demolishing any new construction in extreme circumstances.

Selection of architects and other professional advisers

It is normally in your organisation's best interests to commission established professional advisers – such as solicitors, architects, surveyors and engineers – to handle particular aspects of the project's development. Their fees should comprise a relatively small proportion of your total project costs but will be vital to its success.

You may want to use firms with which your organisation has previous experience, or companies with a track record in the particular type of project. It is normally best to ask a number of companies to tender for your business, so as to get the best possible deal. You should also be aware of the European Procurement Regulations which affect service contracts above a certain size (see below).

Design

You must work with your professional advisers in order to achieve a high-quality design – paying particular attention to initial big decisions rather than subsequent small details. Good architecture need not cost more than bad, especially measured over the lifetime of a building. Various design questions you should take into account include:

- Will the building be fit for the purpose you intend?
- Are statutory and other requirements met?
- Are there proper access provisions for people with a disability?
- How expensive will it be to manage, maintain and run over its intended lifespan?
- How will you compromise between speed and quality of construction?
- Will the building be welcoming, safe and attractive?
- Will the building enhance its immediate surroundings?

You should then seek the approval of your members for the proposed design.

Funding

Once you have completed the design you should go about finding a builder. You will probably want to do this through a tendering process – you should ask a number of builders to submit an estimate of how much it would cost for them to complete your design. Your professional advisers will be able to suggest the best way to do this, but you should be aware of the European Procurement Regulations which affect works contracts above a certain size (see below).

When you have selected the 'most economically advantageous' tender, in terms of quality not just price, you will at last know the cost of your proposed facilities. You can then go about raising the funding for the capital and revenue elements of your project.

Construction and management

Before you sign any building contract, you should ensure that you have completed all the stages outlined above and that all the necessary capital funding is secured and ready to use. You must have guarantees of funding before commencing construction, as few funders, and in particular lottery distributors, will be willing to bail your organisation out financially.

When funding is secured, the contract can be signed and construction can commence. If you want to visit the site during building works you should always tell the constructor first, and whilst on site you should never give instructions direct to the contractor but instead should get one of your professional advisers to do so. Once work gets under way you will have to pay the constructor regularly on the basis of the work done to date.

When the building work is completed, it will be inspected by the local authority to check that it is in line with the plans they approved. Your design adviser will issue a Certificate of Practical Completion to the contractor, who will hand the building over to your organisation for necessary interior work. At this stage you must make certain that your organisation has insurance for the building, its contents and its users. For a period after practical completion, you have a chance to check for any defects in the construction, which should be rectified by your contractor if caused by faulty workmanship or materials. Once any necessary work is done, you have reached final completion of the building stage.

You can then open your new facilities. Now it's time for the hard work to begin!

Access for people with a disability

When setting out policy directions for the distributing bodies in the areas of arts, sport, heritage and for the Millennium Fund, the Secretary of State for National Heritage (now Culture, Media and Sport) specified that all lottery funded projects must have suitable access for people with disabilities. Not only does this involve physical access to these facilities, but also equality of opportunity. This section contains brief guidance on the key disability issues which should be addressed by your organisation. These notes are only intended as a brief introduction, and you should undertake more detailed consideration of these issues. You may find it useful to contact some of the organisations listed below, who may be able to offer you detailed advice.

As a bare minimum, the following disability issues should be taken into consideration:

Physical access

New and refurbished public buildings must provide access for wheelchair users to all floors, and provide facilities for people with sensory impairments, in order

European Union procurement regulations

In an attempt to ensure that a competitive market exists within the European Union, procurement regulations have been introduced which affect contracts issued by public sector bodies for works or services above a certain size. In order to permit international competition for these public contracts, they must be put out to public tender (by placing advertisements in appropriate European journals) so that any company in Europe can bid for the contract.

Because the National Lottery distributing bodies are defined under these rules as contracting authorities, if you receive substantial lottery funding these regulations will affect your organisation. All recipients of money from the National Lottery must comply with the procurement regulations where lottery funds contribute over half of the costs of:

- A works contract (i.e. construction costs) worth more than ECU 5 million (about £3.5 million).
- A services contract (i.e. professional fees for advisers) worth more than ECU 200,000 (about £40,000).

You can select the most suitable company on the basis of either the lowest cost, or the 'most economically advantageous tender' taking into account other longer-term factors such as design quality. These regulations have applied to public sector bodies and local authorities for some time, but now apply to all recipients of lottery proceeds above these thresholds – including charities.

to comply with Building Regulations. There may be cost implications, but such expenses need not be enormous as minor changes can make significant differences to accessibility when considered sooner rather than later.

Awareness of needs

Be aware of the needs of users who may have a disability. Staff should receive ongoing disability awareness training, and managers in particular should have a good working knowledge of disability issues. Even the most accessible building in terms of physical design needs effective management to ensure full access.

Information about access

Provide information about access for people with a disability in all publications as part of your marketing strategy.

Recruitment

Be aware of the possibilities for actively recruiting people with disabilities to work for your organisation, and keep employment policies under review.

Decision-making

Take steps to ensure that people with a disability can play a full part in your internal decision-making process. You should undertake consultation with people with disabilities who make use of existing or planned facilities.

The checklist shown in the box opposite can help your organisation assess the degree to which it has considered the needs of people with disabilities.

Sources of information and advice on disability issues:

British Blind Sport (BBS)	01926-424247
The British Deaf Sports Council	01943-850214 (Voice); 01943-850081 (Minicom)
The British Paralympic Association (BPA)	0181-681 9655
Disability Sport England (DSE)	0171-490 4919
The British Wheelchair Sports Foundation (BWSF)	01296-484848
Centre for Accessible Environments (CAE)	0171-357 8182 (Minicom)
Council for the Advancement of Communication with Deaf People (CACDP)	0191-374 3607
Disability Action (Northern Ireland)	01232-491011
Disability Scotland	0131-229 8632
Disability Wales	01222-887325
Equal Opportunities Commission	0161-833 9244
Equal Opportunities Commission for Northern Ireland	01232-242752
Federation of Sports Associations for the Disabled	01873-830533
RADAR (Royal Association for Disability and Rehabilitation)	0171-250 3222
Scope Cerebral Palsy Sport	0115-940 1202
Scottish Sports Association for the Disabled	01592-771700
Special Olympics UK	0171-416 7257
UK Sports Association for People with Learning Disability	0171-250 1100

Disability access checklist

- ❑ Physical access
- ❑ Dedicated car parking spaces
- ❑ Drop-off points
- ❑ Unobstructed external routes into facility
- ❑ Level or ramped public and staff entrances, including main entrance
- ❑ Internal and external ramps, handrails and lifts meet Building Regulation standards
- ❑ Access to all levels and areas of building (public and non-public)
- ❑ Dedicated wheelchair spaces in performance seating areas
- ❑ Dedicated toilet facilities
- ❑ Box office and/or reception area of accessible height and width
- ❑ Facilities for people with sensory impairment
- ❑ Induction loop in performance areas and at box office/information desk
- ❑ Infra red enhancement in performance areas
- ❑ Visual fire alarm system
- ❑ Braille, large print and/or raised lettering used for signage
- ❑ Sign language interpretation or lipspeakers provided
- ❑ Audio description and 'touch and feel' elements provided
- ❑ Facilities to accommodate guide dogs
- ❑ Organisational policy
- ❑ Ongoing disability awareness training for staff
- ❑ Accessibility information published and marketed
- ❑ People with disabilities employed and actively recruited
- ❑ Decision-making process involves people with disabilities

Conditions of grants

If you are successful in obtaining lottery funds for a capital project from the arts, sport, heritage or Millennium funds, there will be a number of standard terms and conditions attached by the distributing body:

- The grant must be used for the purpose specified in your application form, and is non-transferable. The grant may have to be repaid if there is a change in purpose or ownership during or after the project.
- Lottery funds will also have to be repaid if:
  1. Your organisation ceases to operate for any reason.
  2. You fail to apply your grant for the purpose it was awarded or you fail to complete the project.
  3. You fail to comply with the conditions of the grant.
  4. Your application contained information that was fraudulent, incorrect or misleading.
  5. You have acted in a fraudulent or negligent way at any time during the completion of the project.

- If there is an underspend on your project, you must return the appropriate share to the distributing body. However, if there is an overspend on your project, your grant will not be automatically increased.
- You must supply the distributing body with regular reports on your project's progress, monitor its success when completed, and provide the distributing body with any other information they might require.
- Depreciating assets acquired through lottery funding cannot be sold without written permission from the distributing body.
- Appreciating assets are subject to similar restrictions, with written distributing body approval needed before they may be sold (at any time), and the vendor must show that the proper market value has been received. The distributing body may insist that any such assets are transferred to another appropriate eligible body.
- If lottery-funded items are sold, or if a lottery-funded project realises a distributable profit (which should be rare given that projects should not be for private gain), a proportion from the proceeds/profits must be paid back to the distributing body. This proportion should be equivalent to the distributing body's original contribution towards the overall project cost.
- Assets acquired through lottery funding cannot be used as security for a mortgage or other loan without the prior written permission of the distributing body.
- You must ensure that your lottery funded project operates an Equal Opportunities Policy, and that the public are given full appropriate access to the facility with no person unreasonably denied access.
- Where a grant is for the acquisition of a particular item or collection, the applicant must normally retain ownership of the item(s) and maintain it appropriately.

Each individual distributing body also adds its own particular terms to these standard conditions which relate to their own specialist fields.

Chapter 8
The Foundation for Sport and the Arts

··

For further details contact:

The Secretary, The Foundation for Sport and the Arts, PO Box 20, Liverpool L13 1HB (0151-259 5505)

The Foundation for Sport and the Arts expects to give around £7–£9 million a year to sport.

The Foundation for Sport and the Arts (FSA) is one of the largest backers of sport. It was set up in July 1991 using money from football pools competitions. (Spot-the-ball revenue is directed to the Football Trust; see separate entry in chapter 12.) Despite heavy competition from the National Lottery (launched in November 1994), it remains a vitally important funder of sport both in the amount it gives, and in its determination to support as many sports and communities as possible. Support is directed to every level of sport and the arts, but the Foundation is driven by a desire to put money back into those areas and communities where pools punters can see and enjoy the benefits.

The Foundation's income

The Foundation was set up by football pools promoters with the help of a government agreement to reduce betting duties and redirect them towards helping sports and the arts. The FSA gives a third of its income to arts projects, with the remaining two thirds directed to sports and related facilities. The FSA is independent of both the pools companies and the government. It is controlled entirely by its trustees (see list below). The Foundation has helped over 130 different sports. The biggest individual sector of beneficiaries has been the voluntary sports clubs – the trustees are very supportive of grass-roots activities.

The FSA and the National Lottery

In the previous edition of the Sports Funding Guide published in 1995, the National Lottery had arrived as the new kid on the block. FSA income was hit hard by the competition as the national obsession with the lottery took hold. The pools companies – Littlewoods, Vernons and Zetters – saw their takings fall by about 17% following the lottery launch. As a result both the Football Trust and FSA witnessed a sharp reduction in the amount available for distribution to sports clubs and arts projects.

123

With a further reduction in subscriptions from the pools companies following the introduction of a mid-week lottery draw, weekly income is now around £100,000, compared to a pre-lottery level of £1.4 million each week. Whilst the FSA will probably never regain pre-lottery income levels of £68–£70 million, the £10–£12 million remains very important to those looking to support their sport.

FSA trustees

The Foundation's trustees are a combination of sporting, artistic and pools industry figures. This glittery group is advised and informed by Gratton Endicott, the Secretary since the Foundation started. The trustees are: Sir Tim Rice, Chairman; Lord Brabazon, Deputy Chairman; Nicholas Allott; Lord Attenborough; Dame Janet Baker; Sir Christopher Chataway; Lord Grantchester; Clive Lloyd; Geoffrey Russell; Gary Speakman; Robert Upsdell.

The Chairman, lyricist (and sports enthusiast) Sir Tim Rice plays a particularly active role in that there is a Chairman's Fund from which he can individually and quickly authorise grants of up to £1,500 (though the applications will still have gone through the normal vetting procedure). There is a professional staff (27 people in 1998) who apply the guidelines described below. Pam Bennett leads the Sports Team and Lila Thomas is in charge of Non-Athletic Sports.

Capital and revenue grants

The FSA has always supported capital costs, with grants given mainly towards new buildings and the refurbishment of old ones. It has also helped with equipment or competition costs. However, with the National Lottery taking some of these clothes and funding capital items, the FSA has had to consider supporting running costs.

In an interview in early 1996, Grattan Endicott pondered on the relationship with the National Lottery, observing: 'There is a real concern that all these sports palaces are being built, and there is no way of running them … there will come a time when we have the facilities, but there is no means of staffing and running them. There aren't simple answers. We have to be accountable to people who do the pools, and obviously it's easier to monitor a capital grant and say, "That's where your money went" than it is to point to salaries. But in the long term, this may be part of what the FSA does.'

Revenue support

The long term was not far away. Later that year the FSA issued the following guidelines on revenue support: 'In the past we have avoided commitments to core funding and, in general, to payment of wages. Where we can deal with cases on a two-year or three-year basis with no prospect of further funding subsequently, we have now made exceptions. The trustees are now prepared to look with interest at further applications coming forward.

'In preparing an application for revenue funding the following should be noted:

1. It is expected that a Business Plan will be required with closely detailed assessments of the revenue expenditure envisaged. Specify staff to be employed and why. The application should incorporate a plan in outline showing key figures or alternatively the full plan accompanied by a summary of key proposals.
2. Trustees will look for lean administration, economic and essential in its structure and practices.
3. Trustees should be given detail of the other revenue funding anticipated with information as to the extent to which it has been structured. Bodies that should evidently contribute to be designated and their position statements attached to the plan. (Local authorities in particular please note.)
4. Our reporting accountants will be asked at some stage to explore the proposals in the business plan.
5. To require prominent ongoing acknowledgement of any substantial grant-aid accepted from the Foundation.

'When discussing the subject, trustees indicated that revenue funding bids should be for schemes with a duration of not more that three years with no implication that the Foundation would provide further funding beyond that.' They have some particular anxieties about the 'ground level' management of facilities and resources already existing. They see the Foundation's best use of revenue funding directed to the wider enjoyment of facilities and the more effective management of resources. However, there could also be scope in selected cases for start-up revenue funding in the first two or three years of a project.'

Recent examples include:

- A salary paid to Scope East Recreation Forum to employ a Leisure, Training and Development Officer. The salary was over a two year period, with a commitment from the FSA of £18,400 in the first year and £18,900 in the second.
- Annual grants of £3,000 a year for three years for a mini-basketball programme to be run by Sheffield Hatters Basketball Club.
- £60,000 over three years to Inverness District Indoors Bowling Club as start-up funding for a new indoor bowling stadium.

Capital support and the National Lottery

The FSA is not stopping its capital funding, and this is likely to remain the main element of the FSA's support. The FSA prefers projects where it is the lead funder, but will in some selected cases be involved in partnership funding where the lottery is also supporting. 'In particular the Foundation may be prepared to take on the principal funding of a discrete segment of a project where this can be distinguished as a significant, self-contained Foundation exercise.'

Applicants considering approaching both the lottery and the FSA should note the following from the 1998 Annual Report: 'The Trustees are curbing the size of grants and extending the benefit of grants as far and wide as possible; a side effect of this is their extreme reluctance to put relatively small sums into projects which call for seven-digit grants from the lottery. A feature of recent experience has been the number of times a grant has been awarded and subsequently the grantee has decided to go to the lottery with a much bigger scheme and has wished to take our offer with him as part of the proposal.'

Liverpool Cricket Club has recently applied for FSA support for one element of its redevelopment plan. Following an amalgamation of the Liverpool Collegiate Rugby Club and the Liverpool Ladies Hockey Club, the Cricket club has submitted an extensive upgrading plan for lottery support. It successfully applied to the FSA for help with upgrading the ground floor changing rooms as this would be a stand-alone element of the club's refurbishment and would help the club to offer facilities to its members while the larger upgrading work continued.

The FSA liaises regularly with the Sports Councils in England, Wales, Northern Ireland and Scotland.

Loans

In December 1996, the Foundation announced that it was considering making interest-free loans where appropriate. The potential borrower would have to show how the lease or purchase of land or property would make enough income available to repay the loan.

The Bristol Lawn Tennis Club was given an interest-free loan in February 1998. The loan is worth £35,000 and will contribute towards the cost of buying the clubhouse buildings and clubhouse. The total value of the project is £390,000.

Maximum and minimum awards

The Foundation no longer gives awards of millions as it once did when it was founded and was little known. The maximum is currently £75,000 although the trustees have stated that they now rarely consider an award of more than £50,000. Grants can be for as little as a few hundred pounds, and there has been a consistent determination to support 'a lot with a little' rather than 'a few with a lot'.

'Bids for help arrive in great numbers and it is evident that there are needs that the FSA is more readily able to meet than is the Lottery. We rarely now consider an award of over £50,000, but generally the lower the total number of pounds given away, the more certain we can be that most of the pounds will be wisely and constructively spent.' Sir Tim Rice, Chairman of the FSA Trustees

Sports supported by the FSA

The FSA gives to a very wide spectrum of sporting activities. They range from the mainstream such as golf and cricket to less well-known activities of kabbadi and korfball. Originally, the FSA could only support 'athletic' sports (an unenviable task for the trustees to distinguish between athletic and non–athletic sports). Now it can give to sports that 'do, or are likely to, promote or enhance physical health or physical fitness'. The FSA says that 'any sport or game entailing fairly vigorous or brisk physical exercise is likely to be within the definition'.

Football used to be excluded as it was extensively covered by the Football Trust. However, in 1995, the FSA decided that although professional football was still out, grass-roots and community soccer could come under its umbrella for support. Given the decline in the funds, and perhaps the anticipated response, the Foundation made it very clear that grants were not likely to be over a few hundred pounds, nor would they be made in great numbers. Support would be directed towards local amateur sides, local authority facilities, schools and neighbourhood initiatives. The monthly grants lists bear this out. A large number of local schools and teams have been supported with awards averaging around £500.

The status of golf has been under discussion at the FSA for some time. It is supported, but the trustees are clear that support will not be given to 'exclusive' clubs where facilities are not made available to the widest public possible. Pay and play schemes are therefore given priority, as is the development of the game in areas which will have the most impact upon the young, disadvantaged and 'unpretentious' players generally. Awards have been made to enhance clubhouse facilities and extend courses from nine to eighteen holes.

Sports which are not supported by the FSA

There are a few sports that the FSA does not support, and it has a flexible and responsive approach to the development of sport generally. Shooting, for example, has been supported in the past, but the guidance notes suggest a more cautious approach in the light of recent publicity. The trustees consider applications on a case by case basis. Pistol, rifle and clay pigeon shooting have been grant-aided. The guidance notes warn however: 'Recent events may cause these precedents to be reviewed'.

Sports *not* covered by FSA grants:

Angling	Fishing	Motorised sport
Croquet	Horse racing	

Horse racing is definitely not supported; it is covered by the Horserace Betting Levy. Grants are not given for croquet, angling or motorised sport. The FSA does support bowls, archery, and sailing and yachting, to a limited extent. Parascending, parachuting and gliding can be helped if they benefit people at a community level. Equipment for adventure playgrounds is in, as are swings (but only for very young children).

A sporting index of recent grants

The FSA's giving to sport in the five months January–May 1998 was as follows (this list is ordered by sport; number of grants in the period; range; total value of grants given and examples of what the money was given for):

- *Archery*   3 grants   Range: £350–£2,500   Total: £3,200
  individual archer's expenses; archery club building

- Association *football* 180 grants Range: £200–£3,000   Total: £114,800
  largely to schools, with a few grants to local teams (including an asylum seekers' team), for equipment and kit. £500 was by far the most popular award.

- *Athletics*   3 grants   Range: £500–£10,000   Total: £11,500
  regional development project; equipment; training costs

- *Badminton*   1 grant   Range:£500   Total: £500
  home match expenses

- *Basketball*   3 grants   Range: £3,000–£4,000   Total: £8,000
  new wheelchair basketball club; junior basketball programme

- *Bowls*   29 grants   Range: £340–£20,000   Total: £190,700
  clubhouse; ditches; automatic watering system; mower; youth team away matches; short mat indoor bowls; drainage

- *Boxing*   6 grants   Range: £1,000–£30,000   Total: £58,100
  club roofing and refurbishment; equipment; tournament boxing ring; training facilities

- *Canoeing*   6 grants   Range: 1,200–£12,000   Total: £29,700
  lightweight sprint boat; refurbishment of clubhouse; canoe slalom championships expenses

- *Caving/mountaineering/climbing* 2 grants Range: £1,700–£13,000 Total: £14,700
  equipping vehicle store for search and rescue team; upgrade of indoor climbing wall

- *Cricket*   24 grants   Range: £680–£40,000   Total: £333,600
  re-thatching a pavilion roof; junior coaching programme; nets; artificial pitches; village cricket ground; wicket cutter; pitch covers; new cricket square; mower; new pavilion

- *Cycling*   1 grant   Range: £500   Total: £500
  competitor's training, travel and equipment costs

- *Equestrian*   1 grant   Range: £2,000   Total: £2,000
  competitor's travel, training and maintenance of a horse

- *Fencing*   4 grants   Range: £500–£3,000   Total: £8,500
  scoring equipment; foils; starter kit; competitor's expenses

- *Gaelic sports*   3 grants   Range: £5,700 – £20,000 Total: £37,700
  establishing under-10 hurling club; pitch widening; floodlighting training pitch

- *Gliding*   2 grants   Range: £35,000–£40,000 Total: £75,000
  winch; second towing aircraft

- *Golf*   5 grants   Range: £500–£35,000   Total: £88,500
  amateur's competition expenses; extension of a clubhouse; course improvements; greenkeeper's workshop

- *Gymnastics*   3 grants   Range: £1,600–£8,000   Total: £12,000
  floor mats; equipment; safety matting; gym floor

- *Health/fitness* 1 grant   Range: £6,100   Total: £6,100
  fitness equipment for young people's resource centre

- *Hockey*   1 grant   Range: £3,000   Total: £3,000
  hosting 1998 European club championship finals;

- *Ice hockey/ice skating/skater hockey* 3 grants Range: £500–£6,700 Total: £21,200
  safety padding; equipment and kit for skater hockey team; shorts and helmets for women's team; training, travel and competition costs

- *Judo*   3 grants   Range: £300–£2,000   Total: £4,100
  training costs; mats

- *Martial arts*   1 grant   Range: £300   Total: £300
  training equipment

- *Multi-sport*   61 grants   Range: £330–£65,000   Total: £626,800
  floodlit, multi-play sports surface (Prestatyn); disability sports programme (Forth Valley); Sports Club of the Year awards (national); vehicle repairs (Liverpool); buying of five acres of playing field (Stafford); youth games (Glasgow); salary costs of a sports worker on an estate (Sheffield); awards for sportsmen and women (Wales); skateboard and rollerblade park (Rother); swimming programme for children with hemiplegia (Northern Ireland); sports equipment for new community centre (Isle of Lewis); pilot project educating young people in ethics and fair play (national); sports development in rural areas (Cornwall)

- *Netball*   4 grants   Range: £400–£8,000   Total: £10,900
  set-up equipment for new club; travel costs; kit and equipment; training and competition costs

- *Parascending*   1 grant   Range: £75,000   Total: £75,000
  buying of tow paragliding site

129

- *Rowing*   3 grants   Range: £5,800–£16,000   Total: £37,300
  trailer; juniors' and novices' equipment; racing boats and sculling blades

- *Rugby (Union and League)* 8 grants Range: £500–£20,000 Total: £53,400
  minibus; junior tour; Little League kits; British student championships;
  training equipment

- *Sailing/yachting* 16 grants   Range: £500–£50,000   Total: £261,500
  rescue boat and trailer; safety equipment for Round Britain and Ireland Yacht
  Race; club house repairs; pontoon for disabled access; dinghies

- *Schools/colleges*   16 grants   Range: £450–£75,000   Total: £234,700
  sports barn extension; solar panels; minibuses; wicket; artificial pitch; gym;
  outdoor multi-sports club; PE equipment; showers

- *Speed skating*   5 grants   Range: £4,200–£ 6,300   Total: £25,500
  safety padding for five clubs

- *Sub-aqua*   15 grants   Range: £2,500–£15,000   Total: £81,800
  compressors; storage; dive boat

- *Swimming*   5 grants   Range: £1,000–£6,600   Total: £21,500
  minibus for disabled swimming club; community use of school swimming
  pool; life-saving training

- *Table tennis*   2 grants   Range: £4,700–£5,000   Total: £9,700
  costs of participation in world schools championships; match and practice
  facilities upgrade

- *Tennis*   28 grants   Range: £1,000–£40,000   Total: £905,800
  resurfacing tennis courts; floodlighting; training, equipment and competition costs

- *Trampolining*   1 grant   Range: £5,300   Total: £5,300
  trampolines

- *Volleyball*   1 grant   Range: £250   Total: £250
  posts and net

- *Walking/orienteering* 2 grants Range: £600–£700   Total: £1,300
  printing orienteering map; waterproof clothing for walking group

- *Watersports (barefoot, water ski, snorkelling,*
  water polo, general) 4 grants   Range: £3,000–£34,000   Total: £50,100
  barefoot water ski championships staging costs; water polo team's training
  costs; safety boats; dinghies

In addition to those listed above the Foundation has also given grants for *aikido,
boardsailing, bicycle motocross, camogie, cycle speedway, fives, handball, human performance
(sports science), hurling, jujitsu, kabaddi, korfball, life saving, luge, modern pentathlon,*

movement and dance, nordic biathlon, pétanque, polo, rounders, sand and land yachting, shinty, skateboarding, skiing, surfing, surf life saving, taekwondo, rackets, tug-of-war, water skiing, weightlifting, and wrestling. A range of disability sports is also supported.

Individuals

The FSA liaises with the SportsAid (see chapter 14) and only supports individuals in exceptional circumstances. It previously helped to fund a joint initiative for self-development sports grants with the Prince's Trust (see chapter 14), but funds are no longer available for this.

The FSA does give a few grants to individuals, such as recent grants of £300 towards equipment costs for a martial arts competitor, £500 for a cyclist's travel, equipment and training, and £1,900 for a triathlete's bike and wet suit. 'In such cases it is essential that the exceptional nature of the application is attested to in unqualified terms by an organisation of substance. In cases where the Foundation finds it possible to help it is almost always because trustees fear real potential may be blighted by the difficult financial background of the persons concerned.' Much more often the grant is for a small group of sportsmen or women to take part in an event in their field.

The FSA is not particularly interested in élite performers. These are the preserve of the Sports Council. It mainly gives grants to facilities which will encourage everyone to participate and enjoy sport, rather than for sporting excellence.

Geographical spread of FSA grants

The FSA looks to support all areas of the country. The whole enterprise is Liverpool based, with local advisers throughout the country. In 1997/98, money was given away throughout the four countries in the following amounts: £5,616,700 in England (compared to £12,575,000 in 1996/97), £444,900 to Northern Ireland (£1,586,000 in 1996/97), £799,500 in Scotland (£1,884,000 previously), and £651,600 in Wales (£1,178,000 the preceding year). There is an even distribution throughout the country and, unusually for a national Foundation, no noticeable bias towards London and the south east. In 1997/98 a total of £7,512,700 was given to sports and non-athletic sports projects. Overall, there were 2133 successful applications for sports projects, 214 of which were non-athletic.

The FSA does not allocate budgets to particular sports or geographical regions. The amount given to each activity or area is likely by and large to reflect the number of applications coming in. Where the FSA feels that a particular geographical area has been under-represented in recent grant giving, it gives preference to schemes from that area to maintain a rough balance. The distribution is totally in response to applications. The Foundation makes no pretence at being proactive in its giving.

Applications

The amount

Grants can be up to £75,000, although in practice most grants are between £1,000 and £50,000. The FSA has wise words for applicants: 'The Foundation has noted that applicants sometimes seem to lack confidence to ask for the full sum they need; this does not help their case. If your proposal is well thought out and it requires £20,000 rather than £10,000 to see it through you should apply for the full amount.'

The Foundation has always preferred to make a large number of smaller grants, rather than a small number of large grants. Its philosophy has been to help 'a lot of people a little' and to distribute funds as widely as possible, in keeping with the ethos of supporting projects and activities that pools customers would approve of.

In March 1998, for instance, £867,000 was given in 141 grants. 58 grants were for amounts up to £1,000; 55 were for amounts between £1,001 and £10,000; 24 were between £10,001 and £30,000; and 4 were between £30,001 and £50,000.

The following from the March grants list are typical.

£2,500 to Bowmen of Bosworth Archery Club for a new building.
£35,000 to Seckford Golf Club for upgrade of clubhouse.
£6,100 to Wyborn Youth Trust for fitness equipment.
£1,000 to Wishford C of E School for play equipment.
£500 to Collaton St Mary C of E Primary school for playground markings.
£675 to Halewood U3A for waterproof clothing for a walking group.
£25,000 to Cove Cricket Club for a new cricket square.
£12,500 to UOB Sailing Club for three Lark dinghies.
£20,000 to Toddington Tennis Club for resurfacing three tennis courts.
£4,200 to ADKC Action Disability, Kensington and Chelsea for basketballs and five lightweight wheelchairs.
£2,000 for Sport for Youth, Glasgow towards organising Glasgow Youth Games.
£5,000 to Rother District Council for skateboard and rollerblade park.
£11,900 to Uig Community Association for sports equipment in new community centre.
£33,000 to Craigcefnparc Welfare Association for refurbishment of community hall.
£750 to Tramways FC for kit and football equipment.
£550 to Cromarty Primary School for soccer sevens starter kit.
£1,500 to Matthew Sykes for canoe slalom championships.
£1,500 to Alresford Bowling club for a new mower.
£6,700 to Cynon Valley Cardinals Skater Hockey Team for kit and equipment.
£15,500 to Walton Rowing Club for three rowing boats and sculling oars.
£5,700 to Rosconnor Gaels GAC Hurling Club to establish under-10 hurling club for one year.

How to apply

Applicants should first send a letter outlining the project and what they want. The Foundation will then send you a questionnaire asking for more detailed information. The aim and advantage of this two-stage process is that you do not have to spend ages putting together a complete application which the Foundation cannot support. A brief letter saying who you are, what you do and what you need money for is all that is needed in the first instance. Also include a set of your most recent accounts.

Who to write to

Completed applications should be returned to the Secretary at:

PO Box 20, Liverpool L13 1HB (0151-259 5505)

The trust does not respond in any way to direct approaches to individual trustees; all correspondence must be with the secretary. The trust actively seeks not to give any advantage to anyone who tries the 'back door' approach, and says any indirect approach can work against the application.

Information to include in the full application

The FSA will ask for some or all of the following:

- Background to the organisation (e.g. why it exists, how it started, who it is affiliated to).
- Why a grant is wanted. This may need to be backed up with the reports of consultants and professional advisers.
- How many people will benefit from the proposal?
- How many people can be accommodated in the spectator accommodation?
- Who will make it happen? Where available, information on suppliers and contractors should be included.
- Who supports the project (include any big names as well as community supporters)?
- The status of the club/society (e.g. is it a charity?) and who runs it – board of governors, trustees, members' committee or the like?
- The total cost of the project and the amount requested from the Foundation.
- How will the project be funded? Where is other money coming from, apart from the Foundation?
- The latest accounts/financial statements of the organisation.

The Foundation will still want **a summary of the key elements set out on a single sheet of A4 paper.**

They need to see quickly what it is you are applying for, and how they should proceed. Videos and lengthy publications will not help your case. With around 100 to 150 applications a week, there simply is not enough time for trustees to look at supplementary material.

133

Once the completed application is received, it is passed on to the relevant working party. They may come back to you for more information.

Grant applications are decided upon by following general guidelines available from the Foundation. The Foundation is admirably open (and unstuffy) in describing its policies. It tries to 'lead applicants by the hand'.

There are two key factors:

(i) **The project should benefit the general community:** 'The money comes out of the pockets of pools punters: we would like to plough it back largely into things that the general community will experience and enjoy'.

(ii) Therefore, the Foundation is particularly keen to support the **'little clubs'** – i.e. regional and local clubs.

Not surprisingly, the Foundation receives more applications than it can support, even after it has weeded out those which do not fit its policies. It has to choose amongst 'equals'. When they are considering your application, trustees will be asking themselves the following:

- What is to be gained by the community? Are facilities to be shared so that the widest use is to be made of them, and especially by the kind of people who do the pools and contribute the money?
- Are children and young people involved?
- Do disabled, deprived or disadvantaged people benefit?
- Does this application help us spread our money throughout the UK?
- Does it help us fund the whole spectrum of sports?
- Does the application show signs of 'self-help'. For instance, have the applicants made efforts to obtain other funding? If they want money to improve facilities, are they prepared to do work themselves?

Time lags

The Foundation is dependent upon the flow of funds from football pools income. As a result, there has to be money in the barrel before grants can be paid, which can lead to considerable delays between a grant being agreed and the money being released. Currently, there can be a gap of three months to over a year between an application being submitted and the cheque being sent.

Applications that have been approved by the Foundation are sent a letter of intent and updates about the progress of their application from time to time. When a letter has been received, the FSA strongly advises that applicants should not go too far in advancing a project.

The Secretary, Grattan Endicott outlined the FSA's position: 'The length of time that it takes to resolve the outcome of an application once it is received varies greatly, because we do hold some until the funding situation eases in

An application's progress

1. The organisation sends an outline application to the FSA.
2. If the application seems relevant the FSA will send a questionnaire which asks for more detailed information. If it is not relevant, it will be rejected at this stage and the applicant will be told.
3. The organisation fills out the questionnaire and encloses the other information asked for.
4. The FSA tells the organisation that the application has been received.
5. Applications are passed to assessors for external comment.
6. If appropriate, the FSA asks for the views of umbrella bodies and others.
7. Applications are returned to the FSA with comments.
8. Applications are ordered into FSA priorities.
9. Approved applications are passed to the trustees.
10. If agreed, a Letter of Intent is sent to the organisation. If not, a rejection letter is sent.
11. Agreed applications wait for the necessary money to come in.
12. Once money has come in, the grant is sent to the organisation. The time lag from acceptance to payment can vary from days to months. There is a plea from the FSA for applicants not to telephone staff to find out how the application is doing.

the hope that we may be able to assist them even though in the first two or three months that we have them, funds are not available. It is not surprising that a considerable proportion of the rejections are made fairly quickly since we do notify people as soon as we are aware they will not receive sufficient priority with us to be assisted. Some of these turn rounds are very quick indeed and the majority are within two or three months. Because of our uncertain funding arrangements it is inevitable that some of the cases linger much longer and that the answer is then negative. We do make a practice of writing to people from time to time while matters are taking their course to reassure them that progress is being made or to set out for them the difficulties of the situation that are causing the delay.'

Where a grant is turned down, the Foundation writes to applicants. Unsuccessful applicants can reapply, but it is best to leave a suitable gap, perhaps for a year. Ideally, further applications should be for something different, rather than repeating something that has already failed.

What the Foundation looks for in an application

- Is the project well run?
- Is it financially sound?
- Can it show that the project will be financially secure in the future (i.e. is it sustainable)? This is a key requirement.
- Is the need a real one?
- Is the proposed action sensible, and has the applicant taken appropriate advice?
- Is there no obvious extravagance?
- How many people will benefit? What people?
- Are other funders involved?

'We do fund the pursuit of excellence, but our first thought is lower down the order of things – to allow those who enjoy an activity to participate in it, no matter how modest their standards. We believe that quite small sums, pumped into the grass roots of a community, can markedly improve the quality of life.'

Chapter 9

Company sponsorship and Sportsmatch

■■

Sponsorship for smaller organisations

Getting money from sponsors is never easy; but if you are a Premier League football club, a Formula 1 racing team or a Wimbledon tennis champion, major companies will want to associate themselves and their products with you because millions of potential customers follow your every move. The problem for the superstars is 'how much and for how long?' rather than 'can we get any money at all?'.

World-class players and teams are rare, and rarity of any type commands a premium price so the bidding gets higher and higher. They can afford to be selective of their sponsors, choosing only those who offer the best total package, from the multi-million dollar fee to the number of flights and hotel rooms for friends and family.

Sponsors, too, exercise their right to be selective. Their millions are dependent on continued success and the maintenance of corporate and personal standards on and off the field of play. The stakes are high and the potential returns for the sports person and the company are enormous.

On a more down-to-earth level, the smaller sports clubs and societies of Britain are trying to raise money for survival rather than further increase wealth. But it is crucial to remember that the principles of sports sponsorship remain basically the same at whatever level.

Sadly, many small sporting organisations get the principles of sporting sponsorship completely the wrong way round; they then wonder why it is so difficult to raise money. The fundamental mistake often comes from

> Remember, sponsorship is a business expenditure, not a donation. You have to go about it in a business-like way.

the simple fact that sports organisers enjoy their particular sport and think it is the most important thing in the world. Such attitudes do not help them breach the wall surrounding company sponsorship funds. Too often organisers try to get sponsorship by saying, in effect: 'What do we want to do and who are we going to get to pay for it?'

This approach may sometimes raise money but it is not commercial sponsorship. A company may, for example, want to improve its general image in an area. Paying for a few advertising hoardings at the local football club and putting its name on the players' shirts may make everyone feel that bit better but it does not do much more than that.

For many companies that is enough. They have 'done their bit' and can cheerfully reject all other calls for their cash. Such attitudes often exist in smaller companies where the chief executive has a personal, and real, interest in a particular sport in the locality and wants to do some good. In reality it is a dreadful waste of a company's hard-earned profits and in the long term actually limits the amount of money made available to sport because sponsorship is not allowed to demonstrate its real capabilities as a marketing tool for business.

What sports organisers should be saying is: 'What does company X want or need to achieve and how can we help it achieve that objective?' Not only will a company's money then be used more effectively but the organisation is more likely to gain funding, generate continuing investment and make itself attractive to other companies.

Principles of sponsorship

There are two basic rules for sport and sponsor:

Sponsor: What will I achieve from sponsorship that I cannot do in any other way for the same or less money?

Sport: What can I offer that cannot be achieved in any other way for the same or less money?

This is really the same rule looked at from different points of view. And if they look over-commercial, with too much emphasis on money then, sorry! Sports sponsorship is commercial and its success will only be achievable if both sides recognise it; not to do so can only limit the business and sporting development related to any particular venture.

Sports sponsorship must, therefore, be a partnership with the sport becoming a member of the business squad and the company metaphorically putting on its boots or trainers and joining the sporting team.

Being part of the same team may also lead to some changes in the way both members think. If a company thinks, for example, that it can afford £10,000 for a modest sporting sponsorship it should do one of two things:

Either: it should immediately double it to £20,000

Or: halve it to £5,000.

The principle in either case is the same; sponsorship expenditure should be backed by further promotional expenditure to bring the sponsorship to the attention of the company's target market. A reasonable rule of thumb is to spend £1 on promotion for every £1 of sponsorship fee. The Institute of Sports Sponsorship estimates that the ratio is closer to 3:1 when all associated expenditure is included.

It is a tougher decision for the sport to say it would accept half of the original budget, or insist on a doubling of budget for promotion. In the real world the temptation to take what is on offer is almost overwhelming – but if sponsorship is to be a long-term successful venture then these tough decisions have to be made.

Compatibility

As well as the money, there is also the question of compatibility between sport and sponsor; one should feel comfortable with the other. One extreme form would be the sponsorship of an athletics club by a tobacco company. Aside from the fact that this is excluded by the voluntary agreements on sponsorship made by the tobacco industry, it is unlikely that the club would accept it. Equally it is unlikely that tobacco would offer sponsorship, because there is an obvious clash of sport and product that would not sit comfortably in the spectators' mind.

However, there are instances where an initial judgment, for example the sponsorship of Rugby League by the mild cigarette, Silk Cut, might not seem correct, but in fact develop into highly successful events.

Sponsorship is often used to change the perception of a product or company, but its limitations should be recognised. Manufacturers of fish and chips should not try to make themselves look like smoked salmon and caviar because no-one will believe them. Neither should a sport take sponsorship money from a company whose market they do not reach; it is all a waste of time and money for everybody.

There will never be enough sponsorship money for sport because there is always something more that needs doing. But there is still something around £350 million spent annually in Britain by companies and the Government's Sportsmatch scheme has generated £34 million of new sponsorship money.

So there is money for the having; but to find a way in, sport has to understand why businesses sponsor sport.

Why do businesses sponsor sport?

Companies are not charitable institutions; they exist to generate profits and in so doing create useful products for society, jobs for people, tax revenue for government and a return for their shareholders.

Yet many companies do give to community organisations. Total company support for charities was about £350 million in 1996/97. They are not obliged to, but like many individuals they feel that some charitable expenditure is a sensible and responsible use of their profits (or wages). As well as the purely humanitarian aspect of charitable donations, such gifts help establish a company's reputation as a responsible corporate citizen just as an individual's actions establish his or her reputation in the community. Whilst there is strictly no commercial return on charity there is a benefit to the way a company is perceived by the public and, importantly, its own existing and potential employees.

Sponsorship investment is a different kettle of fish. It is designed to give a clear and measurable commercial return on marketing expenditure that is designed to reach and influence potential customers or other audiences that have an impact on its business. Companies spend money on sponsorship because it can achieve commercial objectives that other marketing techniques cannot:

Advertising makes a direct proposition to the customer. An advertisement effectively says: 'Here is our product, this is what it does and this is why you will like it.'

A **sales promotion** gives a direct incentive to buy a product instead of its competitor. The offer can be two pence off, buy two and get one free or buy ten and get a free T-shirt. The permutations are limited only by the marketing department's imagination.

Direct mail personalises the sales message with a direct communication to groups of individuals.

Sponsorship is a more subtle process. It is rarely linked with direct sales objectives; rather it seeks to create an environment where the existing or potential customer feels more favourably disposed to the sponsoring company or product. This can be direct, for example at a sponsored golf match when there is ample time to talk to customers individually about their needs and how the sponsor's product may help, or indirect, which is when the spectator is left with the feeling that because a company has sponsored 'my' sport then the product is 'my' sort of product.

There is a crucial difference between the two types of sponsorship. One merely seeks to create the opportunity for a sales message; the other seeks to use the sport to translate its values to the product. This latter technique is image marketing and can add the excitement and skill of sport to the product values of, say, a fizzy drink or an estate agent which, with the greatest of respect, can be rather dull on their own!

Many sponsorship executives or agencies would disagree but sports sponsorship is basically a branch of public relations. PR is about getting a third party to tell a consumer that a product is a good thing. If a manufacturer says a product is good in any of the paid for media then the consumer is rightly sceptical; if a journalist tests the products and says it is good then this is seen as independent endorsement.

By associating a product with a sport, a company or product can assume some of the values of that sport. Sport can represent achievement and excellence. If Coca-Cola wishes to reinforce its positioning as the world's favourite soft drink (and it does) then it is a natural for it to be seen at the Olympic Games or the World Cup, which are pinnacles of international sporting achievement. It is equally appropriate for a local company to associate itself with the equivalent local team or event; the scale may be different but the principles are the same.

If the consumer/spectator enjoys a sponsored sporting event, he or she can be more favourably disposed to the product. They will not rush out and buy it immediately but when touring the supermarket or walking down a high street full of estate agents the successful sponsor's brand name will be favourably noted. Communication has been achieved with the consumer through the third party agency of the sporting event.

Sponsorship does not – or at least should not – exist in a vacuum. Used properly it can add depth and texture to a company's marketing communications. Paid for advertisements are more effective if their claims are backed by actual events which reflect and support the advertising message; equally the advertising can use and develop messages and images from a sport which allow the creation of more interesting and attractive propositions.

There are also specific objectives of sponsorship and any given project may contain some or all of them.

Brand/corporate awareness

The object is simply to put the company or its product's name in front of the consumer and make him or her remember it. If that is all it does then the sponsorship money is wasted, because the consumer does not know what to do; so awareness sponsorships must be backed with advertising or public relations support to explain the name further and create a reason to buy the product or understand the company's business. For example, Cornhill's sponsorship of Test Cricket was backed up with newspaper advertisements stating 'It's time you tested Cornhill Insurance' and giving contact addresses and telephone numbers. Naturally, these advertisements were placed in the sports pages.

Green Flag spent four years, and around £4 million sponsoring the England football team. The company gained high awareness of the name – up from zero to 53% – but not many knew what the company did. Subsequently the company pulled out, claiming it had achieved its awareness objective and wanted to move to other means of communications to explain its services. (The fact that the cost of the sponsorship quadrupled had, of course, nothing to do with the decision!)

Brand/corporate image

Image sponsorship is concerned with maintaining or enhancing the image – or the way in which the consumer views – the product or company. Many companies want to go or keep their products up-market. This means establishing an image of quality and dependability that justifies charging a premium (expensive) price. It can be vital in establishing a difference between one product and its competitors. Whilst sponsorship cannot do this alone, it is a valuable support to other product components such as advertising, packaging and point-of-sale material. There are also potential pitfalls for a company that links its image to a particular individual: Paul Gascoigne, Stan Collymore and John Daly are just a few examples of sportsmen whose antics caused their sponsors to tear up their contracts.

Reasons a company may sponsor

- Name awareness
- Enhancement of a corporate image
- Opportunities to entertain customers, clients and VIPs
- Improved investor relations
- Services or facilities which benefit staff
- Involvement with the community
- Improved staff relations/morale
- Recruitment incentives
- Association with a high-quality event
- Access to a specific market i.e. targeting an audience very precisely
- Product or service promotion – cost-effective advertising

Customer relations

Many companies are involved in selling high-value products of considerable complexity that cannot just be put on a shelf with a price sticker. Computer companies do not just sell jazzed-up calculators; they sell networked systems, installation and backup services that are tailor made to their customer's needs. They need to establish a long-term relationship of trust and confidence which can be fostered in the relaxed surrounding of entertainment at a sponsored event. Sport is a common language in business and is used to encourage good relations, as well as saying thank you for an order. Hospitality packages can be purchased at many events, but there is a special cachet in being invited to a sponsor's 'own' event. But beware: there are increasingly strict government and corporate guidelines on the acceptance of hospitality which can be interpreted, in some circumstances, as a bribe.

Employee relations

Sponsorship can help employees identify more closely with their firm by following the fortunes of its sponsorships. They can also attract new employees who feel comfortable with the idea of working for a company which sponsors a sport they are interested in.

Community relations

Companies want to get on well in the areas where they have factories or offices. They are subject to all sorts of regulations and requirements and while sponsorship of the local football team will not exclude them from any of their obligations such involvement will indicate that they are not just there to make a quick buck, but do see themselves as a good, local corporate citizen. It might, one day, just make the difference between a no and a yes to a planning application.

What are companies looking for?

Modern business sponsors have developed strategies for their brand or corporate communications. They will seek to identify or create support activities which enhance that strategy rather than tailor their strategy to match available events.

Some events are so important in the sporting calendar – The Grand National, Test Matches, Cup Finals – and attract such large audiences that they are very important to sponsors. Indeed, some will not accept sponsorship, so far. Some sponsors are happy to associate their name with a really major event (although gaining an association of company or product names to an existing event can prove extremely difficult), but a sponsor will generally prefer an event or programme that is unique to its company or product. This can create problems in that some sporting events can appear contrived and not really reflect the true nature of the sport. At other times, a created event can become too popular – the Gillette Cup in cricket eventually meant only cricket to consumers who had no associations with razor blades, so the sponsors pulled out.

Whatever the choice of sport, a sponsor is looking for an event that will enhance the reputation of its product by association with quality, enjoyment and good performance. For many companies it is important to be associated with winners. Motor companies sponsor motor racing to demonstrate the excellence of their road cars by association with performance and reliability. Other companies seek to demonstrate their role in the community. British Telecom, for example, sponsor many sporting events, particularly for disabled people, that emphasise a caring, service-led company.

> The sponsor will look for an event that is compatible with its product. Bells Whisky and Johnny Walker Whisky have been significant sponsors of golf because the image of a sociable drink at the 19th hole after a game is very much part of the golf culture. Pizza Hut were and Wagon Wheels biscuits are now substantial supporters of Football in the Community because their restaurants and products are aimed at young people who are interested in football and they have a clear presence in hundreds of communities and shops in Britain.

Generally, a sponsor will seek to achieve these objectives through attracting publicity among its target market. For consumer goods companies the target market is the general public, or specific segments of it, so media coverage in the press and television and radio is the most immediate and wide-ranging means of communication. Financial services companies will have a much narrower segment of the market as a target, people with money to invest; brewers will want to communicate with people who go into pubs; double glazing companies want to impress home owners. For some of these companies widespread media coverage is wasted because they are not talking to their market. It can be far more useful for a sponsor to reach 10 real customers than 1,000 or 10,000 of the general public who have no interest in a particular product.

One of the secrets of gaining sponsorship is to know who the sport reaches, who is involved and what are their interests. Then, and only then, should the search for a sponsor begin, and the first priority there is to discover the company's target markets, strengths and weaknesses and to see if what you have matches what they want.

How to develop a sponsorship package

In an ideal world, sponsors and sports would sit down together and discuss their mutual plans and problems. Sponsors would outline their marketing plans and reveal the gaps and weaknesses that they need to remedy; sports would discuss their development plan, outline past performance and future potential. After considerable discussion, areas of common ground would be identified, sport would develop an event or programme to meet the sponsor's needs and the sponsor would set aside a budget to fund it. The two sides would then work happily together towards a successful event, monitor and evaluate its performance and then, with suitable modifications, renew the contract for a further year.

Real life isn't like that. Business executives are extremely busy running their current workload and companies are using fewer people and expecting them to do more, so for most executives doing what they have already been asked to do is often the limit of their realistic ambitions. Arriving on their doorstep, therefore, with a new idea that only promises more work for uncertain returns is unlikely to gain an immediate favourable response.

The solution is that the sponsorship seeker has to do the majority of the preliminary homework and demonstrate an understanding, or at least a sensitivity, to the company's needs. This is obviously difficult as the sports body is not a part of the company and does not know its commercial priorities or its sensitivities. Indeed, the company may regard these policies as extremely confidential. You may well have the answer to a company's communications problem, but if it does not tell you what the problem is then mutual cooperation is unlikely.

To develop a sponsorship package you first need to analyse what you have to offer and secondly analyse what you think the company needs. The latter is more difficult for you as it is really guesswork, but forget your sporting role for a moment and act as a consumer. What do you think of a company or its products? Do you use them and why (or why not)? Companies spend thousands of pounds on market research and your view is as valuable to them as the people the researchers have questioned.

Whether you are looking for local or national sponsors will affect the way you go about the process but the principles are the same and start with what we shall call the sponsorship audit.

What are companies looking for?

Sports organisations should be able to offer at least some of the following:
- A **respectable partner** (with the right image).
- A real **partnership**. Is there scope for partnership, or is the applicant simply seeking money? What involvement is being looked for from the sponsor, and how well does this meet the needs of the sponsor?
- A **proven track record** (preferably in securing and delivering sponsorships) and a **professional approach**. Has the applicant approached the business of getting sponsorship in a professional way, and can he/she demonstrate a similar professionalism in the running of their organisation?
- Genuine **value for money**. What are the benefits and how much money is being asked from the sponsor? How does this rate as compared with other possible sponsorships that the company might consider? The relationship of cost to return and the importance of the return to the company are **the** dominant factors affecting the decision to sponsor or not to sponsor.
- An **interesting project** (at least to the company management and possibly also company staff) and **initiative**. Does the sponsorship represent a new initiative, something that would not happen without the company's support? Is it interesting and lively? It is much more attractive to back an interesting proposal and an interesting organisation.
- **Continuity**. Is there scope for a continuing relationship (over the next few years), or is the activity/event just a one-off?
- **Visibility**. How 'visible' will the event be, and what specific publicity and PR benefits will accrue to the sponsor? Will the company name be given a high profile?
- **Appropriateness**. Is the activity/event appropriate to the sponsor? Also, are you approaching the right company (e.g. not asking one motor manufacturer to provide a vehicle produced by a rival, an all too common occurrence)?
- **Targeted audience** (possibly leading to direct marketing e.g. providing the company's wine in the directors' box after the game).
- **Other tangible benefits** (e.g. good publicity; media coverage; link with brand advertising; entertainment opportunities for company directors and staff; access to VIPs; involvement of company employees or retirees; training or experience for employees etc.).

The sponsorship audit – 1

What do we have to offer?

No doubt you believe that your sport and the project you want sponsored is the best thing since sliced bread. Others will not. Don't worry, because your enthusiasm will be important but you have to back your basic belief with facts and figures that will persuade doubters.

You need dispassionately to audit your sport and the part your organisation plays in the game and the town, region or country in which you operate. The following is a list of questions to which you will need answers. It is not comprehensive but will start the process. No doubt more questions will emerge as you progress.

- How many people play and watch your sport?
- What type of people are they (age, sex, social group, income)?
- Who else is interested (newspapers, television, radio)?
- What is your track record? Are you league champions or trying to avoid relegation? (Either can present an opportunity to a sponsor.)
- What are your (realistic) ambitions? How are you going to achieve them?
- Who runs your organisation? Are they any good? Do you have strong financial controls?
- Have you been sponsored before? What were the results for you and the sponsor?
- What would be the benefits of your sponsorship proposal (to your sport, to participants, to spectators, to the general public)?
- Have you sounded out interest in the project? Have you asked newspapers, television and radio if they will give you regular coverage?
- How do you plan to support the project? Will you produce programmes, posters, leaflets, support manuals, training packages?
- What exposure can you offer a sponsor? Where will the sponsor's name appear, how large will it be, how often will it appear?
- What opportunities are there for the sponsor (attendance, entertainment, free tickets, presentation of prizes)?
- Will your project qualify for a Sportsmatch Award or for funding from the National Lottery, or the Foundation for Sport and the Arts?
- What will the project cost? Where will the money go, what amount will be spent on administration, how much goes to the sport directly?
- What reporting systems do you have? How will you account for expenditure? How will you monitor attendance, press coverage, attitudes to the sponsor before and after the event?

And so on. The more questions you can have answered before the sponsor has to ask them, then the greater your chances of success.

The sponsorship audit – 2

What does the company need?

The communications needs of companies vary greatly from product to product and over time. Because you will need to gain a good understanding of the company you approach, it is better to limit your search to a few companies and tailor make your proposal rather than making hundreds of copies and casting them on the waters; they will almost inevitably sink.

> As with all fundraising and income generation, a relevant approach to an appropriate person works far better than a general letter to everyone. Target a few companies and give them individual attention rather than writing to every company in your local *Yellow Pages*.

You need to do some research. Start by thinking about the compatibility of your event with a company's products and consumers. Are both of interest to young or old people, men or women? Is your sport or the company modern, fashionable or traditional; is it of interest to the higher social groups or the lower? Are you fish and chips or caviar consumers? Pick the companies that are selling either of those products to your participants and spectators.

Once you have established the type of company you want to approach you must do a lot of reading. Start with general newspapers, either national or local. Read the business pages and the *Financial Times* to see what 'your' companies are doing. Look at the marketing press and particularly the three sponsorship publications *Sponsorship News*, *Sports Marketing* and *Hollis Sponsorship Newsletter*. Investing in the *Hollis Sponsorship and Donations Year Book* could prove worthwhile as it gives you named contacts in companies, details of their sponsorship interests and budgets. The Institute of Sports Sponsorship produces a comprehensive *Sponsorship Update* every month that reviews all press and broadcast media coverage of sponsorships and sponsors. The Directory of Social Change publishes the journal *Corporate Citizen* three times a year, with the latest developments in corporate community investment. Consider sharing the costs of all these publications with other sports who are different enough from yours not to be competing for the same money.

> ## A successful sponsorship from a company's point of view
>
> - It has the right **image**
> - It has the **correct target audience** or target area
> - It **sells the benefits** of the sponsorship to the company (especially how the sponsorship would meet the company's commercial objectives).

147

Hold a few brainstorming sessions with your members to talk about target companies and what you think they might need. Remember to include some of your younger members in these sessions. They usually have a much clearer idea of what is happening and selling in the high street that any number of older and 'wiser' heads.

If you are looking for support from local companies, an early approach to discuss their activities and your sport might actually work and be extremely beneficial to you. Do not expect necessarily to get to talk to national companies – they just do not have the time.

As with all fundraising, start with the people you know. It is much better to approach people who know you, like you and trust you than people whose first reaction is 'Who are this lot?' Ask your members, supporters, parents etc. to see who works for a local company or who knows someone who does. Even if they do not work in the PR department themselves, they may be able to make the initial approach on your behalf. If the company turns them down, they risk alienating a member of their own staff, not a club they have never heard of. By using personal contacts you get a foot in the door a little more easily.

If you haven't got a personal contact you will have to get in touch by letter. Write to the public relations departments of the target companies to get a copy of their annual report, employee newspaper and other publications to get some idea of their activities.

By now, you should be beginning to get an idea of the activities and priorities of your target companies. The next task is to match these to what your sporting organisation has to offer. It is not enough to offer 1,000 contacts to a company sponsoring your event – many of them may be totally irrelevant to the company. You need to say which 1,000 people will be involved and how. A simple list based on the findings of the audit of your organisation and sport next to the company and product requirements should start to produce areas of overlap.

The following example is an approach you might develop:

Audience/Consumer	Sport	Company/Product
Male	✓	
18–24	✓	✓
25–34		
35–45		
Single	✓	✓
Married		
Professional		✓
Manual	✓	
Homeowner	✓	✓

A quick glance will establish if you are both talking to the same people, or whether it is time to look at another company!

The next thing you need to look at is the range of sponsorship benefits you can offer the company. For example, could you offer some or all of the following?

	Yes	No
Goodwill in the local community	❏	❏
Contact with opinion formers	❏	❏
Contact with government departments	❏	❏
Contact with celebrities	❏	❏
Opportunities for company directors	❏	❏
Opportunities for company staff	❏	❏
Other (specify)	❏	❏

What about publicity material? Would the company's name and logo be on any of the following?

	Yes	No	
Letter heading	❏	❏	How many? ....
Envelopes	❏	❏	How many? ....
Press releases	❏	❏	How many? ....
Posters	❏	❏	How many? ....
Promotional flyers	❏	❏	How many? ....
Programmes	❏	❏	How many? ....
Newsletters	❏	❏	How many? ....
Website	❏	❏	How many hits? ....

Can you deliver any media coverage? Before you say 'yes' ask yourselves how much coverage you already receive in the following:

	Frequent	Occasional	Possible
National television	❏	❏	❏
Regional television	❏	❏	❏
National radio	❏	❏	❏
Local radio	❏	❏	❏
National press	❏	❏	❏
Local press	❏	❏	❏
Free press	❏	❏	❏
Specialist press	❏	❏	❏
Magazines/journals	❏	❏	❏
Your own publications	❏	❏	❏
Internet links	❏	❏	❏
Other (specify)	❏	❏	❏

Also, don't forget about advertising possibilities at the entrance to your club, on the team coach, on your team strips, in the programme etc.

Such work is fairly basic, but it is a good starting point for discussions with a potential sponsor. The more facts and figures you can give them the better, especially if they are backed up by a track record of delivery.

If the company senses that common ground exists between sport and their market more detailed and sophisticated requirements will start to emerge. This is when sport and sponsor start to work together to address the real concerns of a company. At this stage, you should be pretty close to some form of agreement. A company might well insist on – and you should offer – to sign a confidentiality agreement.

First though, you have to get into the company. Telephone to find the name of the person responsible for sponsorship. Write an outline of your scheme emphasising how you think you can help the company. Remember, many sponsorship proposals fail because they concentrate too much on the needs of the sports club rather than stressing the commercial benefits to the company. You should request a meeting and follow up with a telephone call.

Put together a brief presentation that gets your message over in under 20 minutes; allow 10 minutes for questions so that the entire session can be over in half an hour. If it goes on longer than that it should be only because the company wants it to and you will know they are interested.

The crucial part of the proposals will concern money; not surprisingly this is one of the most difficult areas for both parties.

How to cost a sponsorship package

There are two basic starting points in putting together costings for a sponsorship:

- How much do you need?
- How much do you think you can get?

The two figures may not be totally different but it is obviously a waste of time to offer a £100,000 sponsorship to a small company whose annual profits may be not much more than that. However, a key issue is how much the company would have to pay for such publicity. One simple method of estimating the value of a sponsorship is to count up the number of column centimetres gained in press coverage or the amount of broadcast time achieved and calculate how much this would have cost the company to buy as advertising space. In reality this does not stand up to close scrutiny because the sponsorship coverage is not as direct a hard sell as an advertisement, but it helps.

Another way is to calculate the number of 'impacts' achieved by the sponsorship coverage. This is simpler as you only have to total the circulation figures of newspapers or magazines and the number of listeners or viewers of broadcast media. Again, it is a crude measure but it helps companies get an idea about what you have to offer. At this point, it may be worth talking to a PR agency about how much they think the sponsorship is worth, but you will have to pay to find out.

You can try to get more than one sponsor for the same project, but this can be difficult. The sponsorship is worth less if you don't have exclusive rights to it. Certainly you should never offer a sponsorship to companies who operate in the same market as competitors.

There are three further factors in costing a sponsorship:

- Is the event dependent on raising a certain sum of money which, if not found, means it will not take place?
- Is the event going ahead anyway and sponsorship money is needed only to increase its size, number of participants or impact?
- Is the event of sufficient importance that the sponsorship money is only an 'entry fee' for the company to attach its name to the event?

These three factors determine the way costings are put together, the amounts needed and the amounts asked for.

The sponsorship audit of the sport and the proposed sponsored event will have highlighted other factors that can add value to the sponsorship. If you have a promise of television coverage then it would be reasonable to expect more than just the money to stage the event, but it would be useful to give an idea of how that extra money will be used. If it can be shown to be directed, say, to training and coaching or encouraging young people to play the game then the sponsor can see further returns from the investment.

Think ...

- Sponsorship is a business expenditure, not a donation. You have to go about it in a business-like way.
- When costing a sponsorship package the issue is what is the value of the sponsorship to the company, not how much will it cost you to provide it.
- A good sponsorship that meets a company's objectives could be worth a lot more than you think.
- Evaluate what the sponsor will get from the sponsorship that they cannot get in any other way for the same or for less money.
- Evaluate what your organisation can offer that could not be achieved in any other way for the same or for less money.
- Why are you offering the sponsorship to that particular company (as opposed to the one down the road)?
- How do you get over the prejudice that you are just a small sports club and that it's too risky being associated with you?
- How do you show that you are well run and that you understand the sponsor's needs and aspirations?

Costings need to be as detailed as possible covering every aspect of the event. These will vary depending on the sponsorship package, the sport concerned and not least the participation of amateur or professional players.

Ways of reducing the cost of sponsorship should also be investigated. Ticket sales, for example, can be underwritten by the sponsor and their commitment reduced according to the number sold. If nothing else this gives an incentive to the in-house advertising and public relations teams to prove they can do their jobs!

The sport should always reveal other sources of funding such as sports governing bodies, the Foundation for Sports and the Arts, Sportsmatch and the National Lottery.

> If you are expecting to charge a premium for guaranteed TV coverage then it is prudent to get it in writing from the television contractor. Failure to deliver will certainly entail a return of the television premium, so do not spend it in advance!

The ability to stage payments can be attractive to companies. It can help them manage their cash flow or spread it across financial years. Also, remember that company budgets are planned on a 12 to 24 month basis so it is no use expecting support for an event that is scheduled to happen in a fortnight's time.

If a company works on a calendar financial year it will begin to put together outline plans for overall financial targets around June. These figures will be fed down to the cost and profit centres during the summer and the departments will begin to respond to them in September. In October the sum of the parts will be examined by senior management for formal agreement in October. Fine tuning then will result in a locked down budget sometime in November that will take some shifting, particularly if it involves extra expenditure. In reality, the only budget changes that happen at this stage are cuts. The clear message is to think well ahead and remember that there are many layers of approval to go through in a company before a go-ahead can be given.

Running a sponsorship

One of the best ways of attracting new sponsorship is to demonstrate that you have done so successfully in the past. In practical terms this means you should maintain a record of your sponsorship quest. Start by preserving in a binder your original audit of your own activities, follow it with your audit of the sponsor's business and the presentation to the company. If the bid is successful include the contract and begin to develop a full record of the event and the surrounding activities.

Include photographs, programmes, posters, press clippings, transcripts and tapes of radio and TV coverage (if you can afford them) or at least details of programme, channel, transmission time and length.

The sponsor may be able to provide expertise instead of cash. The obvious areas are in public relations, advertising, design and print buying, marketing and even accounting. They should be costed by the sport in its proposal and the value of this in-kind support be clearly identified and treated as part of the deal. Exchange of skills brings sponsor and sport closer together and can bring valuable commercial expertise to a sports organisation that will be extremely useful for future events as well as the current project.

An initiative from Sportsmatch was launched in 1998 to encourage large companies to open their sports facilities to sports organisations. The value of the use of the facilities is calculated according to an established formula and Sportsmatch will match the amount in order for the organisers to pay for coaching, transport or other needs to make the event happen. The advantage for companies is that it allows them to gain extra value from their facilities by using them as a promotional tool and, it is hoped, the steady decline in corporate sports facilities will be slowed.

After the event, sit down with the sponsor and produce a post–mortem report, what went well, what went badly and how it could be improved. Most companies will want to do this anyway for their own purposes but willing participation by the sport organiser will give a reassuring impression of professionalism.

A successful sponsorship budget proposal

Hockey Coaching Clinics

ITEM	DESCRIPTION	COSTS (£)
Pitch Hire	4 synthetic pitches @ £45 per hour x 2hrs	360.00
Portaloos	2 @ £70 per pitch (University sites)	140.00
Transport	Hire 4 minibuses @ £100 per day incl. fuel	400.00
Coaching Fees	10 coaches per pitch x 4 pitches @	
	£20 per session (International free of charge)	800.00
Equipment	200 cones, 300 balls @ £5, 10 sets of bibs	2,000.00
	Sticks for new corners (50 x £10)	500.00
PA Systems	Hire and installation x 4 @ £150	600.00
First Aid	3 venues @ £50	150.00
	Promotional Posters 2,000 @ £0.25	500.00
	Certificates of participation 600 @ £0.50	300.00
Prizes	Across all ranges and ability groups	270.00
Photographers	3 @ £30 per hour x 2hrs	180.00
Uniforms	100 staff and coaches @ £5.00 printed	500.00
T-shirts	600 participants @ £3.00	1,800.00
TOTAL		£8,500.00

This document will become a valuable selling tool in future bids for sponsorship and it is well worth the time and money spent to assemble it, even though in the frantic activity that usually surrounds a sponsorship it may not seem quite as important to record it for posterity as to concentrate on making the thing happen in the first place. It is, as the old joke goes, difficult to remember, when you are up to your armpits in alligators, that the original objective was to drain the swamp.

Getting sponsorship – 10 practical tips

1. **Identify the right person** in the company to contact. You need the name of the marketing manager.
2. **Stress the benefits** of the sponsorship to the sponsor. This should be done as often and clearly as possible and backed up with statistics or other supporting information.
3. **The size of the payment will be dependent upon the value of the sponsorship to the sponsor**, not the cost of the work for you. The payment may be more or less than the cost of the project.
4. **Help companies use their own resources to make the sponsorship work**. Suggest, for instance, that they might like a picture story in their house magazine or in the trade press. Most are very keen to impress their colleagues and their rivals, but few think of this without prompting.
5. Sponsorship, especially long-term deals, is all about **working together**. Promise only what you **know** you can deliver, and always try to deliver a little bit more than you promised.
6. When you first start talking about sponsorship, your friends will equate your local project with the FA Carling Premiership and suggest you take a good long holiday. Tell them that **most sponsorship money comes in sums of under £10,000** and that we're talking horses for courses. You do not intend to compete with international championships but you have got a lot to offer at the local level.
7. **Get into the habit of reading adverts**. Look particularly at local papers and trade press. Who has got money to spend on promotion? What kind of image are they trying to promote? Who are they trying to reach? How can you help them?
8. **Name drop!** One satisfied sponsor can help you get another.
9. **Before you begin, think about an ethical code**. Are there some companies you wouldn't wish to be associated with?
10. **Keep at it!** It is hard work but sponsorships can be really valuable. After every negative letter remind yourself there's another post tomorrow!

The way you run the sponsored event has two important consequences for the future:

■ It will encourage your existing sponsor to continue. Despite all the corporate jargon about innovation and breaking new ground, a lot of companies – or at least their managers – are much happier repeating a proven success than risking a new, unproven activity.
■ It will prove attractive to other companies and demonstrate your professionalism and commercialism.

It is also important to remember that sponsorships have a sell-by date. You may have a very successful relationship with a particular sponsor for three years, after which the company says it wants to pull out. This does not mean that you have suddenly become unattractive to sponsors, but rather that the particular company has obtained the desired commercial benefit from the association and wants to move on.

Therefore, it is important to give yourself time to renegotiate new deals. Do not assume that a sponsor will automatically sign up for next year. Write in a time limit (at least nine months before the event) for the company to commit itself. If it does not you are then free to find another company. The fact that the sponsorship has been very successful will be attractive to a new company, but you need to give yourself time to develop a new relationship.

Two examples below give good ideas for integrating sport and commercial promotions.

A McDonald's franchise in Birmingham sponsored a mini-league soccer programme run by the local police. Total sponsorship was only £1,250 but because the scheme was aimed at young people in deprived areas it attracted a similar Sportsmatch award. Part of the scheme involved simple attendance slips for the youngsters. On the back of each was a voucher offering a special price meal at the McDonald's branch, which was not valid without the signature of the mini-league organiser on the front.

Both parties were happy as it gave an easy attendance check, an incentive to turn up and a direct benefit to the sponsor's business – particularly as the 7–11 years old were more than likely to bring along friends or parents to help them 'save' money.

Pizza Hut, on the other hand, has put hundreds of thousands of pounds into the Football in the Community scheme. They also attracted a Sportsmatch grant, but for £75,000 this time. Part of the programme involved training and coaching days on a Saturday which involved a small payment from parents – to cover amongst other things lunch in the local Pizza Hut! It was a small price to pay for a day of freedom, safe in the knowledge that the children were being entertained in a secure environment. For the youngsters the day culminated with a tour of the local Premier League club which certainly left favourable impressions of Pizza Hut amongst thousands of potentially very long-term customers.

The benefit to sport, as well as the sponsor, should not be underestimated. Both parties are in the business of promoting themselves. Participation in football may gain a youngster a free hamburger or pizza but while they're eating it they're sure to tell friends how they too can get a free lunch!

The true scope of joint promotions is dependent on the product or company concerned and the imagination of the organisers. Cost need not be a factor because the examples cited were self-liquidating – that is the costs of the promotion were paid for by the direct increase in sales.

Other joint ventures can involve the production of event programmes or other literature for training and coaching. These should obviously be a vehicle for the sponsor's branding but here is also scope for involving other non-competing businesses.

Advertising and joint promotions

Companies become weary with continuous approaches to place advertisements. The actual cost for space may be quite small but production of the advertisement can be very expensive. Companies invest thousands, sometime millions, of pounds in their corporate identity and they do not want to appear in public in any other clothes. So to produce an advertisement in a programme which has a space cost of £100 may cost them ten times that amount in design and artwork.

Many approaches for advertising are in fact a request for some kind of donation. However, they are rarely accompanied with the necessary information about target audiences and events numbers. If the market data that first convinced the sponsor to sponsor is presented to the advertiser you may get a better result.

Some advertisers will not have such exacting standards and will be more than happy just to see their name in print to demonstrate support. Others may be content with 'sponsoring' a page of a programme and gain a credit for relatively low cost. The resulting relationship between the company and sports club is very short-term. In some circumstances this may be exactly what the club wants, but by making a professional approach using the kind of information previously discussed, your chances of success are much greater and the resulting package may well be longer-lasting.

The important tactic is to develop a range of options with a scale of charges. It is easy to say no once, but when three or four options are wheeled out there is a good chance of an eventual yes, albeit a weary one!

You may be able to farm out advertisement sales. There are many specialist agencies who will undertake to produce a programme at no cost to the organisers and sell the advertisements. They will keep the majority of the revenue but you will have a powerful promotional tool at no cost and little effort.

Local, and even national, newspapers are keen on joint promotions. You could run an event-related quiz in several editions of the paper with free tickets as the prize. Radio stations with hundreds of hours of airtime to fill also look kindly on promotions that let them talk about something to their audience at no cost.

All of these joint promotions, and there are many more, are aimed at making the sponsorship work for the sponsor and for the sport. They are commercial because sports sponsorship is commercial. The future of many sports depends on a recognition of what business needs and an understanding of the true value of sport as a vehicle for corporate and brand promotion.

Sponsorship and schools

The government's sports policy goes under the title 'Sport for All', but it has put particular emphasis on sport in schools and has encouraged extending business sponsorship in schools.

As an incentive to companies and clubs, £1 million of Sportsmatch money (see below) will be earmarked as funding for schools projects. Leaflets are available from Sportsmatch which give guidance to schools seeking sponsorship and for companies looking to move into sponsorship.

Sportsmatch and schools

Business sponsorship of sporting activity in schools is increasing. Therefore, £1 million of Sportsmatch money is being earmarked as funding for schools projects.

For example, Beckenham RFC held sessions for teachers from schools in the Beckenham area to train as rugby coaches. The scheme was sponsored by the Woolwich Building Society, whose £1,000 was matched by Sportsmatch. The money has been used to buy equipment such as rugby balls and coaching videos. The project will end with an inter-school competition. Around 6,250 children in 40 schools will benefit.

Sportsmatch

A source of business and government funding for grass-roots sport

More than £34 million of new money has been generated for grass-roots sport since Sportsmatch was launched in November 1992. More than 70 sports have received awards and over 2,000 sponsoring companies, the majority of them new to sponsorship, have participated. Around 10 million people, mostly youngsters, have participated in Sportsmatch-backed sponsored sports activities.

The purpose of the Business Sponsorship Incentive Scheme for Sport, to give Sportsmatch its full title, is to improve the quality and quantity of business sponsorship of grass-roots sporting and physical recreation events and activities in Great Britain.

Sportsmatch is aimed at encouraging existing business sponsors of major sporting events to extend their involvement with sport and physical recreation into the grass-roots areas. It is also aimed at bringing businesses who have not sponsored sport or physical recreation before into grass-roots sponsorship.

The scheme is funded by the government under the provisions of Section 3 of the Physical Training and Recreation Act 1937. Separate budgets have been established for England, Scotland and Wales, with the funds made available for England by the Department for Culture, Media and Sport and for Scotland and Wales by the Scottish and Welsh Offices, respectively. Whilst many applications will be for funding from the individual home country budgets, it is possible for business sponsors and organising bodies to apply for an award for a sponsorship to be operated at grass-roots level throughout Great Britain.

The scheme is administered in England by the Institute of Sports Sponsorship (ISS), a national non-profit making organisation representing business sponsors of sport, which also coordinates any GB sponsorships. In Scotland and Wales these are jointly administered by ISS and the respective Sports Councils.

The benefits

Sportsmatch has been created to:

- enable grass-roots sponsorships to take place that may not otherwise have been affordable by a business sponsor alone; and
- enhance the value of the sponsorship.

A business sponsor will be able to enjoy all the commercial benefits of the particular sponsorship, whilst contributing only half the cost. Similarly the organising body will be able to enjoy all the benefits created by the sponsorship and an event or activity that may otherwise not have taken place.

As Sportsmatch award winners, the extra benefits include:

- The prestige of receiving an award and commemorative certificate;
- The increased publicity to be gained from Sportsmatch press releases issued by the Department for Culture, Media and Sport, the Scottish and Welsh Offices, and by the ISS or the Scottish Sports Council or the Sports Council for Wales announcing the awards;
- Government endorsement received through receptions held for award winners.

Sportsmatch schemes are as varied as the sports and sponsors involved but a few examples may help to give a flavour of the type of project that qualifies. The examples below are winners of the 1998 annual Sportsmatch awards which are made to show examples of best practice in the scheme.

Sportsmatch Awards 1998

Community Category Winner

Organiser: Saracens Football Club
Sponsor: Kenwood Electronics
Sportsmatch Award: £50,000

Grass-roots sports sponsorship reinforced Kenwood's sponsorship of the first team and has begun to create a new interest in rugby at the Saracens' new home in Watford. The scheme reached 2,500 young people and school teachers and included drug awareness elements as well as coaching and participation.

Disability Sports Category Winner

Organiser: Meteors Wheelchair Basketball
Sponsor: Ashdale MSP
Sportsmatch Award: £2,060

The sponsors achieved practical endorsement of their products' reliability and allowed the club to increase the number of participants significantly and extend participation to girls.

Schools Category Winner (and overall winner)

Organiser: Manchester City Football Academy
Sponsor: Co-operative Bank PLC
Sportsmatch Award: £50,000

A community sponsorship to bring the bank's services to the attention of its youth market. The scheme provided coaching opportunities at 10 centres spread over Manchester for after school activities. Coaching during school time supplemented curriculum activity and publicised the coaching centres.

Youth Category Winner

Organiser: Molesey Boat Club
Sponsor: Cargill plc
Sportsmatch Award: £4,500

Sponsorship enabled purchase of a purpose built boat for young rowers for the club to extend its involvement with local schools. Provision of a part-time coach also increased the numbers of youngsters who could be introduced to the sport.

How Sportsmatch works

The scheme is designed to be as simple as possible. Applicants must meet certain criteria for receiving an award before an award is approved. Then every pound put up either by a new business sponsor for a grass-roots event or activity or by an existing business sponsor increasing the level of sponsorship will be matched on an equal basis. The minimum level of sponsorship is £1,000 (£500 in Scotland in Wales and for schools-based projects in England) and the maximum award is £50,000 (£25,000 in Wales).

The criteria for assessment are as follows:

1. The sponsored event or activity must fall within the definition of sport and physical recreation that has been agreed by government for the purposes of the Sportsmatch scheme. Basically, the sport or physical recreation should be competitive or otherwise challenging and should involve physical effort or skill. At the end of the chapter there is a list of sports and physical recreation activities which all qualify under the Sportsmatch definition. The decision of the Sportsmatch award panel on whether or not the applicant's sponsorship proposal falls within the definition will be final.
2. To qualify as a grass-roots sponsorship, the benefits derived from the sponsorship must not extend to professional sport. This does not necessarily exclude a professional body from applying, provided the event or activity being sponsored is for the benefit of non-professionals; for example, coaching schemes utilising professional coaches/players to teach sporting skills. Where the coaching services provided do not already form part of that person's normal job, then it would be reasonable to build into the sponsorship costs suitable remuneration charges.
3. International events and major national events will not qualify. However, nationally organised schemes aimed at the grass roots would be acceptable. In the event of demand for awards exceeding funds available over that particular time period, priority would be given to 'special need' groups such as young people, schools, disabled people and ethnic minorities, or events or activities

in urban and rural deprived areas. In all cases the sponsored event or activity should encourage increased participation or improved performance at grass-roots level and not apply unduly restrictive membership criteria.

4. Both parties to the application must provide evidence that the event or activity either would not take place without the financial support available from Sportsmatch (i.e. that the business sponsor would not have been in a position to provide the sponsorship support required), or that the event or activity will be significantly enhanced by the Sportsmatch award.

5. The business support must be commercial sponsorship, not patronage or a donation.

6. The sponsorship must give the business sponsor appropriate publicity and facilities for the support involved and it should be beneficial to both parties.

7. The Sportsmatch award panel must be satisfied of the eligibility, legal status and financial accountability of both the business and the organising body.

8. The business sponsor should indicate an interest in developing or continuing a grass-roots sports or physical recreation sponsorship programme.

Sportsmatch budget proposal

Learn to Swim Scheme

	Organising body: Fast Swimmers	Event: Water Babies	Dates: From 1/7/98 to 10/7/98
Expenses	Budget 1 Without Sponsor or Sportsmatch	Budget 2 With Sponsor Only	Budget 3 With Sponsor and Sportsmatch
Trophies	500	1,000	1,000
Posters	500	1,000	1,000
Coaches' wages	1,000	5,000	10,000
Travel	100	1,000	1,000
Pool hire	1,000	3,000	5,000
Equipment 1			1,000
Equipment 2			700
Advertising		1,000	1,900
Printing	300	1,400	1,800
Total expenses	3,400	13,400	23,400
Income			
Own sources	3,000	3,000	3,000
Sponsor		10,000	10,000
Sportsmatch		10,000	
Tickets	400	400	400
Total income	3,400	13,400	23,400

Conditions to be abided by should a Sportsmatch award be made:

1. Proper credit should be given to the award. This will be taken into account when considering future applications.
2. Evidence of payment and receipt of the sponsorship money being put forward by the business sponsor must be provided before the Sportsmatch award can be paid.
3. An audited or certified statement should be provided showing how the Sportsmatch award has been used.

Eligible sports

American football	Hang gliding	Rounders
Angling	Highland games	Rowing
Archery	Hockey (field)	Rugby league
Association football	Hockey (ice)	Rugby union
Athletics	Hockey (roller)	Sailing and yachting
Badminton	Hockey (street)	Sand and
Ballooning	Hurling	land yachting
Baseball	Judo	Shinty
Basketball	Keep fit/Aerobics	Shooting
Biathlon	Korfball	Skateboarding
Bicycle polo	Lacrosse	Skating (ice)
Billiards	Lawn tennis	Skating (roller)
Bobsleigh	Luge	Skiing
Bowls	Martial arts	Snooker
Boxing	Modern pentathlon	Softball
Camogie	Motor cycling	Squash rackets
Canoeing	Motor sports	Sub-aqua
Caving	Mountaineering	Surfing
Cricket	Netball	Swimming
Croquet	Orienteering	Table tennis
Crossbow	Parachuting	Tenpin bowling
Curling	Paragliding	Trampolining
Cycling	Pétanque	Triathlon
Fencing	Polo	Tug of war
Fives	Pool	Volleyball
Gaelic football	Quoits	Water polo
Gliding	Racketball	Water skiing
Golf	Rackets	Weightlifting
Gymnastics	Real tennis	Wrestling
Handball	Riding	Yoga

How to apply for a Sportsmatch award

The Sportsmatch annual budget is allocated at eight panel meetings which take place at approximately six week intervals. Applications are normally processed according to the date they are received. Whenever possible, applications should be received at least twelve weeks before the start of the sponsored event or activity.

Applications for awards for sponsorship taking place only in England, Scotland or Wales should be sent to the appropriate office (see end of chapter). Applications for GB awards should be sent to the Scheme Manager for the country in which the organising body is based.

The Scheme Manager or his/her deputy will discuss each application with the nominated coordinator before presenting the application to the Sportsmatch award panel.

Sportsmatch addresses

England
The Sportsmatch Scheme Manager
Warwick House
25/27 Buckingham Palace Road
London SW1W 0PP
0171-233 7747; Fax: 0171-828 7099

Scotland
The Sportsmatch Scheme Manager
The Scottish Sports Council
Caledonia House
South Gyle
Edinburgh EH12 9DQ
0131-317 7200; Fax: 0131-317 7202

Wales
The Sportsmatch Scheme Manager
The Sports Council for Wales
Sophia Gardens
Cardiff CF1 9SW
01222-300500; Fax: 01222-300600

Institute of Sports Sponsorship
Warwick House
25/27 Buckingham Palace Road
Victoria
London SW1W 0PP
0171-233 7747

This chapter has been written by Martin Cannon, head of Cannon Communications, which acts as a public relations consultant to the Institute of Sports Sponsorship and Sportsmatch.

Chapter 10

Raising money from the government 1

Central and regional government

■■

Government money is now spent on three levels: central, regional and local. This chapter looks at how to money is distributed by central and regional government; the next chapter concentrates on local government.

Background

Regional government is a new phenomenon in British life. Previously government existed only on two levels – central and local. There is now a concerted effort to bring government closer to the people by moving away from centralised government giving where spending decisions are made wholly by Whitehall departments. Regional offices and agencies have become key players in determining funding priorities. There are now more regional opportunities for voluntary organisations to become involved in strategic regional planning.

At the same time, organisations have to be fleet-footed in keeping up with the many structural changes that have occurred and to get to know a variety of decision-makers and funders. This chapter takes you through how the system works before moving onto individual sources of money.

A large part of government money is now administered through regional offices. These offices incorporate a number of programmes that were included in the last edition of this guide, such as the National Rivers Authority which is now part of the Environment Agency. The Rural Development Commission will become part of the new Regional Development Agencies in April 1999/2000. Some funding programmes have disappeared altogether such as Urban Development Corporations and Safer Cities initiatives. These may have already been replaced by a new funding scheme, or will be in the future. Generally, responsibility for any new programmes is likely to be devolved to the regional offices.

Some programmes support building costs, whilst others will fund the running costs of a project. Partnership with other bodies is now a feature common to a number of the programmes. You may also find that government money can be used to match funds from other schemes such as Europe or the National Lottery.

The Department for Culture, Media and Sport

The Department for Culture, Media and Sport (DCMS) is the central government department responsible for sport. It has an annual budget of £910 million (1997/98). This is spent in a number of areas including the arts, libraries, museums, royal estates, heritage, as well as sport and recreation. It currently funds 45 non-departmental bodies representing these interests. In 1997/98 the department's allocation to sport was over £50 million with a projected budget for 1998/99 of £49 million.

DCMS gives grants to sport primarily through its funding of Sport England and the UK Sports Council. These two bodies then allocate resources to 'foster, support and encourage the development of sport and physical recreation and the provision of sporting facilities in England and at the United Kingdom level. Sport England's aims are for more people to be involved in sport, more places to play sport and more medals through higher standards of performance in sport.'

The UK Sports Council is responsible for the achievement of excellence in the United Kingdom. In 1997/98, Sport England received £33.7 million, and the UK Sports Council £11.8 million. (The Sports Council for Northern Ireland is funded by the Northern Ireland Department of Education; the Scottish Sports Council by the Scottish Office and the Sports Council for Wales by the Welsh Office.) Chapter 6 has further information on the Sports Councils.

As well as allocations to the two Sports Councils, DCMS also funds the Sportsmatch scheme which matches sponsorship money for grass-roots sports development. (See page 158.) Since its establishment in 1992, £34 million has been generated in new sponsorship money. The department gives £3.2 million to the scheme each year.

A government agreement to reduce pool betting duty has helped the work of both the Football Trust (see page 233) and the Foundation for Sport and the Arts (chapter 8). Income for both these bodies has declined with the emergence of the National Lottery and its impact upon pools income. The 3% reduction in betting duty remains vital for both bodies and is annually worth about £10 million each to Football Trust 1998 and the Foundation for Sport and the Arts. (The Football Trust also received a £55 million funding package from Sport England and the Football Association Premier League announced in 1997 to improve facilities and safety throughout association football.)

The department also oversees the running of the National Lottery. (See chapter 7.)

Applications for support should **not** be made direct to DCMS.

Either way, any money obtained from these sources will **not** be given on account of your project's sporting merits. Each department and government body detailed below has its own set of priorities which are very unlikely to include sports development. Your project or activity must contribute to their priority areas and fit in with their existing policies. Where your activities contribute to main government focus areas such as social exclusion, crime prevention, job creation, enterprise or training for example, more funding opportunities may open up to you. However, it will be the strength of your ability to deliver training, regeneration, new enterprise or environmental improvement that will secure funding, rather than your commitment to sporting excellence. You will need to think more widely about your project's benefits if doors to central and regional government grants are to open up to you.

Many regionally-administered schemes are also part of locally defined strategies and priorities. Where this is the case we have tried to say so, but a general principle applies: find out as much as possible about what is happening locally and regionally, and try to find ways to influence economic planning and local development.

The following programmes are covered in this chapter:

Enterprise
Highland and Islands Enterprise

Environmental improvement
ENTRUST
Environment Agency

Health
Drug Action Teams

Rural Regeneration
Rural Development Programme
Rural Challenge

Urban Regeneration
English Partnerships
Single Regeneration Budget
The Urban Programme (Scotland)

Regional administration

The Department for the Environment and the Regions has overall government responsibility for the democratic and economic development of the English regions. To establish more regional accountability, a number of grant programmes have been devolved to ten government offices in the regions. These government offices (GOs) aim to be a one-stop shop within a region for all regeneration initiatives. The GOs respond to local needs and initiatives and set strategic economic objectives that will help target resources for the most urgent problems. They look to work with, and through, a wide range of organisations. 'Partnerships', 'multi-agency approaches' and 'linkage' are key phrases. Sports projects looking to be part of regeneration programmes will have to work closely with bodies such as local authorities and TECs if they are to be considered for regional funds.

Government offices have responsibility for European Structural Funds in their areas, together with the programmes detailed below. In addition, they have oversight of infrastructure and general economic development within their region. They will become the holders of the keys of a number of funding programmes covering current government concerns: social exclusion; crime prevention; and the new deal for communities for example. This development role is set to be strengthened with the dawning of Regional Development Agencies (RDAs) which come into force in April 1999.

All change in 1999

Much will alter in 1999. Government Offices for the Regions will contribute to the development of the Regional Development Agencies in England (RDAs). These will have the same geographical boundaries, although there will be changes in the North West, and London will not be in place until 2000. (A separate Merseyside presence will remain to administer European money allocated through Merseyside's Objective 1 status.) As well as domestic funding changes, these offices will also have to adapt to changes in European funding in the light of EU Agenda 2000 proposals (see chapter 13 on Raising money from Europe).

The RDAs will have the following core functions:

- regional economic strategies
- regeneration
- rural areas
- European Structural Funds

- inward investment
- business support
- reclamation and preparation of land
- skills.

RDAs will also contribute to policies and programmes on:

- transport
- land use
- environment and sustainable development
- further and higher education

- crime prevention
- public health
- housing
- tourism
- culture and sports infrastructure projects.

These functions reflect ongoing concerns, and elements of a number of old funding programmes will be included in meeting objectives. The RDAs pull together rural initiatives (such as Rural Challenge and the Rural Development Commission) and urban strategies (such as English Partnerships and the Single Regeneration Budget). This chapter details those programmes where sports initiatives are mostly likely to find a welcome.

The role of sport

In addition to economic priorities, there is also room within the RDAs' wide brief for culture, media and sport initiatives. Their contribution to the economic life of a region is seen as central: 'The cultural sector has a major role to play in economic development. It contributes significantly to the quality of life in the regions, and makes them more attractive to investors. Nearly 700,000 people work in the cultural sector – more than in banking and building societies and nearly twice as many as in motor manufacturing. The creative industries contributed approximately £9.6 million to Britain's exports in 1996...

'The interests of the sector are currently represented in each region by a cultural forum. The membership of these groupings varies from region to region, but at the broadest level brings together representatives of the Regional Arts Board, Area Museums Council, Sports Council, English Heritage, Regional Tourist Board, Regional Film Commission and other media organisations, public libraries and information, and local authority culture and leisure departments. These cultural agencies will act as partners to the RDAs to ensure that regional support for the cultural sector and creative industries form part of a coherent economic development strategy. In recognition of this close relationship, those with experience of the cultural sector may well be appropriate candidates for membership of the RDA board.'

DETR report *Building Partnerships for Prosperity*.

The cultural forum in each region was still to be finalised at the time of writing.

RDAs will follow similar regional boundaries and a number of the contacts will remain the same as those of the Government Offices for the Regions. RDAs' coverage will be as follows:

North East: counties of Durham and Northumberland; unitary authorities of Cleveland, Darlington, Gateshead, Hartlepool, Middlesbrough, Newcastle-upon-Tyne, North Tyneside, Redcar, South Tyneside, Stockton-on-Tees and Sunderland

North West: the counties of Cheshire, Cumbria and Lancashire; unitary authorities of Bolton, Bury, Knowsley, Liverpool, Manchester, Oldham, Rochdale, St Helens, Salford, Sefton, Stockport, Tameside, Trafford, Wigan and Wirral

Yorkshire and Humber: counties of East Riding of Yorkshire and North Yorkshire; unitary authorities of Barnsley, Bradford, Calderdale, Doncaster, Kirklees, Kingston-upon-Hull, Leeds, North East Lincolnshire, North Lincolnshire, Rotherham, Sheffield, Wakefield, and York

West Midlands: counties of Herefordshire, Shropshire, Staffordshire,

Warwickshire and Worcestershire; unitary authorities of Birmingham, Coventry, Dudley, Sandwell, Solihull, Stoke-on-Trent, Walsall and Wolverhampton

East Midlands: counties of Derbyshire, Leicestershire, Lincolnshire, Northamptonshire, Nottinghamshire and Rutland; unitary authorities of Derby and Leicester

Eastern Region: countries of Bedfordshire, Cambridgeshire, Essex, Hertfordshire, Norfolk, Suffolk; unitary authority of Luton

South West: counties of Cornwall, Devon, Dorset, Gloucestershire, Isles of Scilly, Somerset and Wiltshire; unitary authorities of Bournemouth, Bristol, North East Somerset, North Somerset and Bath, Poole and South Gloucestershire

South East: counties of Berkshire, Buckinghamshire, East Sussex, Hampshire, Kent, Oxfordshire, Surrey and West Sussex; unitary authorities of Brighton & Hove, Isle of Wight, Milton Keynes, Portsmouth and Southampton

London: 32 London boroughs and City of London.

Sport and Community Regeneration

YOUTH WORKS, East Lancashire is quoted as a successful idea in a report published by the Social Exclusion Unit looking at neighbourhood renewal and the way forward.

'The project is supported by a national partnership between Marks and Spencer, Crime Concern and Groundwork. Additional partners, such as the local authority and housing associations support the project locally. Within East Lancashire the programme has provided training in areas such as youth work skills and parenting sessions, first aid courses, community sports leadership courses, football training (in association with Blackburn Rovers Football Club), and assertiveness training. The programme has extended its areas of operation from one estate to four over the past three years, targeting some of the most disadvantaged communities in Lancashire.

'Impact: In the first year there was a 35% reduction in crime across an estate targeted by the programme. This reduction has been sustained in the second and third years. On the same estate there has been a cost saving to the local housing association of over 50 per cent of repair and management costs.' *Bringing Britain Together – a national strategy for neighbourhood renewal,* produced by the Social Exclusion Unit

Current government reviews of regeneration strategies suggest that these new regional bodies will continue along previously defined paths. There will be more focus on the areas of greatest economic and social need within a region, and continued direction of resources to these areas over a greater period of time. Partnerships will continue to be central to successful projects.

169

To be considered under regeneration programmes, sports projects need to think how their activities or facilities contribute to wider social concerns than just the pursuit of sporting excellence. The chances of success under a number of different headings will increase as the appeal of a sports project widens. Does an activity give new skills (e.g. vocational qualifications) to target groups? Are new uses created out of unused, derelict land? Do the activities include hard to reach groups? Are there new ideas to tackle social exclusion? Is there a crime prevention element to the project? Does the activity offer value for money by combining with existing facilities (schools, surgeries, youth centres)? Is the organisation working with other bodies (such as health authorities, the local authority, TECs)? Does the project bring new partners to a regeneration strategy?Government Offices and the emerging Regional Development Agencies administer the following programmes which may have space for sports activities that contribute to their objectives:

Urban regeneration	*Rural regeneration*
English Partnerships	Rural Development Programme
Single Regeneration Budget	Rural Challenge

These are detailed below. Integrated government offices also have responsibility for the European Structural Funds such as the European Regional Development Fund. (See chapter 13.)There are additional programmes which may support specialised sports projects that fit criteria such as conservation, land management or health. These are listed in the second half of the chapter.

Single Regeneration Budget (SRB) Challenge Fund

This is the largest concentration of statutory support for local communities and is now into its fourth funding round. It brings together 20 previously distinct schemes under one heading. (Other programmes detailed in the first edition of this guide may eventually find shelter under the SRB umbrella.) A large part of the budget is directed towards existing projects under City Challenge and English Partnerships. The remaining funds are allocated to the Single Regeneration Budget to be made available for new projects run over the next three years.

The total amount available for distribution is expected to gradually increase as commitments under old grant programmes are fulfilled. In 1995/96, £1.1 billion was given to support 164 proposals (with an average grant of around £300,000). The second round made £2.4 billion available for new proposals in 1996/97 and for 1997/98. The third round to run from April 1997 to March 1999 awarded around £200 million. Round four running from April 1998 to March 2000 will give new funding of around £800 million. Under the Comprehensive Spending Review a further £2.3 billion was directed towards SRB over the next three years.

What it funds

The SRB is for local regeneration projects. It complements and attracts other resources which can be private, public or voluntary. The projects can last between one and seven years. So far there have been three grant rounds to support projects which improve the quality of life in their area by supporting one or more of the following priorities:

- enhancing the employment prospects, education and skills of local people, particularly the young and those at disadvantage, and promoting equality of opportunity;
- encouraging sustainable economic growth and wealth creation by improving the competitiveness of the local economy (including support for new and existing businesses);
- improving housing through physical improvements, better maintenance and greater choice and diversity;
- promoting initiatives of benefit to ethnic minorities;
- tackling crime and improving community safety;
- protecting and improving the environment and infrastructure and promoting good design and landscaping;
- enhancing the quality of life of local people, including their health and cultural and sports opportunities.

In July 1998, the Comprehensive Spending Review included plans for a reworked SRB. There will now be two strands:

- New Deal for Regeneration
- New Deal for Communities

Over £2.3 billion has been committed from 1999 to 2002. Most of this total will cover commitments already made under the previous four rounds, although £800 million is new funding. Of this new money, 80% will be directed towards areas of greatest need, with the remaining resources used to regenerate other areas including rural areas and former coal field communities.

New Deal for Communities

This strand of the SRB will support initiatives that tackle social exclusion, particularly in the 'Worst Estates' (one of the Social Exclusion Unit's main priorities). It will only operate in communities where there is the greatest deprivation. The NDC programme aims to:

- bring housing and regeneration spending together
- improve job prospects and link with Welfare to Work New Deals and, where applicable, Employment Zones
- improve neighbourhood management and delivery of local services.

In September 1998, 17 Pathfinder authorities were invited to prepare bids to shape future NDC programme rounds. As this is in the very early stages of development it is too early to report on the content of the bids. It is possible that where sports organisations are working with hard-to-reach groups and in areas of social exclusion, they may find support within the programme. The 17 authorities are: Birmingham, Bradford, Brighton and Hove, Bristol, Hull, Leicester, Liverpool, Manchester, Middlesbrough, Newcastle-upon-Tyne, Norwich, Nottingham, Sandwell and the London boroughs of Hackney, Newham, Southwark and Tower Hamlets. The timetable is:

December 1998 – submission of bids
Mid January 1999 – offers of support to successful bids
Mid June – detailed delivery plans to be submitted
End June – ministerial announcement of approved bids

How SRB works

Applications are made through the 10 Government Offices for the Regions, which distribute funds to successful bids. (Responsibility for SRB will be transferred to RDAs in April 1999.) They produce full guidance notes on how to organise and prepare bids, and assess applications in the light of local strategies and priorities. At every stage it is up to those bidding for funds to prepare their case and present it effectively. You must be clear about what you will do and why; how you will do it and with whom, and include other funders. You will have to show how your bid will give value for money and complement existing private and public sector activities, and how local development strategies are supported by your proposals.

Partnerships are essential

At the heart of the SRB are partnerships between different bodies. This is not to say that local voluntary organisations cannot apply or lead a bid; it is just that they will have to apply in conjunction with other bodies. The most obvious partner is a local authority or TEC, but it may be another body such as a housing association or health authority.

In the early days of the SRB it was anticipated that the voluntary sector would be a main player in constructing bids. Experience to date suggests otherwise. The first round (1994) involved 200 successful bids, of which 92 included voluntary organisations. The second round (1995) incorporated 172 successful schemes, including 98 where voluntary organisations were represented. The third round (1996) supported 182 bids, of which 107 involved voluntary organisations.

As voluntary organisations had a lower profile in applications than was expected, more emphasis is to be placed upon their involvement in the future. Recent guidance notes stated: 'Bids should harness the talents and resources of the voluntary sector and volunteers... in the preparation and implementation of bids'.

To participate you will have to be in touch with local decision-makers who are involved in the bidding process. Success with the Challenge Fund will depend on how strong relationships are with other local bodies.

To help make your organisation part of a bid you should highlight any added value that you bring. You may have additional trust funding for instance, or long-term relationships with specific funders, expertise in certain areas or be part of a European network.

Making it work – successful partnerships

SRB bidding is time-consuming and can be frustrating where bids are not approved despite your best efforts. Key factors for success are largely to do with creating successful partnerships. Where voluntary sector bids have worked there are some common features:

- good partnerships with other bodies were already in place;
- those bidding, including the voluntary organisation, kept in touch with the government office and worked with the advice that it offered;
- the projects were well thought out and offered real benefits that fitted in with local strategic plans;
- an early start had been made on the bid and there was a long preparation period;
- local bodies such as authorities and TECs worked together with voluntary organisations and officers supported voluntary involvement.

Bidding timetable for SRB Round 5

Collaboration with GOs/RDAs will be a prerequisite for funding. Potential partners and bidders should speak as early as possible to the regional contact to discuss their proposal. You should consult your nearest RDA to find out the most up-to-date timetable. Ask to be added to their mailing list to be kept in touch with programme developments. The following gives an idea of how long the process takes. Potential applicants need to bear in mind that this does not include the lead in time for creating and agreeing a partnership.

September 1998	GOs issue Regional SRB Frameworks
October/November 1998	Bidders start to prepare bids, and discuss proposals with GOs
By end November	Deadline for submission of expression of interest to GOs
End of April 1999	Deadline for final bids to RDAs (GO in London)
May 1999	RDAs (GO in London) assess final bids and make recommendations to London
June 1999	Bidders informed of decisions
From June onwards	Approved bids begin to be implemented subject to agreement

Examples where sports/cultural facilities have been incorporated in recent successful SRB bids:

Leicester – Strategic Regeneration of Belgrave

This is a crime prevention and job creation programme to tackle social exclusion among young unemployed people in a deprived area of Leicester. Alongside new jobs and training opportunities nine new sports/cultural facilities were created with improvements to a further four facilities. The scheme's total cost will be £5.4 million with the Challenge Fund contributing £2.5 million of the overall total.

Netherley Valley development

This is a successful round three bid, which used elements from an unsuccessful round two project. The bid is largely concerned with housing initiatives, but has also incorporated the development of the National Academy of Sport for Disabled Athletes. The Challenge Fund has contributed £5.1 million towards the total cost of the scheme of £50 million.

Government Office contacts

Readers should bear in mind that Regional Development Agencies (apart from London) will come into play on 1 April 1999. Addresses are likely to remain the same, and staff will be deployed from the Government Offices for the Regions, English Partnerships and the Rural Development Commission.

East Midlands Region: Colin Packman, Government Office – East Midlands, SRB Unit, The Belgrave Centre, Stanley Place, Talbot Street, Nottingham NG1 5GG (0115-971 2449; Fax: 0115-971 2558)

Eastern Region: Keith Allen, Government Office – Eastern Region, Room 115, Heron House, 49-53 Goldington Road, Bedford MK40 3LL (0123-479 6135; Fax: 0123-479 6110)

London Region: Malcolm Sims, Government Office – London, Room 7.3, Riverwalk House, 157-161 Millbank, London SW1P 4RR (0171-217 3062; Fax: 0171-217 3461)

North East Region: Derek Burns, Government Office – North East, Room 1206, Wellbar House, Gallowgate, Newcastle-upon-Tyne NE1 4TD (0191-202 3624; Fax: 0191-235 3768)

North West Region (excluding Merseyside): Helen France, Government Office – North West, Room 1224, Sunley Tower, Piccadilly Plaza, Manchester M1 4BE (0161-952 4351; Fax: 0161-952 4365)

North West Region (Merseyside only): Peter Mattison, Government Office – North West (Merseyside), Cunard Building, Pier Head, Liverpool L3 1QB (0151-224 6448; Fax: 0151-224 6339)

South East Region: Marie Griffiths, Government Office – South East, Bridge House, 1 Walnut Tree Close, Guildford, Surrey GU1 4GA (01483-882 322; Fax: 01483-882 309)

South West Region: Denise Jones, Government Office – South West, The Pithay, Bristol BS1 2PB (0117-900 1873; Fax: 0117-900 1918)

West Midlands Region: Jane Tietjen, Government Office – West Midlands, 2nd Floor, 77 Paradise Circus, Queensway, Birmingham B1 2DT (0121-212 5280; Fax: 0121-212 5301)

Yorkshire & the Humber Region: Richard Norbury, Government Office – Yorkshire & the Humber, 12th Floor West, City House, New Station Street, Leeds LS1 4US (0113-283 5268; Fax: 0113-283 6653).

English Partnerships

English Partnerships is a government sponsored body which aims to regenerate derelict, vacant and under-used land and buildings. Readers should note that when Regional Development Agencies are launched in 1999, English Partnerships will be included under their umbrella. The information below covers the current position. Some, if not all, elements may change next year. The scope of English Partnerships is all of England, although the areas listed overleaf have priority.

- European Objective 1 and 2 areas (these will change following EU directives)
- Coalfield closure areas
- City Challenge and other inner city areas
- Other Assisted Areas
- Rural areas, mainly those covered by European Objective 5b (these will change following EU directives)
- Other areas of severe economic need identified by English Partnerships regional offices.

As the name suggests, organisations should be linked in partnership with local strategic bodies such as local authorities, TECs, private developers, or regional development bodies, if bids for large scale project funding are to be successful. Support is given for schemes which create or protect jobs, offer regeneration and economic development, and improve the environment.

The project should give good value for money, be designed with local people in mind, enhance the environment and, if it is a large project, make an impact on the economy and help run-down areas become more attractive. Sports organisations may be interested in two areas of support, the Community Investment Fund and the Land Reclamation Programme.

The Community Investment Fund

Organisations looking for grants of between £10,000 and £100,000 and are working within one of the geographically defined areas, can apply to the Community Investment Fund administered by English Partnerships. The investment fund is for capital items for small initiatives started by and benefiting local communities. Each year, around £3 million is made available for voluntary or community led capital projects. To be eligible, groups must be looking for capital investment (buildings, renovation, new facilities for example), be part of the local community, and be working with and for them. Revenue costs are not supported.

Support is given for projects which:

- will provide or significantly improve land and buildings, and therefore add to a local community's asset base;
- are proposed by voluntary groups which are based in, and closely involve, local communities;
- are not profit-making;
- contribute to English Partnerships and other local regeneration plans;
- give economic or social benefits at a community level;
- need support from English Partnerships of less than £100,000;
- are practical and financially sustainable.

A recent project which received support was Ashington YMCA with £18,000 to upgrade community facilities including a community gym. The publication *Brick by Brick: How to develop a community building* to help organisations building or refurbishing property for community use is available from English Partnerships corporate and regional offices.

Environmental improvement and area regeneration

English Partnerships also encourages environmental improvement in the designated areas. These are supported by the Land Reclamation Programme, or if they are capital projects which need more than £100,000 they will be covered by the English Partnerships Investment Fund.

Large sports developments have been supported, but smaller environmental projects may include improvements to a previously derelict piece of land through developing a play area, sports field, cycle track etc. for the benefit of the community.

English Partnerships is also involved in 20 area regeneration strategies. One current project is the development of the Royal Docks in East London. The agency is contributing £24 million to create an international rowing course in the Royal Albert Dock.

English Partnerships has also supported sports specific projects, partly because the agency 'recognises the contribution that cultural, leisure and sporting activities can make to economic development and urban regeneration', but also no doubt because of the arrival of the National Lottery as an investor in capital facilities. Tipton Sports Academy in Sandwell demonstrates the multi-partner approach. The £5 million project is a leisure centre with a new athletics track, tennis courts, football pitches and a cricket pitch. English Partnerships' contribution was £200,000, with further support raised from the Tipton Challenge Partnership, the Lawn Tennis Association, the Sports Council Lottery Fund and the Foundation for Sport and the Arts.

Information on all forms of English Partnerships support, including the Community Investment Fund, is available from six regional offices. An initial enquiry to a regional office will lead to a detailed discussion if the project is eligible. There will then be a formal application, and additional information will be given if required. The grant decision will follow. One of the advantages of this process is that there is no formal deadline. Once organisations are in discussion with their regional office, the application procedure starts and moves towards a conclusion.

There is a Community Development Manager in each office who will advise you on whether your project is eligible:

Midlands: Osiers Office Park, Braunstone, Leicester LE3 2DX (0116-282 8400; Fax: 0116-282 8440)

North East: St George's House, Kingsway, Team Valley, Gateshead, Tyne & Wear NE11 0NA (0191-487 8941; Fax: 0191-487 5690)

North West: Lancaster House, Mercury Court, Tithebarn Street, Liverpool L2 2QP (0151-236 3663; Fax: 0151-236 3731)

South East: Devon House, 58-60 St Katherine's Way, London E1 9LB (0171-680 2000; Fax: 0171-680 2040)

South West: North Quay House, Sutton Harbour, Plymouth PL4 0RA (01752-251071; Fax: 01752-234840)

Yorkshire & Humberside: Hall Cross House, 1 South Parade, Doncaster, South Yorkshire DN1 2NY (01302-366865; Fax: 01302-366880)

Corporate offices: 16-18 Old Queen Street, London SW1H 9HP (0171-976 7070; Fax: 0171-976 7740); 3 The Parks, Lodge Lane, Newton le Willows, Merseyside WA12 0JQ (01942-296900; Fax: 01942-296927).

Rural regeneration

Rural Development Commission
The Rural Development Commission (RDC) is the current body administering rural regeneration in England. Its brief is to stimulate economic development which will create jobs and improve services in the English countryside. Resources are presently concentrated in designated Rural Development Areas (RDAs) which cover over 35% of England and take in 29 counties.

177

In April 1999, a new Countryside Agency will be formed by merging the Countryside Commission and the RDC. At the same time, Regional Development Agencies will be formed to administer both rural and urban regeneration. RDAs (areas) will then come under RDAs (agencies), linked with the Countryside Agency, under the administration of the Department of the Environment and Transport and the Regions.

How policy will change is not clear. Presumably the RDC's main priorities will continue to be the provision of new opportunities and services for key groups within those rural areas with the greatest concentration of economic and social problems.

The current position

The RDC states: 'The Commission would not normally expect to fund projects which were clearly the responsibility of other bodies or agencies (e.g. local authorities). However, there may be occasions when Commission resources could be provided to enhance projects or enable adaptation to suit rural conditions and which were aimed at disadvantaged groups. These are: elderly people, sick and/or disabled people (and their carers); low income families; women, especially mothers with young children, or those seeking to join or rejoin the labour market, and children/young people with problems of isolation and limited access to services.'

The Rural Development Programme (RDP)

This is the Commission's main programme for rural development. In general terms, 'Enterprise, jobs and access to services are seen as the principal ingredients for successful rural economies'. All projects must be located in Rural Development Areas and focus on the priorities and needs set out in the local RDA Strategy. Support is not generally available for projects located in towns with populations over 10,000 (although there are exceptions).

RDC funds are used to lever financial support from the private, voluntary and/or local authority sources. Under the Social/Community Projects heading, 'Commission resources are targeted to areas and groups in greatest need and to projects which redress social disadvantage related to rurality. Projects are encouraged to:

(i)   Raise the level or quality of rural services, particularly those aimed at overcoming problems of isolation and access;
(ii) Stimulate local voluntary action including self-help schemes; and
(iii) Promote community development.'

Support is given to projects that are extra to mainstream provision. Grants can be over three years up to a maximum of 50% of the project costs or a total of £50,000. The RDC suggests that a common weakness in applications is that projects are not sufficiently precise in setting out how the performance of the project is to be reported on.

The RDP responds to local concerns with local partnerships shaping how funds are allocated. Alongside central regeneration strands, there has also been support for green tourism, training and environmental projects that help to improve the economic prospects of an area. Projects related to Community Development should gain the support of the local Rural Community Council. Applications can be made at any time and applicants should discuss the project with the RCC as early as possible in their planning.

Rural Challenge

Rural Challenge aims to encourage innovative partnerships to make a difference to rural areas which have a number of economic and social problems. All RDAs are invited to compete for yearly prizes of up to £1 million each to be spent in their areas. This prize is paid out over three years. In the most recent round of the competition, the judges were looking at proposals aiming to achieve at least some of the following:

- increased community involvement in service provision and the encouragement of regeneration;
- better quality of life for local people through reasonable and affordable access to services and facilities, including transport, childcare, housing and healthcare;
- diversification of the local economy, particularly extending the range of industries and occupations;
- improved performance of the local economy to make it more competitive;
- a reduction in unemployment, increased economic activity and a reduction in the outward migration of economically active young people;
- training for additional vocational and other qualifications;
- reduction in the crime rate and fear of crime;
- enhancement of the natural and built environment;
- promotion of energy conservation and in particular renewable energy projects, making use of sustainable resources.

The Rural Challenge competition is in two parts. Firstly, in each eligible RDA, any local partnerships may put forward proposals as they wish. One of these is then selected by the RDA to enter the national contest. The most recent round awarded a total of £5 million, giving £1 million to each project. Applications for the most recent round were closed in June for decisions to be made in November.

RDAs compete in alternate years, except for the four largest which compete each year. The RDAs eligible for the most recent round were:

East Anglia: Cambridgeshire, Essex, Norfolk

East Midlands: East Derbyshire, Lincolnshire

North: Durham, Lancashire, Northumberland

South East: East Sussex, Kent

South West: Cornwall and Isles of Scilly, Devon, Wiltshire

West Midlands: Hereford and Worcester, Midlands Uplands (covering Staffordshire and West Derbyshire)

Yorkshire and Humberside: East Riding of Yorkshire, North Lincolnshire; South Yorkshire

The RDC suggests: 'Successful bids are likely to:
- lever in significant funding from other sources, particularly the private sector;
- demonstrate a novel approach and offer the prospect of effective action;
- respect and where possible, enhance the environment;
- involve partnerships drawn from the private, voluntary and public sectors;
- strengthen the capacity of local communities.'

Sports representation in bids depends on how sport and leisure is included in local regeneration plans or on community umbrella bodies, as these tend to be consulted in helping to shape the proposals. It may, for instance, be part of green tourism initiatives such as the racehorse training element of the successful round two bid in Middleham, North Yorkshire. The Middleham Key Partnership included Richmondshire District Council, Middleham Trainers' Association, English Heritage, Middleham Town Council, and Doncaster College. Another successful bid where sport and sustainable leisure elements were included was Watchet Harbour in the Bristol Channel with its proposal to regenerate the area through tourism. Watchet Harbour will be rebuilt to support a wide range of amateur boating. The planned marina will include a registered sailing school and full access for people with disabilities. Partners in the scheme include: West Somerset District Council, Somerset TEC, Watchet Boatowners' Association, Watchet Town Council, Watchet Association of Commerce.

Water sports will also be included in a successful round three bid worth £1.8 million to revive the sea front at Saltburn by Sea in Cleveland.

To be involved in the bidding process, you should contact your local RDA to find out what proposals are in progress and who is taking them forward.

Please note: at the time of writing the future of the RDP and Rural Challenge had not been clarified in the light of proposed changes with the new Regional Development Agencies. Organisations need to keep in touch locally for new policy announcements.

General information on the RDP and Rural Challenge, together with a bidding guidance booklet are available from: Rural Development Commission, Marketing and Information Unit, 141 Castle Street, Wiltshire SP1 3TP (01722-336255; Fax: 01722-332769).

Local and regional enquiries should be directed to the Commission's regional offices, although you should bear in mind that these may change when Regional Development Agencies come into force in April 1999:

East Anglia (Cambridgeshire, Essex, Norfolk, Suffolk): Lees Smith House, 12 Looms Lane, Bury St Edmunds, Suffolk IP33 1HE (01284-701743)

East Midlands (Derbyshire, Leicestershire, Lincolnshire, Nottinghamshire): 18 Market Place, Bingham, Nottingham NG13 8AP (01949-876200)

North (Cumbria, Durham, Lancashire, Northumberland, Redcar & Cleveland): Haweswater Road, Penrith, Cumbria CA11 7EH (01768-865752)

South East (Kent, East Sussex, Isle of Wight): Sterling House, 7 Ashford Road, Maidstone, Kent ME14 5BJ (01622-765222)

South West (Cornwall & Isles of Scilly, Devon, Dorset, Somerset, Wiltshire): 3 Chartfield House, Castle Street, Taunton, Somerset TA1 4AS (01823-276905)

West Midlands (Hereford & Worcester, Gloucestershire, Shropshire, Staffordshire/West Derbyshire): Strickland House, The Lawns, Park Street, Wellington, Telford, Shropshire TF1 3BX (01952-247161)

Yorkshire and Humberside (East Riding of Yorkshire, North Yorkshire, South Yorkshire, West Yorkshire, North Lincolnshire): Spitfire House, Aviator Court, Clifton Moor, York YO3 4UZ (01904-693335).

Environment and land management

The Environment Agency

This government agency was formed in 1995 to oversee the protection and enhancement of the environment in England and Wales. A number of agencies were incorporated including the National Rivers Authority (which was included in the first edition of this Guide). As well as responsibilities for fisheries, navigation, flood defence, water resources and pollution control, it also aims to promote the recreational use of inland and coastal waters throughout England and Wales.

The agency is not a grant-making body, but works with others, including those in the voluntary sector, in supporting environmental projects. These include Recreation and Conservation projects which fit with regionally defined needs. Support for such projects is limited, and the Environment Agency will not be the sole funder. Rather it will work with others, such as the National Lottery, water companies, local authorities, English Nature, charitable trusts, European support programmes and sports organisations. As well as over 1,000 sites that are managed for recreational use, it is also currently involved in over 540 collaborative projects involving recreation, conservation and river restoration. A number of these include groups such as angling associations, sailing and rowing organisations and others using the water for sports. In the past, there

181

has been support for groups promoting wider uses of waterways, such as footpath and cycleway creation, and increased access for disabled water users.

Recent sports projects where the Environment Agency has contributed include:

- provision of fishing platforms for disabled anglers in Preston and Darwen in collaboration with the local authority and a local angling club;
- provision of a visitors' pontoon at Newcastle Quayside to encourage safe mooring on a tidal reach;
- building a new clubhouse for Marlow Sailing Club;
- buying a new lightweight scull boat for Walton Rowing Club.

The agency's head office is in Bristol with a further eight regional offices covering 26 areas in England and Wales. Contact with the regional office should be made as early as possible to discuss the proposal. Not all offices have a nominated recreation manager, but a telephone enquiry should result in contact being made with the appropriate officer.

Head Office: Rio House, Waterside Drive, Aztec West, Almondsbury, Bristol BS12 4UD (01454-624400; Fax: 01454-624409)

Regional offices

Anglian: Kingfisher House, Goldhay Way, Orton, Goldhay, Peterborough PE2 5ZR (01733-371811; Fax: 01733-231840)

Midlands: Sapphire East, 550 Streetsbrook Road, Solihull, West Midlands B91 1QT (0121-711 2324; Fax: 0121-711 5824)

North East: Rivers House, 21 Park Square South, Leeds LS1 2QG (0113-244 0191; Fax: 0113-246 1889)

North West : Richard Fairclough House, Knutsford Road, Warrington WA4 1HG (01925-653999; Fax: 01925-415961)

South West: Manley House, Kestrel Way, Exeter EX2 7LQ (01392-444000; Fax: 01392-444238)

Southern: Guildbourne House, Chatsworth Road, Worthing, Sussex BN11 1LD (01903-832000; Fax: 01903-821832)

Thames: Kings Meadow House, Kings Meadow Road, Reading RG1 8DQ (0118-953 5000; Fax: 0118-950 0388)

Environmental Trust Scheme Regulatory Body Ltd (ENTRUST)

ENTRUST is the regulator of Environmental Bodies (EBs) under Landfill Tax Regulations. This green tax, introduced in 1996, is collected by HM Customs and Excise, with the amount varying depending on the type of waste. Built into the tax is a mechanism for diverting up to 20% of a landfill operator's tax liability to environmental projects. Companies receive no income from this environmental support. Instead, the benefits to the company are a more environmentally conscious image, improved local community relations and a tax benefit. For every £1 donated, a further £9 is deducted from their tax liability up to a maximum credit of 20% of their annual liability.

ENTRUST is not a grant-giving body. Local EBs have to contact and negotiate with a local landfill operator (addresses are available through the local authority, the Environment Agency, and website) to agree a project that has mutual benefits. However, for EBs to benefit from Landfill Tax Credits, they must be registered with ENTRUST. EBs have to be non-profit making, and spend any contributions they receive on approved activities which include:

- land reclamation, remediation or restoration for economic, social or environmental use
- pollution reduction
- education and research and development, to encourage sustainable waste management
- improvement, maintenance or provision of a public park or other public amenity in a landfill site vicinity
- protection of a building of historical or architectural interest which is open to the public and in the vicinity of a landfill site
- provision of financial, administrative and other services to EBs.

'Vicinity' is interpreted as a project or activity that takes place within 10 miles of an active landfill site which is owned by an organisation registered for Landfill Tax. Former landfill sites are not included, nor are transfer stations.

The fee for enrolling is £100. EBs are advised to consult with their landfill operator before applying to enrol. This is particularly the case where the EB is small, or they are looking for contributions for one project, as the £100 enrolment fee is not refundable.

There are currently over 1,000 EBs enrolled with ENTRUST, and there have been over 4,000 projects approved. The value of contributions up to October 1998 was £95 million. Examples of sports organisations enrolled as EBs include:

Bute Shinty and Amateur Athletic Sports Club
Chichester and District Angling Society
Mid-Ulster Flying Association
Ruabon Sports Association
Ripley Ski Club, Harrogate

There are a number of approved projects that include a sustainable leisure element or reclamation of land for sport and play. Examples include:

- restoration of land at the Lodmoor Landfill Site including sports and leisure facilities
- Old Bristolians Sports Club, disabled facilities

- Auldcathie Trust, riding arena for those with disabilities
- Global Wildlife Trust, multi-purpose sports area as part of Jubilee Field development
- Buckinghamshire EB, all weather sports facility at Marsh Gibbon
- Albany Architectural Heritage Trust, repair to Fladbury Sports Pavilion
- SWEET, multi-purpose sports hall and indoor cricket facilities for Frenchay Cricket Club.

Enrolment application forms and project submission forms are available from: ENTRUST Head Office, Suite 2, 5th Floor, Acre House, 2 Town Square, Sale, Cheshire M33 7WZ (0161-972 0044; Fax: 0161-972 0055) Website: www.entrust.org.uk

Local contacts are:

Glasgow: Jim Graham and Margaret Starling – 0141-561 0390
London: Judith Jackson and Michaela Pearce – 0181-950 2152
Manchester: Neil Carrigan and Pallavi Mavani – 0161-610 1219

Health

Drugs Action Teams

The government's anti-drugs strategy builds upon the foundation of previous initiatives and has determined that there shall be a progressive shift by local and central government away from reactive expenditure dealing with the consequences of drugs misuse, towards positive investment to prevent drug-related problems.

The strategy has four elements:

- to encourage *young people* to resist drugs and to achieve their full potential;
- to protect *communities* from drug-related behaviour;
- to offer *treatment* to overcome the consequences of drugs misuse;
- to prevent the *availability* of illegal drugs

The strategy is under the direction of the UK Anti-Drugs Coordinator, Keith Hellawell, and the Cabinet Sub-Committee on Drugs Misuse. Partnerships are essential to the strategy with links with other government departments and agencies such as the Social Exclusion Unit.

At a local level, Drugs Action Teams (DATs) are 'the critical link in the chain' in coordinating local initiatives to combat drugs misuse. Under a previous programme (the Drugs Prevention Initiative which has now finished as a funding body), local initiatives included diversionary activities to offer real alternatives to young people at risk from drugs. These often included sports, with the setting up of local leagues, conferences on sport and drugs and support for local clubs and sports organisations. There are currently 105 DATs and they will vary in their approach according to the communities they are working with. Durham DAT has committed resources to a Drugs in Sport Clinic to look at the effects of Performing Enhancing Drugs. Sports organisations working with those at risk from drugs misuse should contact their local DAT to find out more about local initiatives. For the nearest DAT, contact the UK Anti-Drugs Coordination Unit: 0171-270 5776.

Scotland

The Urban Programme (Scotland)
The overall purpose of the Urban Programme is to help to improve the social, economic and environmental conditions within the areas of greatest deprivation in Scotland. There are currently 12 Priority Partnership Areas (PPAs) and 11 Regeneration Programme (RP) areas where Urban Programme money is targeted. In these areas local regeneration partnerships have been set up to develop local regeneration strategies. Each of these partnerships is made up of representation from the local council, Scottish Homes, the Local Enterprise Company and other appropriate agencies. There are also representatives from the private, community and voluntary sectors.

The Urban Programme allocated a total of £34 million to partnerships in PPA and RP areas in 1998/99. Decisions on how to spend the money are taken locally with detailed plans being drawn up by the partnership. Some partnerships have included sports projects within their strategic plans, on the basis of their contribution to regeneration of the local area. Examples include:

- a Sports Motivation Team supported by North Ayr Partnership;
- Stirling Sport Start which provides sport, leisure and fitness opportunities for all age groups, supported by Stirling Regeneration Programme;
- a pilot Sports Development Project has been set up in Dundee PPA.

Priority Partnership Areas	*Regeneration Programmes*
Ardler, Dundee	Angus
Craigmillar, Edinburgh	Dundee
Glasgow East End	East Renfrewshire
Glasgow North	Edinburgh
Greater Easterhouse	Falkirk
Great Northern, Aberdeen	Fife
Inverclyde	Glasgow
Motherwell North	North Ayrshire
North Ayr	North Lanarkshire
Paisley	South Lanarkshire
West Dunbartonshire	Stirling

185

Priorities for the programme are decided at an area level. Those looking to be involved in the partnership should approach their appropriate council to discuss their proposals and to find out about local arrangements for funding.

The Scottish Office states: 'The Government has announced its intention to review the Urban Programme and set up new Social Inclusion Partnerships. The characteristics of these new Social Inclusion Partnerships will be that: they focus on the most needy members of society; they coordinate and fill gaps between existing programmes to promote inclusion; and they seek to prevent people becoming socially excluded. They will retain the key features of the existing PPAs, and are expected to start work in April 1999. Further details of the new arrangements can be obtained by contacting The Scottish Office.'

Contact: Ann McVie, The Scottish Office Development Department, Area Regeneration Division, Area 2 F, Victoria Quay, Edinburgh EH6 6QQ (0131-244 0808; Fax: 0131-244 0810).

Highlands and Islands Enterprise

Grants are available to help with economic development and social, community and cultural development projects. Sports projects are supported through Community Action Grants as part of a 'Strengthening Communities' programme. These grants range from £10 to a normal maximum of £15,000. They are given through the ten Local Enterprise Companies (LECs). Applications will need to show local involvement; how the project will benefit the community; details of any jobs that will be created, and the general contribution the project will make to community life.

Recent grants have included:

- £100 from Shetland Enterprise for Shetland Men's Hockey Club;
- Help with developing sponsorship and promotional material for martial arts clubs in the areas covered by Inverness and Nairn Enterprise and Moray, Badenoch and Strathspey Enterprise;
- Support from Caithness and Sutherland Enterprise to start the Highland League Wick Academy's Youth Team:
- Support from Inverness and Nairn Enterprise towards the cost of new changing rooms for Glenurquhart Shinty Club;
- Support for the Bettyhill swimming pool.

As well as the Community Action Grants, all LECs aim to develop businesses and create jobs. Where sports projects contribute towards these aims, they may be eligible for other grants. The British Association for Ski Instructors at Glenmore for example, gained support for new headquarters on the strength of its business contribution to the region.

For the nearest LEC, contact: Highlands and Islands Enterprise, 20 Bridge Street, Inverness IV1 1QR (01463-234171; Fax: 01463-244469).

Chapter 11
Raising money from the government 2
Local authorities

■■■

At some point during their lifetime, most voluntary sports organisations will look to the local town hall for help. You may need equipment, help with understanding the law, buildings, running costs, training, contacts or advice. In many cases the local authority may have someone who can answer your question or know support you can apply for.

Although local authorities budgets for sports and recreational facilities have fallen throughout the nineties (Sport England estimates a decline of around £40 million between 1991/92 and 1996/97, or 7.5%) it remains an important supporter of local sports activity. Direct expenditure by local authorities on sport and recreation is currently around £960 million.

Local authority support for sport comes in a number of forms:

- Capital, for buildings, refurbishment, playing fields, equipment and the like.
- Revenue, for what it costs to run your activity, from salaries and telephone calls to coaching fees and courses.
- Rate relief.

The climate of local authority support is changing. Voluntary organisations, community groups and local sports clubs need to recognise that local authorities have many different functions and competition for all resources is becoming fiercer. Sectors such as sport and community development will have to compete against local authority responsibilities such as education, housing and mainstream social services. Unlike charitable trusts, local authorities do not exist just to give money away and are not solely interested in the development of sport. Like never before, questions are being asked about effectiveness and the value for money that grants budgets bring to the local authority. Local groups have to bear in mind that they must offer added value or something extra to increase their chances of success in winning local authority support.

Lots of people and organisations are competing for local authority support. This chapter will tell you how best to compete and how you can improve your chances of winning. Your relationship with the local authority will be made up of many parts: lobbying, profile-raising, partnership-building as well as fundraising. You will need to be clear about what you do and what you need.

You must then make sure that the people who matter in the local authority become equally clear. You will also need to be clued up on the local authority's priorities and what they are looking for from the relationship. This will take time and effort, but it usually pays dividends.

Money's too tight to mention?

Local authorities are similar to other funders in this Guide in that personal relationships count. Increasingly, you have to build your relationship with your local authority as you would any other potential supporter. The days of widespread grant aid for anything and everything are over, and few local authorities now want to be cheque-writing machines. Particularly if you are a new project, you should not start by asking the local authority for money. You need to work with them, ideally in that much overused word – partnership – to develop a project and win support for the idea. All too often sports organisations begin their relationship with the local authority on the wrong foot, by asking for money rather than winning support for their proposal.

What local authorities can support

Rate relief

Local authorities can give valuable indirect support to local sports clubs through rate relief. Sport England estimates the total value to sport to be around

---

How local authorities support sport

These are some examples of what local authorities support. Each area and authority will be different, and yours may support sport in other ways as well.

- Advice
- Equipment – to buy or loan
- Salaries
- Running costs – heating, lighting etc.
- Project start-up costs
- Training
- Bursaries
- Buildings
- Transport
- Refurbishment
- Sports leaders' qualifications
- Coaching
- Help with programme development
- Access to other funders and programmes
- Publicity
- Endorsement

£16 million. The level of relief varies greatly from area to area, but it can be up to 100%. The amount will be governed by the authority's policy and may depend upon the type of organisation. A club does not have to be registered as a charity, but to qualify there may have to be evidence of the extent of a club's community benefit (links with schools, open facilities, coaching sessions, youth policies and so on).

Contact the local authority for further details of their policy and how to apply. Claim any rate relief you are entitled to while you can. The government is currently reviewing Local Authority Discretionary Rate Relief.

Which local authority?

Local government in England has been transformed in recent years. This chapter is a snapshot of the situation as it is now; it may be very different in two to three years. It may also be the case that as authorities change, patterns of who has responsibility for what, take time to emerge.

The structure of local government will be different in each part of the country. In Scotland, Wales and Northern Ireland there is one tier of local government, although you may be working in more than one local authority area. In England you may have several levels to take into account: your county council, a district council, a borough or city council. There may be a further level still if you have a parish or town council. Or you may have just one, say a London borough, a metropolitan district such as South Yorkshire or one of the new unitary authorities such as Bristol. (At the end of the chapter is a list of the different local authorities.)

The situation is still changing. Where you are not sure how your local authority is structured, ask around. Someone on your committee, a member, a volunteer or a parent may know. You can also ring your local councillor and ask about the local authority and how it works. (You will need get to know him or her sooner or later, so this will be a useful introduction.) If you do not already have their number, the town hall will. Ask for the Chief Executive's department and they will inform and direct you from there.

Contacting the appropriate office in your local authority can be time-consuming and frustrating. How your local authority is set up will directly affect who you apply to, and what you ask for. So it is worth spending some time getting to know the system. Once you are inside the gates, understanding how the authority works and making progress should become easier.

If you work within a unitary authority (these include London boroughs and metropolitan districts, as well as many towns and cities), you have one authority to think about. In each of these cases, it will be a matter of making contact with the appropriate offices to talk about your proposal.

District or county?

Where you are working with a county council which also includes district, borough and possibly city councils, you need to take account of the two-tiered structure. Here, the responsibilities and functions of the local authorities are divided between the two levels.

The county council will have responsibility for the large services and facilities which benefit the whole county. These include education and social services;

District and borough councils on the other hand are responsible for services and resources that benefit their local areas. These include housing, environmental services and local planning.

There will be some cross-over in the responsibilities of county and district councils.

Whether you apply at the county or district level will depend upon what you are applying for. You should consider how wide the geographical area is that you cover. This is particularly the case with sports activities. Does your project have a county-wide interest with large numbers of participants, or is it more local? A regional sports organisation for example may be setting up mini-leagues in schools in a number of towns and more than one district. A local basketball club is more likely to focus on its local area. One will have a county-wide appeal, the other will link more easily with the district council.

If you are looking for county support you may have to lobby strongly. At this level it can help to have councillors, key officials and local politicians arguing the merits of your case and persuading others of the county-wide benefits of your scheme. Council committees where decision-making powers lie are not just made up by councillors. There may also be representatives of voluntary organisations, trade unions and similar local interests, all of whom can usefully be lobbied.

Once you have decided how your local authority is organised, you need to approach the appropriate officials. The named office which has responsibility for sport varies from authority to authority. Some authorities will include the local voluntary sports sector under Leisure Services, some will have a wide-ranging function called Community Services, or Cultural and Community Services where leisure and recreation will be found.

However your local authority is organised, find out:

- Who takes the lead in leisure and recreation facilities and initiatives? Which council, county, district etc. and then, which departments?
- Who makes the policies which affect sports provision? Councillors or committees?
- Who makes these policies happen? Officers or offices?

Parish and town councils

In some villages and county towns in England and Wales there can be a further tier of local government. Parish or community councils work at a very local, parochial level. Called community councils in Wales, parish or town councils in England (and neighbourhood or community councils in some urban areas), these bodies are responsible for maintaining and providing leisure and recreation facilities. In practice they look after village halls and playing fields as well as car parking, street lighting and such like. They must also be consulted in any local planning applications.

This local council will decide on local priorities for spending and fix its own rate which will be collected by the district council. The parish council will not have vast sums of money available, but it will direct the money to very local concerns. A small sports club managing a community resource such as a sports field, pavilion or athletics track or wanting to build changing facilities may well find the parish council a welcoming supporter. Often in villages there will be a Village Plan which may include details of recreation facilities, both actual and planned. Make contact with your parish council, either by attending the open meetings or by meeting parish councillors.

Council officers will be able to tell you how much is available, if anything, and how it is spent. Councillors may also be able to lobby on your behalf. Some parish council meetings are attended by local authority councillors. They may use meetings as a sounding board to find out what the local priorities are. If your name is mentioned here and wins support, there may be more note taken at a district level. Lists of local parish councillors will be posted in town and county halls, in your village hall (if you have one), or your local post office, parish church or library. The local citizen's advice bureau may also have information.

Who does what in the local authority?

Fundraising at any level is most effective when you connect with key people who are enthusiastic about your cause. You may need to enthuse them first and then get them to enthuse others. Writing endless letters is often the least effective way of raising funds. It is more helpful to your cause to meet with people face to face. In local authorities the key people to contact are:

- local authority officers
- local councillors

You should not leave making these contacts until it is too late. Too often groups leave meeting the people who can influence and help until the eleventh hour or even after their application has failed. It is far better to involve local authority staff, councillors, MPs and other local people at an early stage to help the process along. If you do not yet know of any local people that have influence in the community, ask around your members, parents, volunteers and staff to find someone who does. If you have someone connected with the organisation who has particular experience or knowledge of making things happen locally, use them to make introductions for you and to promote the project themselves.

Local authority officers

Your first point of contact with the authority will usually be an officer within one of the departments. These are very important to your cause and can help your project in many ways. They are paid members of staff employed to implement council policies. You should also bear in mind that administrative officers often have detailed knowledge of what is happening, and may have the most information.

You need to think more widely than just sports officers to find other staff who may be able to help. There may be other staff working in other departments that can also advise. For instance, if you are running a wheelchair basketball tournament, you may need to talk to both the sports development officer and to the disability officer within the authority (who may be in social services). If you are involved in after-school clubs, social services may be interested. Links with curriculum development may interest the education department. Activities for young people may be appropriate to a youth officer. Work with people from a particular under-represented group may involve officers with specific responsibilities. Birmingham City Council, for instance, focuses on Women and Girls, People from Ethnic Minority Groups and People with Disabilities as under-represented groups in the community.

In all cases you will need to keep officers informed about your organisation and ensure that your activities are promoted within their department. If you are unsure which officer you should speak to, contact the Chief Executive's office which will be able to give you a name as a starting point. More and more local authorities are now establishing External Funding Units to help with liaison and signposting to appropriate offices and personnel.

Officers make recommendations to councillors to act upon and you should brief them well and update them regularly. They will want to know how your proposal is to work; what resources (not just money) will be required; whether there is community support; whether there is opposition; and any possible repercussions from supporting your activity. Try to make sure that officers are well informed and enthusiastic about your proposal.

If your activity is modest, support may be directly authorised by officers, although this is less the case now than it used to be. Councillors more than ever are keen to control spending decisions and to make sure that the council's support for projects is politically and financially transparent. Where the proposal needs further endorsement, officers can recommend it for councillors' support at the committee level. It may be, however, that you need to persuade councillors personally to give their backing when it reaches their committee(s).

When contacting councillors and local authority officers, follow up telephone calls and meetings with a letter, summarising the key points you wish to make. Copies are often passed on to other local authority colleagues with notes written on.

Councillors

Councillors are representatives of a ward or a county division. They are also politicians with an agenda. They serve on committees and decide policy following briefings given by local authority officers. The fact that they are local representatives gives you the greatest point of leverage as their first duty is to represent the people in their ward. Sport is a good way to build up and unite communities; they should be interested in what you have to say. They should be particularly keen where your activities reach groups such as young and old people or where you have an approach for tackling crime prevention or social exclusion for example.

Where you need help from a number of different departments within the local authority, councillors can sponsor your application, oil the local government wheels, and generally help the progress of a proposal. They may help to broker a deal between departments that can give larger funding to a project than could be given by a single department. Where you are looking for county funding (as opposed to district), councillors can also help to cross district council lines. You may need to promote the regional benefits of your proposal. Local councillors on your side will help to identify which county officers to speak to and the channels to go through. They can also make a difference on the committees they participate in.

Local councillors are listed in the local press, your town hall, the citizen's advice bureau which will also give details of their surgery hours, or the *Municipal Yearbook* available in your local library. Some local authorities list councillors and committee members on their websites. You can contact your local ward councillor at their home address (they expect this) or through the local authority. You should write care of the local authority when contacting other councillors. Letters are always helpful. Busy councillors can attach a quick note and pass it on to the relevant officer.

Be realistic in your approach and consider the scale of your activity and what you are asking help for. Remember that whilst the chair and vice-chair of any committee are obviously central to any decision-making, they are also the busiest people. They will be key contacts, but you will have to work around committed schedules. Many committee meetings are open to the public and publicised daily in the town hall.

Remember that the balance of political power can be very different between the various tiers of local government. It is important to be able to present your case in different ways to attract the support of politicians in different parties. Keeping informed and aware of political and structural change will help your approach. One local authority officer observes: 'Local authorities are, at the end of the day, political organisations, and political priorities and considerations will often come into play. However, there is a move in many authorities towards having clear policy and funding priorities for grants and resisting pressure to support projects outside these priorities (thus reducing the scope for political patronage).'

Promoting your cause may seem daunting at first. However, if you are clear about why they should support you, your enthusiasm and a well-argued case will at least guarantee a hearing. Local authorities are like other funders, and will want to know why they should support you and what they are getting for their support. Briefing councillors and officers is part of this process.

> When briefing councillors, ensure that what you say is based on facts, and argue your case on its merits. Do not assume they have background knowledge of your organisation, the issue or approach you are taking, or where sport fits in to the community. Councillors may not have the papers or information to hand and will need filling in. Relationships built up with councillors over time will prove the most valuable, so try and involve then in your work: invite them to address a meeting of your supporters for example. As politicians, councillors like being loved, and few will resist the temptation to say positive things about you that they know will please the audience – and that you can hold them to in the future. Early evening appointments are often best.

Which departments should you approach?

Local authorities organise their departments in different ways. They have various functions such as housing, community services, social services, education and so on. Each of these functions includes a number of different responsibilities. For example, leisure services (which may be a separate department or may come under education, or be part of community services) will be responsible for parks, gardens, cemeteries, arts and libraries as well as sports development and recreation. It is likely that this will be the first local authority department you make contact with.

Depending upon your project there may also be a number of other departments that may be interested in your project. Some are obvious, others less so. In each case you should research their current priorities. You also need to think who benefits from your project and how it fits in with current local authority concerns.

Each local authority is different and will reflect local issues and priorities. The following is therefore a brief outline of the departments that cover sports facilities and sports development. There is also information on other offices which may also be supportive of your approach.

Leisure services, including sports development

Most sports funding will come from the leisure services department (sometimes called leisure and recreation, or leisure). Around two thirds of authorities will have their own sport development team or committee as part of this department. If there is a sports development team or officer, they will have a say in how sports projects are helped and how departmental priorities are decided (see sports development below).

Each local authority has a different approach to supporting sports activities. Most money for sports is spent on the authority's own activities such as buildings, maintaining indoor and outdoor sports facilities and administering sports development programmes. The same leisure and recreation department will also be responsible for museum and gallery provision, theatres, concert facilities, promoting tourism and maintaining public parks and open spaces. You will have to compete with organisations other than sporting ones for a share of the money.

You can apply for grants, but these are usually small-scale to cover equipment, training fees, establishing local leagues, small events and the like. Larger-scale projects such as buildings, sports programmes and international events will need a more creative approach. You may need other supporters as well as the local authority, and within the authority you may need more than one department to help.

Sports development

Local authorities differ in their approach to sports development. In many cases an officer or officers will be responsible for sports development. Policies can be very general or concentrate on certain groups e.g. élite performers, ethnic minorities, women, old and young people.

At its simplest, sports development is about increasing and improving opportunities to participate and compete at all levels in sport. Some will use the foundation, participation, performance and excellence levels to channel resources. Many will target resources at particular groups or ages. Southampton City Council's sports development team for instance has developed a Stay with Sport initiative to encourage and sustain participation. The Sports Steps programme for under 12s and the Sports Wise for over 12s links young people and sports opportunities in the city. They are looking to a programme of accreditation for local sports providers.

Local authority sports officers now link up regularly with schools, clubs, community groups, governing bodies, welfare agencies and previously under-represented groups such as women, young and older people, ethnic minorities, the disabled, the economically disadvantaged.

Check whether your local authority has a sports development officer (SDO) or team and contact them (they are usually called sports development, action sport, sport specific development, youth or community recreation teams). Find out about the priorities and interest groups that may connect with your sport or those who participate in it. Tell them what you do and what you need.

Sports development officers will have a number of responsibilities and tasks. In particular they will help with training and coaching, advise on helpful contacts, work with specific groups and market and publicise events, activities and information. A large part of some SDOs' work is to promote coaching and training qualifications. They can use the Community Sports Leader Awards or governing body qualifications to encourage more home-grown sports leaders from within the community. Birmingham City Council, for example, has developed a database of local voluntary coaches for its Coach Train programme. Training courses are given free of charge to accredited clubs.

A different approach has been taken by Nottingham County Council in its promotion of volunteer resources. A 'semi-volunteer' hockey coach is paid by the council to coach and coordinate hockey in the county. The payments do not amount to a full salary, but do recognise the volunteer's significant help towards promoting the game in the area.

Sports development check list

The following questions will help in developing your relationship with the local authority:

- Does our local authority have a sports development officer or team?
- Have we contacted them for advice or other support?
- Who is the first point of contact?
- Are there officers with a specialism in our sport or in groups who are already involved in our project, or who we would like to involve?
- Do they produce guidelines for those applying for grants?
- Have we got up-to-date information?
- What is the maximum and minimum grant available?
- Is there help with equipment costs; revenue or running costs such as salary and administration; or with capital such as building or site development?
- Do we know of any sports clubs who have had help, and what was it for?
- Is in-kind support available, such as help with coaching or the loan of equipment?

Making the case for your project

What features of your project make it attractive to your local authority?
How do any of the following apply to your organisation or project?

- Fits in with local authority priorities (essential)
- Local benefits
- Regional benefits
- Large number of different groups benefit (which ones?)
- Community run
- Innovative approach
- Addressing special needs
- Matching funds raised
- Established track record
- Excellence
- Sound finances
- Fills a gap or augments local authority service provision
- Number of different bodies/organisations involved (which ones?)
- Established and enthusiastic membership
- Large number of benefits from a small grant (what benefits?)
- Local support
- Good publicity for the local authority
- Value for money
- Other (list)

Education

Local Management for Schools (LMS) has changed how money is spent on education by the local authority. Individual schools hold the purse strings and you need to approach them, not the local education authority. However, schools are not grant-givers. They are buying in a service which you are providing.

Schools can be responsive to approaches from other groups in the community to use the school. They can also be open to help from sports clubs with teaching the sports part of the curriculum, or running playground activities. There can be new opportunities to work with individual schools to share facilities and to develop new partnerships.

Sports organisations can benefit greatly from good school links. Apart from the use of facilities, you can also use the school community to widen your activities and increase participation and membership. The benefits are not hard to see. A small sports club can run conventional after-school leagues, tournaments and clubs which can lead to new activities. You might be able to start fitness programmes, with parents' groups for example, or women's taster days for your sport. There are new possibilities for marketing and publicity. Furthermore, your club will be operating in partnership with another body and efficiently using its resources. All these points can be also be underlined when you approach other funders, particularly those wanting to see a community base to your project.

Schools want to generate income by charging for their facilities. They also want to give their children the widest range of activities they can. Many are looking at National Lottery funding for their sports activities, but to succeed they need to show how their facilities would be used by the community. It will also help your fundraising to show the widest possible community links.

A schools liaison officer in Tameside Borough Council works to encourage contact between schools and local sports clubs. This promotes the local use of school facilities and helps young people continue in sport after school. A school with a particularly good basketball court hires it for one evening a week to a local club. The first hour is used for introductory sessions for children, and the second hour for junior squad training. The school earns income from the club's hire, whilst at the same time improving its reputation for sports provision as an added attraction for young people considering the school.

Other departments
Depending upon what your project is there may be further departments in the local authority that you could approach. Some are obvious, others less so. In each case you will need to look into their current services, priorities and timetables for applications. You also need to look closely at who benefits from your activities, and whether there are other parts of the local authority that may be interested in your proposal. Whilst support may first come from leisure (which may be under education, community and so on), there may also be help under the following:

- education
- social services
- youth services
- opportunities for those with disabilities
- ethnic minorities
- women
- health promotion
- increasing awareness of the local authority
- urban development and regeneration
- rural isolation
- environmental improvement
- voluntary sector liaison
- community safety.

Each local authority is different. The following are some examples of projects that may support the current priorities and concerns of a particular department. It is by no means exhaustive, and each local authority and each department within that authority will have its own approach to relationships with voluntary organisations.

The Social Services department for example, may be interested in projects such as:

- After-school clubs
- Work with young mothers
- Counselling and information services
- Work with young people leaving care
- Work with young refugees
- Reducing youth crime.

General grant-giving

As well as the specific departments, most councils will have a general grant-giving committee. Bear in mind that all local authority grants are discretionary, but this particular source has wider discretionary powers and can give to a range of organisations for events and activities which are not necessarily covered by other departments. The fund is sometimes called the Community Chest and can be applied for by any organisation within the authority's area. Grants for sport may well be small (up to £500) and for items such as equipment or course fees.

The scheme is often operated from the Chief Executive's office, which may also be responsible for events and activities that are not covered by other functions, including marketing of the local authority. Conferences, festivals or tournaments for example may have authority-wide benefits and may be supported more on the lines of a sponsorship, particularly if there are publicity and increased profile opportunities or links with other countries, through town-twinning and the like.

There may be restrictions on how many times a year you can apply. This need not alter your application for football nets for example, but if you have trainee officials and coaches looking to attend courses at different times in the year, you will need to plan accordingly. All departmental budgets have allocations to be spent by the end of each financial year. If you apply towards the end of a budgetary period there may be too little money in the coffers, or 'too much'. Where there is a surplus, officers will be keen to see it spent before the next financial year; your application may be received particularly warmly. However, if the cupboard is bare you will have to wait until the next financial year. If you get to know your council officers they may be able to tell you how much money is left within a particular budget.

Local authorities and other bodies

Local authorities often work in partnership with other organisations and often apply for funding themselves (e.g. for SRB funding or European grants programmes). They generally work with other organisations such as TECs, businesses, health authorities and probation services to achieve a variety of aims and to draw up and implement locally defined strategies on a wide range of issues. In many of these large funding programmes, small groups going it alone will not stand much chance of winning bids on their own. Where they are known and trusted by large bodies however, their chances of being included in regeneration plans for the area increase greatly.

Increasingly, local authorities are gatekeepers to other forms of funding and influence. Where local authorities are working closely with other bodies on funding bids or service provision, there may be opportunities for voluntary organisations to become involved, including sports bodies. It is the case, however, that to be involved at any meaningful level you will have to be at the right meetings and in the right networks to get an invitation to the bidding table.

Local authorities have regular meetings with a host of other public agencies such as the probation service, police authorities and the local health authority. These meetings propose and advise on approaches to local issues and concerns and how services will be delivered. Where your activities reach groups targeted by these bodies or you have an approach that is innovative and professional, you can make a strong case for being included in any consultation, and then being considered as part of any service delivery.

The significance of local authorities

- May give core funding
- Can publicise activities and events
- Access to networks
- Lead bodies e.g. in SRB, European bids
- Relationships with health authorities, police authorities, TECs etc.
- Expertise on form filling
- Policy and legislation issues e.g. health and safety.

In some cases the absence of a local authority from a partnership bid can cause suspicion. Some of the larger funding programmes will want to see the authority's involvement if they are to take the application seriously.

Again, each area is different, but health authority initiatives may include health promotion, fitness campaigns and the like. (Each area draws up a local health strategy detailing health priorities for the area.) These may link with local authority environmental and education programmes and priorities. A multi-agency initiative combining with the probation service and police force for example, may include diversionary activities for young people which may use sports activities.

Applications

By the time you fill in any application form you will know how your local authority works. You should be able to enlist the support of officers and local councillors. The application procedure will differ from authority to authority, although in almost every case there will be an application form to fill in. This may be specific to leisure services or named department or be a general form for the whole of the authority.

In general you need to know:

- the maximum and minimum grants available;
- current priorities and criteria, either for the council as a whole or the funding programme in particular;
- how you should fill in the application form;
- what information is needed and how it should be presented;
- the application timetable and deadlines for submission.

Where you are applying for a large project with other funders involved you need to allow for time lags and delays in submission and approval. Lead-in times differ according to which partners are involved, how many, and how good the relationship is. If a proposal is to go before a committee for a decision, you need to find out the timetable and to lobby for your cause well in advance.

Be clear and concise. Take advice from officers as to how the form should be filled in. Once submitted, a regular (although not too frequent) telephone call will keep you in touch with how the application is progressing. If by this time you are on good terms with the relevant officers this can be a friendly, informal chat that can help to keep the application 'live'.

Basically, there are three ways of getting a project supported by the local authority:

- Applying for a grant, but amounts are limited and available money is generally used up on commitments made in previous years. There is now more emphasis on 'priority-driven' support rather than historic funding.
- Through service agreements or contracts, where you are competing with a whole range of organisations – including commercial ones.
- Getting the local authority to include your project in an SRB, safer cities, ESF or other bid. Many local authorities now act as gatekeepers for external funding. But all this takes time and forward planning.

Remember, local authorities are like other funders in what they want to know from you:

- What do you want to do?
- Why do you want to do it?
- How will you make it happen?
- Who will be accountable?
- What difference will the work make to the local area?
- What do you want from the local authority?

In other words, they will look to see if you:

- Have identified a clear need.
- Have produced a good and workable plan.
- Have costed your work.
- Will be able to measure the value and outcomes of your work.

Think differently

The key thing is that when you meet with your local authority, don't talk about funding; talk about collaboration. Local authorities are not cheque-writing machines. They do not see themselves as there to underwrite your core costs year in, year out. They have their own views on what service provision they want to see happen in the area. Show how you fit into and understand their priorities and concerns, rather than expect them just to support you to do whatever you like.

Local authorities also appreciate credit and recognition for their contribution to a project. Show how you will publicise their grant and generally help people to view their local authority more positively.

Do
- Find out how your local authority works
- Find and contact key local officers
- Build good relationships with local councillors across the party divides
- Find out about and understand authority/department priorities
- Think creatively about your project
- Use local media to raise your profile
- Attend meetings regularly
- Be clear and to the point
- Keep well informed about changes in criteria/priorities
- Be persistent
- Budget realistically
- Find out about application procedure and deadlines.

Don't
- Give up
- Leave talking to councillors and officers until you need money
- Limit your project to one narrow departmental interest
- Forget in-kind support from your local authority
- Be bashful about what you can offer
- Let information become out of date
- Plan in the short-term – look to the future
- Waffle

Sport England produces a number of Policy Briefings. Some of the examples quoted above are from *Policy Briefing 3* on *Local authority support for the voluntary sector in sport*. For further information, contact Sport England's Policy Unit: 0171-273 1698.

A list of local authorities 1998/99

As outlined above, the map for local authorities has been redrawn over recent years. Sports organisations may want to apply for support at a district, borough city, or county level. Alternatively, they may come under a unitary authority. Listed below are all the local authorities in England, Northern Ireland, Scotland and Wales. To find the appropriate authority in your area, look firstly under the country. Next, look up the general geographical region (e.g. South West England; Mid Wales; Central Scotland). Find the county, listed in alphabetical order. Finally, look up the unitary authority or county council and then districts, boroughs or city councils if they exist.

The authorities start with the county and are followed by its district, borough or city authorities (these are indented with a bullet point). Then come the unitary authorities which are not indented.

A directory of contacts for local authorities is on the internet at www.tagish.co.uk

England

North East

Durham
Durham County Council
- Chester-le-Street District Council
- Derwentside District Council
- Durham City Council
- Easington District Council
- Sedgefield Borough Council
- Teesdale District Council
- Wear Valley District Council
Darlington Borough Council
Hartlepool Council
Stockton-on-Tees Council

East Yorkshire
East Riding of Yorkshire Council
Kingston-upon-Hull City Council

North Yorkshire
North Yorkshire County Council
- Craven District Council
- Hambleton District Council
- Harrogate Borough Council
- Richmondshire District Council
- Ryedale District Council
- Scarborough Borough Council
- Selby District Council
Middlesbrough Borough Council
Redcar & Cleveland Borough Council
York City Council

Northumberland
Northumberland County Council
- Alnwick District Council
- Berwick-upon-Tweed District Council
- Blyth Valley Borough Council

203

- Castle Morpeth Borough Council
- Tynedale District Council
- Wansbeck District Council

South Yorkshire

Barnsley Metropolitan Borough Council
Doncaster Metropolitan
    Borough Council
Rotherham Metropolitan
    Borough Council
Sheffield City Council

Tyne & Wear

Gateshead Metropolitan
    Borough Council
Newcastle-upon-Tyne City Council
North Tyneside Council
South Tyneside Metropolitan
    Borough Council
Sunderland Metropolitan
    Borough Council

West Yorkshire

Bradford Metropolitan Borough Council
Calderdale Metropolitan
    Borough Council
Kirklees Metropolitan Council
Leeds City Council
City of Wakefield Metropolitan
    District Council

North West

Cheshire

Cheshire County Council
- Chester City Council
- Congleton Borough Council
- Crewe & Nantwich Borough Council
- Ellesmere Port & Neston
    Borough Council
- Macclesfield Borough Council
- Vale Royal Borough Council
Halton Borough Council
Warrington Borough Council

Cumbria

Cumbria County Council
- Allerdale Borough Council
- Barrow-in-Furness
    Borough Council
- Carlisle City Council
- Copeland Borough Council
- Eden District Council
- South Lakeland District Council

Greater Manchester

Bolton Metropolitan Council
Manchester City Council
Oldham Metropolitan
    Borough Council
Rochdale Metropolitan
    Borough Council
Salford Metropolitan
    Borough Council
Stockport Metropolitan
    Borough Council
Tameside Metropolitan
    Borough Council
Trafford Metropolitan
    Borough Council
Wigan Metropolitan
    Borough Council

Lancashire

Lancashire County Council
- Burnley Borough Council
- Chorley Borough Council
- Fylde Borough Council
- Hyndburn Borough Council
- Lancaster City Council
- Pendle Borough Council
- Preston Borough Council
- Ribble Valley Borough Council
- Rossendale Borough Council
- South Ribble Borough Council
- West Lancashire District Council
- Wyre Borough Council
Blackburn and Darwen Council
Blackpool Council
Bury Borough Council

Merseyside

Knowsley Metropolitan
     Borough Council
Liverpool City Council
St Helens Metropolitan
     Borough Council
Sefton Metropolitan
     Borough Council
Wirral Metropolitan
     Borough Council

Midlands

Derbyshire

Derbyshire County Council
- Amber Valley Borough Council
- Bolsover District Council
- Chesterfield Borough Council
- Derbyshire Dales District Council
- Erewash Borough Council
- High Peak Borough Council
- North East Derbyshire
  District Council
- South Derbyshire
  District Council
Derby City Council

Herefordshire

Herefordshire Council

Leicestershire

Leicestershire County Council
- Blaby District Council
- Charnwood Borough Council
- Harborough District Council
- Hinckley & Bosworth
  District Council
- Melton Borough Council
- North West Leicestershire
  District Council
- Oadby & Wigston District Council
Leicester City Council

Lincolnshire

Lincolnshire County Council
- Boston Borough Council
- East Lindsey District Council
- Lincoln City Council
- North Kesteven District Council
- South Holland District Council
- South Kesteven District Council
- West Lindsey District Council
North East Lincolnshire Council
North Lincolnshire Council

Northamptonshire

Northamptonshire County Council
- Corby Borough Council
- Daventry District Council
- East Northamptonshire Council
- Kettering Borough Council
- Northampton Borough Council
- South Northamptonshire Council
- Wellingborough Borough Council

Nottinghamshire

Nottinghamshire County Council
- Ashfield District Council
- Bassetlaw District Council
- Broxtowe Borough Council
- Gedling Borough Council
- Mansfield District Council
- Newark & Sherwood District Council
- Rushcliffe Borough Council
Nottingham City Council

Rutland

Rutland District Council

Shropshire

Shropshire County Council
- Bridgnorth District Council
- North Shropshire District Council
- Oswestry Borough Council
- Shrewsbury & Atcham
  Borough Council
- South Shropshire District Council
The Wrekin District Council

205

Staffordshire
Staffordshire County Council
- Cannock Chase District Council
- East Staffordshire Borough Council
- Lichfield City Council
- Newcastle-under-Lyme
    Borough Council
- South Staffordshire District Council
- Stafford Borough Council
- Staffordshire Moorlands
  District Council
- Tamworth Borough Council
Stoke-on-Trent City Council

Warwickshire
Warwickshire County Council
- North Warwickshire Borough Council
- Nuneaton & Bedworth
    Borough Council
- Rugby Borough Council
- Stratford-upon-Avon District Council
- Warwick District Council

West Midlands
West Midlands
Birmingham City Council
Coventry City Council
Dudley Metropolitan Borough Council
Sandwell Metropolitan Borough Council
Solihull Metropolitan Borough Council
Walsall Metropolitan Borough Council
Wolverhampton Metropolitan
    Borough Council

Worcestershire
Worcestershire County Council
- Bromsgrove District Council
- Malvern Hills District Council
- Redditch Borough Council
- Worcester City Council
- Wychavon District Council
- Wyre Forest District Council

South West
Cornwall
Cornwall County Council
- Caradon District Council
- Carrick District Council
- Kerrier District Council
- North Cornwall District Council
- Penwith District Council
- Restormel Borough Council

Devon
Devon County Council
- East Devon District Council
- Exeter City Council
- Mid Devon District Council
- North Devon District Council
- South Hams District
- Teignbridge District Council
- Torridge District Council
- West Devon Borough Council
Plymouth City Council
Torbay Borough Council

Dorset
Dorset County Council
- Christchurch Borough Council
- East Dorset District Council
- North Dorset District Council
- Purbeck District Council
- West Dorset District Council
- Weymouth & Portland
    Borough Council
Bournemouth Borough Council
Poole Borough Council

Gloucestershire
Gloucestershire County Council
- Cheltenham Borough Council
- Cotswold District Council
- Forest of Dean District Council
- Gloucester City Council
- Stroud District Council
- Tewkesbury Borough Council

Bristol City Council
South Gloucestershire

Somerset
Somerset County Council
- Mendip District Council
- Sedgemoor District Council
- South Somerset District Council
- Taunton Deane Borough Council
- West Somerset District Council
Bath and North East Somerset
North Somerset Council

Wiltshire
Wiltshire County Council
- Kennet District Council
- North Wiltshire District Council
- Salisbury District Council
- West Wiltshire District Council
Swindon Borough Council

South East
Bedfordshire
- Bedfordshire County Council
- Bedford Borough Council
- Mid Bedfordshire District Council
- South Bedfordshire District Council
Luton Borough Council

Berkshire
Bracknell Forest Borough Council
Newbury District Council
Reading Borough Council
Slough Borough Council
Windsor & Maidenhead Council
Wokingham District Council

Buckinghamshire
Buckinghamshire County Council
- Aylesbury Vale District Council
- Chiltern District Council
- South Buckinghamshire
    District Council
- Wycombe District Council
Milton Keynes Council

Cambridgeshire
Cambridgeshire County Council
- Cambridge City Council
- East Cambridgeshire District Council
- Fenland District Council
- Huntingdonshire Borough Council
- South Cambridgeshire
    District Council
Peterborough City Council

East Sussex
East Sussex County Council
Brighton & Hove Council
- Eastbourne Borough Council
- Hastings Borough Council
- Lewes District Council
- Rother District Council
- Wealden District Council

Essex
Essex County Council
- Basildon District Council
- Braintree District Council
- Brentwood Borough Council
- Castle Point Borough Council
- Chelmsford Borough Council
- Colchester Borough Council
- Epping Forest District Council
- Harlow District Council
- Maldon District Council
- Rochford District Council
- Tendring District Council
- Uttlesford District Council
Southend-on-Sea Borough Council
Thurrock District Council

Hampshire
Hampshire County Council
- Basingstoke & Deane Borough Council
- East Hampshire District Council
- Eastleigh Borough Council
- Fareham Borough Council
- Gosport Borough Council
- Hart District Council
- Havant District Council

- New Forest District Council
- Rushmoor Borough Council
- Test Valley Borough Council
- Winchester City Council
Portsmouth City Council
Southampton City Council

Hertfordshire
Hertfordshire County Council
- Broxbourne Borough Council
- Dacorum Borough Council
- East Hertfordshire
    District Council
- Hertsmere Borough Council
- North Hertfordshire
    District Council
- St Albans District Council
- Stevenage Borough Council
- Three Rivers District Council
- Watford Borough Council
- Welwyn Hatfield
    District Council

Isle of Wight
Isle of Wight Council

Kent
Kent County Council
- Ashford Borough Council
- Canterbury City Council
- Dartford Borough Council
- Dover District Council
- Gravesham Borough Council
- Maidstone Borough Council
- Sevenoaks District Council
- Shepway District Council
- Swale Borough Council
- Thanet District Council
- Tonbridge & Malling
    Borough Council
- Tunbridge Wells
    Borough Council
Medway Towns Council

Norfolk
Norfolk County Council
- Breckland District Council
- Broadland District Council
- Great Yarmouth Borough Council
- King's Lynn & West Norfolk
    Borough Council
- North Norfolk District Council
- Norwich City Council
- South Norfolk District Council

Oxfordshire
Oxfordshire County Council
- Oxford City Council
- Cherwell District Council
- South Oxfordshire District Council
- Vale of White Horse
    District Council
- West Oxfordshire District Council

Suffolk
Suffolk County Council
- Babergh District Council
- Forest Heath District Council
- Ipswich Borough Council
- Mid Suffolk District Council
- St Edmundsbury Borough Council
- Suffolk Coastal District Council
- Waveney District Council

Surrey
Surrey County Council
- Elmbridge Borough Council
- Epsom & Ewell Borough Council
- Guildford Borough Council
- Mole Valley District Council
- Reigate & Banstead
    Borough Council
- Runnymede Borough Council
- Spelthorne Borough Council
- Surrey Heath Borough Council
- Tandridge District Council
- Waverley Borough Council
- Woking Borough Council

West Sussex

West Sussex County Council
- Adur District Council
- Arun District Council
- Chichester District Council
- Crawley Borough Council
- Horsham District Council
- Mid Sussex District Council
- Worthing Borough Council

London

Barking & Dagenham
Barnet
Bexley
Brent
Bromley
Camden
Corporation of the
        City of London
Croydon
Ealing
Enfield
Greenwich
Hackney
Hammersmith & Fulham
Haringey
Harrow
Havering
Hillingdon
Hounslow
Islington
Kensington & Chelsea
Kingston upon Thames
Lambeth
Lewisham
Merton
Newham
Redbridge
Richmond-upon-Thames
Tower Hamlets
Waltham Forest
Wandsworth
Westminster

Northern Ireland

Antrim Borough Council
Ards Borough Council
Armagh City & District Council
Ballymena Borough Council
Banbridge District Council
Carrickfergus Borough Council
Castlereagh Borough Council
Coleraine Borough Council
Cookstown District Council
Craigavon Borough Council
Derry City Council
Down District Council
Dungannon District Council
Fermanagh District Council
Larne Borough Council
Limavady Borough Council
Lisburn Borough Council
Magherafelt District Council
Moyle District Council
Newry & Mourne District Council
Newtownabbey Borough Council
North Down Borough Council
Omagh District Council
Strabane District Council

Scotland

Aberdeen & Perthshire

Aberdeen City Council
Aberdeenshire Council
Angus Council
Dundee City Council
Moray Council
Perth & Kinross Council

Central

Clackmannanshire Council
Falkirk Council
Fife Council
Stirling Council

Edinburgh, the Lothians & Scottish Borders

City of Edinburgh Council
East Lothian Council
Midlothian Council
Scottish Borders Council
West Lothian Council

Glasgow & West of Scotland

Argyll & Bute Council
Dumfries & Galloway Council
East Ayrshire Council
East Dunbartonshire Council
East Renfrewshire Council
Glasgow City Council
Inverclyde Council
North Ayrshire Council
North Lanarkshire Council
South Ayrshire Council
South Lanarkshire Council
Renfrewshire Council
West Dunbartonshire Council

Highland & Islands

Council of the Isles of Scilly
Highland Council
Orkney Islands Council
Shetland Islands Council
Western Isles Council

Wales

North Wales

Conwy County Borough Council
Denbighshire County Council
Flintshire County Council
Gwynedd Council
Isle of Anglesey County Council
Wrexham County Borough Council

Mid Wales

Ceredigion County Council
Powys County Council

South Wales

Blaenau Gwent County
    Borough Council
Bridgend County Borough Council
Caerphilly County Borough Council
City & County Council of Cardiff
Carmarthenshire County Council
Merthyr Tydfil County
    Borough Council
Monmouthshire County Council
Neath Port Talbot County
    Borough Council
Newport County Borough Council
Pembrokeshire County Council
Rhondda Cynon Taff County
    Borough Council
City & County Council of Swansea
Torfaen County Borough Council
Vale of Glamorgan County
    Borough Council

Chapter 12

Raising money from grant-making trusts

▪▪▪

Sports organisations are increasingly looking towards grant-making trusts as a source of support. To be effective, organisations need to understand how the world of grant-making trusts works and to plan their approach accordingly. This chapter gives some tips and ideas to help with research and applications. It also gives information on a number of trusts which give specifically to sport.

> The largest grant-making trust for general sport is the Foundation for Sport and the Arts. It currently gives around £7–£9 million a year to sport. For details, see chapter 8.

Grant-making trusts (also called foundations) come in many shapes and sizes. They exist to give money to other organisations or individuals. Two trusts detailed in this book – the Foundation for Sport and the Arts and the Football Trust – are grant-making trusts but are not registered charities. More usually, grant-making trusts are charities themselves, and they will only be able to give money for charitable purposes. This does not necessarily mean that they can only give to registered charities. There is scope for giving to individuals and to non-charitable causes, but the purpose of the grant must be charitable as defined in law.

There are probably over 10,000 grant-making trusts in the UK. Most of these are very small and only able to give in a tightly defined local area. The top 1,000 trusts give over £1 billion in grants a year.

Why trusts exist

Trusts are set up for a number of reasons. Some are fundraising charities such as BBC Children in Need, or Charity Projects who run the biennial Comic Relief Red Nose Day Appeal. Money that is raised from the public is then distributed in grants to organisations. Other trusts are set up by wealthy benefactors, often by transferring cash or shares in their companies to a charitable foundation. Members of the Sainsbury family, for instance, have set up grant-making trusts with shares in J Sainsbury plc. These trusts reflect the founder's interests and enthusiasms in the organisations and causes that they support.

Many trusts are set up with money left in wills. For example, Jim Joel, a racehorse owner, left over £40 million of his personal fortune to the Childwick Trust. Not surprisingly, the Childwick Trust's interests include support for 'charities or charitable objects associated with thoroughbred horse racing and breeding'.

Some trusts are established as a memorial to an individual and their interests. The Ayrton Senna Foundation for example, was established following the driver's death, to support the education, health care and medical treatment of children worldwide. Tiger Woods has founded a trust with income from a $300,000 master class. Proceeds will help disadvantaged young people. One of the most written about trusts in recent times is the Diana, Princess of Wales Memorial Fund set up to receive money given by the public following her death. At the time of writing it was expected that funds of over £100 million would be administered by the trust. Grant-making decisions have come about slowly, but the initial wave of grants reflected causes associated with Diana at the time of her death. These included some sporting causes alongside the expected medical, homeless and artistic charities. Initial beneficiaries were those she had a link with: the All England Tennis and Croquet Club, British Sports Association for the Disabled, English Women's Indoor Bowling Association, Gloucestershire County Cricket Club, David Lloyd Slazenger Racquet Club, Lyford Cay Club, Royal Highland Yacht Club and the Welsh Bowling Association.

Each trust has its own set of restrictions about what it can and cannot give money to. Very few are interested in sport specifically, although many more may support a project that happens to be sport-based, but which clearly helps disadvantaged people or improves society. (This may be, for example, through teaching a sport to people with disabilities; breaking down ethnic barriers in communities or through diverting young people away from crime and into other activities.) The trick is to show the social and community rather than the sporting benefits of the project. This chapter will concentrate on that.

What kind of grants do trusts give?

Cash
Most trusts simply make cash donations. These vary in size depending on the annual income of the trust. However, most major national trust grants will be in the £500 to £5,000 range, although some give up to £1 million. Small local trusts may give as little as £10, especially where the trustees have decided to give a little to a lot, rather than large amounts to a few applicants.

Short-term/start-up help
Most grants are given for one to three years. Trusts do not see their role as paying for core services for a long period of time; rather, they like to kick start new

and exciting projects into life and then expect someone else to take on the long-term funding. Once you have come to the end of your trust grant, it will rarely give more money for the same thing. However, you can go back for funding for a different project. Therefore, unless you are new or very small, do not ask trusts to support your organisation as a whole, rather ask them to support a particular piece of work or meet a well defined need. (See chapter 3 for more information on Fundraising for projects.)

Revenue and capital

Trusts will give grants both for revenue (salaries, rent, rates etc.) and for capital (e.g. building and equipment costs). If you are applying for revenue costs, try to show how the project will be self-funding once the trust money runs out. If it is for a capital project, show how the facility will be used and how the running costs will be met.

Innovation/difference

One of the most important parts of any application to a grant-making trust is where you show what is new about your project. What makes it stand out from the crowd? Is it a brand new project? Are you moving into a new area? Are you reaching a new group (e.g. young people at risk, elderly people)? Are you using new ways to solve old problems (e.g. mini-sports leagues for school refusers as part of their reintroduction to education)? Are you giving disadvantaged people new skills (e.g. setting up basketball leagues for unemployed people to give them coaching and refereeing qualifications and training them to organise and run the league themselves)? Are you breaking down barriers in communities in new ways (e.g. organising family sports days to bring divided communities together)?

Not statutory

Grant-making trusts will not fund things that they see as the responsibility of the state (i.e. that central or local government should be funding). Trusts will not automatically step in where the state is cutting back and funding is drying up. Trust funding is certainly not a substitute for lost local authority or sports council funding.

How are trusts run?

Trustees

The key players in the trust game are the trustees. They are generally unpaid, responsible for running the trust and, crucially, making the grant decisions. They meet every month, every three months, once a year or whenever there are enough applications to make it worthwhile – it depends on the trust.

Staff

Most of the larger trusts have paid staff to administer the trust. They may have a full or part-time Secretary, Clerk or Director (the name varies). These people are not trustees, so they do not make grant decisions. However, they receive all correspondence, may visit applicants or request more information and make recommendations to trustees about whether a project is worth supporting or not. Bear in mind, though, that the trustees always have the final say on what is and is not supported.

Policies

Most larger trusts will have grant-making policies. These will say:

- what general areas of activity they support (e.g. environmental charities, projects for ethnic minorities);
- the geographical area they support (e.g. throughout the UK, only on Merseyside, or wherever);
- what kinds of grants they like to give (capital or revenue);
- and what they will definitely not support.

Trusts with such policies almost never give grants outside their stated policy. If you do not fit the criteria, do not apply. A large number of trusts do not have defined priorities and give grants according to their general charitable objects (that is, one or more of the following: relief of poverty, sickness or distress, advancement of religion, advancement of education or other purposes beneficial to the community in a way recognised as charitable).

Written applications

Most trusts receive written applications. On the basis of these applications they decide who they will give a grant to and for how much. Some trusts, however, do not consider any applications at all, rather they go out and find the projects they want to support. There is nothing wrong with this. However, when a trust states that it does not respond to applications or that it only supports projects known to the trustees, unless you have a personal contact with one of the trustees, leave the trust alone.

Most grant-making trusts are swamped with applications. They could easily give their money two or three times over on the basis of applications they already receive. This does not mean that you should not apply, but rather that you will have to put time and effort into making a good application to an appropriate trust. So you need to know who to apply to and how to make your approach. Research is essential.

Who do we apply to and how do we do it?

The crucial question in deciding whether or not to apply to a trust is: 'What do we and the trust have in common?' What you want to do must coincide with what the trust is looking to fund. This may be in terms of geography, where you and a local trust operate in the same area. There may be a particular target group (e.g. young people, older people, those with disabilities, or disadvantaged people) who you want to involve in your activity and the trust wants to help. The sport itself may be an area where the foundation has a track record of involvement, although this is much less common. As in most fundraising, the motto with charitable trusts might be: 'Only connect.'

With this is mind, you should consider the following:

- **Read** chapter 4 on Preparing and writing a good fundraising application. The six essential elements of an application are all highly relevant when approaching trusts. It helps to be clear about all the information you need to put in before you start your serious planning.
- **Look hard** at the work you do. Read chapter 3 on Fundraising for projects. Funders like to see individual projects that they can support. It is much easier for them to decide on where their money will be going and what good it will do. Can you devise one of a series of projects or activities that you need money for? Unless you are very new or very small, the trust is unlikely to support your entire organisation. It is far more likely that they will want to support a particular – and finite – piece of work that fits in with their specific interests. You will need to show them how this project is a part of what they are interested in supporting.
- **Define** what is new or innovative about your activity or project. Trusts are not interested in picking up the tab to meet existing costs: they want to see something new about a project. Does it reach people who are not participating in sport elsewhere? Does it try to solve a long-standing problem in a new and pioneering way? Is it developing a new service or activity or promoting a good use of resources in a town or village? If there is nothing new about the project, your chances of raising money from trusts are slim.
- **Plan** for the future and decide how the project can be funded in the long term. Trusts generally only give grants for up to three years, but they like to see that an organisation is well managed and there is a long-term future for their investment. You will need to persuade them that you can pay for and run the work once their grant has been spent.
- **Maximise** the impact of your personal contacts. Ask around your organisation, your management committee, staff, members, members' families, supporters, anyone! Does anyone know any charity trustee or trust administrator personally? If so, get them to make contact with the trust and see how the land lies. Personal applications are always the best.
- **Look through** the guide books. There are various trust guide books (see box on page 218) which can help you target your applications. These can also be inspiring where there are examples of work that have been funded. It may be that you are running an activity that is better than something which is currently funded, or you may have an approach that is more imaginative.
- **Get hold** of guidelines published by the trusts themselves. Read them carefully and address the points they raise in your application. For example, if the guidelines ask how the project will be evaluated, you need to give

them a clear idea. Go with the grain rather than against it. In many cases trusts will be supporting sport as a low priority amongst many others. Bear this in mind when making your case, and show the added benefits that come from supporting your sports project. Grants may be small and one-off, so tailor your approach and expectations accordingly. If the trust prefers to give support for equipment or an event, apply for that, rather than for a salary.

- **Contact** the trust by telephone if there are paid administrators. Discuss your application before you write formally (e.g. is your project eligible, do you have to be a registered charity, when would it be considered, do you need to fill out an application form?). Most of the larger trusts are prepared to have a preliminary chat over the phone. However, if you get the impression that they do not want to talk, do not push it.

- **Write** to the trusts you have identified. The letter should be not more than two sides of A4. In this letter you should state clearly:

- Who you are
- What you do
- Why it is important
- What you need
- What it will achieve
- Where you will get the money from.

You should also send a budget for the particular project, a set of accounts for the organisation as a whole, an annual report and maybe one or two other documents to support your application. See chapter 4 on Preparing and writing a good fundraising application for more information on putting a letter together.

The above is the most basic strategy. The following should help you stand out from the crowd.

- Build contacts. You will probably be able to identify 10 or 15 key trusts who you have a good chance of getting support from, maybe now or maybe in the future. If you can, warm them up by sending some information before you actually write to them for money. This could be through your annual report, some press coverage or a newsletter. The main purposes are: (a) to show yourselves in a positive light; (b) to try and get your name known before you write for money; and (c) to show that you are committed to a longer-term relationship with the trust. Many trusts complain that the only time they hear from people is when they want money. They actually like to know how things are going.

Avoid the scatter-gun approach

Too many organisations try to write to too many trusts. It is much more effective to write a carefully targeted letter to about 15 trusts than it is to write a 'Dear Sir/Madam' circular letter to 150. Circular letters are almost never read.

Some dos and don'ts when writing to trusts

Do
- Plan a strategy
- Plan ahead
- Select a good project
- Believe in what you are doing
- Select targeted trusts
- Write an application tailored to the needs of the trust you are approaching
- Use personal contacts
- Prepare a realistic and accurate budget for the project
- Be concise
- Be specific
- Establish your credibility
- Keep records of everything you do
- Send reports and keep trusts informed
- Try to develop a partnership or long-term relationship
- Say thank you

Don't
- Send a duplicated mail shot
- Ask for unrealistic amounts
- Assume trusts will immediately understand the work you are doing or the need you are meeting
- Make general appeals for running costs
- Use jargon
- Beg

- The information does not need to be fat and glossy. Most trusts are run by busy people with little time to wade through long project descriptions. A letter saying: 'In May, 1994, you supported us with ..., and we are now able to report that ...' is all you need. Remember, this is not an appeal letter; you are not asking for money. Be brief, upbeat and informative. Practice writing your update on a postcard to keep the length down. Send the trust this kind of information once or twice a year. If you do not know trust people personally, this is the next best thing. Sports organisations will need to stress the community aspects of their work rather than only the sporting ones when writing to general non-sports specific trusts. Show what strides you have made in working with young people, older people, those with disabilities, excluded groups or how you have helped the regeneration of an area of interest to the trust.
- If the project is new or unknown to the trust, ask well-known sponsors or supporters to say how effective the project is and how much it is needed.

This helps create a bridge between you and the trust. Remember too, that whilst you may know everything there is to know about your project, organisation and your sport, trust administrators and trustees may know nothing about it at all. Do not assume too much knowledge about your activities and how these help the community.

■ Offer to visit the trust to explain your work, or better still try to get them to come and see you. Put them on your VIP list for any events you may be running. They probably will not come, but they might. If they do, you will be on your way to securing a grant so long as you take time to show them round, introduce the kind of people they want to meet and generally enthuse them about what you are doing.

■ When you are successful in receiving a grant, remember this is the beginning of the relationship, not the end. Remember to say thank you for the grant. Keep the trustees informed about how things are going (they will probably ask for information anyway). Always try to be positive and upbeat. If you get one grant and spend it well, you have a good chance of getting another grant for something different later on.

Where to get information

The main sources of information are those produced by trusts themselves. (Only the largest publish reports or guidelines for applicants.) There are also a number of published grants directories, which include:

A Guide to the Major Trusts Volumes 1 & 2 1999/2000, published by the Directory of Social Change: detailed information on the top 1,000 trusts

Guides to the Local Trusts 1999 (London, North, Midlands, South) published by the Directory of Social Change: detailed information on local trusts in England

The Scottish Trusts Guide 1996 published by the Directory of Social Change: detailed information on 350 trusts in Scotland

The Directory of Grant-Making Trusts, published by the Charities Aid Foundation: brief information on about 2,500 trusts

Other local guides may be available from your local council for voluntary service. Ring the National Association of Councils for Voluntary Service (0114-278 6636) for the address of your nearest one.

For further information, ring the Directory of Social Change (0171-209 5151) or the Charities Aid Foundation (01732-520 000).

Keep records

You will need to keep a check on who you wrote to and what for. You also need to keep records of who did and did not fund you. You should keep a record of at least the following:

- Name of trust
- Do we have any personal contacts with this trust? If so, who?
- Do we send them regular information? If so, what and when?
- Have we applied to them before? If so, what happened?
- What are we currently applying to them for?
- When did we write?
- Who wrote the letter?
- What happened?

Remember, the ideal letter starts something like: 'In May 1996 you kindly supported us with £5,000 for our multi-purpose all weather pitch. I'm delighted to say that this is now fully used by over 300 young people a week. We are now writing with a new project which ...' However, this can only be done if records are kept.

Do we need to be a charity to get money from trusts?

Not necessarily, but it helps. Most charitable trusts state that as a matter of policy they will only give to registered charities. By law they can only give for charitable activities. Therefore:

- If you are a registered charity, fine. Apply in your own name and the cheque will be paid to you.
- If you are not registered, you will need to do two things: (a) show that the project you are proposing is charitable in law, and (b) find a registered charity to receive the donation on your behalf. This means that when you apply for funds you ask that the cheque is paid to registered charity, Anytown Charitable Trust, who will then write a cheque to you for the same amount. This is clumsier than being a charity yourself, but it works.

Local councils for voluntary service are often happy to receive cheques on behalf of groups in their area. Councils for voluntary service (CVS) are charities which are set up to support and advise voluntary groups in their town or city. You should get to know your local CVS in any case – they can be useful sources of information and advice. Ring the National Association of Councils for Voluntary Service (0114-278 6636) for the address of your local CVS.

For further information on the pros and cons of registration as a charity see chapter 17 on Sport and charitable status.

Raising money from local trusts

Most trust grants for sporting activity are given by general purpose local trusts (i.e. trusts who can give to a wide range of activities but only in a certain geographical area). Therefore, when compiling a list of trusts to write to, see if there are any trusts active in your area and find out their policies. It stands to reason that these can only give within a certain area and therefore to a limited number of organisations. They may therefore receive fewer applications than the more well-known national trusts. However, unfortunately not all areas have local trusts. If your area does not, you will have to apply to trusts which can give throughout the UK.

Much local giving is done on a contact basis where trustees give to projects they know and like. Sometimes they give to the same organisations year in year out. If so, try to work your way onto their list. You should make a real effort to get to know local trustees personally. At least, you should send them regular information.

Community Foundations

These are local foundations that have been set up to cover a specific geographical region or town (e.g. Cleveland, Tyne and Wear, Birmingham Airport, Bristol). Like other local trusts, they can only give in these areas. The foundations work to attract charitable resources to an area and to channel these to local causes. Some are proactive in their giving and look for specific concerns to give money to. Others respond to applications as they are received.

Sports organisations need to keep informed about developments in their area and where new trusts are being formed to think about applying. Local sports clubs are often supported, particularly where there is clear community benefit or the project fits in with an interest area such as youth or disability. Previously, Cleveland Community Foundation as part of a youth development programme supported the costs of a seven foot American basketball player to coach young people in the region.

The Association of Community Trusts and Foundations (ACTAF) is not a grant giving body, but will be able to give contact information for any community trusts and foundations active in your area. Contact: 4 Bloomsbury Square, London WC1A 2RL (0171-831 0033).

A local charity and its giving to sport

This charity gave £965,000 in grants to over 60 groups and organisations; a substantial amount for a local trust. This trust gives grants to organisations within its geographical area of benefit which is a part of the West Midlands. The trust supports a range of local causes including churches, old people's clubs, schools, residents' associations, theatres and young people's organisations, as well as local sports clubs.

Sports grants given in 1996/97

Cricket club – £2,000 for fencing
Cricket club – £19,300 for artificial wicket and equipment
Recreational trust – £2,000 for floodlighting
Rugby Football Club – £13,500 for a junior section for mini-rugby pitch and
   equipment
Special Olympics – £1,000 for athletes' expenses
Squash club – £12,000 for replastering and replacement of floor
Tennis club – £2,500 for fencing
Tennis club – £20,000 to improve courts and changing facilities

Airport Trusts

A number of international airports have established foundations to support their local communities. This makes good business sense to invest in the local neighbourhood where there is disturbance from aircraft noise. Birmingham International Community Trust for instance was established in 1998 and its area of benefit is defined as those areas affected by the airport's operations. The airport contributes £50,000 each year to the trust which is then supplemented by fines imposed on airlines which exceed the night noise violation level. The fund has now been increased to £160,000 by this mechanism. One of the trust's four areas for contribution is: 'Bringing the community closer together through facilities for sport, recreation and other leisure time activities.' Manchester Airport Trust Fund is also new and has recently given grants to Moss Side Boxing and Athletic Association (£1,500) and Prestbury Bowling Club (£4,000).

National trusts

You may want to cast your net wider than local trusts. National trusts usually have more money but are the most heavily applied to. They also tend to be narrower in their focus, and many of the larger trusts have articulated priorities for their grant-giving. Circular letters to them almost always fail; carefully targeted applications to relevant trusts have a much greater chance of success.

Your appeal to the trust must show how your project fits in with one or more of the trust's interests. You may be offering activities under one or more of the following:

- Young people
- Older people (50+)
- People with disabilities
- Education
- Community facilities
- Disadvantaged people
- People at risk from e.g. crime, drugs

National trusts can be particularly sceptical about applications from sports organisations. Some are explicit in their non-support for sport. You will need to stress that you are not writing about sport, rather about women's welfare, drug prevention, young outreach, school refusal or whatever.

Examples of grants paid by large trusts

The following trusts are detailed in the *Guide to the Major Trusts Volumes 1 and 2*. Some are national, others are large local foundations. The overwhelming majority of the following trusts do not give sport any kind of priority. However, they still gave the following grants:

Athletics   NBC Sixfields Athletics Club (£100,000 for new clubhouse and track, Horner Foundation)

Aviation   Guild of Pilots (£40,000, Air Charities Trust)

Basketball Llanderlyn Community Development Association (up to £1,000 for a young people's basketball project, Noel Buxton Trust)

Boxing   Merthyr Tydfil Boxing Club (£2,000, the Former Mid Glamorgan Welsh Church Act Fund)

Coaching and sports education London Coaching Foundation (£6,000, Sir John Cass's Foundation)
Boy's Brigade (£2,000 for sports education, Sir John Cass's Foundation)
Bedford schools (£25,000 for coaching for young people, Harpur Trust)
City of Westminster Sports Scholarship Scheme (£6,000 for running costs, John Lyon's Charity)

Canoeing Wye Bother Canoe Club (Up to £1,000, Girling (Cwmbran) Trust)

Cricket   Surrey County Cricket Club (£2,000, Sir John Cass's Foundation)
Muckamore Cricket and Lawn Tennis Club (£1,500)
Sussex Young Cricketers Educational Trust (Friarsgate Trust)
Tiverton Heathcoat Cricket Club (up to £1,000, Heathcoat Trust)
English Schools Cricket Association (Hobson Charity Ltd)
Scottish Cricket Union (£8,000, Stanley Morrison Charitable Trust)
Hallam Cricket Club (£5,000, Sheffield Town Trust)

Cycling   Cyclists Touring Club (£10,000, Rees Jeffreys Road Fund)

Disability Kirklees and Calderdale Wheelchair Basketball Club (up to £500 for equipment, Percy Bilton Charity Ltd)
British Sports Association for Disabled (£20,000, Sir John Cass's Foundation)
Handicapped Anglers Trust (£3,700, Draper's Charitable Fund)
British Wheelchair Sports Foundation (£5,000, Lord Leverhulme's Charitable Trust)

Mark Lees Foundation (£20,00 for rowing facilities for young people with disabilities, Rufford Foundation)

British Disabled Water Ski Association (£8,000, Jill Kreitman Foundation)

Cricket Federation for People with Disability (£1,000, MJC Stone Charitable Trust)

Equestrian Various (£56,000, Saddlers' Company Charitable Fund)
Jockey Club Charitable Trust (Macdonald–Buchanan Charitable Trust)

Football Moulton Football Club (£5,000, Horne Foundation)
Dailly Football Club (over £1,000, Blair Foundation)
Oxford City Football Club Trust (up to £1,000, DLM Charitable Trust)
Colchester United Football in the Community (over £1,000, Divert Trust)
Save the Family Footy Project (over £1,000, Divert Trust)
Ten football projects (£42,000, Divert Trust)

Golf Moseley Golf Club (£500, Lillie Johnson Charitable Trust)
Golf Fanatics International (£800, Talteg Ltd)
Golf Foundation (over £1,000, A&R Woolf Charitable Trust)

Hockey National Hockey Foundation (£37,600, Kirby Laing Foundation)

Gymnastics Brunswick Boys Club Trust (£2,000 for refurbishment of gym floor, John Lyon's Charity)

Lacrosse IFWLA Word Cup Lacrosse (£3,000, Stanley Morrison Charitable Trust)
Scottish Lacrosse Association (£5,000, Scottish Lacrosse Association)

Martial Arts Samurai Judo Club (up to £500 for equipment, Percy Bilton Charity Ltd.)
Age Concern, Northumberland (£600 for tuition of older people in Japanese martial arts, Great Britain Sasakawa Foundation)

Rowing Oxford University Boat Club (£24,000, Palgrave Brown Foundation)

Rugby Wavell Wakefield Trust (£60,000 to youth training scheme, Save & Prosper Educational Trust)
Randalstown Rugby and Hockey Club (£1,500, Enkalon Foundation)

Sailing Ocean Youth Club (£20,000 for round the world voyage for young people, Dulverton Trust)

Rona Trust (£51,000 for sailing activities for young people, Viscount Amory's Charitable Trust)

Christian Sailing Centre (£9,000, Maurice Laing Foundation)

Jubilee Sailing Trust (£10,000, John Coates Charitable Trust)

UK Sailing Academy (£158,00, Lister Charitable Trust)

St Mawes Sailing Club (£250, Vec Acorn Trust)

Shooting Dorchester Rifle and Pistol Club (£1,000, Duke of Cornwall's Benevolent Fund)

Skiing British Ski Federation Trust (Up to £1,000, Northumberland Village Homes Trust)

Sports clubs Mickleover Sports Club (up to £1,000, 10th Duke of Devonshire's Charitable Trust)

Hythe and Dibden Sports Club (£5,000, Dibden Allotments Charity)

Wallingford Sports Trust (£20,000, Christopher Laing Foundation)

Tongue and Farr Sports Association (£2,500, MJC Stone Charitable Trust)

Shipston Sports Club (£1,000, Stella Symons Charitable Trust)

Swimming Solent Dolphins (£25,000, Dibden Allotments Charity)

Tennis Lawn Tennis Association Trust (£1,800, Mrs LD Rope Third Charitable Settlement)

General sports facilities Perth Leisure Pool (£514,000 for improvements, Gannochy Trust)

Hendon Youth Sports Centre (£200,000, Milly Apthorp Charitable Trust)

Hampton Pool (£70,000, Hampton Fuel Allotment Charity)

National Playing Fields Association (£10,000, Dulverton Trust)

East Anglian Sports Park (£50,000, Norwich Town Close Estate Charity)

Festival of Sport (£2,000 for Richmond event, Richmond Parish Lands Charity)

Birmingham City Council Department of Leisure and Community Services (£26,400 for a sports wall, Sutton Coldfield Municipal Charities)

Refurbishment of sports and education centre in Brent (Sir Jules Thorn Charitable Trust)

These are general trusts whose main interests will be in areas other than sport. A large number can only give in a certain geographical area. Do not use this list for indiscriminate mailing to trusts. Read the full details of these trusts and their policies from their own guidelines and the entries in *A Guide to the Major Trusts, Volumes 1 & 2*, available from the Directory of Social Change.

Sports specific trusts

The following 28 trusts give to sport. Some give to a range of sports and facilities, others give to one particular sport. Two give only in a particular geographical area, whilst the majority give throughout the country. Some only give to individuals and those competing at a high level. Some do not support individuals at all, but only give to organisations. A number are the charitable arm of the sport's governing body and work closely with the parent organisation.

Archery

The Worshipful Company of Fletchers' Trust

Contact: John Owen-Ward, Clerk to the Company, 11 Aldermans Hill, London N13 4YD (0181-882 3055; Fax: 0181-882 5851)
Beneficial area: UK
Grant total: £9,000 in 1996/97
Policy: One of this livery company's charitable aims is the relief of poverty among those who are involved in making arrows. This call on the company's funds is now negligible and the company's charitable giving is directed towards support for archers who are disabled.

In 1996/97, the company's income totalled £7,900 and almost £9,000 was distributed in grants. The major part of this total (£7,000) was spent in grants to disabled archers with a further grant of £600 towards the costs of an annual competition. Grants are usually for amounts up to £500 for initial, and sometimes replacement, equipment.

Exclusions: The company only gives grants for equipment.
Applications: In writing to: The Hon Almoner, The Worshipful Company of Fletchers c/o GNAS, 7th Street National Agricultural Centre, Stoneleigh, Kenilworth, Warwickshire CV8 2LG.

Athletics

Athletics for the Young

Contact: Geoff Clarke, Honorary Treasurer, 'Dunrunin', 9 Whitehouse Avenue, Great Preston, Woodlesford, Leeds LS26 8BN (0113-286 2590; Fax: 0113-286 2590)
Beneficial area: England
Grant total: £101,000 in 1997
Policy: The trust is funded by the Amateur Athletics Association of England and works closely with the three English Regional Associations. Support is given through these regional bodies to develop young athletes in county teams, Sportshall Athletics and coaching squads.

In 1997, the trust's income was £91,000 (including a grant of £50,000 from the AAAoE). Grants totalled £101,000. Support included: grants to North of England AA (£20,000); South of England AA (£15,000); Midland Counties

225

AA (£15,000); almost £49,000 for the Five Star Awards and Standards; and £2,500 towards the costs of a county development officer.

Exclusions: The trust is confined to developing young athletes up to the age of 23. There is no financial limit imposed.

Applications: Applications should be made through the appropriate regional body.

The British Athletics Foundation

Contact: Mr A Farrell, Secretary, 30a Harborne Road, Edgbaston, Birmingham (0121-456 5098; Fax: 0121-456 4998)

Beneficial area: Great Britain

Grant total: £64,500 in 1997

Policy: The foundation aims to provide and help with facilities and resources to support young people under 25 years of age to enjoy and be trained in athletic pursuits.

In 1997, the foundation's income available for distribution totalled £112,300. £64,500 was directed towards regional athletics associations and to local councils to support regional development officers, competitions and other events. Remaining funds were used to employ development officers and to coordinate development initiatives throughout the UK.

Applications: Applications are made by affiliated regions, national associations and clubs, in writing to the correspondent. The trustees usually meet quarterly to consider applications.

The Ron Pickering Memorial Fund

Contact: Mrs Jean Pickering, 11 Wendover Drive, Welwyn, Hertfordshire AL6 9LT (01438-715814; Fax: 01438-714250)

Beneficial area: UK

Grant total: £35,000–£40,000

Policy: The fund was established in 1991 in memory of Ron Pickering and his substantial contribution to sport. The fund helps young aspiring athletes to reach their potential. They must be between the ages of 15 and 23 and still be in some form of education. Up to this year, over £250,000 has been distributed to more than 600 individual athletes.

The fund relies on donations and income fluctuates accordingly. The main source of income is sponsorship raised by a team in the London Marathon. All the money raised is given in grants the following year. The annual grant allocation is around £30,000. Grants range between £100 and £300. In recent years a further £6,000 has been given towards providing Sports Hall Athletics equipment for children to be introduced to athletics.

Exclusions: Applicants receiving major sponsorship from other sources will not be supported.

Applications: In writing to the correspondent.

Canoeing

The Jubilee Canoeing Foundation

Contact: Paul Owen, John Dudderidge House, Adbolton Lane, West Bridgford, Nottingham NG2 5AS (0115-982 1100; Fax: 0115-983 1797)

Beneficial area: UK

Grant total: £5,600 in 1997/98

Policy: The foundation incorporates the James Turner Legacy Fund and supports youth canoeing and canoeing for disabled people.

The foundation prefers to support a larger number of projects by giving smaller awards of between £200 and £500.

Projects for young people

Support is given for:

a) Equipment and facilities which help young people to participate and develop in the sport. 'We like to see a large number of people helped by the little money we can make available and therefore we do not generally support the purchase of equipment for an individual.'

b) Canoeing expeditions and activities which involve young people. There is a clear preference for those projects which show that young people have been involved in the planning and organising as well as taking part.

Credit must be given to the foundation where a grant has been awarded, and a report of the activity must be submitted within three months of completion before a grant can be released.

Projects for disabled people

Support is given for:

a) Specialist equipment and facilities to help people with disabilities to participate and develop in the sport. The same conditions about individuals' equipment apply as above.

b) Training for leaders 'to encourage appropriate sensitive leadership and good practice. For example, we often fund members to attend a BCU Endorsement Course in canoeing with Disabled People.'

c) Canoeing expeditions and activities which involve people with disabilities. The same conditions apply as outlined above.

Applications: On an application form available from the British Canoe Union at the above address. The trustees meet in June and December to consider applications. Applications must be received by the end of April or the end of October. When successful, 'the grant will not normally be released until the applicant provides proof of having spent the grant as agreed.' Successful applicants are given up to 18 months to claim their award.

Cricket

The Cricket Foundation

Contact: Terry Bates, Secretary to Trustees, c/o ECB, Lord's Cricket Ground, London NW8 8QZ (0171-432 1200; Fax: 0171-289 5619)
Beneficial area: British Isles
Grant total: £2.5 million in 1998/99
Policy: The foundation received a total of £10 million from the English Cricket Board to be spent over a four year period, 1996–2000. Grants have been given to a number of priority areas to develop every level of the game.

Coaching and development

County cricket boards were required to draw up county development plans to submit to the foundation for strategic investment. Pitch improvement, equipment, scoring and umpiring training, strengthening of club junior sections, teacher support, increased access to women and those with disabilities have all been supported within the plans.

No grants were given for capital projects, contracted full and part-time coaches, administration, publications, clothing, trophies and under 11 county cricket. In 1998/99, awards to the county cricket boards totalled £2.5 million, the lion's share of the foundation's income.

To further support the county development of the game, the foundation has established a network of eight regional cricket development officers. Each RCDO has a discretionary fund of £4,000 to support modest applications within their region. Awards are up to a maximum of £350 and are given for costs such as repairs to machinery, overhead projectors and specifically adapted balls for blind cricketers.

The foundation is also committed to Durham University's Cricket Centre of Excellence, with an annual grant of £45,000 for three years.

Kwik Cricket

The foundation works closely with other funders, particularly the Lord's Taverners (see below), to distribute kits as widely as possible. In 1997/98, the foundation contributed £20,000 to make the kits available at half price (£25 each).

Non-turf pitches

The foundation works in partnership with the National Lottery Sports Fund and individual clubs and schools to provide non-turf pitches. The foundation's contribution is £88,000 per 50 pitches. (The National Lottery Sports Fund contributes £137,000, with club/school contributions totalling £25,000 in 1996/97, or £500 per club/school. Clubs and schools can apply individually to the ECB for Lord's Taverners funding for a non-turf pitch where a maximum grant of £1,000 per pitch can be given.)
Applications: Through County Cricket Boards.

Brian Johnston Memorial Trust

Contact: Chris Atkinson, Chief Executive, 71 Baker Street, London W1M 1AH (0171-224 1005; Fax: 0171-224 0431)
Beneficial area: UK
Grant total: £8,500 in 1997
Policy: This trust was founded in 1995 to commemorate the cricket commentator, Brian Johnston by providing recreational facilities for cricket. The trust supports the promotion of cricket in schools and clubs' youth sections; helps talented young cricketers and provides sporting opportunities for those with disabilities, particularly for blind cricketers.

The trust depends upon subscriptions and fundraising for its income. In 1997, income totalled £207,000 and grants totalled £8,500. Awards are given to schools and clubs promoting cricket in their communities. Capital projects are normally excluded.

In 1997, grants ranging between £100 and £500 were given to 18 schools throughout the country. Four cricket clubs received grants of between £300 and £1,000. £2,500 was given to British Blind Sport. Some support is ongoing over three years.

The trust also awards scholarships to young talented cricketers between the ages of 11 and 19 who are in financial need. Help is given towards equipment, travel and coaching costs. In 1997, 10 scholarships ranging between £500 and £750 were awarded.

Exclusions: Large scale capital projects and overseas tours are not supported.
Applications: On an application form available from the correspondent. Trustees meet in March and September to consider applications.

The Lord's Taverners Limited

Contact: Patrick Shevington, Director, 22 Queen Anne's Gate, London SW1H 9AA (0171-222 0707)
Beneficial area: UK
Grant total: £1.36 million in 1997
Policy: The Lord's Taverners Limited's charitable mission is 'To give young people, particularly those with special needs, a sporting chance'. It is well known for its fundraising work to support cricket, sport for young people with disabilities and to supply minibuses.

In 1997, the foundation distributed £1.36 million in grants. These awards were allocated in the following proportions: 50% to cricket (£519,600); 40% for minibuses (£521,900); 10% towards sport for young people with disabilities (£79,600).

Cricket

The foundation works hand in glove with the Cricket Foundation (see above) which received the main grant of £274,000. This income is then disbursed to individual projects and organisations. In 1997, around 900 grants were given

229

for 38 coaching and competition projects; distribution of 800 red (juniors under 13) and blue (for those between 13 and 16) bags of equipment to schools and youth sections of cricket clubs; and the installation of 38 non-turf pitches. Grants are given up to a maximum of £1,000 for a non-turf pitch, £500 for a non-turf practice 'end' and £300 for netting. Priority is given to projects where there are working links between a club and school(s), or where good links would be established by installing a pitch.

The English Schools Cricket Association is an annual beneficiary and received £95,000. A further £103,600 was given in direct cricket grants to the Arundel Castle Cricket Foundation, the London Playing Fields Association (Peter May Memorial) and the MCC Indoor School.

The foundation is a major supporter of Kwik Cricket and in 1997, £20,000 was allocated to supplying around 500 kits to primary schools and youth organisations.

Other sports

The National Playing Fields Association has been a regular beneficiary of the foundation, and received an annual grant of £25,000 for its programme of building multigames walls.

Sport for young people with disabilities

The foundation received over 1,000 applications and awarded 33 grants totalling almost £99,500. Beneficiaries included hydrotherapy pools, sailing and canoeing equipment, gymnastic equipment, sports wheelchairs and specialised play equipment. Further information is not available about individual grant amounts.

Exclusions: No grants to individuals. Under the youth cricket programme, the following would not receive support: building or renovation of pavilions; site screens; bowling machines; mowers/rollers; overseas tours.

Applications: Applications for cricket grants are handled by the National Cricket Association, and clubs must be affiliated at the county cricket level. Schools, clubs and youth organisations can apply individually for Lord's Taverners funding for non-turf pitches. Application forms for projects covering sport for young people with disabilities are available from the foundation.

Disability sports

The British Paralympic Trust

Contact: J Swan, Secretary, Impact House, 2 Edridge Road, Croydon, Surrey CR9 1PJ

Beneficial area: UK

Grant total: £25,800 in 1997/98

Policy: This trust was formed in 1990 to manage a government grant of £500,000 to promote sport for the disabled. Income comes from interest earned on the investment and fluctuates from year to year.

In 1996/97, income was £32,000 and grants totalled £25,800. No grants list is attached, so further details about beneficiaries and the size and purpose of individual grants are not available. The trustees give some very general outlines concerning the trust's activities in saying that grants committed by the trusts are to 'groups and individuals promoting a wide spectrum of sport for the disabled'. The trust received 28 applications, of which 22 were supported with a grant. The grant total is distributed across three impairment sectors: physical (£16,800); sensory (£6,200); and learning disability (£2,800).

Applications: In writing to the correspondent.

See also entry for The Lord's Taverners Limited in the Cricket section above, for other grants for disability sports.

Football

The Football Association National Sports Centre Trust

Contact: Mike Appleby, 9 Wyllyotts Place, Potters Bar, Herts EN6 2JD (01707-651840; Fax: 01707-644190)

Beneficial area: National

Grant total: £631,000 in 1997

Policy: The trust is chiefly concerned with 'preserving and protecting the physical and mental health of the community, and providing recreation and leisure facilities for public use in the interests of social welfare.' It administers two grants schemes: The Hard Surface Play Scheme and The Football Association Grant Aid Scheme.

In 1997, the trust's income totalled £1.94 million. This was made up of £113,000 from investments; £1.17 million from the Football Association and a further £75,000 in a regular donation from the receipts of the FA Charity Shield pre-season match. Around half the grant total of £631,000 was given for Hard Surface Play Areas. Under this scheme grants totalling £320,000 were given to clubs, schools and community centres to provide play areas for community use.

(a) Hard Surface Play Scheme

This scheme aims to provide small floodlit multi-sports areas to be used by football clubs and other organisations in the local community where football is a major user group. As well as the playing surface, help is also given towards the cost of fencing and floodlighting on full-sized synthetic surfaces. Help can also be given for indoor facilities.

The minimum recommended size for a small sided area is 36m x 23m surface in tarmacadam, rubber crumb or artificial grass. The facilities must be fully enclosed and must include floodlighting so that the area is used to the full during the winter months; fencing should also be included. It should be made available as widely as possible to other sports and community groups.

Grants will be up to a maximum of £25,000 and must be matched on a £ for £ basis by funding from other sources such as the funders listed in this Guide or from funds raised internally.

Applications will be considered from affiliated football clubs and from

231

organisations where football is a major user group. Application forms are available from the above address.

As the scheme is very popular, there is a backlog of applications and it will take around six to eight months for a decision on the application to be made. However, in certain cases applications for grants of less than £5,000 can be considered earlier.

(b) The Football Association Grant Aid Scheme

This scheme was launched with the Football Trust (see below) to give grants of up to £5,000 to grass-roots football clubs and other organisations where football is a major user group. These grants are designed to help with the development and/or improvement of facilities. This would include assistance with improvements to fencing, floodlighting, pitch levelling/drainage and changing facilities. Grants given under the scheme must be matched on a £ for £ basis by funds from other sources. In 1997, grants totalled £311,000.

An application form is available from the National Sports Centre Trust at the address above. Applications will only be considered from clubs which are affiliated to a County Football Association, or from organisations whose membership includes a club affiliated to a County Football Association, which will be asked to complete a section of the form in support of the application. The club/organisation should have been in existence for at least three years. Grants will not be given for work that has already been completed.

The Football Association Youth Trust

Contact: Mike Appleby, Secretary to the Trustees, 9 Wyllyotts Place, Potters Bar, Herts EN6 2JD (01707-651840; Fax: 01707-644190)
Beneficial area: UK
Grant total: £290,000 in 1997/98
Policy: The trust supports schools and universities in their development of football. Those benefiting from the trust must be under 21, unless they are in full-time education. Grants are given to organisations throughout the United Kingdom to help with equipment and training facilities.

As well as income from investments, the trust receives support from the Football Association, and a regular share of the receipts from the pre-season Football Association Charity Shield match. Income has been steadily rising and totalled £1.13 million in 1997/98. The trust awarded £290,000 in grants for the year. Unspent income continues to increase steadily and now totals over £1 million. Beneficiaries are largely school, university and county football associations. Grants range between £1,200 and £100,000. The largest beneficiaries were the University of Wales, Cardiff (£100,000 towards a national schools anti-racism campaign) and the English Schools FA (£84,000). Other awards were: £9,000 to the British University Sports Association; £7,500 to the Independent Schools Football Association and £4,000 each to Cambridge and Oxford University football clubs. All these are regular beneficiaries. A number of grants of less than £2,000 were given to a variety of football associations.

Exclusions: No grants towards the cost of overseas matches, trips or projects. The trust does not support individuals.
Applications: In writing to the correspondent.

The Football Trust 1998

Contact: Peter Lee, Chief Executive, Walkden House, 10 Melton Street, London NW1 2EB (0171-388 4504; Fax: 0171-388 6688)
Beneficial area: UK
Grant total: £52.3 million in 1996/97
Policy: The Football Trust was founded in 1979 by the pools companies, Littlewoods, Vernons and Zetters. Income has been raised through a reduction in the pool betting duty, Spot the Ball, and contributions from the football associations of England, Scotland, Wales. The trust took on the funding of ground improvements following the Taylor Report recommendations made in the shadow of the Hillsborough disaster in 1989.

Since 1990, the trust has distributed over £150 million to clubs in the FA Premier League, the Football League and the Scottish Premier League. This money has helped to fund improvements such as relocation, new stands, and seating and roofing initiatives. In all, the trust's contribution has enabled over £500 million to be invested in projects related to Taylor's recommendations. The Football Trust is to be wound up, but its work will be continued by the new Football Trust 1998. This change is due almost entirely to the emergence of the National Lottery and its impact upon the pools companies' income. Under a new arrangement, the Football Trust 1998 will be funded by the following:

- The FA Premier League will provide £5 million annually over the next three years to be matched by £5 million annually from Sport England to continue the programme of Taylor Report improvements. (The Premier League will also give a further £4 million to support Southampton and Wimbledon.)
- Lottery money of at least £2.5 million will be provided by Sport England annually for the next four years to ensure the trust can continue its support for all levels of the game.
- £10 million will be contributed by the Football Association over the next four years, with the intention of continuing its support into the future.
- The 3% reduction in pool betting duty will continue. This is currently worth around £10 million to the trust each year.
- The Football League have agreed to transfer the administration of their Ground Improvement Levy scheme to the trust.

Support from the Professional Footballers' Association for football in the community schemes and for the development of the game generally will also be routed through the trust.

The following are the current priorities for the trust and it seems likely that these activities will continue as before.

Ground and facility improvements

The major part of the trust's income of £52.3 million in 1996/97 was allocated to ground improvements, including help with four new stadia at Stoke City, Bolton, Derby and Sunderland. 19 clubs benefited with grants ranging from £2.5 million to £6,000.

Grants are available for a range of safety measures, extending community facilities and widening access to families and those with disabilities. As well as league clubs, grants are also available to all Pyramid clubs (which includes those in the Conference, Ismian, Northern Premier and Southern leagues). Grant aid is available for approved and eligible expenditure for safety work subject to appropriate permission. The level of award is at the trustees' discretion. £500,000 was given in total to Pyramid clubs in 1996/97.

The trust supports pitch and changing room upgrades at the grass-roots level. In 1996/97 a total of £500,000 was allocated to improvements, with a further contribution of £1 million from the FA. Grants are up to £5,000 and given on a matching basis to the club. The trust also supports women's football and the development of Hard Surface Play Areas (see entry under Football Association National Sports Centre Trust), and for many years has supported the dual use of educational facilities and charitable playing fields organisations.

Coaching and youth development

The trust has been committed to developing and strengthening young people's participation in the game throughout England, Scotland, Wales and Northern Ireland. Training facilities and youth development programmes have been supported throughout the UK including in 1996/97 the development of women's football in Northern Ireland; £200,000 for coaching in Wales; and £4.25 million for a National Community Development Programme with a further £1.2 million committed to Scotland.

Beneficiaries receiving smaller grants included the Crown and Manor Soccer Academy for a football coaching scheme linked to academic and vocational education (£14,000); the British Deaf Sports Council towards team training and travel costs to compete in the World Summer Games for the Deaf in Copenhagen (£7,600); the Arran Sports Association for a new all-weather pitch as part of the Ormidale Park complex (£100,000) and continued support for anti-racism initiatives including £4,000 towards a research project 'Asians Can't Play Football'. The trust has invested substantially in the Football in the Community Programme with around £5.5 million.

The Chairman's Discretionary Fund which previously gave small grants for equipment and kit for under 18's teams is to be replaced by the **Football Charitable Trust.** This will give grants for training, five-a-side, development, education, and recreation facilities at all levels of the game. In 1996/97, the fund gave over 300 grants of up to £250 and totalling £72,000. Subject to the trustees' discretion these amounts are likely to be similar under the new Football Charitable Trust.

Exclusions: The trust does not give grants to individuals, and does not support running costs.

Applications: An application form is available from the trust. Organisations should include a detailed project description with information on any funding that has already been secured. Applications are considered throughout the year.

The Goaldiggers Charitable Trust

Contact: Jean Wenger, Secretary, 25 Ovington Square, London SW13 1LQ (0171-584 6445; Fax: 0171-581 2402)

Beneficial area: National

Grant total: Not known

Policy: The trust supports the provision of areas for kickabout games and five-a-side football pitches. The Kickabout Scheme, launched in 1995, is the trust's most recent initiative. The last accounts on file at the Charity Commission predate the scheme, so it is not clear how much is available for distribution, or the type of beneficiary.

The trust has given the following information: 'The trust focuses on facilities accessible to communities without restrictions being imposed. Grants are awarded on merit and normally would not exceed £10,000.'

The minimum grant is £500.

Applications: On an application form available from the correspondent. Very full and helpful notes are attached detailing recommended surfaces and fencing.

General sports

The Arsenal Charitable Trust

Contact: Alan Sefton, Community Department, c/o Arsenal Football Club, Arsenal Stadium, Abnell Road, Highbury, London N5 1BU (0171-704 4140)

Beneficial area: National, with a strong preference for the London boroughs of Islington and Hackney.

Grant total: £71,000 in 1995

Policy: The trust's charitable objects include the relief of need of those injured whilst participating in sport, or the dependents of those killed whilst participating in sport; and also the provision of general welfare recreational facilities in Greater London boroughs, principally Islington and Hackney. As no list of grants and beneficiaries is included in the accounts on file there is no further information about the trust's priorities or how it directs its grant-giving.

In 1995, the trust's income, raised largely from donations, totalled £68,000 (compared to £114,000 the previous year). Grants totalled almost £71,000 (£92,000 in 1994). There are no further details concerning beneficiaries, purpose of grants, or typical amounts. Further information would be welcomed.

Applications: In writing to the correspondent.

This entry has not been confirmed by the trust.

The Colson Fellowship Fund

Contact: The Secretary, Central Council of Physical Recreation, Francis House, Francis Street, London SW1P 1DE (0171-828 3163; Fax: 0171-630 8820)

Beneficial area: UK

Grant total: £1,200 in 1997/98

Policy: The Colson Fellowship Fund gives grants to individuals who 'can demonstrate a need and willingness to help themselves; who wish to develop their leadership skills; and who wish to give service to the community, through the medium of sport'. The trustees of the fund are the CCPR.

At 1st April 1997, the fund totalled £77,900, with contributions and interest adding a further £7,100. With over £85,000 available for distribution the grant total of £1,200 for the year is surprisingly modest. In previous years the totals have not been significantly higher: £3,000 in 1996/97; £1,900 in 1995/96 and almost £8,000 in 1994/95. No grants list is attached to the accounts and there are no further details concerning the number and size of grants, type of beneficiaries or purpose of award. There was almost £84,000 available for distribution in 1998/99.

The CCPR states: 'The trust is soon to merge with the British Sports Trust, the charitable arm of the CCPR'. This trust runs the Community Sports Leader scheme which spent £663,700 on the four awards in 1997. Over 35,000 young people benefited. The British Sports Trust accumulated funds totalled £1.5 million in 1997/98. Those looking to apply should watch to see how the Colson Fellowship Fund develops its role under the new arrangement.

Applications: In writing to the correspondent.

The London Marathon Charitable Trust Ltd

Contact: David Golton, Treasurer, 2 The Square, Richmond, Surrey TW9 1DY (0181-940 0102; Fax: 0181-940 5798)

Beneficial area: London

Grant total: £1.33 million in 1997

Policy: The trust was set up in 1981 and has built steadily upon the success of the London Marathon. London Marathon Limited pays over its entire income to the trust. As well as staging the London Marathon, the company also generates income from the management of the Chase Corporate Challenge (on behalf of Chase Bank), held in Battersea in July. The trust gives grants towards sport, recreation and leisure facilities for those living in London. Since 1981, the trust has given an impressive £4.5 million towards such causes. 1997's grant distribution alone totalled £1.33 million.

Much of the trust's income is channelled through the London boroughs, and there was previously a particular interest in those which hosted part of the marathon course. This area of benefit has since been widened and in 1997 a total of 15 London boroughs received amounts ranging from £2,500 (Ealing) to £109,500 (Tower Hamlets). The remaining 13 authorities were: Bromley, Camden, Croydon, Enfield, Greenwich, Hillingdon, Hounslow, Kingston on

Thames, Merton, Newham, Redbridge, Sutton and Wandsworth. Grants approved to the boroughs totalled £598,000 in 1997, a large part of the £1.33 million given in total in the year.

Beneficiaries can include youth groups, schools, tenants' and community associations as well as sports organisations. A number of these were supported under borough applications, although organisations can apply individually.

Support is given for all levels of sporting ability and participation, from the very local and specific (sports equipment to a local group or school for example) to the more general (such as a local authority all-weather, multi-sports play surface). Grants are given for new facilities, or to improve existing buildings or areas. There are a number of exceptions where the trustees do not give grants, which are detailed below.

In 1997, the largest non-borough grants were to the Featherstone High School in Ealing (£88,600 for an artificial turf pitch and hard court multi-play area); London Playing Fields Society (£48,400 for changing rooms at a new sports centre); and the London Coaching Foundation (£37,500 in continuing support for a coaching programme). Other awards included:

£34,000 to Lennox Youth Group for an all-weather pitch;
£33,000 to Brixton Top Cats Basketball Club for four basketball hoops and seating;
£20,000 to Royal Albert Dock Trust for training boats;
£18,000 to Corbets Tey School for a swimming pool;
£10,000 to Ruislip Bowls Club for a pavilion extension and provision of changing facilities;
£8,000 to Eton Manor Cricket Club for two non-turf practice wickets;
£5,800 to Bluebirds Wheelchair Basketball for three sports wheelchairs and computer equipment;
£5,000 to Ealing, Southall & Middlesex Athletic Club for gym equipment;
£5,000 to Northwood (Dulwich) Bowling Club for new lockers and bar;
£600 to Wimbledon & Merton Swimming Club for lane ropes;
£250 to South Lewisham Little League for football nets, flags and trolleys.

The trust's designated fund to be carried forward totals £1.77 million.

Exclusions: No grants to organisations outside London. There is no support for revenue costs such as salaries, property or pitch rental and markings, travelling expenses and small items such as team strip. The trust does not support individuals.

Applications: Through the local authority or in writing to the treasurer.

The RIBA Community Projects Fund
Contact: Joan Watson, RIBA Community Projects Fund, PO Box 640, Newcastle-upon-Tyne NE99 1QY (0191-232 9292)
Policy: The Community Architecture Group of the Royal Institute of British Architects runs the RIBA Community Projects Fund, with additional support from two grant-making trusts, the Tudor Trust and City Parochial Foundation.

The fund gives money towards feasibility studies for building projects. The fund supports a range of community developments, not just sport, although a small number of sports projects have been helped with a grant. Applicants should note that at the time of writing, future funding was uncertain.

The fund gives grants of up to £1,000 to community-led organisations looking to employ an architect or appropriate professional adviser. Grants are awarded according to the scale of the project and are towards the cost of the feasibility study for a building and/or environmental improvement. Many different types of projects are supported, not just those developing sports.

'A feasibility study will investigate whether your ideas for a building project are possible and how much they will cost. The report will usually contain a project history, details of funding sources, legal and planning implications, suggestions for project management and future action together with costings and drawings. The study is aimed to help you secure capital funding for the building costs. The architect will present your ideas in a professional manner, helping your project to succeed. There is no one standard type of study, it will depend on what your project needs.'

Recent projects which have been supported include:

■ Hayle Watersports Association, Cornwall for a major watersports facility on the site of an outdoor swimming pool;

■ Fred Knight Sports Ground, London, for the regeneration of a former British Gas sports ground to provide sports and leisure training and accessible facilities in an area of high social and economic deprivation.

The fund only gives grants to community organisations which are representative and properly constituted. The project must show wide community benefits. 'There must be no gain for a small number of individuals involved.' Priority is given to those projects which would be unlikely to be started without help from the fund. You cannot apply for help from the fund retrospectively. That is, work on the feasibility study must not have started before the application is submitted to the RIBA.

Grants will not be given for:

■ Projects where detailed design work only is required;

■ Projects which require basic repair work only;

■ Organisations funded by statutory bodies such as educational and health authorities;

■ Groups with sufficient financial reserves to cover the costs of the feasibility study;

■ Organisations who have a national parent body where funding is available;

■ Preservation/conservation groups where the primary aim is to preserve the building;

■ Projects where the feasibility study is already underway or completed.

Applications: Applications must be made on a form available from the contact above. You should enclose an annual report and if possible a photograph of the site or building. The assessment panel meets quarterly and applications will normally be assessed within twelve weeks. Applicants may be contacted by one of RIBA's regional coordinators, who can also be contacted for guidance relating to an application.

The Torch Trophy Trust

Contact: Mrs P Smith, Honorary Secretary, 16 Lancaster Gate, London W2 3CW (0171-262 4542; Fax: 0171-402 0486)

Beneficial area: Great Britain

Grant total: £1,500 (Torch Trophy awards); £1,700 (bursaries)

Policy: The Torch Trophy awards are given in recognition of voluntary effort in developing sport. In 1948, Commander Bill Collins organised the Olympic torch relay from Greece to the games in Wembley and each year miniature replicas of the torch are awarded to those making an unpaid contribution to sport and its development. In 1994/95 there were 20 recipients representing a wide range of sports throughout Great Britain.

Attached to the trust is the **Commander Collins Bursary Fund** which supports coaching, refereeing or similar qualifications and educational projects connected with sport. The bursaries are not given to enhance an individual's performance, and are given through governing bodies on the condition that no other funding for the project is available.

In 1994/95, the trust's Accumulated Fund totalled £23,500 and the Bursary Fund had an additional £18,800 available for distribution. In the year, three bursaries totalling £1,800 were given. The three beneficiaries were the British Baseball Federation (£500); the Sussex County Badminton Association (£900) and the English Schools' Table Tennis Association (£400). Unspent income totalled £17,000 for the year.

Benefiting sports in 1997 were: gliding (£370 for an international gliding congress in France); ice hockey (£500) and baseball (£500 for ABCA Coaching Convention in USA).

Applications: In writing to the correspondent.

Golf

The English Ladies Golf Association

Contact: Marian Carr, Secretary, Edgbaston Golf Club, Church Road, Birmingham B15 3TB (0121-456 2088; Fax: 0121-454 5542)

Beneficial area: National

Grant total: £21,000 in 1996/97

Policy: The association supports women's golf with grants to both individuals and clubs.

In 1996/97, the association's income totalled £29,000. It gave a total of almost £21,000 in grants for coaching, equipment and players' expenses at championship events. Grants were given to counties, golf clubs and individuals.

239

Awards to individuals ranged between £40 and £400.
Applications: In writing to the correspondent.

Wentworth Golf & Tennis Scholarships

Contact: David Oakley, Secretary, Wentworth Club, Wentworth Drive, Virginia Water, Surrey GU55 4LS (01334-842201; Fax: 01344-842804)
Beneficial area: National
Grant total: £27,000 in 1994/95
Policy: The scholarship fund helps promising young golfers and tennis players with coaching, clothing and travel costs.

The fund is supported by annual donations, which totalled £26,600 in 1994/95. In 1994/95, golfers received a total of almost £8,000 and tennis players £19,000. No grants list was attached to these accounts, so the number of beneficiaries is not known. However, in the previous year 15 golfers and 11 tennis players benefited, with a further 8 nominees from the Golf Foundation receiving a week's coaching.
Applications: In writing to the correspondent.

This entry has not been confirmed by the trust. Contact details are correct.

Motor Sport

The RAC British Motor Sports Training Trust

Contact: The Secretary and Administrator, Riverside Park, Colnbrook, Slough SL3 0HG (01753-681736)
Beneficial area: UK
Grant total: Over £59,000 is expected to be distributed during 1998
Policy: This trust supports education and training initiatives to reduce accidents in motor sports. Since its inception the trust has received a large Gift Aid donation from the Motor Sports Association of the United Kingdom. During 1998, the trust is expecting to receive about £124,000 in donations and deposit interest.

The trust has scheduled to give grant aid to over 20 motor sports clubs as a contribution towards their expenses of providing over 90 safety days for 5,400 volunteer officials during the year.

The trust currently has over £1.2 million available for distribution.
Applications: In writing to the correspondent.

Netball

The All England Netball Association Youth Trust

Contact: Mrs Janet Wrighton, Chairman, Netball House, 9 Paynes Park, Hitchin, Herts SG5 1EH (01462-442344; Fax: 01462-442343)
Beneficial area: England

Grant total: Not known

Policy: 'The Youth Trust supports activities that benefit all young people – particularly those that support their education and development.' The trust promotes the training and development of those playing netball. Although the total given in individual grants appears to be decreasing (£8,350 in 1994; £3,500 in 1995; and £210 in 1996), this amount is supplemented by proactive support for specific projects targeting different areas of the game.

Currently, the trust has agreed to award a 'development grant' towards a coaches' resource manual; an 'enablement grant for seminars' ; an 'encouragement grant' for training; and a 'tournament grant' for the England under 18's and under 21's squads. Further information about the projects would be welcomed.

Applications: In writing to the correspondent. Applications should include a project outline with full costings.

Rowing

The Alan and Rosemary Burrough Charitable Trust

Contact: Alan Burrough CBE, Manor Garden, Henley-on-Thames, Oxfordshire RG9 2NH

Beneficial area: National

Grant total: £50,000 in 1997

Policy: This is a general charitable trust giving to a wide range of charitable causes, including specific rowing organisations which receive the lion's share of the trust's awards. The settlor, senior trustee and correspondent was an oarsman, rowing for Jesus College, Cambridge University, and Thames Rowing Club. (He was also disabled in the war and is a Christian. These three area of his life are reflected in the causes supported by the trust.)

In 1997, the trusts's assets totalled £1.27 million, generating an income of £49,500. Grants distributed by the trust totalled almost £50,000. In 1997, the trust gave 39 grants to a wide range of organisations, which included churches and ex-service charities as well as rowing. Six grants were given to rowing organisations, and a number are regular beneficiaries. The largest grant of £34,000 was given to Cambridge Rowing Trust. Other smaller grants for rowing were given to the University Athletics Central Committee CUBC Appeal (£2,500); Jesus College Boat Club (£1,000); the Rowing Foundation (£500); Cambridge University Boat Club (£250); and the Oxford and Cambridge Rowing Foundation (£100).

Exclusions: Support is only given to organisations with charitable status. No support is given to individuals.

Applications: In writing to the correspondent. However, applicants should note that much of the trust's support is committed to specific beneficiaries.

The Mark Lees Foundation

Contact: The Secretary, 8 Purfield Drive, Wargrave, Berkshire RG10 8AP
Beneficial area: UK
Grant total: £21,000 in 1997
Policy: The foundation supports rowers under 23 years of age aiming for selection to national teams and who are facing hardship. In 1997, income totalled nearly £21,000 (half that of the previous year). Grants were similarly halved and totalled £16,000 for the year. 39 individuals benefited, with awards of between £150 and £500. Grants are given to help with training, travel and living costs.
Exclusions: Only rowers aiming for selection to national teams and experiencing hardship are supported.
Applications: In writing to the correspondent.

The Rowing Foundation

Contact: Mrs M P Churcher, Secretary, The Priory, 6 Lower Mall, Hammersmith, London W6 9DJ (0181-748 3632)
Beneficial area: UK
Grant total: £22,000 in 1997
Policy: The foundation supports the development of rowing and water sports at junior level, for those in full-time education and for those with disabilities. In 1997, the trust's income totalled £22,000 and grants totalled almost £22,000. Accumulated funds available for distribution now total £105,000. Grants range between £200 and £7,500.
In 1997, beneficiaries included the Rupert Guinness Training Camp (£6,000); the National Schools Regatta (£4,000); the Amateur Rowing Association (£2,200 for disabled rowing); Liverpool Victoria Rowing Club (£7,500) and Loughborough Boat Club (£500).
Applications: In writing to the correspondent.
Exclusions: Grants are only given to organisations. Individuals are not supported.

The Stewards' Charitable Trust

Contact: R S Goddard, Secretary, Henley Royal Regatta, Regatta Headquarters, Henley on Thames, Oxfordshire RG9 2LY (01491-572153)
Beneficial area: National
Grant total: £67,500 in 1996/97
Policy: This fund which supports the development of rowing among the young by encouraging grass-roots participation is currently being built up. Accumulated income totalled £1.1 million in 1996/97, which the trustees argue 'is still a good way short of being self-sufficient'. Total income coming into the trust in the year was £343,000, largely made up by a £300,000 contribution from the Henley Royal Regatta.
With the stated caution of the trustees, grants are not widespread. £67,500 in total was spent in 1996/97, the majority of which supported the cost of a Chief National Rowing Coach of Juniors (£42,500). The remaining £25,500 was

spent on British Junior Rowing, although it is not clear from the accounts what costs or projects were supported. Unspent income for the year totalled £270,000. Accumulated funds available for distribution now total over £1.1 million.

Readers should note that this trust was initially reluctant to appear in this guide. The correspondent states: 'The Stewards' Charitable Trust gives money mainly, although not exclusively, to rowing projects of a charitable nature ... we are inundated with applications for grant aid for completely unrelated activities. It is to avoid such inappropriate applications that we would propose not to appear in such a wide ranging publication.'

As is stressed elsewhere in this guide, applications to charitable trusts should be directed to those interested in your work. Poorly researched and indiscriminate applications to inappropriate trusts help neither the applicant or the trust, and in the long run may lead to changes in a trust's policies which leave the sector poorer as a result.

Applications: In writing to the correspondent. Applicants should note the comments above and contact the trust before making an application to find out if their project is eligible for support.

Rugby Union

The Wavell Wakefield Rugby Union Youth Trust
Contact: Robert Horner, Honorary Treasurer, Linden Lea, Greenhill Road, Otford, Sevenoaks, Kent TN14 5RR (01959-522024; Fax: 01959-522838)
Beneficial area: UK
Grant total: £1.5 million in 1996/97
Policy: The trust supports the development of rugby union football for young people. In 1996/97, the trust's assets totalled £894,000 and income totalled £1.3 million. Grants totalled £1.5 million for the year.

The major part of the trust's income, totalling £914,000, was spent in supporting Rugby Football Union Youth Development Officers. A further £482,000 was given to support the insurance costs of young players at clubs and schools. The English Rugby Football Schools Union received £70,000, and £10,000 was given to the Students Rugby Football Union to cover coaching, administration and competition costs. Both are regular beneficiaries. A further generic heading in the grants list is 'Constituent Body Youth Support Grants' which totalled £94,400 in the year. Further details about beneficiaries or what the grants were given for, are not included in the accounts, although it seems likely they were given to support youth sections in clubs and organisations. These may be given directly or through the 'Constituent Bodies'.

Applications: In writing to the correspondent, or through the 54 youth development officers around England. Contact details are available by telephoning 01484-866363.

Squash

The Women's Squash Trust

Contact: Mrs Ann Jackson, Trustee, Ivy Cottage, Willow Bridge, Cockfield, Bury St Edmonds, Suffolk IP30 0JA (01284-828018)
Beneficial area: UK
Grant total: Not known
Policy: This relatively new trust was established in 1996, and as yet no accounts are on file at the Charity Commission. The trust states: 'The Women's Squash Trust has at present very limited funds from which to award grants. However, we have made small grants to young players throughout the country to assist with coaching, training and travel costs.'
Applications: In writing to the correspondent.

Tennis

The Cliff Richard Tennis Development Trust

Contact: Sue Mappin, Harley House, 94 Hare Lane, Claygate, Esher, Surrey KT10 0RB (01372-470648; Fax: 01372-470645)
Beneficial area: UK
Grant total: £217,000 in 1996/97
Policy: The main area of the trust's activity is the Cliff Richard Tennis Trail which promotes tennis through state primary schools with initial coaching sessions involving children and teachers. Each school receives equipment and follow-on coaching plus a teacher's resource pack. (The Tennis Trail is sponsored by Direct Line Insurance which has been involved with the scheme since 1992.) In 1996/97, the trust's income totalled £144,000 (£57,500 from deeds of covenant and £73,600 from coaching fees). Expenditure totalled £217,000, made up of: Tennis Trail venue costs (£98,300); scholarship fees (£16,800); academy costs (£19,500); squad, coach and clinic costs (£8,600); equipment and storage (£28,100); travel (£2,700); and consultancy (£25,000).
The trust does not give grants directly to organisations. It does support individual players who show potential. One-off grants of between £100 and £300 are given to players of all abilities up to the age of 18.
Exclusions: Only UK citizens are eligible for awards. Children funded by the LTA or Rover scheme are not eligible for support.
Applications: On an application form available from the correspondent. Applications are considered quarterly. Write to: Cliff Richard Tennis Development Trust, PO Box 46C, Esher, Surrey KT10 0RB

See also entry for Wentworth Golf & Tennis Scholarships in the Golf section above.

Chapter 13
Raising money from Europe

■■■

Raising money from Europe is not easy and requires a considerable investment of time. There is only one relatively small programme (Eurathlon) that is designated specifically for sport, and this has recently been suspended following a ruling from the European Court of Justice (see below). However, with careful thought and creativity, some sports activities may also be eligible for non-sports European money. As with other sources of money detailed elsewhere in this Guide, organisations need to think hard about what they do, how they do it and who it involves and benefits. They should also assess the impact their activities have on the local area and region, and highlight any Europe-wide dimension there is to the work.

European funding can be a key to unlocking funding in the UK. This can include central and local government funds and the National Lottery. The reverse is also true, where matching funding raised domestically is not only attractive to those running European funding programmes, but in a number of cases, essential for an application to get off the ground.

The following is a brief guide to some of the different European funds that are available. Whilst the European Union budget seems large (around £170 billion), much is tied to general priority areas such as agriculture, poor countries or regions, research and so on. A large part of the European cake is also taken up with large infrastructure projects, economic development, vocational training and job creation. The mechanisms for allocating these funds are currently being reviewed (see below).

Europe – The bad and the good

The good
- ✓ New sources of funding
- ✓ Matching money for other funders
- ✓ Increased profile for the organisation
- ✓ New skills
- ✓ New ideas
- ✓ Partnerships
- ✓ Exchange opportunities

The bad
- ✗ Greater administration
- ✗ Red tape to get through
- ✗ Large investment of time
- ✗ Commitment of resources to uncertain outcomes
- ✗ Programmes change frequently
- ✗ Some programmes need match funding
- ✗ Time lags and delays

Agenda 2000

Many current EC funding programmes and priorities run until 1999, and most of these will have already committed money to selected projects. New programmes under the reshaped Structural Funds (see below) will run from 2000 to 2006 and follow redefined priorities. The EU has now to prepare for the new millennium; expansion in the number of Member States with central and Eastern European countries keen to join; increasing economic integration and monetary union, whilst facing the challenges of continuing disparities between its Members States. All this has to be accomplished within an unchanged budget of 1.27% of Gross Domestic Product. It follows that money will be spread more thinly, and probably towards more tightly defined targets. Competition for support is already fierce and will become more intense, both between countries and between regions. At the time of writing, much of the detail was still to be decided, and will not be confirmed until spring 1999. What follows gives some ideas of which spaces to watch and where you might get the best view from.

Current EU Member States

Austria	Germany	The Netherlands
Belgium	Greece	Portugal
Denmark	Ireland	Spain
Finland	Italy	Sweden
France	Luxembourg	United Kingdom

New Member States by 2003

Cyprus	Estonia	Poland
Czech Republic	Hungary	Slovenia

Preliminary research

There are plenty of European funding sources. You have to decide which ones, if any, are appropriate to you. This may be straightforward and based on advice and expertise within your organisation or that given by a consultant. Increasingly, matching your project to the right fund needs specialised knowledge. You should do some preliminary research first. Take soundings from any groups you know that have been successful or who have failed in their bid. This will be invaluable in giving an insider's view of the process. Euro Info Centres throughout the country will have all you ever wanted to know about Europe, and a large amount that you did not (see page 274 for contact details). You may also find it useful to refer to *A Guide to European Union Funding*, published by the Directory of Social Change (0171-209 5151).

'Prior systematic investigation works much better than "rushing in" – fewer and fewer EU funds are available through personal contacts, or because you happen to be in the right place at the right time.'
A Guide to European Union Funding for NGOs, ECAS

Remember, a large part of European money has already been ear-marked for particular countries and regions. This money is then distributed through existing networks based on published policies. You need to explore what is already out there and work within that. You should find out what local economic strategies are in place in your area and how any bid you make would fit in. This will strengthen any application. If, for example, you can show how a young people's sports project contributes to local employment training initiatives, your chances of success with certain EU programmes will increase.

The regional sports council office, local authority (economic development department), TEC or regional government office (European officer) may have experience and knowledge and can give advice. You should also talk to Commission officials, Members of the European Parliament and technical staff to collect as much information as possible. There are a number of consultants working in and out of Brussels who will be able to help put a bid together and iron out some of the wrinkles. Whether you favour the custom built consultant-crafted model, or the do-it-yourself flat pack assembly approach, get as much advice as you can.

The following can help with preliminary advice before you start brushing up your French in Brussels:

United Kingdom Sports Council, International Relations and Events, 10 Melton Street, London NW1 2EB (0171-380 8021; Fax: 0171-380 8025)

NCVO European Funding Team for all voluntary organisations (0171-713 6161; Fax: 0171-713 6300)

Wales Council for Voluntary Action European Office (01938-552379; Fax: 01938-552092)

Scottish Council for Voluntary Organisations (0141-332 5660; Fax: 0141-332 4225)

Budget lines, DGs and programmes

European funding is divided into two streams. There is money attached to named funding programmes (ESF, ERDF, Eurathlon and so on), but there is also money given under certain budget lines. As with central and local government money in the United Kingdom, European funds are administered by different departments. Each department or Directorate General (DG) has responsibility for an area of European policy and its own budget line(s). There

247

are 24 DGs and sport comes under DGX which is responsible for audiovisual media, information, communication and culture. It may be the case that you can apply under a particular budget line rather than a specific programme. DGV, for example, has responsibility for health initiatives within the Community. If you are running a health project, look at both the DG's budget line and specific programmes to see which, if any, are appropriate.

DGX

DGX is currently headed by Director General, Spyrros Pappas. The head of the Sports Unit is Jaime Andreu. The Sports Unit has responsibility for the following:

- cooperation and liaison between around 18 DGs whose policies have implications for sport;
- management of sports specific funding programmes, which until recently were: Eurathlon and Sports for People with Disabilities;
- working with national and international representatives in yearly meetings of the European Sports Forum;
- meeting with sports federations, organisations and institutions;
- running an information and help service: Sport Info Europe.

The Sports Unit
The European office administering sports information within the community runs a helpdesk, Sport Info Europe, which can be contacted at:

European Commission, DGX Unit Sports, Rue de la Loi, B-1049 Brussels
Fax: 00 322 2 295 77 47
e-mail: jaime.andreu-romeo@dg10.cec.be
Contacts: Jaime Andreu 00 32 2 299 92 52
Karel Govaert 00 32 2 299 90 45
Patricia Lambert 00 32 2 296 89 10
Rudy Mathijs 00 32 2 299 39 57

Sports specific funding

The Eurathlon Programme
Since 1994, Eurathlon and Sport for People with Disabilities have been the sports specific programmes within the European Union. Around £2 million a year (3 million ECU) has been allocated to around 150 projects across the EU. Both programmes are currently suspended (see below) and if they continue in the future, they are likely to change significantly.

The present Eurathlon programme (up to 1998) has focused upon transnational projects involving at least three Member States. Support has been for one year and projects have been concerned with the following:

- Sporting activities aimed at improving ties between people within the Community. This applies particularly to young people, women, elderly and disadvantaged people. Events and activities should be non-élitist and promote the ideas of sport for fun and for all.
- Training for athletes and others actively involved in sport such as coaches, monitors, umpires.

The most recent Eurathlon round in 1998 included 18 successful applications from the United Kingdom (out of 31 total applications). The European Commission's contribution totalled £108,000 with an average award of £6,000. The 1998 projects reflected the European interest in football in the year of EURO 98, but other sports such as climbing, aikido, curling and angling were also represented.

Successful projects in 1998

Adur Eurathlon Project 1998 – Sompting, West Sussex – various sports

British Aikido Federation European Summer School 1998 – British Aikido Federation

DEST 98 (Dalton-Euro-Sports Train 98) – Moldgreen Rugby Club – various sports

EUREKA Sports Programme – South Bank University, London

Euro Walk 2000 – Birmingham City Council Health and Fitness Section, Sports Development

EURO 98 Youth Football Tournament – Buxton and Bad Nauheim Twinning Association

European Netball U-17 Festival – Federation of European Netball Associations

European Symposium on Gender Equity in Running Sport – Yorkshire and Humberside Federation of Sport and Recreation

European Volley-Fest – Yorkshire Volleyball Association

European Women's Climbing Seminar – c/o British Mountaineering Council

European Women's Football Festival – Cheshire County Football Association

Hackney EURATHLON 98 Multinational Youth Sport Programme – London Borough of Hackney Regeneration and Partnership Unit – various sports

Professional Football Opportunities for Disadvantaged Groups – Cypriot Football League in England, London

Royal Caledonian Curling Club International Summer Camp – Royal Caledonian Curling Club, Midlothian

SPORT FUSION 98 – South East Derbyshire College – various sports

Welsh Castles Relay – Les Croupiers Running Club, Cardiff – Jogging

1998 Flexeys World Youth Fly Fishing Championship and Angling Festival – Welsh Salmon and Trout Angling Association

1998 Games of Friendship – Christchurch Borough Council, Dorset – various sports

Selection of projects to date has taken into account the following:

- Innovation, quality, originality and trendsetting elements of the activity. Does the project do something no other sports organisation is doing? Is it well managed? Is it well designed and is it being delivered in a way that promotes confidence?
- European dimension, encouraging the broadest possible participation from the Community. Does the project or event involve ordinary people, sportsmen and sportswomen, trainers and officials?
- Public interest and response. Does the project promote the Community and reach significant numbers of people through attendance at the event, publicity and media coverage?

The current picture

'Following a complaint from the British Government against the Commission, the Court of Justice in Luxembourg has ruled that the Commission should stop all programmes without legal base, as is the case for "Sports". The consequences are that our current budget has been frozen and that the budget line "Sports in Europe" has been withdrawn from the budget in 1999. We will not be able to run both programmes [Eurathlon and Sport for People with Disabilities] next year.

'The Commission is currently negotiating with Parliament to see what new actions may be possible. But any such actions will require a specific legal base...Once a final decision is taken, the Commission will provide information about the detailed arrangements.'
Sport Info Europe, November 1998

If, subject to negotiations, the Sports in Europe budget line is unfrozen, programmes are likely to be reshaped following a review. In October 1998, the following information was available from the Commission:

'The programme will have much more specific objectives, placing particular emphasis on the use of sport to combat social exclusion. The minimum amount the Commission can award will be increased substantially but the number of projects receiving subsidies will be cut by two thirds: ideally 50-60 projects receiving an average of ECU 30,000 to 50,000. Proof of the Community dimension will be the participation of at least six Member States.

'Federations' routine activities – championships for example – will no longer qualify. Projects can be for a maximum of two years. A single European panel of judges will assess the projects. The programme devoted to sport for the disabled will be included in the new pilot scheme which will run for three to four years.'

Application forms are usually issued in the autumn of the year before the project is due to start, and there has been one grants round each year. In previous years, those with internet access could download application forms from the Sports Info website: europa.eu.int/comm/dg10/sport

Information is available from the Commission Offices at the following addresses:

England: Jean Monnet House, 8 Storey's Gate, London SW1P 3AT (0171-973 1992; Fax: 0171-973 1900).

Northern Ireland: Windsor House, 9-15 Bedford Street, Belfast BT2 7EG (01232-240708; Fax: 01232-248241).

Scotland: 9 Alva Street, Edinburgh EH2 4PH (0131-225 2058; Fax: 0131-226 4105).

Wales: 4 Cathedral Road, Cardiff CF1 9SG (01222-371631; Fax: 01222-395489).

Currently, applications are not being accepted as the budget line is frozen. Sports Info Europe will have the most up-to-date information as it becomes available.

Sports events for people with disabilities

For four years up to 1998, small EC grants have been made available to help with the organisation of sports events for disabled people. Currently the Commission is negotiating with the European Parliament to determine new funding arrangements. Decisions are unlikely before spring 1999, and organisations should keep in touch with lead bodies in their Member States. Some elements of the current programme may well remain, so a brief outline of current criteria is included here.

Events must have a European dimension, should involve disabled participants from at least four Member States, raise awareness of their sporting abilities and promote the EC.

Priority will be given to projects which:

- introduce new sports or forms of sports;
- stimulate participation in new sports;

251

- have a positive effect on the dissemination and exchange of experience, knowledge and information;
- aim at people with more severe disabilities or others that will never have the possibilities to participate in international championships and paralympics; and/or
- promote sport for people with a disability in general, in some new way.

Grants have generally ranged from £1,500 to £15,000. The total budget has been around £100,000.

Recent UK projects receiving grants

World Team Cup (Tennis)

The British Tennis Foundation organised this annual event (Davis and Federation Cups of wheelchair tennis) in 1997. It was the second time that Nottingham had hosted the competition. 32 men's teams and 15 women's teams from 32 countries competed. European representation included teams from Austria, Belgium, Denmark, Finland, France, Germany, The Netherlands and Spain.

International Wheelchair Games

This event was organised by the Welsh Paraplegic and Tetraplegic Sports Association in Cardiff. Over 160 competitors from nine Member States and two other countries took part. Disciplines included track and field events, powerlifting, table tennis and bowls. There was also a 10K Grand Prix road race won by David Holding (UK) and Tanni Grey (UK).

Applications can be made at any time up to 1st September in the year before the event. Applications should be sent to: Jaime Andreu at DGX Unit Sports, Brussels (see Eurathlon address above), and to the National Committee of the Member State in which the project will take place. The project must come from a properly established body or organisation and take place in one of the EC Member States.

It must be open to participation from all Member States and include proposed participation from at least four EC countries. The EC cannot be the sole funder and the application must include an indication of how the Community's support will be made known (e.g. in printed materials and through the media).

The applications should include background, justification, aims and objectives, a statement of benefits to be achieved, the disability group(s) involved, number of participants and a budget.

The Secretariat to the UK (National Committee) on Sport for People with Disabilities relating to European Commission business is the United Kingdom Sports Council. Contact: Dave McCrae, United Kingdom Sports Council, Walkden House, 10 Melton Street, London NW1 2EB (0171-380 8013; Fax:0171-380 8015).

If, subject to negotiations, the Sports in Europe budget line is unfrozen, there will be one budget line for sport which will bring together Eurathlon and Sport for People with Disabilities. The likelihood is that disability sport will become a policy target group within the reshaped Eurathlon programme.

Organisations should note that applications are not currently being accepted as the budget line is frozen. Sports Info Europe will have the most up-to-date information as it becomes available.

> European officials and all Commission switchboard staff speak good English. Commission offices are as approachable as central government departments, and are often easier to get clear information from.

Money for deprived areas and for training

The European Structural Funds

Whilst the above are dedicated schemes for sport, anyone looking to Europe should remember that the lion's share of European money for projects is routed through a number of programmes called Structural Funds. The two main funds are:

- The European Regional Development Fund (ERDF) for capital investment in deprived areas.
- The European Social Fund (ESF) for training schemes.

(There are also two smaller Structural Funds which will not apply to sport: the European Agricultural Guidance and Guarantee Fund (EAGGF) for agricultural and forestry regions; and the Financial Instrument of Fisheries Guidance (FIFG) to cover fishing.)

Structural Funds may be relevant to sports organisations where their activities include training opportunities and/or are part of the economic development of certain tightly defined geographical areas (which are the 'least favoured' areas hit hardest by economic change or isolation or underdeveloped regions).

> The European Community is largely an economic entity. Many of its activities centre on the economic development of the Community with job creation encouraging economic competitiveness. Europe will be more welcoming if your organisation can help to further these ends. If you secure funding from these schemes it will be because your proposal has real economic or training benefits rather than because you are a sports project. In other words, you will have to be helping to create jobs, providing training or initiating enterprise, to be considered.

Beyond 1999

Current commitments under the Structural Funds run until 1999. What happens beyond that point is still being worked out, and regulations will not be finalised until 1999. The principles that will guide the regulations are that the funds should:

- concentrate resources on the poorest regions of the EU;
- simplify procedures;
- clarify who does what between the European Commission and the Member States. This should increase accountability, transparency and value for money.

Although detail is still to be worked out, clear statements of intent can be seen in the slimming down of the current six objective areas to a more manageable three. The old structural fund objectives translate into the new ones as follows:

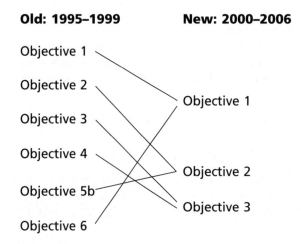

Old: 1995–1999 **New: 2000–2006**

Objective 1

Objective 2

Objective 3 Objective 1

Objective 4

Objective 5b Objective 2

Objective 6 Objective 3

From 2000

- Objective 1 resources will be limited to areas where the Gross Domestic Product per head is less than 75% of the European Union average. These regions will receive two thirds of the Structural Funds budget in total.
- Objective 2 will concentrate on the economic and social conversion of those areas (other than those covered under Objective 1) which are undergoing structural difficulties. These areas will account for around 18% of the EC's total population and will take in:
    - areas in decline through changes in industrial and service sectors
    - rural areas in decline
    - areas reliant upon fisheries
    - deprived urban areas.

- Objective 3 will bring together all initiatives that promote the development of human resources outside regions that are eligible under Objectives 1 and 2. Unlike the other two objectives, it is not geographically defined, and will include training, education and employment initiatives.

Currently, decisions on which regions come under which objective and how much will remain from previous ERDF and ESF incarnations are still being taken. Government offices in the regions and regional development agencies will have responsibility for Structural Funds in their areas and should be the first with local details once the Agenda 2000 dust finally settles.

Current areas in the UK covered by Objectives 1,2,3 and 5b

Objective 1: Highland & Islands; Merseyside; Northern Ireland.

Objective 2 (industrial): West Midlands (including Birmingham); East England (Yorkshire and Humberside and East Midlands); North West England; West Cumbria; North East England; Industrial South Wales; East Scotland (administered by the Scottish Office Industry Department); West Scotland (administered through the Scottish Office Industry Department); East London and the Lea Valley; Thanet; Stoke-on-Trent; Burton-on-Trent; Plymouth; Barrow; Gibraltar.

Objective 3: Throughout the UK for projects under the European Social Fund only.

Objective 5b (rural): Devon, Cornwall and West Somerset; Dumfries and Galloway (administered through the Scottish Office Industry Department); Rural Wales; The Northern Uplands; East Anglia; English Marches; Lincolnshire; Derbyshire/Staffordshire; Borders (administered through the Scottish Office Industry Department); Rural Stirling (administered through the Scottish Office Industry Department); Grampian (administered through the Scottish Office Industry Department); Tayside (administered through the Scottish Office Industry Department).

The European Social Fund (ESF)

This fund deals with employment not welfare as the name might suggest. It gives money for vocational training so that people are more likely to gain or retain a job. The Fund pays for the running costs of vocational training schemes (for employed or unemployed people), not capital expenditure as the ERDF does. There has to be an expectation that a reasonable number will go on to find employment or on to further training at the end of the course. The minimum age for participants is usually 16.

ESF after 2000

From 2000 ESF will cover five general areas:
- promotion of social inclusion
- fighting of unemployment
- promotion of lifelong learning and training to encourage employment prospects
- anticipation and easing of economic and social change
- improvement of women's participation in labour markets.

The training opportunities being offered clearly have to make people more employable. Trainees should gain recognised qualifications or credits towards them, or be able to go on to further training, keep employment or become self-employed. Training should lead to vocational qualifications, be suited to the needs of the labour market, and provide good value for the money spent. In a number of ESF projects, particularly under the current YOUTHSTART there have been elements of sports training, with pre-vocational schemes leading to community sports leaders awards, outdoor pursuits training and sports instructors' training.

Currently, any legally constituted organisation such as a TEC, college, local authority or voluntary organisation can apply for ESF support as long as it can secure matched funding for a given project. ESF will usually provide up to 45% of the cost of the project (although this may be higher in current Objective 1 areas). Matched funding must include contributions from a recognised public match funder which can include one or more of the following:

- a central government body;
- a local government body;
- a registered charitable trust;
- any organisation which directly or indirectly receives over 50% of its money from central government, local government or levies raised for training purposes.

Most items, apart from capital expenditure and interest charges, can be funded. Eligible costs include staff costs for trainers and others, childcare or the care of dependents, subsistence, travel, rent and leasing, rates, heat, light, telephone, stationery and training materials, depreciation of equipment, advertising and publicity, project evaluation, distribution of project results, costs of transnational working. Individuals may not apply for ESF money.

How to apply: Competition for all ESF awards is fierce and is likely to be more competitive after 2000. Good partnerships, preparation, research and long lead in times will improve the chances of success. Application forms and extensive guidance notes are available from the Department for Education and Employment or the Scottish Office Development Department at the addresses below. It is strongly advised that applications should be made after consultations with sector managers and regional government offices who are the first point of contact for ESF applicants. A list of contacts is included in the guidance notes from the DfEE.

European Social Fund Unit, Department for Education and Employment, Level 1 Caxton House, Tothill Street, London SW1H 9HF (0171-273 3000; Fax: 0171-273 5540).

The EMPLOYMENT Support Unit provides central information and newsletters on employment and training initiatives and may well continue in this role with new Community Initiatives. Interested organisations can be added to their mailing list to keep in touch with developments. Contact: The EMPLOYMENT Support Unit, ECOTEC, Priestly House, 28–34 Albert Street, Birmingham B4 7UD (0121-616 3661; Fax: 0121 616 3680).

The European Regional Development Fund (ERDF)

The Structural Funds are one of the main levers to influence economic change in the European Community. They constitute around a third of the entire EU budget totalling £23 billion, of which around 47% is ERDF. The UK allocation for all Structural Funds between 1994 and 1999 totalled £9 billion. It is likely that the amounts allocated to the UK will change when budget lines become tighter in light of the Union's expansion.

The European Regional Development Fund is a capital investment fund which aims to reduce regional economic differences between the poorest and most affluent parts of Europe. The Fund concentrates on the least favoured regions of the Community. These include areas of acute industrial decline and remote rural areas. These are currently defined by the Objective 1 (areas lagging behind); Objective 2 (industrial) and Objective 5b (rural) areas listed in the box on page 255. (These will be streamlined into three new objectives to run from 2000–2006 – see above.) Support is given to job creation projects, the development of small- and medium-sized enterprises; infrastructure projects; initiatives which improve the attractiveness and image of the region, tourism, and research and development.

The maximum grant for Objective 1 areas is 75% of the total project cost. For Objective 2 areas it is 50%. However, the precise level of grant varies according to the type of project being funded. ERDF grants must be matched and can include a combination of any of the following:

- Public money (e.g. national or regional Sports Councils, sports governing bodies, central or local government, City Challenge, development corporations);
- Charitable trusts;
- Private sector finance;
- The organisation's own resources including mortgages, loans and earned income.

Applications must identify the specific economic benefits their scheme will achieve and identify the local benefits of the project. They will also be expected to show how the benefits were estimated and how they will be monitored to guarantee success. This is much more exacting now than in the earlier days of the Fund, and from 2000 onwards the likelihood is that outcomes will have to be even more precisely measured to ensure value for money.

Until recently the most likely area for funding for sports groups was under the tourism and image heading. In some areas this may be tied closely to job creation with precise measurement required of the number and nature of the jobs created. Applications in support of an event or facility must be able to make a convincing case for:

- the number of visitors attracted;
- the number of overnight visitors attracted;
- square metres of new/improved facilities;
- amount of private sector investment levered in £s;
- the number of full-time equivalent jobs directly created;
- the number of full-time equivalent jobs indirectly created.

Examples of sports projects funded under ERDF in the past include: athletics tracks, marinas, tennis centres and leisure pools.

Contact: The current Objectives 1 and 5b are eligible for support up to 2001. Programme administrators are likely to commit all grants early in 1999. For information on arrangements for 2000 onwards, and the application process contact the regional government office (for addresses see page 174). A large number of ERDF applications are submitted by local authorities in partnership with regional bodies. For sport this may be the local authority, regional Sports Council or a governing body for instance. You will need to consult with them extensively to strengthen your application.

In Scotland, the Scottish Office will give you the nearest regional contact to discuss your proposal: The Scottish Office Industry Department, European Funding and Coordination Division, Room 5/89, New St Andrew's House, St James' Centre, Edinburgh EH1 3TG (0131-556 8400; Fax 0131-244 4785).

For Northern Ireland, contact: Industrial Development Board for Northern Ireland, IDB House, 64 Chichester Street, Belfast BT1 4JX (01232-233233; Fac: 01232-545000).

Use of farm land

There are currently small grants available for farmers in some areas looking for alternative economic uses for their land in Objective 5b areas (which will be absorbed into Objective 2 from 2000 onwards). Grants are made to the landowner not the sports organisation involved in the business plan. Examples include a sailing club using an under-used water area and the conversion of a barn of an indoor cricket club. Details are available from your Regional Service Centre. Where you do not have details of the local RSC, contact the Ministry of Agriculture, Fisheries and Food Helpline for the nearest one: 0645 335577.

Vocational training for young people

LEONARDO da Vinci

LEONARDO was launched in January 1995 to run until December 1999, and supports training and cultural exchange programmes for young people. A further phase has been announced to take the programme beyond 2000. Details about the nature of this next stage had not been confirmed at the time of writing. However, it is likely that it will build upon the first phase of LEONARDO and some familiar elements will remain.

DGXXII which has responsibility for vocational training and education has announced that subject to the agreement of Member States governments, ECU 1,000 million will be made available for the new phase of LEONARDO and its development of training. This compares with a total of ECU 620 million for the present LEONARDO programme. A further 600 million will be channelled into the European Community action programme 'Youth' which will incorporate exchanges and promote young people's mobility between Member States.

The present LEONARDO programme concentrates on sustaining quality and supporting innovation in Member States' vocational training through transnational exchanges, placements and partnerships. Projects may include:

- pilot projects involving more than one Member State;
- exchange programmes of trainees and trainers between Member States;
- work experience placements for young trainees, young workers or job seekers;
- development of language skills and innovative practice;
- surveys, analyses and data exchange.

Some of the activities covered by grants are transnational projects that, for example, develop common training modules; provide training for trainers and those who manage training; and encourage lifelong learning and the promotion of lifelong learning.

Young people covered by the present LEONARDO programme are defined as people under 28 years of age, who are undergoing training, or who are searching for work.

Transnational exchanges and placements are for:

- short work placements for young people in initial vocational training (3 to 12 weeks);

259

- long work placements for young people in initial vocational training (13 weeks to 9 months). Applications for these traineeships are particularly encouraged;
- work placements for young workers or young job seekers (3 to 12 months);
- exchanges of trainers (2 to 8 weeks), concentrating on the exchange of good practice. Note that in this case exchanges do not have to be reciprocal, as exchange here can mean the transfer of expertise.

Successful applications to date answer the following questions:

- **Why** do the activity? How does it meet a defined need, or offer a solution? How does it fit into a wider training or academic strategy?
- **Who** are the partners? What types of organisation will be involved and what will they bring to the project?
- **How** will the project be managed? What is the timetable, and who will be responsible for the project? How will the partners' roles be defined and how will you communicate with one another and the Commission? How has the project been costed?
- **What** are the intended outcomes? What difference will the completed project make in this country and in Europe? How will you measure the outcome and the results? How will it help a target group or solve a training problem?

You should also have clear ideas and strategies for spreading the word about your project and its outcomes and results.

There will be further calls for proposals under the current phase of LEONARDO through 1999. For further information and clear and full guidance notes, contact: Central Bureau for Educational Visits and Exchanges, Seymour Mews House, Seymour Mews, London W1H 9PE (enquiries: 0171-389 4389; Fax: 0171-935 1017).

Exchange programmes

Town Twinning

Sports events can play a central role in strengthening links between twin towns. Currently, the European Commission office responsible for town twinning does not fund links that are exclusively about sport. The European Commission Grant is available for events which advance the mutual understanding of twinning partners in Europe. The grant may apply to events in which sport is only one element of a larger event.

The grants are small, but with an enthusiastic local twinning association and the help of your local authority twinning officer, there can be help for hosting and travel costs for those attending an event. A twinning association in Lancaster was given a small grant towards the cost of hosting delegates from a new twin attending the annual youth games.

Application forms are available from: the International Links Team, Local Government International Bureau, 35 Great Smith Street, London SW1P 9BJ (0171-664 3116; Fax: 0171-664 3128).

To discuss a particular project before applying, contact the (multilingual) Town Twinning Office in Brussels for help and advice: Anne Blanche Haritos, Town Twinning, DGX Unit D, Rue de la Loi 200, L1/53 Brussels.

Youth for Europe III

The Youth for Europe programme which runs until 1999 promotes exchanges of young people within Europe, especially those who are disadvantaged. These exchanges help young people to learn from each other, to share experiences and to build bridges between Member States. Applicant organisations need to show how their project helps this process of understanding and cooperation. Sports organisations should note that the programme does *not* support festivals or sports gatherings. Successful projects may include sport as an element of the exchange, but projects will not be supported on the strength of their sporting activity. Sport may be a programme element but not the main focus. Projects should first and foremost be about the development of young people and their understanding of other Member States.

As with the programmes outlined above, the programme will continue but new arrangements for 2000 to 2004 are currently being decided by the European Commission.

The current programme supports the following:

- exchanges between projects in two or more Member States, with groups of young people aged 15 to 25 and where the exchange lasts at least a week;
- projects where young people are involved in innovative or creative initiatives, especially those that combat all forms of exclusion, as well as projects which foster the cultural and artistic interest of young people;
- the development of networks and partnerships involving different Member States;
- projects which encourage young people to participate in voluntary service which benefits the Community;
- youth worker exchanges which increase awareness of practice and experience in other Member States;
- study visits, seminars which increase awareness of other countries' practice and experience;
- projects which help Member States generally to cooperate on youth programmes;
- building links with non–Member States.

Grants are available, generally for 50% of eligible travel or hosting costs. Recently supported projects include:

- Havering Youth Service, where members worked with local authorities in Seville towards environmental protection, including encouraging cycling. Following campaigning in Seville, the group also went Spanish hill-walking.
- St Neots Twinning Association organised a multilateral event involving groups of around ten young people from France, Italy, Germany and Greece. There was a planning meeting in Italy. The self-funding twinning association with support from volunteers, the youth service and the local MEP, organised a two-week programme of workshops on unemployment, drugs and family violence, together with sports and music activities.

The above projects received grants which covered over half the cost of their outward travel and around 40% of the costs of hosting the visit from their partners. The St Neots project also received a grant towards half of the costs of their partners' travel costs to England.

For further details contact: Indra Bahadur, Information Officer, Youth Exchange Centre, The British Council, 10 Spring Gardens, London SW1A 2BN (0171-389 4030; Fax: 0171-389 4033).

Further information

Lobbying and seeking funders in Europe can be linked processes. In the same way that there is no magic key to unlock funding in Europe, so there is no easy way to lobby for change on sports policy and its implementation. Getting to know your Member of the European Parliament is a good start. Elections for the parliament will be held in June 1999, and much may change following the results. A full list of MEPs is available from: the London Office of the Parliament, 2 Queen Anne's Gate London SW1H 9AA (0171-222 0411; Fax: 0171-222 2713).

Euro Info Centres (EICs): The EU produces large amounts of paper on a range of policy concerns and directives. Some of these have a bearing on sport, either directly or indirectly. There are a number of Euro Info Centres (EICs) throughout the UK, often in universities and libraries or chambers of commerce, where European information can be easily accessed. Contact numbers for EICs are:

Belfast:	01232-491031	East Anglia:	0345-023114
Birmingham:	0121-455 0268	Exeter:	01392-214085
Bradford:	01274-754262	Glasgow:	0141-221 0999
Bristol:	0117-973 7373	Hertfordshire:	01727-813407
Cardiff:	01222-229525	Hull:	01482-464940/35
Chelmsford:	01245-437519	Inverness:	01463-715400

Kent:	0345-226655	Nottingham:	0115-962 4624
Leeds:	0113-283 3126	Sheffield:	0114-953 2126
Leicester:	0116-255 9944	Slough:	01753-577877
Liverpool:	0151-298 1928	Southampton:	01703-832866
London:	0171-489 1992	Stoke-on-Trent:	0345-202122
Manchester:	0161-237 4000	Sussex:	01444-259259
Newcastle:	0191-261 0026/5131	Telford:	01952-208213

There are also six Rural Development Information and Promotion Centres (CARREFOURS):

Ayr:	01292-520 331	County Tyrone:	016625-488 72
Carmarthen:	01267-224 859	Garstang:	01995-601 207
Cirencester:	01285-653 477	Inverness:	01463-715 400

Internet sites: The EC is committed to distributing as much information as possible through the internet. DGs and a number of programmes regularly post updates and programme details, including application forms on the net. As Agenda 2000 becomes more sharply defined it will be particularly useful to keep up to date with changes as these appear. A starting point for EU surfing is the European Union site: http://europa.eu.int

Information about all aspects of the European Community is also available at the UK offices of the Commission which have an information service, although it can take time to get through on the telephone.

England: Jean Monnet House, 8 Storey's Gate, London SW1P 3AT (0171-973 1992; Fax: 0171-973 1900)

Northern Ireland: Windsor House, 9-15 Bedford Street, Belfast BT2 7EG (01232-240708; Fax: 01232-248241)

Scotland: 9 Alva Street, Edinburgh EH2 4PH (0131-225 2058; Fax: 0131-226 4105)

Wales: 4 Cathedral Road, Cardiff CF1 9SG (01222-371631; Fax: 01222-395489)

The United Kingdom Sports Council produces a newsletter on European affairs, *EuroCommuniqués*. Contact: Rachel Wilson, United Kingdom Sports Council, International Relations and Events, 10 Melton Street, London NW1 2EB (0171-380 8021; Fax: 0171-380 8025).

Chapter 14
Raising money for individuals

■■

Most of this book deals with grants to sports clubs and societies rather than individual sportsmen and sportswomen. However, probably over £16 million a year is given to help individual sportspeople competing at every level from schools and other junior events right through to Olympic and world champions.

In Britain, unlike many other countries, sportsmen and women do not receive any direct support from government. The main sources of help to individuals are as follows:

- **The World Class Programme:** Funded by the Lottery Sports Fund, this governing body-led programme is by far the largest source of money available for individuals. Under the World Class Performance element of the programme (supported by the four home country Sports Councils and the UK Sports Council), 33 different sports have received almost £30 million worth of Lottery money (up to and including November 1998). Almost £13.5 million of this has been in the form of subsistence funding for individuals.
- **SportsAid (formerly the Sports Aid Foundation):** An independent fundraising organisation and registered charity. SportsAid gave a total of just over £1 million in grants to over 2,100 individuals during 1997/98.
- **Sports governing bodies:** Some of these give help either from their own resources or from related funds. They are also a vital link in the World Class Programme distribution chain (see below).
- **Sports grant-making trusts:** A small number of sports-specific trusts give grants to individuals. (See chapter 12 for a full list.)
- **Foundation for Sport and the Arts (FSA):** The FSA is a large grant-giver to organisations (see chapter 8). It also gives a very small number of grants to individuals.
- **Local and national relief-in-need charities:** There is a large network of local charities which can give grants to individuals for all kinds of financial needs. These can include poor sportspeople and young people with a developing interest and talent in sport.

Over the next six months many changes will be implemented to the World Class Programme and SportsAid. These changes will significantly alter – and hopefully improve – the quality of support available to individuals. At the time of writing, elements of the programmes were still under debate. The information provided in this chapter gives an indication of where and how things are changing. It is strongly recommended, however, that individuals seek further information from their relevant national governing body of sport to keep up with the changes that will take place.

It is the governing bodies which have the responsibility to put together a World Class Plan (see below) and will have the clearest idea about how individuals will be developed in each sport. Individuals named by the governing body under the plan are eligible to be considered for subsistence funding. At Performance and Potential levels of the plan, funding will come from the Lottery Sports Fund. At the Start level, individuals apply to SportsAid.

The World Class Programme

The World Class funding programme aims to give the national governing bodies (NGBs) of sport and their performers the best ever opportunity to achieve consistent success in significant major international competitions and events. It follows three inter-related stages of performer development:

World Class Performance

This level supports the training and preparation programmes of élite performers who have the potential to win medals (or equivalent) in significant international competitions and events now and within the next six years.

World Class Potential

This stage helps the development of talented performers who show the potential to win medals (or equivalent), in significant future international competitions and events within the next ten years.

World Class Start

At this level, NGBs can be given help to identify and nurture a specific number of performers who have the necessary characteristics to achieve future World Class success.

An important note

Individual sportspeople **cannot** apply directly for awards under the World Class Programme. Only National Governing Bodies can apply for help from the programme. To receive individual support, performers must be part of the National Governing Body's World Class Plan.

Awards given under World Class Performance between May 1997 and November 1998

	Performance Plan Costs	Subsistence Costs	No. of Athletes	Total Awarded (UK)	English Element of Award
Athletics of which:	£2,237,400	£2,597,000	344	£4,834,400	£4,250,300
Disabled Athletics	£301,300	£968,800	106	£1,270,100	£1,085,500
Badminton	£975,100	£352,000	64	£1,327,200	£1,327,200
Bobsleigh	£197,300	£102,000	6	£299,200	£256,400
Boxing	£75,500	£73,800	12	£149,300	£149,300
British Paralympic Association	£33,900	-	-	£33,900	£28,200
Commonwealth Games Council for England	£155,700	-	-	£155,700	£157,700
Canoeing	£1,052,200	£689,300	74	£1,741,600	£1,505,700
Cricket (Women's)	£95,000	£62,400	14	£157,400	£157,400
Cycling	£994,900	£798,200	79	£1,793,100	£1,607,900
Diving	£202,500	£95,000	11	£297,500	£277,200
Equestrian of which:	£539,600	£450,000	53	£1,015,800	£918,400
Disabled Dressage	£107,100	£109,100	10	£216,200	£190,800
Golf (Men's)	£65,000	£66,100	12	£131,100	£131,100
Golf (Women's)	£46,000	£69,800	22	£115,800	£115,800
Gymnastics	£1,677,300	£572,300	133	£2,249,600	£1,946,700
Hockey	£591,000	£485,500	84	£1,076,500	£1,076,500
Ice-skating	£186,700	£165,400	46	£352,100	£320,300
Judo	£310,300	£782,000	63	£1,092,400	£909,900
Karate	£402,800	£197,400	27	£600,200	£600,200
Modern Pentathlon	£147,400	£196,900	21	£344,400	£306,500
Netball	£985,000	£334,000	57	£1,319,000	£1,319,000
Orienteering	£86,400	£152,700	19	£239,100	£207,000
Rowing	£1,233,900	£719,800	138	£1,953,700	£1,687,500
Rugby (Women's)	£207,500	£107,200	35	£314,700	£314,700
Sailing	£1,560,800	£1,045,300	78	£2,606,100	£2,447,000
Shooting	£63,000	£145,800	20	£208,800	£208,800
Skiing of which:	-	£60,000	12	£60,000	£40,000
Disabled skiing	-	£30,000	6	£30,000	£25,000
Squash	£1,118,000	£783,300	85	£1,901,300	£1,901,300
Swimming of which:	£2,114,600	£1,485,900	118	£3,600,400	£3,163,700
Disabled Swimming	£450,300	£680,500	44	£1,130,900	£975,400

	Performance Plan Costs	Subsistence Costs	No. of Athletes	Total Awarded (UK)	English Element of Award
Table Tennis	£1,207,200	£203,600	98	£1,410,800	£1,410,800
Ten-pin Bowling	£17,200	£23,800	4	£41,000	£41,000
Triathlon	£180,500	£86,100	39	£266,600	£239,700
Water Skiing	£100,300	£176,600	21	£276,900	£276,900
Weightlifting	£29,700	£47,600	8	£77,300	£77,300
Wheelchair Basketball (Men's)	£226,500	£336,300	17	£562,800	£468,800

World Class Events

Awards given up to November 1998

	Year	Cost	Sport England Award
Junior Hockey World Cup	1997	£272,300	£90,000
European Disabled Sailing Championships	1997	£34,400	£10,500
Sports Acrobatics World Championships	1997	£142,800	£42,900
European Short Course Swimming Championships	1998	£138,300	£40,000
World Disability Athletics Championships	1998	£1,393,000	£534,000
World Cup Orienteering – Events 3 & 4	1998	£71,500	£12,800
Soccer World Cup for Players with Learning Disabilities	1998	£956,700	£150,000
European Show Jumping Championships	1999	£1,376,800	£481,900
Junior European Target Championship (Archery)	1999	£25,900	£9,100
World Wheelchair Basketball Championships	2002	£43,900	£14,500
Soccer World Cup	2006	£9,420,000	£3,140,000

Transitional arrangements

A number of NGBs have received World Class Performance awards, some of which have now finished. The process of preparing Potential and Start applications for World Class Potential and World Class Start is time consuming. Therefore, where athletes are currently benefiting from a Performance award but are more likely in the future to be classified as Potential award beneficiaries, they will be covered in the interim by World Class Performance.

Eligible applicants

All NGBs of sport recognised by the Sports Councils are eligible to submit a World Class application.

Initially, World Class Performance was funded separately by the relevant home country Sports Council or a combination of the home countries for the UK and GB national governing bodies. If you are a British or UK governing body of sport, it is recommended that you discuss your World Class Programme with the UK Sports Council first, before applying for Lottery funding. English governing bodies should approach Sport England direct.

Potential and Start funding is an initiative of Sport England and as such will only be available to support performers who qualify to represent England. Governing bodies in Northern Ireland, Scotland and Wales should contact their home country Sports Council for domestic arrangements.

Disability sports

Where possible NGBs of sport are expected to integrate the training and preparation of their talented disabled sportsmen and sportswomen into their World Class Plan. In some cases it will also be acceptable, in the interim, for the disability element to be included as a separate section of the World Class Plan.

If there is not an appropriate NGB, the home country Sports Council and the UK Sports Council, with the advice of the Disability Advisory Group and the English Federation of Disability Sport, will determine which organisation is eligible to apply.

World Class Plans

An eligible application will include one **World Class Plan** for the sport, made up of the constituent parts of Performance, Potential and Start, as appropriate. Where a NGB is not applying for all the constituent parts, they should provide a strategic overview. As part of this overview a **Performer Development Model** must be provided. This will define how a talented individual is expected to progress to a World Class performer.

The performer development model should show how World Class Start provides a solid foundation for World Class Potential, and Potential for World Class Performance. The plan must describe clearly the relationship between each part of the programme.

A World Class Plan should:

- incorporate a performer development model and the relevant constituent parts for which you are seeking funding;
- provide details of the disciplines being included as well as details of the named men, women and disabled performers.

Eligible Performance Plan costs

Through Performance funding the aims are to:

- set **performance goals** to win more medals in significant international competitions;
- establish **performance standards** required to achieve the performance goals;
- **identify and select** the performers with the potential to win medals;
- develop and implement detailed **training and preparation** programmes, incorporating the necessary sports science, sports medicine, personal development and other training support to help performers to achieve their goals;
- provide appropriate **international competitive** opportunities;
- access the **necessary facilities** and equipment;
- support the **personal development** of performers;
- employ **World Class coaches** and other staff;
- create and implement effective **selection** processes;
- provide **post performance** advice.

Eligible Potential Plan costs

Through Potential funding the aims are to:

- establish **performer development** guidelines identifying attainment targets at certain development stages;
- develop and implement **training and competition** programmes to give performers the best chance of reaching this level;
- establish **talent development** programmes, incorporating the necessary sports science, sports medicine, personal development, and other training support;
- specify and implement the measures and additional support required to **remove any barriers** and inequalities faced by talented performers;
- review the quality and appropriateness of **competition structures**;
- access the necessary **facilities and equipment**;
- support the **personal development** and education of performers;
- employ **World Class coaches** and other staff;
- create and implement effective **selection** processes.

Eligible Start Plan costs

Through Start funding the aims are to:

- set up **development programmes** incorporating the necessary sports science, sports medicine, personal development and other training support for the nurturing of talent;

269

- support the **personal development** and **education** of young performers;
- specify and implement the measures and additional support required to **remove any barriers** and inequalities faced by talented performers;
- employ **World Class coaches** and other staff;
- create and implement effective **selection** processes;
- determine the **talent characteristics** necessary to be a world class performer;
- establish methods of **measuring** the talent characteristics of potential performers;
- develop a systematic approach to searching for and **identifying talent.**

Ineligible Plan costs

The World Class Programme does **not** provide funding for the costs of running an applicant organisation. These include:

- employment of staff **un**related to the World Class Programme e.g. regional development officers;
- management and administration costs incurred by the NGB **not** associated with the World Class Programme;
- training of governing body personnel **un**related to the World Class Programme;
- marketing and promotional activities;
- membership services;
- review and development of coaching and leadership services **not** associated with the programme.

Partnership funding

Normally, support of up to 90% of the total cost of a World Class Plan will be considered. NGBs of sport must contribute at least 10% towards the total cost from their own resources, or from other sources.

A financial need assessment will be carried out to determine whether an applicant is in genuine need of World Class Funding and is:

- capable of generating 10% partnership funding; or
- capable of generating more than 10% partnership funding.

NGBs are required to enclose evidence of confirmed partnership funding with their application.

The NGB contribution does not have to be made up entirely of cash. Items such as donated goods and services can also be counted. This can include for example, a grant from a local authority or services given by the local university, and can be in kind support or help given directly. A figure will be accepted that represents what the cost would be if the NGB had to pay for the service, providing the value can be independently verified.

Duration of award

The period of funding being requested should correspond directly to the time period covered by the World Class Plan, up to a maximum of ten years.

If the application is successful, the home country Sports Council (or Sport England in the case of Start and Potential) or UK Sports Council will inform the NGB of the level of the Award, which parts of the Plan have received funding, and how many years the award will cover. All funding will be subject to annual reviews.

Access criteria

Sport England anticipates that the demand for World Class funding will exceed the amount of money available. Therefore, criteria have been set to determine how resources will be allocated. Sport England suggests that before NGBs spend time and money in developing an application, that they first make contact to confirm whether they meet the access criteria.

To help Sport England to develop these criteria, independent research was commissioned to determine the relative value of international success for each sport based on a number of criteria. All recognised NGBs, for both non-disabled and disabled sports, were invited to complete a pro forma indicating:

- status of the primary competition for their sport;
- the degree of likely future success in primary competition;
- the significance placed by the public on success in that sport.

Where a sport meets the access criteria, Sport England can provide individually tailored support from their World Class Team and appropriate advisers to help develop the World Class Plan.

Pre-application support

Application forms for the World Class Programme can be obtained from only one source: The Lottery Line on 0345-649649.

There are two types of application forms for the World Class Programme:

1. National Governing Body Application Form to apply for revenue funding for their World Class Plan, made up of Performance, Potential and Start, as appropriate, for all disciplines which feature within their sport.
2. World Class Performance Subsistence Award form sent to named performers in the applicant's World Class Performance and Potential parts of their World Class Plan. Performers will receive a World Class Athlete pack and subsistence application form at their home address following the submission of the Governing Body's World Class Plan application form.

The Governing Body must complete a separate World Class Plan Application Form for the men and women within each discipline.

Once the form has been completed, applicants should take a copy for their own records and then send it to:

World Class Funding Awards
Sport England
Lottery Sports Fund
PO Box 649
London WC1H 0QS

An integral part of the pre-application support to those sports that are eligible and meet the access criteria is the financial need assessment, as described above.

In addition, a Corporate Governance Audit will be carried out to decide whether the organisation is 'fit for purpose', and that it is capable of implementing a Programme funded by a Lottery Sports Fund Award. The Corporate Governance Audit will normally be carried out before an award is made, unless it has previously been carried out for other purposes.

The audit covers issues such as accountability, conflicts of interest, management structures, financial management, accounting for Lottery Sports Fund awards, and personnel practices. During the life of an award, further similar audits will be carried out as part of a monitoring and evaluation process and the continued funding under the World Class plan will be conditional on satisfactory completion of these periodic audits.

Processing the application
Completed application forms should be sent to Sport England's Lottery Unit where it will be allocated to a Case Officer. The assessment of a NGB's performance plan follows the process below which is carried out by the designated Case Officer:

1. Register application on database and acknowledge
2. Make initial eligibility assessment
3. Seek advice from specialist English or UK Sports Council staff
4. Commission expert adviser to complete appraisal
5. Prepare report to be submitted, initially, to a Case Conference

The appraisal of the application (at points 3 and 4) considers the following:

- where the applicant's squad is currently ranked in the world;
- the overall strength of their opposition;
- the long-term goal;
- whether the annual targets are measurable and attainable;
- the composition of the squad;
- the preparation programme;
- the performance director's reimbursement, appointment and credentials;
- the other performance plan personnel;

- the management structures and processes;
- implementation schedules;
- internal arrangements for monitoring;
- value for money.

Making the decision

Home country applications

Following a review by a Case Conference of Senior Case Officers, chaired by the Head of Revenue Operations, the application is presented to the Lottery Awards Panel. The Panel then makes a recommendation to the home country Sports Council. The Council makes a decision and the applicant is notified.

UK/GB applications

The application, which has been reviewed by a Senior Case Officer's Case Conference, is presented to the UK Sports Council. The UK Sports Council makes a recommendation to the Home Country Sports Councils. The applicant is notified once the Home Country Sports Councils have made their decision.

As with National Lottery capital applications, the decision process will take at least six months. The process can take longer where additional information to support the application is required.

Where the applicant is successful, they must then meet the terms and conditions of the award.

Possible outcomes

Full award

This constitutes a firm financial commitment on behalf of the Sports Council(s) to fund part(s) of the entire World Class Programme for the sport. Conditions are usually attached to full Awards, some to be fulfilled over the duration of the Plan, some before the release of the first payment.

In principle

'In principle' decisions are not an irrevocable commitment. They indicate the Lottery Awards Panel's recommendations to support the application in principle providing that a number of issues are resolved to their satisfaction.

Rejection

This recommendation is for those applications which the Sports Council(s) believe do not meet the criteria for funding within the resources available.

Monitoring the award

Monitoring usually takes place at the end of the sport's competitive season.

Measures of Performance include the following:

- Fitness for purpose of the National Governing Body to deliver the programme;
- Value of performance outcomes;
- Programme integrity;
- Individual athlete programmes.

Business and financial measures include:
- Organisational governance;
- Robust accounting systems for Lottery funds;
- Partnership funding;
- Individual athlete spot checks.

SportsAid

Until 1997, SportsAid, operating under its original name of the Sports Aid Foundation, was the principal contributor to individual sportsmen and women. At that time, SAF supported a wide range of performers, from those expected to perform with distinction in Olympic, World and European championships through to youngsters in junior national squads. However, as an independent fundraising organisation, SAF was always restricted in the amount of money available for distribution.

In 1997/98 SportsAid gave over £1 million in over 2,100 grants. This total was made up of contributions from Barclaycard's Team 2000 initiative (£280,000); the Foundation for Sport and the Arts (£304,500) which set aside funds for SportsAid's administration; and funds raised by SportsAid both regionally and nationally.

Grants administered by SportsAid in 1997/98

Sport	Grant total	Number of sportspeople receiving grants
Archery	£13,900	30
Association Football	£8,500	19
Athletics	£134,000	235
Badminton	£42,000	98
Baseball	£14,900	29
Basketball	£9,900	32
Bobsleigh	£9,800	6
Bowls	£2,500	10
Boxing	£15,200	29
Canoeing	£53,700	68

Sport	Grant total	Number of sportspeople receiving grants
Cricket	£21,300	39
Curling	£11,400	10
Cycling	£28,900	69
Cyclo-cross	£4,800	17
Dancesport	£6,300	16
Disabled	£81,000	193
Equestrian	£7,800	19
Fencing	£19,800	49
Golf	£12,800	43
Gymnastics	£32,500	80
Handball	£1,800	6
Hockey	£26,600	43
Hurling	£200	1
Ice Hockey	£5,400	27
Ice Skating	£30,800	44
Judo	£56,900	110
Karate	£17,700	17
Lawn Tennis	£22,600	45
Modern Pentathlon	£15,700	14
Netball	£5,100	24
Orienteering	£15,200	41
Roller Hockey	£4,100	9
Roller Skating	£9,200	20
Rowing	£42,600	58
Rugby League	£3,000	12
Rugby Union	£1,900	7
Sailing	£44,900	75
Shooting	£12,000	26
Skiing	£18,500	39
Softball	£500	2
Squash	£22,000	52
Swimming	£72,300	139
Table Tennis	£19,800	50
Trampoline	£23,500	46
Triathlon	£9,800	23
Volleyball	£14,500	42
Water Skiing	£19,700	23
Weightlifting	£17,300	40
Wrestling	£3,000	6

SportsAid and the Lottery Sports Fund

The introduction of lottery funding for individuals in 1997 meant that many of the established competitors who would previously have received SAF support are now funded through the World Class Performance programme outlined above. As a result SAF was relaunched as SportsAid, the Charity for Sport. It has a clear focus on young sportspeople who do not yet qualify for individual support under the World Class Programme.

To enable SportsAid to allocate its resources as effectively as possible, national governing bodies have been invited to submit a specified number of applications for support. SportsAid has asked governing bodies to identify youngsters, mainly aged 12 to 18, who clearly have talent but who also need financial support. SportsAid may also consider children under 12 or young people aged 19, 20 or 21, provided that the national governing body can make a special case for them.

SportsAid operates at both a national and a regional level. At present, applicants who do not receive a national grant will be referred to their local SportsAid and may receive a smaller regional grant. On average, a national grant is £500 for one year; a regional grant is between £200 and £250.

'Applications for SportsAid grants have always been submitted via, and endorsed by, the appropriate governing body. This procedure will continue in the future and SportsAid is confident that governing bodies will invite anyone who might qualify for a grant to complete an application form.'

Future plans

In December 1998, just before this Guide was published, it was announced that young sportspeople in England, who are included within a governing body's World Class Start plan, can apply for a SportsAid grant. These grants will be given by the SportsAid regions in England. Nationally, SportsAid will continue to help with the funding of individual performers from a wide range of sports. These will include some of those who do not meet the access criteria for Lottery funding. At the time of writing, details were still being finalised. Interested parties should contact their sport's national governing body for further details as they become clear.

Competitors from Northern Ireland, Scotland and Wales should note that the above information only applies to England. There are SportsAid bodies in each of the Home Countries and contact details are given below.

SportsAid's trustees have identified the following sports as priorities for SportsAid funding:

Archery (Target, Field)
Athletics
Badminton
Baseball
Basketball
Bobsleigh
Boxing
Canoeing (Flat Water, Slalom,
    Wild Water, Marathon)
Cricket
Curling
Cycling
Cyclo-cross
Equestrian (Three Day Eventing,
    Dressage, Show Jumping)
Fencing
Golf
Gymnastics (Artistic, Rhythmic,
    Sports Acrobatics)
Handball
Hockey
Indoor Hockey (*not* Mixed)
Ice Hockey
Ice Skating (Figure/Dance, Speed)
Judo
Karate
Lawn Tennis

Luge
Modern Pentathlon
Mountain Biking
Netball
Orienteering
Roller Hockey
Roller Skating (Artistic, Speed)
Rowing
Rugby League
Rugby Union
Sailing
Shooting
Skiing and Snowboarding
    (Olympic disciplines only)
Softball
Squash
Swimming (Long Course, Synchro,
    Water Polo, Diving, Long Distance)
Table Tennis
Trampolining
Triathlon (Olympic distance)
Volleyball
Water Skiing (Tournament only,
    not Barefoot)
Weightlifting/Powerlifting
Windsurfing (Olympic classes)

The following sports for disabled competitors are also SportsAid priorities:

Archery
Athletics
Badminton
Basketball
Boccia
Canoeing
Cycling
Equestrian
Fencing
Goalball
Ice Sports
Judo
Lawn Bowls

Lawn Tennis
Powerlifting
Racketball
Sailing
Shooting
Skiing (Alpine, Nordic, Biathlon)
Soccer
Snooker
Swimming
Table Tennis
Volleyball
Water Skiing
Wheelchair Rugby

SportsAid contact addresses

National bodies

SportsAid – National Headquarters, Lynton House, 7-12 Tavistock Square, London WC1H 9TL (0171-387 9380; Fax: 0171-380 0283).
E-mail: enquiries@sportsaid.org.uk; Website: www.sportsaid.org.uk
Director: Chris Goldie

Scottish Sports Aid Foundation, 76 Constitution Street, Edinburgh EH6 6RP (0131-555 4584). Director: George Bowmaker.

SportsAid Cymru/Wales, The National Sports Centre of Wales, Sophia Gardens, Cardiff CF1 9SW (01222-397571). Director: Ron Jones.

Ulster Sports & Recreation Trust, House of Sport, Upper Malone Road, Belfast BT9 5LA (01232-381222). Administration Officer: Robin Mitchell.

Regional contacts

SportsAid Northern, University of Durham, School House, Haworth Building, Leazes Road, Durham DH1 1TA (Tel/Fax: 0191-374 1720). Administrator: Marion Bell.
Area covered: Cleveland, Cumbria, Durham, Northumberland, and Tyne & Wear.

SportsAid North West, Belle Vue Athletics & Leisure Centre, Pink Bank Lane, Longsight, Manchester M12 5GL (0161-231 7775; Fax: 0161-231 7705). Administrator : Marva Campbell.
Area covered: Cheshire, Greater Manchester, Lancashire, and Merseyside.

SportsAid South East: at the time of writing, the contact address had not been finalised. For further information, please contact SportsAid Headquarters at the address above.
Area covered: Surrey, East and West Sussex and Kent.

SportsAid South West, Sunset Cottage, Gew Terrace, Redruth, Cornwall TR15 1PF (01209-216784). Regional Director: Roger Luke.
Area covered: Avon, Cornwall, Devon, Dorset, Gloucestershire, Somerset and Wiltshire.

SportsAid Southern, Watlington House, Watlington Street, Reading, Berkshire RG1 4RJ (0118-959 7804; Fax: 0118-957 6111). Administrator: Jean Wathen.
Area covered: Berkshire, Buckinghamshire, Hampshire, Isle of Wight, and Oxfordshire.

SportsAid West Midlands, 3 Beverley Close, Balsall Common, Coventry CV7 7GA (01676-533504/535911). Administrator: Muriel Taylor.
Area covered: West Midlands Metropolitan Authorities, Hereford & Worcester, Shropshire, Staffordshire, and Warwickshire.

SportsAid Yorkshire & Humberside, Coronet House, Queen Street, Leeds LS1 4PW (0113-242 7627). Administrator: Kristina Rafnson-Hall.
Area covered: North, South and West Yorkshire, and Humberside.

SportsAid East Midlands: at the time of writing, the contact address had not been finalised. For further information, please contact SportsAid Headquarters at the address above.
Area covered: Derbyshire, Leicestershire, Lincolnshire, Northamptonshire, and Nottinghamshire.

SportsAid Eastern: at the time of writing, the contact address had not been finalised. For further information, please contact SportsAid Headquarters at the address above.
Area covered: Bedfordshire, Cambridgeshire, Essex, Hertfordshire, Norfolk, and Suffolk.

SportsAid London: at the time of writing, the contact address had not been finalised. For further information, please contact SportsAid Headquarters at the address above.
Area covered: Greater London boroughs.

Other forms of support for individuals

Grants from governing bodies

Each major sport has its own governing body (for more information see chapter 15 on Sports governing bodies). Some, but by no means all, give grants to individuals either from their own resources or from related funds.

For example, the Ivor Montegu Junior Fund gives grants to English table tennis players under 17 who show international potential. The money typically will contribute towards training camp or course fees. The British Sub Aqua Club 'consider all applications from individuals. To be successful, the individual must demonstrate a benefit to scuba diving and the underwater environment.' The British Dragon Boat Racing Association only gives grants to help with travel expenses for those selected for national teams.

Almost all grants given through governing bodies are for excellence rather than participation. If they are given through a related charitable trust there must be evidence of real financial need and these grants are often for young people. One such trust, the Mark Lees Foundation supports rowers under 23 years of age aiming for selection to national teams and who are experiencing hardship. (See chapter 12 on Raising money from grant-making trusts for foundations supporting individual sportsmen and women.)

Chapter 15 on Sports governing bodies includes information on over 90 sports. Wherever possible there is an indication of whether the governing body gives support to individuals. Where this is not clear, or you need further information, a telephone call to the relevant governing body should be enough to establish if there is any help available. If your governing body cannot help, ask if they know of anybody who can.

The Foundation for Sport and the Arts

The FSA is well known for its giving to sports organisations (see chapter 8). As well as an amount set aside for SportsAid support to individuals (see above), FSA also gives a very small number of direct grants to individuals. Recent grants have included £300 towards equipment costs for a martial arts competitor, £500 for a cyclist's travel, equipment and training, and £1,900 for a triathlete's bike and wet suit.

'In such cases it is essential that the exceptional nature of the application is attested to in unqualified terms by an organisation of substance. In cases where the Foundation finds it possible to help it is almost always because trustees fear real potential may be blighted by the difficult financial background of the persons concerned.' Much more often the grant is for a small group of sportsmen or women to take part in an event in their field.

For further details contact: The Foundation for Sport & the Arts, PO Box 20, Liverpool L13 1HB (0151-259 5505).

The Prince's Trust

The Prince's Trust aims to help young people to succeed by providing opportunities which they would otherwise not have. The Prince's Trust is wide-ranging in its national support of young disadvantaged people offering training, support for business start-ups and loans and grants.

Where there is disadvantage or a young person cannot continue effectively in their sport without help, the Prince's Trust may be able to help. Individual sportsmen or women can meet informally with a Local Assessor to discuss their application. The assessor's recommendation is then passed to the local grants committee for approval. Grants are around £500 for individuals.

Grants are given where there is disadvantage and have recently included £500 to a young swimmer with learning difficulties and £450 for sailing lessons for a young person in foster care.

For more information on the Prince's Trust contact 0800-842842, or write to: The Prince's Trust, 18 Park Square East, London NW1 4LH (Fax: 0171-543 1200)

Relief-in-need charities

So far, the funds described in this chapter are those which are mainly interested in promoting sporting excellence. Often however, people playing at county or school team standard are looking for support for costs connected with participating in their sport. Although the funds concerned with excellence will be closed to non-élite sportspeople there may be other local non-specific sports funds which can help. (Chapter 12 details sports-specific trusts interested mainly in élite individuals.)

There are well over 2,000 local and national charities which are set up specifically to help people in financial need. They have all kinds of weird and wonderful origins from helping families of tea planters in the former British colonies to people with certain surnames. Many more are restricted by the geographical areas in which they can give or the age of the people they can help. For example, the Christ Church Fund for Children can only give grants to children aged 17 and under who live in Birkenhead. Anyone older than this or who lives outside Birkenhead cannot be helped.

Because they are charities, these funds can only give money either for the relief of poverty or the advancement of education. They cannot give to affluent individuals who want to do some warm weather winter training, but they can give grants to a promising footballer from a poor family who cannot afford a new pair of boots for the school team.

To list all the funds of possible relevance is well beyond the scope of this book. For further information, see *A Guide to Grants for Individuals in Need* and *The Educational Grants Directory*, both published by the Directory of Social Change, 24 Stephenson Way, London NW1 2DP (0171-209 5151; Fax: 0171-209 5049). They may well be in your local library. Alternatively, copies of *A Guide to Grants for Individuals in Need* are in all citizen's advice bureaux. (The address of your local CAB will be in the telephone directory.)

These books are the only comprehensive guides to such charities. They can look daunting, but do not panic. They are divided into various sections. Firstly, look at the local charities section to see if there is a local charity which serves the county, town, village or parish in which you live. If so, are you eligible to apply?

If there are no local charities, you may be eligible for help from an occupational charity. These are set up to look after people who used to do a certain job (e.g. mechanical engineering) but who have now fallen on hard times. They often can help the children of such people.

Alternatively, if you or a parent used to serve in the armed forces, there is extensive welfare provision for former members and their families. If you have a particular medical condition or disability there are various sickness and disability charities who may be able to help.

Whichever charity you decide to apply to, you need to do one of two things:

- If it is a relief-in-need charity, you must show evidence of real financial hardship as well as the need for the equipment/training or whatever.
- If it is an educational charity, stress the educational benefits of the activity.

Sometimes you will have to fill out an application form for help. Often a letter saying what you need, why you need it and why you cannot afford it yourself will be enough.

Such charities tend not to get applications for sporting equipment. Therefore, it can be very helpful to include a reference from a coach, teacher, youth worker, doctor, church minister, or similar third party saying how you would benefit from the equipment and how you are unable to afford it yourself. Show that your sporting commitment is not a passing fancy, rather it is serious.

Also note that most grants given by such charities are small (under £100) and are one-off. However, they can really help pay for necessary equipment that you could not afford otherwise. As with all charitable trusts, making the effort to stay in touch will help your case. One local relief-in-need charity which helped a promising young tennis player with the costs of a residential tennis school did not extend the support when they heard nothing from the beneficiary beyond an acknowledgement of the grant.

Further help and guidance is contained in each of the books listed above.

Chapter 15

Sports governing bodies

■■

Governing bodies are central to the organisation of your sport. They can be a useful source of information and advice when planning competitions, considering insurance schemes or looking for coaching and refereeing expertise. In some cases there may be small funds which can help with specific costs, either for individuals or for organisations. Whether they can help financially or not, their expertise can be invaluable.

What is a sports governing body?

Sports governing bodies are responsible for running organised sport in Britain. They represent an impressive range of sports (the ones listed below cover over 90 sports) and a large number of sportsmen and women. Their role and influence is extensive, ranging from drawing up the rules and regulations of the game and providing coaching awards/schemes, to organising competitions or events at local, national and international level, and selecting national teams. Under the World Performance Programme they have a vital role in securing support for élite sportsmen and women. (See chapter 14 on Raising money for individuals.)

Many governing bodies receive grants and services from the Sports Councils. In 1997/98 Sport England contributed almost £5 million in revenue grants to over 100 recognised governing bodies. (Recognised governing bodies are those where Sport England has identified sporting activities 'with which it is to be associated and which should be developed'.) Bodies which are not recognised as eligible for direct support by Sport England can still receive grants and services from other sources.

However, all governing bodies, whether they receive funding from Sport England or not, can raise additional money elsewhere. This can be through fundraising activities or events, promotional or sponsorship deals or applying to grant-givers. Some are very active in generating money; others are not. Income can vary immensely which will directly affect how much help they can give.

How can governing bodies help?

Advice
Every governing body should be able to give help and advice to clubs and

individual sportsmen and women. This can be anything from guidance on the rules and laws of the game and how to start or run a club, to where to get funding from or how to deal with tax and VAT issues. For example, the National Rifle Association provides information on the administration of firearms law, while the British Canoe Union issues waterways licences for members. In some sports where safety is particularly important, affiliation to the recognised governing body/bodies of sport is a condition of a National Lottery grant. (See page 69 for the sports this applies to.)

Coaching & sports development

Some governing bodies take a lead role in their sport at the grass roots. The Golf Foundation, for example, subsidises instruction by golf professionals to students at college, university or school. It has also just launched a starter centre initiative to increase coaching opportunities in 350 planned centres throughout the country. Where the governing body runs such programmes you may well be able to link in with them.

Cash help

Many governing bodies can give grants from their own resources or through associated charitable trusts. Amounts available range from £50 to over £50,000. Some give to organisations only, others to individuals. Some concentrate on élite performance, whilst others support participation at all levels. If you are planning a fundraising appeal, ask your governing body early on if they can help. If so, this could be a useful lever in raising funds from the Foundation for Sport and the Arts, the National Lottery or whoever.

Equipment and non-cash support

Help may also be available with equipment (e.g. the British Triathlon Association can provide equipment to event organisers), preferential insurance schemes (e.g. canoeing, cycling, fencing, martial arts), or discounted tickets for events and competitions (e.g. the English Basketball Association).

Support, endorsements & contacts

If the governing body cannot give money, it may be able to make helpful supporting statements, or introduce you to influential people. A letter of support from the governing body can help enormously when you are applying to other funders.

It is worth remembering that many of the above grants and services are only available to individuals, teams or clubs who are members of their sports governing body. The cost of joining can vary, as can the benefits attached to membership. However, as an individual you can expect to pay between £2 and £59 a year depending upon the sport, and receive anything from a magazine/ handbook to a package including competition access, privileged insurance rates, legal advice, ticket discounts, and free information booklets.

The main function of governing bodies remains the running of programmes to develop their sport. The Central Council of Physical Recreation is the representative forum for governing bodies where concerns about sport generally can be raised. The CCPR can make representation on their behalf to government or other interests to ensure that the voice of organised sport is heard.

Questions to ask your governing body

When approaching your governing body for help, the following questions should help you in getting the information you need.

- Do we/I need to be a member? If so, how much does it cost and what are the benefits?
- Does the governing body give financial support? If not directly is there an associated charitable trusts? Are there other bodies known to the governing bodies which can help?
- Does the governing body run coaching schemes or training for officials? If so, how can they be used locally or regionally in clubs or schools?
- Are there any useful publications/leaflets?
- Can the governing body give a letter of endorsement for an activity or project?
- Is there anyone else it would be useful to talk to for help?
- Is there any other help or advice the governing body can give?

A list of the governing bodies

Governing bodies differ enormously and they can give different kinds of help. Each of the governing bodies listed below was approached for information on how they support their sport. Many were very forthcoming and supplied full information. Others were less so. Some governing bodies cover Great Britain, others only England. Where you are looking for information in Northern Ireland, Scotland or Wales, ask the Sports Council for the country (addresses on page 335) for contact details.

We have listed the governing bodies by alphabetical order of the various sports. Some have more than one governing body. You may need to contact them all before you get the help and information you are looking for. Where there are changes in addresses, Sport England Information Centre (0171-273 1500; Fax: 0171-383 5740) should be able to provide further information.

Where the sport is not recognised by Sport England, it is marked with an asterisk: ★

Aikido

The British Aikido Board
Contact: Shirley Timms, Secretary, 6 Halkingcroft, Langley, Slough SL3 7AT (01753-577878)
Beneficial area: Great Britain.

American Football

The British American Football Association
Contact: Gary Marshall, Chairman, West House, Hedley on the Hill, Stocksfield, Northumberland NE43 7SW (01661-843179; Fax: 01661-843179)
Beneficial area: England, Scotland, Wales.
Membership: Membership is £2 for individual members of federations who are affiliated to the BAFA. Benefits of membership are registration, insurance, entry to leagues, and national and international teams. There are currently 2,800 members.
Grants available: None.
Other information: The association can support affiliated members with development plans and grant applications to funders.

Angling

The Angling Foundation
Contact: Vince Lister, Chair, 23 Southdown Road, Benham Hill, Thatcham, Berkshire RG19 3BF
Beneficial area: England.
Grants available: None.
Other information: Leaflets, posters and information sheets covering angling and ecology information are distributed free of charge, mainly to young people. Also, fishing tackle is donated to causes such as those raising funds for charity, and junior or disabled anglers groups.

National Federation of Anglers
Contact: William J Hall, Chief Administration Officer, Halliday House, Egginton Junction, Derbyshire DE65 6GU (01283-734735; Fax: 01283-734799)
Beneficial area: England.
Membership: Membership fees range from £242 each year to £1,650, depending on the size of the association. Benefits include: general and legal advice; scientific service; participation in, or attendance at, local and national events. 439 clubs were affiliated in 1997.
Grants available: None.
Other information: General advice is given through the regions, clubs and members.

Archery

The Association for Archery in Schools
Contact: Christopher Fletcher-Campbell, Hon Secretary, Bloxham School, Banbury, Oxon OX15 4PE (01295-721463; Fax: 01295-721463)
Beneficial area: UK.
Membership: Annual fees are £5 per club with a further £14 affiliation fee to the Grand National Archery Society. Benefits include reduced entry fees for annual outdoor and indoor championships; postal leagues, and an achievement scheme.

Other information: The association does not give grants. It states: 'Grants for development to both clubs and individuals are rare and come from non-sport specific funding bodies'.

The Grand National Archery Society
Contact: John Middleton, Chief Executive, National Agricultural Centre, Seventh Street, Stoneleigh Park, Kenilworth, Warwickshire CV8 2LG (01203-696631; Fax: 01203-419662)
Beneficial area: Great Britain.
Membership: Fees are £20 through clubs or £28 direct.
Grants to organisations: The society only gives one grant which is to the Association for Archery in Schools.

Arm Wrestling

British Arm Wrestling Federation
Contact: David Shead, 20 Lancaster Avenue, London SE27 9DZ (0181-761 0567)

Athletics

The Amateur Athletic Association of England
Contact: Geoff Clarke, Honorary Treasurer, 'Dunrunin', 9 Whitehouse Avenue, Great Preston, Woddlesfold, Leeds LS26 8BN (0113-286 2590; Fax: 0113-286 2590)
Beneficial area: England.
Membership: Currently, 1,300 clubs are affiliated to regional

bodies. Benefits include access to coaching, and entry to championships.
Grants to individuals and organisations: See entry in the chapter on Raising money from grant-making trusts, page 225.
Exclusions: Non-affiliated clubs are not supported.
Other information: The AAA is responsible for promoting annual championships for all age groups (above 11 years of age) in all athletic disciplines: track and field, road running, cross country, fell running, race walking, tug of war etc.

The British Athletic Federation Ltd
Contact: Mrs Koster, Financial Accountant, 30a Harborne Road, Edgbaston, Birmingham (0121-456 5098; Fax: 0121-440 0555)
Beneficial area: United Kingdom.
Membership: Yes, by clubs/ associations to regional associations.
Other information: The federation is in transition at present. It is not currently giving support other than advice and information to member associations. Policies may be reviewed in the future.

The federation is aligned to two registered charities – the British Athletic Foundation (see entry in the chapter on Raising money from grant-making trusts, page 226) and the British Athletic Benevolent Fund.

Badminton

The Badminton Association of England

Contact: Steve Baddeley, Chief Executive, National Badminton Centre, Bradwell Road, Loughton Lodge, Milton Keynes MK8 9LA (01908-268400; Fax: 01908-268412)
Beneficial area: England.
Membership: Fees are £6.50. All members are provided with personal accident insurance and physiotherapy insurance. There are over 50,000 members.
Grants available: None.

Baseball

The British Baseball Federation

Contact: Kevin Macadam, Administration Secretary, PO Box 45, Hessle, North Humberside HU13 0YQ (01482-643551; Fax: 01482-640224)
Beneficial area: Great Britain.
Membership: Junior players under 16, free; junior players 16–18, £12.50; senior players over 18, £25.
Grants available: None.
Other information: Non-cash support is given in the form of advice, a schools development pack, factsheets, publications and roadshows.

Basketball

The British and Irish Basketball Federation

Contact: Mel Welch, Secretary, Carnegie National Sports Development Centre, Beckett Park, Leeds LS6 3QS (01532-832600 Ext. 3574)

Beneficial area: Great Britain and Ireland.
Membership: National governing bodies of basketball only.
Grants to organisations:
Examples of grants are: £1,500 to the British Universities Sports Federation for the GB World Student Games basketball team, and £5,000 to the English Basketball Association for a Basketball Development Guide.
Grants to individuals: None.
Grant total: £9,800 (1993/94)
Exclusions: The federation only supports projects covering the whole of at least one country in the British Isles.
Applications: Written applications outlining proposals to be sent to the contact.
Other information: No non-cash support given.

The English Basketball Association

Contact: Andrew Matthews, General Manager, 48 Bradford Road, Stanningley, Pudsey W Yorkshire LS28 6DF (0113-236 1166; Fax: 0113-236 1022)
Beneficial area: England.
Membership: Fees are: junior £4; senior £10.50 and student £7.50. Benefits include: public liability, all risks and personal accident insurance schemes; bi-monthly newspaper; free information booklets; ticket discounts. There are currently 18,000 members.
Grants available: None.

The English Mini Basketball Association

Contact: Ken Charles, General Secretary, PO Box 22, Royston, Herts SG8 5NB (01223-207213; Fax: 01223-207166)

Beneficial area: UK.

Membership: Fees are £8 per year. Benefits include guidelines and rules, access to coaching awards and entry to competitions. There are currently over 350 members.

Grants available: None.

The English Schools Basketball Association

Contact: Norman E Waldron, Secretary, 44 Northleat Avenue, Kings Ash, Paignton, Devon TQ3 3UG (01803-842289 – work; 01803-523183 – home)

Beneficial area: England.

Membership: Fees are: £8 for individual schools with the benefit of competitions and attendance at national team trials; £30–£70 for associations (depending upon the number of schools in the local authority) with the benefit of competitions and voting rights.

Grants to organisations: 30–40 one-off grants for under 15's development programmes and rallies.

Grants to individuals: Only towards expenses of national team membership.

Grant total: £5,000 (1993/94).

Applications: In writing on a form available from: Stephen Hozier, Development Secretary, 9 Pretoria Cottages, Barton Road, Harlington, Nr Dunstable, Bedfordshire LU5 6LG.

Other information: Non-cash support is given in the form of advice and publications.

The Great Britain Wheelchair Basketball Association

Contact: Miss J M Stone MBE, Treasurer, 39 Orwell Drive, Aylesbury, Bucks HP21 8JL

Beneficial area: Great Britain.

Membership: Benefits include eligibility to participate in wheelchair basketball.

Grants to organisations: Yes. No details given.

Grants to individuals: Yes. No details given.

Other information: Non-cash support is given in the form of information, newsletters and a handbook.

Bicycle Polo

Bicycle Polo Association of Great Britain

Contact: Garry Beckett, General Secretary, 5 Archer Road, South Norwood, London SE25 4JN (0181-656 9724)

Billiards

The World Professional Billiards & Snooker Association

Contact: Martin Blake, Company Director, 27 Oakfield Road, Clifton, Bristol BS8 2AT (01272-744491)

Bobsleigh

The British Bobsleigh Association

Contact: Henrietta Alderman, General Secretary, The Chestnuts, 85 High Street, Codford, Warminster, Wiltshire BA12 0NB (01985-850064; Fax: 01985-850094)

Beneficial area: UK.

289

Membership: Fees are £24 per year. Benefits include: summer training with the BBA athletics coach; attending and participating in national, and if appropriate, international events; and association's annual publication.
Grants available: None.
Other information: Non-cash support is given in the form of advice from administrative and coaching staff, and publications.

Boccia

British Boccia Association
Contact: Dean Thomas, Development Officer, 11 Churchill Park, Colwick, Nottingham NG4 2HF (0115-940 1202; Fax: 0115-940 2984)
Beneficial area: UK.
Grants available: None.

Bowling

The English Bowling Association
Contact: G Shaw, Secretary, Lyndhurst Road, Worthing, W Sussex BN11 2AZ (01903-820222; Fax: 01903-820444)
Beneficial area: England.
Membership: Fees are: £2 per person per year (in addition to club fees).
Grants to organisations: The association provides interest-free green maintenance loans of up to £2,000 for the benefit of member clubs.
Grants to individuals: None.
Other information: The association gives advice on sources of possible funding to member clubs.

The English Bowling Federation
Contact: John Heppel, National Secretary, 84 School Road, Beighton, Sheffield S20 1EH (0114-2477763; Fax: 0114-2477763)
Beneficial area: England.
Membership: Benefits include participation in national indoor and outdoor competitions. There are currently 28,000 members.
Grants available: None.

The English Indoor Bowling Association
Contact: David Brown, Secretary, David Cornwell House, Bowling Green, Leicester Road, Melton Mowbray, Leics LE13 0DB (01664-481900; Fax: 01664-481901)
Beneficial area: England.
Membership: Members pay an annual levy through affiliated clubs. Benefits include: encouraging international representation and competitive participation; and providing development advice.
Grants available: None.
Other information: Non-cash support is given in the form of advice on possible funding sources to develop existing and new facilities. The association publishes an annual yearbook.

The English Short Mat Bowling Association
Contact: Norman Dickenson, Secretary, 10 Bradley Close, Middlewich, Cheshire CW10 0PF
Beneficial area: England.

The English Women's Bowling Association

Contact: Nancie Colling, Honorary Secretary, The Royal Pump Rooms, Leamington Spa, Warwickshire CV32 4AB (01926-430686; Home: 01297-21317)
Beneficial area: England.

The English Women's Bowling Federation

Contact: Mrs I Younger, Secretary, Irela, Holburn Crescent, Ryton, Tyne & Wear NE40 3DH (0191-413 3160)
Beneficial area: England.
Membership: Currently 13 county associations are members. The Federation organises regional and national competitions.
Grants available: None.

The English Women's Indoor Bowling Association

Contact: Margaret Ruff, Secretary, 3 Scirocco Close, Moulton Park, Northampton NN3 6AP (01604-494163; Fax: 01604-494434)
Beneficial area: England.

The British Isles Bowls Council

Contact: John Darling, Honorary Secretary, 2 Pentland Avenue, Gowkshill, Gorebridge, Scotland EH23 4PG (01875-821105; Fax: 01875-821105)
Beneficial area: UK.
Membership: National governing bodies of England, Ireland (including Eire), Scotland, Wales and the Channel Islands.
Grants available: None.

Boxing

The Amateur Boxing Association of England Ltd

Contact: Colin Brown, Company Secretary, Crystal Palace National Sports Centre, London SE19 2BB (0181-778 0251; Fax: 0181-778 9324)
Beneficial area: England.

The British Amateur Boxing Association

Contact: Frank Hendry, 96 High Street, Lochee, Dundee DD2 3AY (01382-611412)

Schools' Amateur Boxing Association

Contact: E A Blow, Honorary Treasurer, Archways, 15 Beacon Avenue, Herne Bay, Kent CT6 6JR (01227-364405; Fax: 01227-364405)
Beneficial area: England.
Membership: Fees are £5 annually per school; associate members and individuals pay £5 a year and life members a one-off fee of £50. Benefits for schools include advice, guidance, access to equipment in some circumstances.
Grants to organisations: The association has recently started a new capital fund. One-off grants are given to schools, resident associations, community associations, leisure centres and social services in areas of deprivation, disadvantage and social exclusion. Amounts are between £200 and £300 for equipment to establish boxing in buildings which are secure.
Grants to individuals: None.
Exclusions: Grants are not given for administration costs.

Applications: In writing at any time to: D Savill, Honorary Secretary, Schools ABA, 11 Beaconsfield Road, Ealing, London W5 5JE. Applicants should include information about the local need, location of the activity and how it is to be sustained.

Canoeing

The British Canoe Union
Contact: Paul Owen, John Dudderidge House, Adbolton Lane, West Bridgford, Nottingham NG2 5AS (0115-982 1100; Fax: 0115-982 1797)
Beneficial area: Great Britain.
Membership: Fees are: £28 for adults (comprehensive), £17 for basic; £16.50 for under 18s (comprehensive), £10.50 for basic. Benefits include: insurance, waterways licence, yearbook, magazine competitions and coaching (comprehensive).
Grants to organisations: Limited help is available through the Jubilee Canoeing Foundation (see entry in the chapter on Raising money from grant-making trusts, page 227.
Grants to individuals: None.

Caving

National Caving Association
Contact: The Secretary, Monomark House, 27 Old Gloucester Street, London WC1N 3XX
Beneficial area: England and Wales.
Membership: Fees are £10 for clubs and £40 for constituent bodies. There are currently 350 members.

Grants to organisations: There may be occasional help with regional conservation and/or access projects. Expedition funding is administered through the Ghar Parav Foundation. Requests are only considered from member organisations.
Grants to individuals: None.

Cricket

The English Schools Cricket Association
Contact: Ken Lake, General Secretary, 38 Mill House, Woods Lane, Cottingham, North Humberside HU16 4HQ (01482-844446)
Beneficial area: England.

The England and Wales Cricket Board
Contact: Lords Cricket Ground, London NW8 8QZ (0171-432 1200; Fax: 0171-286 5583)
Beneficial area: England and Wales.
Membership: £12 per team per year for the recreational game. No fees are payable for professional game.
Grants to organisations: See entry for the Cricket Foundation below and in the chapter on Raising money from grant-making trusts, page 228.
Other information: Non-cash support is available in the form of advice and publications. The ECB produces a free booklet: *Sources of Grant Aid and Development Funding for Cricket.*

The Cricket Foundation

Contact: Terry Bates, Secretary, c/o England and Wales Cricket Board, Lords Cricket Ground, London NW8 8QZ (0171-432 1200; Fax: 0171-289 5619)

Beneficial area: England and Wales.

Membership: Fees are £10 per club. Benefits include: publications, insurance, competition entry and eligibility for grants from Lord's Taverners (see entry in the chapter on Raising money from grant-making trusts, page 229). 6,500 clubs are currently members.

Grants to organisations: The Cricket Foundation is an independent charity for the development of cricket. It works closely with the ECB and funding is directed through county cricket boards. See entry in the chapter on Raising money from grant-making trusts, page 228.

Grants to individuals: None.

Grant total: £2.5 million in 1997/98.

Exclusions: Only county boards can apply.

Applications: Through County Cricket Boards.

The Women's Cricket Association

Contact: Barbara Daniels, Executive Director, Warwickshire County Cricket Club, Edgbaston Road, Birmingham B5 7QX (0121-440 0567; Fax: 0121-440 0520)

Beneficial area: England.

Membership: Benefits include: entry to WCA competitions and players to be considered for county/England teams. Members also receive newsletters, a fixture card, a yearbook and discount prices on cricket balls. Costs vary from £5 per year for associates and schools to £25 per year for clubs.

Grants available: None.

Other information: Non-cash support is given in the form of posters, artwork and leaflets for members to promote women's cricket.

Croquet

The Croquet Association

Contact: Paul Campion, Secretary, Hurlingham Club, Ranelagh Gardens, London SW6 3PR (0171-736 3148; Fax: 0171-736 3148)

Beneficial area: England.

Membership: Membership is £22 per year. Benefits include entry to tournaments, magazine, discount on equipment. There are currently over 1,500 members.

Grants to organisations: One-off grants and loans are available to registered clubs to improve facilities. Grants are up to about £500.

Grants to individuals: None.

Grant total: £1,000 (1993)

Applications: Applications are made using a standard pro forma through the local federation development officer, who should be fully briefed on the club's plans before submission.

Other information: Non-cash support is given through the local federations in the form of advice, equipment and coaching.

Crown Green Bowling

The British Crown Green Bowling Association

Contact: J Crowther, Secretary, 94 Fishers Lane, Pensby, Wirral L61 8SB (0151-648 5740; Fax: 0151-648 0733)

Beneficial area: Great Britain.

Membership: Fees are £5 for life membership.

Grants to organisations: One-off grants between £50 and £500 are given for: new greens (£500); irrigation systems (£250); floodlights (£200); toilets (£100); new pavilions (£250); fences (£100); repairs to any of the above (£100).

Grants to individuals: None.

Grant total: £10,600 (1997)

Exclusions: Grants are not given for green maintenance equipment or 'expendable items'.

Applications: Completed application form to the correspondent stating the cost and purpose of the project.

Other information: The association provides non-cash support for members in the form of advice, equipment, and an annual handbook.

Curling

British Curling Association

Contact: M Kidd, Secretary, Cairnie House, Avenue K, Ingliston Showground, Newbridge, Midlothian EH28 2NB (0131-333 3003; Fax: 0131-333 3323)

The English Curling Association

Contact: Eric Hinds, Secretary, Little Wethers, Sandy Lane, Northwood, Middlesex HA6 3HA (01895-201000; Home: 01923-825004; Fax: 01895-201001)

Beneficial area: England.

Membership: Fees are £18 for full membership; juniors half-price. Benefits include: information, representation in international championships and coaching. There are currently 150 members.

Grants to organisations: Through capitation fees, the association helps to support three English teams (of four players) to compete in European and world championships. Awards of up to £1,000 are available to the teams.

Grants to individuals: None.

Grant total: £2,800 (1997) for English teams.

Exclusions: Awards are only given to English teams.

Applications: Through the contact.

Other information: The association says: 'It seems much easier to get money for a capital project than for annual expenses. We have teams that go abroad to represent England. We have not found anyone willing to help them on a regular basis – which is creating hardships. They are not well-off.'

The World Curling Federation

Contact: Mike Thomson, Secretary General, 81 Great King Street, Edinburgh EH3 6RN (0131-556 4884; Fax: 0131-556 9400)

Beneficial area: Worldwide.

Membership: 32 national associations are currently members. Members are eligible for world championships and the Olympic winter games through qualification.
Grants to organisations: Help is given in kind to member associations through providing equipment such as curling stones.
Grants to individuals: None.
Applications: Through the correspondent.

Cycling

The British Cycling Federation
Contact: Jim Hendry, Chief Executive, National Cycling Centre, Stuart Street, Manchester M11 4DQ (0161-230 2301; Fax: 0161-231 0591)
Beneficial area: Great Britain.
Membership: Fees are: £16 per year for affiliated membership. Benefits include: third party accident insurance; legal advice and assistance; touring information; coaching; and a handbook.
Grants available: None.
Other information: Non-cash support is available in the form of advice and publications.

The English Schools Cycling Association
Contact: Susan Knight, General Secretary, 21 Bedhampton Road, North End, Portsmouth PO2 7JX (01705-642226)
Beneficial area: England.
Membership: Fees are: private membership £4; school or club membership £10; local education authority/county membership £40.

Benefits include participation in the association's racing and touring activities; award scheme; overseas trips; coaching courses; and preparation for joining senior clubs.
Grants available: None.
Other information: Non-cash support is available in the form of advice, including information from LEA's on any new regulations concerning children in sport; publications; and occasionally, event prizes of equipment.

Cyclo-Cross

The British Cyclo-Cross Association
Contact: Brian Furness, General Secretary, 14 Deneside Road, Darlington, County Durham DL3 9HZ (01325-482052; Fax: 01325-482052)
Beneficial area: England.
Membership: By club affiliation. Fees are: £20 per year for an unsponsored club; £40 per year for a sponsored club. Benefits include third party public liability insurance and access to racing.
Grants to organisations: Development is devolved to 10 constituent area associations, which receive development funding via a Sport England grant. No funding is given to external organisations. The association is the governing body for the sport in England, and administers the sport at GB level. Responsibility for cyclo-cross in Wales and Scotland is devolved to the Welsh Cycling Union and Scottish Cycling Union, respectively.
Grants to individuals: None.
Grant total: £3,000 in England

295

(1997).

Other information: Non-cash support is given in the form of advice and publications.

Darts

The British Darts Organisation
Contact: Oliver Croft, Secretary, 2 Pages Lane, Muswell Hill, London N10 1PS (0181-883 5544)

Dragon Boat Racing

British Dragon Boat Racing Association
Contact: David Cogswell, 13 The Prebend, Northend, Leamington Spa, Warwickshire CV33 0TR (01295-770629; Fax: 01295-770629)
Beneficial area: UK.
Membership: Fees are: £130 for a crew, £65 for junior crews, and £20 for individuals (£10 for juniors). Benefits include insurance whilst racing, newsletters, training for officials, selection for GB crews. Total membership is currently 34 clubs and 350 individuals.
Grants to organisations: None.
Grants to individuals: One-off grants of £100 can be given to help with travel expenses for selected GB crew members.
Grant total: £100 for individuals (1998).
Applications: To the BDA secretary to be considered as the need arises.

Equestrian

The British Equestrian Federation
Contact: Colonel J D Smith-Bingham, British Equestrian Centre, Stoneleigh Park, Kenilworth, Warwickshire CV8 2LR (01203-696697)
Beneficial area: Great Britain.
Grants available: None.
Other information: The BEF supports competitors participating in international events and disseminates information on rules from the international federation.

The British Show Jumping Association
Contact: Andrew Finding, Secretary General, British Equestrian Centre, Stoneleigh Park, Kenilworth, Warwickshire CV8 2LR (01203-698800; Fax: 01203-696685)
Beneficial area: Great Britain.
Grants to organisations: None.
Grants to individuals: Grants are given for training of juniors under the age of 21 through the 'Training for Triumph' scheme. However, these grants are not awarded directly. Further details from the contact.
Exclusions: Under the present arrangements the BSJA would not give grants for prize money.

The Pony Club
Contact: Mrs J Clark, General Manager, NAC, Stoneleigh Park, Kenilworth, Warwickshire CV8 2RW (01203-696763; Fax: 01203-696836)
Beneficial area: UK.
Membership: Fees are £23 each

year. Benefits include: insurance, training, competitions and local branch activities. There are currently 37,000 members.

Grants to organisations: Equipment and loans are available to local branches.

Grants to individuals: None.

Other information: Non-cash support is given through advice and publications.

Fencing

The British Fencing Association
Contact: Miss G M Kenneally, Secretary, 1 Barons Gate, 33-35 Rothschild Road, London W4 5HT (0181-742 3032; Fax: 0181-742 3033)

Beneficial area: United Kingdom.

Membership: Fees range from £26 for full adult membership to £6.50 for under 14 'Musketeers'. Benefits include: insurance; coaching; proficiency awards; and a quarterly magazine.

Grants available: None.

Other information: Non-cash support is given through advice, equipment, and publications.

Flying

British Gliding Association
Contact: B Rolfe, Secretary, Kimberley House, 47 Vaughan Way, Leicester LE1 4SE (0116-253 1051; Fax: 0116-251 5939)

Popular Flying Association
Contact: Sheelagh Bailey, Director, Terminal Building, Shoreham Airport, Shoreham-by-Sea, West Sussex BN43 5FF (01273-461616; Fax: 01273-463390)

Beneficial area: UK.

Membership: Fees are £32. Benefits include magazine, expertise on regulations and engineering. Anyone building their own aircraft must belong to the association. There are currently 8,500 members.

Grants available: None.

Football

The English Schools Football Association
Contact: M R Berry, Chief Executive, 1-2 Eastgate Street, Stafford ST16 2NQ (01785-251142; Fax: 01785-255485)

Beneficial area: England.

Membership: Fees are between £20 and £50 per season. Members can compete in 11 national competitions. The association organises a programme of national and international events. 476 associations are currently members.

Grants to organisations: One-off grants between £150 and £500 and averaging £300 are given to member associations applying to the Disbursement Fund.

Grants to individuals: Very occasionally support is given to individuals such as £180 for an under 15 international squad physiotherapist to attend a course.

Grant total: £3,700 in 1997/98

Exclusions: The association does not support individual schools.

Applications: On an application form available from the contact. Applications are considered four or five times a year at trustees' meetings.

297

The Football Association
Contact: Graham Kelly, Chief Executive, 16 Lancaster Gate, London W2 3LW (0171-262 4542; Fax: 0171-402 0486)
Grants to organisations and individuals: See entries in the chapter on Raising money from grant-making trusts, page 231.

The Football Trust
Contact: Peter Lee, Chief Executive, Walkden House, 10 Melton Street, London NW1 2EB (0171-388 4504; Fax: 0171-388 6688)
Beneficial area: United Kingdom.
Grants to organisations: See entry in the chapter on Raising money from grant-making trusts, page 233.

The Women's Football Association
Contact: Kelly Simmons, Coordinator for Women's Football, 9 Wyllyotts Place, Potters Bar, Hertfordshire EN6 2JD (01707-651840; Fax: 01707-644190)

Golf

The English Ladies Golf Association
Contact: Marianne Carr, Secretary, Edgbaston Golf Club, Church Road, Edgbaston, Birmingham B15 3TB (0121-456 2088; Fax: 0121-454 5542)
Beneficial area: England.
Grants to organisations and individuals: See entry in the chapter on Raising money from grant-making trusts, page 239.

The English Golf Union
Contact: Paul Baxter, Secretary, The National Golf Centre, The Broadway, Woodhall Spa, Lincs LN10 6PU (01526-354500; Fax: 01526-354020)
Beneficial area: England.
Membership: Fees are £3 a year. Benefits include advice and a handicap system for all golfers. There are currently 720,000 members.
Grants to organisations: One-off and recurrent grants are given to national bodies and sports organisations for research, training and administration costs. Examples of some recent grants include: £55,000 to the Greenkeeper Training Committee, £10,000 to the Golf Foundation and £4,000 to the English Schools Golf Association. In 1997/98, grants totalling £90,000 were made to nine organisations, and ranged between £150 and £50,000. The union has a preference for recurrent grants.
Grants to individuals: None.
Grant total: £90,000 (1997/98)
Exclusions: The union does not give grants to individuals.
Applications: In writing to the correspondent. Applications are considered in September.
Other information: Non-cash support is given through advice on golf development, careers booklets and etiquette booklets. The union also provides coaching and international representation.

The Golf Foundation
Contact: Trevor Homer, Executive

Director, Foundation House, Hanbury Manor, Ware, Herts SG12 0UH (01920-484044; Fax: 01920-484055)

Beneficial area: United Kingdom & Eire.

Membership: Individual associate life membership is currently £50. Benefits include a bag tag, a tie or brooch and a copy of the Foundation's 'Tee to Green' magazine three times a year.

Grants to organisations: In 1997, recurrent grants totalling £297,000 were made to over 3,000 organisations and ranged between £150 and £550 a year. The foundation provides financial and technical assistance to promote the game at grass-roots level by, for example:

- subsidising instruction by professional golfers to students in schools, colleges and universities;
- subsidising instruction by professional golfers to junior members of golf clubs in full-time education;
- paying for golf instruction for disabled people;
- organising competition at schools' level;
- sponsoring Open Coaching Centres during the holidays.

A starter centre initiative has been launched, increasing the coaching funds available through 350 planned centres throughout the British Isles.

Grants to individuals: Special awards are given to young people who show particularly high attainment levels.

Grant total: £297,000 (1997)

Exclusions: No grants for golfing equipment, travel and tournament expenses, or university/college scholarships.

Applications: Applications, on a form available from the Foundation, are considered all year round. However, potential applicants are advised to make arrangements direct with a local golf club professional and to contact the Golf Foundation to register on the coaching scheme before classes commence.

Other information: Various publications and visual aids relating to golf are published by the Foundation.

The Royal and Ancient Golf Club

Contact: M F Bonallack, Secretary, St Andrews, Fife KY16 9JD (01334-472112; Fax: 01334-477580)

Beneficial area: Worldwide, excluding USA and Canada.

Membership: There are currently 102 member associations.

Grants to organisations: Grants are divided into three general areas: coaching (total grants £250,000); grass roots development (£198,000) and facilities (£991,000). One-off and recurrent grants, as well as loans, are given for capital items and equipment costs. Awards range from £12,000 to £198,000 and can be a grant, an interest-free loan or a combination of both. Loans are repayable over ten years.

Appeals which are likely to be considered favourably are: prevention of coastal erosion; repairs to a golf course after a disaster;

299

extending to eighteen holes; new course built in an area where no course presently exists; land purchase to keep course; greenkeepers' facilities required under Health and Safety regulations; installation of new irrigation systems or upgrading existing ones; course improvements; and provision of practice facilities where none exist.

Factors which will help an application: work on the course being given priority over everything else (e.g. clubhouse); available resources committed to project; entry fees, subscriptions and number of members being appropriate to available facilities; extent to which course is available for amateur championships; extent to which junior golfers are encouraged; extent to which course is open to visitors; prudent financial management; other financial help available.

Factors which will be unlikely to receive sympathy: improvements to clubhouse or carpark; extending beyond eighteen holes; building a new course in an area already well served; replacement of existing irrigation systems owing to wear and tear; normal course maintenance work.

Grants to individuals: No direct support is given. Grants are given to unions which may pass on support to individuals.

Grant total: £2.79 million (1997)

Exclusions: Commercially operated clubs that are exclusive.

Applications: On an application form to Ms C Corbett, External Funds Supervisory Committee.

Financial details of the project should be included with the latest accounts. Applications are considered in February, May and November.

Gymnastics

The British Schools Gymnastics Association
Contact: Clive Hamilton, Secretary, Orchard House, 15 North Common Road, Uxbridge, Middlesex UB8 1PD (01895-233377; Fax: 01895-814031)
Beneficial area: Great Britain.
Membership: Affiliation is £3 per school and £2 for each individual. There are currently 1,800 affiliated schools. Benefits include a handbook and entry to competitions.
Grants to organisations: The association provides affiliated regional bodies with grants to run courses and events. The association does not directly fund any individual or other organisation.
Grants to individuals: None.

Handball

The British Handball Association
Contact: Jeff Rowland, Chairman, 40 Newchurch Road, Rawtenstall, Rossendale, Lancashire BB4 7QX (01706-229354; Fax: 01706-229354)

Hang Gliding

British Hang Gliding and Paragliding Association
Contact: Jennifer Burdett, Secretary, The Old School Room, Loughborough Road, Leicester LE4 5PJ (0116-261 1322; Fax: 0116-261 1323)

Hockey

The English Hockey Association
Contact: Stephen Baines, Chief Executive, The Stadium, Silbury Boulevard, Milton Keynes, Bucks MK9 1HA (01908-544644; Fax: 01908-241106)
Beneficial area: England.
Membership: All male hockey teams are required to affiliate to the association in order to enter national competitions, receive the range of technical and administrative services, and play against any affiliated team. Fees range from £25 per season for juniors, to £122 for adult teams.
Grants to organisations: Grants of £1,000 have been made to divisions and counties to assist in administering competitions, coaching, and schools and youth activities. In 1995, grants totalling £3,000 were given to clubs such as Teddington and Havant, participating in European club championships.

Loans are given to clubs for capital improvements and the installation of artificial turf pitches. Ben Rhydding Hockey Club for example received a loan of £3,000 in 1995.

Grants to individuals: The Hockey Association Youth Trust makes grants to young players of potential, to assist in leadership training.
Exclusions: Non-affiliated bodies and clubs.
Applications: For development loans, applications should be made on a form available from the association. Otherwise, by letter at anytime.
Other information: The association gives advice on fundraising, and provides an annual handbook free to all affiliated clubs. Various publications are available on areas such as: coaching, rules of the game, and artificial turf.

Horse Racing

The Jockey Club
Contact: John Maxse, Public Relations Officer, 42 Portman Square, London W1H 0EN (0171-486 4921; Fax: 0171-935 8703)
Beneficial area: England, Scotland and Wales.
Grants available: None.

Hovercraft

Hovercraft Club of Great Britain
Contact: Rev Granville Spedding, 26 Milverton Close, Lostock, Bolton, Lancashire BL6 4PR (01204-841248)
Beneficial area: UK.
Membership: Fees are £30. Benefits include a monthly magazine, insurance, regulation of racing and cruising in UK. There

301

are currently 400 members.
Grants to organisations: None.
Grants to individuals: Very occasionally, research grants of up to £500 are given to students between 18 and 25 specialising in light sports hovercraft only.

Ice Hockey

The British Ice Hockey Association
Contact: David Pickles, General Secretary, Second Floor Suite, 517 Christchurch Road, Boscombe, Bournemouth BH1 4AG (01202-303946; Fax: 01202-398005)
Beneficial area: Great Britain.
Membership: Fees of between £5 and £25 are paid to local associations. Benefits include a coaching programme and selection of national teams. There are currently 7,500 players represented by the association.
Grants to organisations: Grants of between £10,000 and £50,000 are given to local associations for junior development, particularly for equipment costs.
Grants to individuals: None.
Grant total: £75,000 in 1997/98
Exclusions: No support for individuals.
Applications: Only registered clubs can apply. Applications are considered throughout the year.

Ice Skating

The National Ice Skating Association of UK Ltd
Contact: Celia Godsall, CEO, First Floor, 114-116 Curtain Road,

London EC2A 3AH (0171-613 1188; Fax: 0171-613 4616)
Beneficial area: UK.
Membership: Fees are: £16 for juniors and £20 for adults. Benefits include mailings, insurance, group travel discounts and priority tickets. There are currently 5,000 members.
Grants to organisations: None.
Grants to individuals: 'National and élite level performers may be eligible for grant aid. Skaters that receive grant aid will be national squad members. The amount is variable dependent on performance.'
Exclusions: Non-national squad skaters are not supported.

In-line Skating

British In-line Skater Hockey Association
Contact: Jan Millichip, Hornbeams, 4 Queens Road, Yardley, Birmingham B26 2AH (0121-680 4099)
Beneficial area: England, Scotland and Wales.
Membership: Benefits include: starter pack, mailings, coaching and referee courses, rule books and insurance. There are currently 8,000 members.
Grants to organisations: A development grant is given to regional associations.
Grants to individuals: None.
Other information: The association gives advice on development and sponsorship.

British In-line Skating Association
Contact: The Secretary, Suite 479, 2 Old Brompton Road, South Kensington, London SW7 3DQ (01860-345953; Fax: 01860-345953)
Beneficial area: UK and Eire.
Membership: Fees are £6.75. Benefits include insurance, newsletter and product discount card.
Grants available: None.
Other information: There is an information service available to all skaters, including a website: www.bisa.co.uk

Ju-Jitsu

The British Ju-Jitsu Association
Contact: M Dixon, 5 Avenue Parade, Accrington, Lancs BB5 6PN (0114-266 6733; Fax: 0114-266 6733)
Beneficial area: Great Britain.
Membership: Fees vary according to associations. Benefits include coaching qualifications, recognised grades, SNVQ. There are currently 25,000 members.
Grants available: None.

Judo

The British Judo Association
Contact: Shirley Startin, Office Manager, 7a Rutland Street, Leicester LE1 1RB (0116-255 9669; Fax: 0116-255 9660)

Kabaddi

National Kabaddi Association (UK)
Contact: Makhdoom Ahmad Christi, Birmingham City Council, Department of Leisure and Community Services, PO Box 2122, Baskerville House, Board Street, Birmingham B1 2NE (0121-303 2094; Fax: 0121-303 1542)
Beneficial area: UK.
Membership: Fees are £5. Benefits include insurance, training, championships and coaching. There are currently around 200 members.
Grants available: None.

Karate

The English Karate Governing Body
Contact: Brian Porch, General Administrator, 58 Bloomfield Drive, Bath BA2 2BG (01225-834008; Fax: 01225-834008)
Beneficial area: National.
Membership: Fees are £2.20 per year. There are currently 100,000 members.
Grants available: None.

Kendo

The British Kendo Association
Contact: Mrs J Hazelwood, Secretary, Coppice Lodge, Stafford Road, Teddesley, Nr Penkridge, Staffordshire ST19 5RP (01543-466334)

Korfball

British Korfball Association
Contact: Graham Crafter, PO Box 179, Maidstone, Kent ME14 1LU (01622-813115; Fax: 01622-813148)
Beneficial area: UK.
Membership: Membership is through clubs. Each team pays £85

with an additional £1 for each player. Benefits include coaching and refereeing courses, league competitions and international representation. There are over 1,000 affiliated members.

Grants to organisations: One-off grants are given for specific events in the association's designated areas only.

Grants to individuals: One-off grants are given to players representing Britain and for coaching.

Grant total: Figures are not disclosed.

Applications: In writing to the finance officer/development officer. Details should be included about how the person would benefit the sport. Applications can be considered throughout the year.

Lacrosse

English Lacrosse Association
Contact: Anita Chesses, Administrator, 4 Western Court, Bromley Street, Digbeth, Birmingham B9 4AN (0121-773 4422; Fax: 0121-753 0042)
Beneficial area: England.

The English Lacrosse Union
Contact: David Shuttleworth, Chief Executive, Winton House, Winton Road, Bowdon, Altrincham, Cheshire WA14 2PB
(0161-928 9600)

Lawn Tennis

The All England Lawn Tennis & Croquet Club
Contact: C J Gorringe, Secretary, Church Road, Wimbledon, London SW19 5AE (0181-944 1066)

The British Schools Tennis Association
Contact: Gilly Crump, Executive Director, c/o British Tennis Foundation, The Queens Club, Barons Court, West Kensington, London W14 9EG (0171-381 7000)
Beneficial area: Great Britain.
Membership: Direct affiliation costs £16 for secondary schools and £8 for primary schools per year. However, this can vary if via local county schools associations. Benefits of membership include: national schools coaching programme; badge award scheme (compatible with national curriculum); free entry to all national schools competitions; financial assistance with tennis facilities; and a regular magazine.
Grants to organisations: Grants of £100 (up to £150 for two different tennis schemes) are given annually to local county school associations for administration and specific programmes. In addition to these recurrent grants, the Schools Association also jointly administers an LTA budget of grants or loans for tennis facilities in education establishments and the like. Between 1995 and November 1998 grants totalled £937,260. Loans totalled £1.17 million (1995–1998).
Grants to individuals: None.
Grant total: £9,600 (1993/94)

Exclusions: Individual financial assistance.

Applications: A detailed information pack and form is provided to potential applicants for additional association grants covering facilities. Applications are considered quarterly by the facilities committee.

Other information: Non-cash support is provided as follows: coaching programmes – includes payment of coaches' fees, and resource packs and equipment to selected schools;

Match Points – points awarded to schools which can then be exchanged for equipment; publications, including a schools tennis magazine; and subsidised in-service training courses.

The International Tennis Federation

Contact: Alun James, Bank Lane, Roehampton, London SW15 5XZ (0181-878 6464; Fax: 0181-392 4747)

Beneficial area: Worldwide.

Membership: There are 196 member countries.

Grants to organisations: Support is distributed through the Grand Slam Development Fund. In 1997 this totalled $4,000,000, or around £3 million. Loans and one-off or recurrent grants are given for facilities, travel, equipment, coaching and promotional events.

Grants to individuals: Travel and coaching grants are given to juniors, particularly young players from less developed countries.

Grant total: £3 million in 1997

Applications: By contacting the development department. There are regular quarterly meetings.

The Lawn Tennis Association

Contact: John James, Secretary, The Queens Club, West Kensington, London W14 9EG (0171-381 7004; Fax: 0171-386 0234)

Beneficial area: Great Britain.

Membership: Fees vary. Benefits include funding, competitions and tournaments, development programmes, coaching schemes and club loans. There are over 5,600 affiliated organisations and over 67,000 registered members.

Grants to organisations: Support is given for the Indoor Tennis Initiative, educational facilities, training centres, county development and facilities, international training and club loans. There is a preference for recurrent support, loans and capital items.

Grants to individuals: Support is not given directly to individuals. Help is given to selected squads of players for training costs. This can be given at county level as well.

Grant total: £4.17 million in 1996/97.

Applications: In writing to the contact.

Long Distance Walking

Long Distance Walkers Association

Contact: Les Maple, Honorary Secretary, 21 Upcroft, Windsor, Berks SL4 3NH (01753-866685)

Beneficial area: UK.
Membership: Fees are: £7 for an individual, £10.50 for a family and £21 for affiliated group. Benefits include: mailings and reduced entry fees to challenge events. There are currently over 4,800 individual members and 39 affiliated groups.
Grants available: None.

Luge

The Great Britain Luge Association
Contact: The Secretary, 61 West Malvern Road, Malvern, Worcestershire WR14 4NE (01684-576604; Fax: 01684-891063)
Beneficial area: UK.
Membership: Fees are £10. Benefits include newsletters, access to training (including novices), access to equipment and British championships. There are currently 60 members.
Grants to organisations: None.
Grants to individuals: Help is given with track fees and travel to international events. Awards range between £100 and £1,000.
Grant total: £3,500 in 1997/98 to individuals.
Exclusions: Grants are not given to organisations.
Applications: In writing to the GBLA office. Applicants should include details of the proposed event and their experience.

Martial Arts

The British Council of Chinese Martial Arts
Contact: Bob Weatherall, General Secretary, 110 Frensham Crive, Stockingford, Nuneaton, Warwickshire CV10 9QL (01203-394642; Fax: 01203-394642)
Beneficial area: UK.
Membership: Fees are £5 per member. Benefits include insurance cover, access to NVQ and national and international events. There are 88 affiliated associations.
Grants available: None.

MADEC (Martial Arts Development Commission)
Contact: The Secretary, PO Box 381, Erith, Kent DA8 1TS (01322-431440; Fax: 431465)
Beneficial area: United Kingdom.
Membership: A fee is charged for individual membership licences from student to instructor level. The fee includes insurance at preferential rates.
Grants available: None.
Other information: MADEC administers the sport of martial arts. It also runs coaching and medical courses (paid for by the individual), issuing coaching licences to successful participants. As MADEC is not funded by the Sports Council it is reliant upon the money raised through courses and the issue of licences to carry out its activities. Website address: www. madec.org

Model Flying

British Model Flying Association
Contact: Graham Lynn, Chacksfield House, 31 St Andrews Road, Leicester LE2 8RE (0116-244 0028; Fax: 0116-244 0645)
Beneficial area: UK.

306

Membership: Fees are: seniors £20 and juniors £12. Benefits include insurance cover. There are currently 27,400 members.

Grants to organisations: None.

Grants to individuals: One-off grants are given to support competitors in world championship competitions.

Grant total: £28,000 to individuals in 1997.

Exclusions: Grants are not given to organisations.

Applications: Applicants must be a member of the model flying team representing the UK at a world championship event. Applications are considered by the BMFA council as they arise.

Modern Pentathlon

The Modern Pentathlon Association of Great Britain
Contact: Diana Wilson, Honorary Secretary, Pentathlon House, Baughurst Road, Baughurst, Tadley, Basingstoke, Hants RG26 5JF (0118-981 7181; Fax: 0118-981 6618)

Motorsport

The RAC Motorsports Association Ltd
Contact: John Quenby, Chief Executive, Motorsports House, Riverside Park, Colnbrook, Slough SL3 0HG (01753-681736; Fax: 01753-682938)
Beneficial area: UK.
Membership: Club membership fees are £44. Benefits include mailings and a yearbook. There are

currently over 700 member clubs and 31,600 individual members.

Grants to organisations: One-off grants between £500 and £2,500 are given for member clubs' equipment and capital projects.

Grants to individuals: None.

Grant total: £37,000 (1997)

Exclusions: Only member clubs are eligible. No grants are given for computer equipment. No grants are given to individuals.

Applications: On an application form available from Colin Hilton, Director, Sporting Services. Applications should include membership details, joint funding, and how the proposal fits within the regional plan for motorsport. Applications are considered up to October.

Mountaineering

British Mountaineering Council
Contact: Roger Payne, 177-179 Burton Road, Manchester M20 2BB (0161-445 4747; Fax: 0161-445 4500)
Beneficial area: GB/UK (individual members); England & Wales (club members).
Membership: Fees are £15 for individuals. Benefits include insurance, mailings, information service, discounts and training. There are currently over 38,000 members.
Grants to organisations: None.
Grants to individuals: One-off awards are given for expeditions and competition climbing. Individuals must meet the excellence programme criteria. Awards range

between £200 and £700 and totalled £40,000 in 1997.

Grant total: £40,000 for individuals (1997)

Exclusions: Only competitors meeting the excellence programme criteria are eligible. Grants are not given to organisations.

Applications: On an application form available from the BMC National Office. Applications are considered on 31st December and 31st August.

Netball

The All England Netball Association

Contact: Elizabeth Nicholl, Chief Executive, Netball House, 9 Paynes Park, Hitchin, Herts SG5 1EH (01462-442344; Fax: 01462-442343)

Beneficial area: England.

The All England Netball Association – Schools' Committee

Contact: The Chairman, Netball House, 9 Paynes Park, Hitchin, Hertfordshire SG5 1EH (01462-442344; Fax: 01462-442343)

Beneficial area: England.

Membership: Individual schools affiliate via their county association. Fee per school is £8.50; secondary schools £4.00, although fees vary according to local need. Benefits include: affiliation to AENA; competition structure; and the opportunity to trial for county, regional and national squads.

Grants to organisations: None.

Grants to individuals: Support is given to individual players via the Alex Barlass Trust Fund to cover expenses such as travel, clothing and footwear. Applications are approved by a small committee. In 1993/94, four grants of £50–£60 were given to individual players aspiring to England squad standard. There is a preference for one-off grants which range from £50 up to a maximum of £75. Individuals can also apply to the AENA who also have a Youth Trust Fund. (See entry in the chapter on Raising money from grant-making trusts, page 240.)

Exclusions: Individual schools/ projects.

Applications: Applications, in writing, are considered as they are received, and should include a full description of costs and the applicant's ability and potential.

Other information: Non-cash support is available in the form of advice. Information is circulated regularly and leaflets are available explaining awards, and association structures. Umpires and coaches can also advise, and will officiate at local competitions. Locally, courses may be run for free or for a nominal fee.

Orienteering

The British Orienteering Federation

Contact: Don Locke, Secretary General, Riversdale, Dale Road North, Darley Dale, Matlock, Derbyshire DE4 2HX (01629-734042; Fax: 01629-733769)

Parachute

British Parachute Association
Contact: Tony Butler, Technical
Officer, 5 Wharf Way, Glen Parva,
Leicester LE2 9TF (0116-278 5271;
Fax: 0116-247 7662)
Beneficial area: UK.
Membership: Fees vary. Typical full
membership is £59.50 annually.
Benefits include insurance, and
mailings. There are currently 4,500
full members and 3,200 student
members.
Grants to organisations: None.
Grants to individuals: Support is
given to teams and individual
competitors selected to represent
the UK in world class competition.
Competitors have to meet stringent
performance criteria to qualify for
support. Financial help usually
covers costs such as flights, entry
fees and training jumps.
Grant total: Around £15,000 for
UK team support.

Pétanque

British Pétanque Association
Contact: David Kimpton, National
Administrator, 12 Ensign Business
Centre, Westwood Park, Coventry
CV4 8JA (01203-421408;
Fax: 01203-4222269)

Polo

Hurlingham Polo Association
Contact: John Crisp, Secretary,
Winterlake, Kirtlington, Kidlington,
Oxford OX5 3HG (01869-350044;
Fax: 01869-350625)

Pool

The English Pool Association
Contact: Ivor Powell, Secretary,
44 Jones House, Penkridge Street,
Walsall WS2 8JX (01922-635587;
Fax: 01922-635587)
Beneficial area: England.
Membership: Fees vary. Benefits
include entry to international
events. There are currently 350,000
members.
Grants available: None.

Quoits

National Quoits Association
Contact: B Thomas, Secretary, 20
The Lane, Mickleby, Saltburn-by-
the-Sea, Cleveland TS13 5LX
(01947-841100)

Racketball

British Racketball Association
Contact: I Wright, 50 Tredegar
Road, Wilmington, Dartford, Kent
DA2 7AZ (01322-272200;
Fax: 01322-289295)
Beneficial area: Great Britain.
Membership: Fees are £10 per
club per year. There are currently
100 members.
Grants available: None.

**Great Britain Racquetball
Federation**
Contact: Wendy Hackett, General
Secretary, 10 Waverley Gardens,
Barking, Essex IG11 0BQ
(0181-925 9842)
Beneficial area: England, Scotland
& Wales.
Membership: Fees are £5 each year.

Grants to organisations: None.
Grants to individuals: Occasional one-off grants to national players competing in international events.

The Tennis and Rackets Association

Contact: Brigadier A D Myrtle CB CBE, Chief Executive, c/o The Queens Club, Palliser Road, West Kensington, London W14 9EQ (0171-386 3448)

Roller Hockey

National Roller Hockey Association (England) Ltd

Contact: Keith Allen, President, 42 Croft Lane, Letchworth, Herts SG6 1AP (01462-464022; Fax: 01462-677555)

Roller Skating

The British Federation of Roller Skating

Contact: Margaret Brooks, Chairman, Lilleshall National Sports Centre, Newport, Shropshire TF10 9AT (01952-825253; Fax: 01952-825228)
Beneficial area: Great Britain.
Membership: Fees are: under 18s £16; over 18s £20; competitive members £8. Benefits include: details of, and entry to, competitions; quarterly magazine.
Grants to organisations: None.
Grants to individuals: Yes.
Applications: Through the contact.
Other information: Non-cash support is given through advice and publications.

Rounders

The National Rounders Association

Contact: Brian McKinney, General Secretary, 3 Denehurst Avenue, Nottingham NG8 5DA (0115-978 5514; Fax: 0115-978 5514)

Rowing

The Amateur Rowing Association

Contact: Rosemary Napp, National Manager, The Priory, 6 Lower Mall, Hammersmith, London W6 9DJ (0181-748 3632; Fax: 0181-741 4658)
Beneficial area: England for domestic rowing; Great Britain for international rowing.
Membership: Membership fees range between £8.50 and £40, and benefits include an insurance scheme, a magazine and competition licences. There are currently around 16,000 individual members and 500 affiliated clubs.
Grants to organisations: None. A small number of grants are administered separately by the Rowing Foundation. (See entry in the chapter on Raising money from grant-making trusts, page 242.)
Grants to individuals: None. A very small number of grants to international rowers are administered separately by the Mark Lees Foundation. (See entry in the chapter on Raising money from grant-making trusts, page 242.)
Other information: The ARA gives advice and information, and is active in encouraging links between schools and rowing clubs.

The Women's Rowing Commission

Contact: Mrs Di Graham, Chairman, 30 Denton Grove, Walton-on-Thames, Surrey KT12 3HE (01932-240 459)
Beneficial area: England.
Membership: Fees are £35 per year, although students and first year competitors pay less. Benefits include a regular magazine, a preferential insurance scheme and eligibility to enter competitions.
Grants available: None.
Other information: The Women's Rowing Commission is part of the Amateur Rowing Association and involves all areas of women's rowing from grass-roots to international level. It has an ongoing programme of development and has instigated many events for women such as women's sculling and Henley Women's Regatta.

Rugby League

The British Amateur Rugby League Association

Contact: Ian Cooper, West Yorkshire House, 4 New North Parade, Huddersfield HD1 5JP (01484-544131; Fax: 01484-519985)
Grants to organisations: None.
Grants to individuals: Grants are given to individuals.
Applications: Through the contact.

The English Schools Rugby League

Contact: R Unsworth, Honorary Secretary, 6 Brook House, Warrington Lane, Wigan WN1 3RP (01942-39588)
Beneficial area: England.

Membership: Nominal fee of £25 per region. Benefits include full participation in all competitions, and eligibility to be selected for international sides.
Grants to organisations: Funding is made available to enable regions to organise their own competitions, particularly in the area of development. For example, £1,200 was given to Yorkshire & Humberside to cover 'Development Rallies'. In 1993/94, grants totalled £37,500 of which £10,000 was given to two organisations. There is a preference for recurrent grants.
Grants to individuals: None.
Grant total: £37,500 (1993/94)
Exclusions: Support is not given to individual local associations, nor to incidental expenses such as refreshments and the like.
Applications: On an application form. Applications are considered in June/July.

Rugby Union

The England Rugby Football Schools' Union

Contact: Ron Tennick, Secretary, National Centre for Schools & Youth, Castlecroft Stadium, Castlecroft Road, Wolverhampton WV3 8NA (01902-380302; Fax: 01902-380311)
Beneficial area: England.
Membership: Fees are £10 per school. Benefits include: information on laws, publications, videos, clothing, principal fixtures and ticket application forms for Twickenham. There are currently 3,200 members.

Grants to organisations:
Recurrent grants of between £600 and £1,500 are given to the county and district unions.
Grants to individuals: None.
Grant total: £50,000 to organisations in 1997.
Exclusions: Grants are not given to individuals.
Applications: Through the contact.
Other information: Non-cash support is given through advice, a handbook, laws book, and information sheets.

The Rugby Football Union
Contact: The Director of Communications, Rugby Road, Twickenham, Middlesex TW1 1DZ (0181-892 2000; Fax: 0181-892 9816)

The Rugby Football Union for Women
Contact: Veronica Wilson, National Administrator, National Headquarters, Newbury Sports Arena, Monks Lane, Newbury, Berks RG14 7RW (01635-42333; Fax: 01635-42333)
Beneficial area: England.
Membership: Fees are: £150 for the first team, £25 for subsequent teams, £25 for a youth team and £10 for a school team. Benefits include: entitlement to play RFUW and representative sides; handbook; help in organising/setting up a club; and fixture information.
Grants available: None.
Other information: Non-cash support is given through advice and publications such as a starter pack, handbook, and a history of women's rugby.

Sailing

British Federation of Sand and Yacht Clubs
Contact: Mike Hampton, Secretary, 23 Piper Drive, Long Whatton, Loughborough, Leics LE12 5DJ (01509-842292)

The Jubilee Sailing Trust
Contact: Lindsey Coleshill, Director, Test Road, Eastern Docks, Southampton, Hants SO1 1GG (0170-363 1388)

The National School Sailing Association
Contact: Martyn Styles, South Kent Professional Development Unit, Chart Road, Folkestone, Kent CT19 4EW (01303-278621 Ext.23)

The Ocean Youth Club
Contact: Martin Rewcastle, The Bus Station, South Street, Gosport, Hampshire PO12 1EP (01705-528 421/422)
Beneficial area: Great Britain
Membership: Members (aged 12–24) £10 per year; friends (25 years plus) £27.50 per year.
Grants to organisations: Bursaries to help young people to go sailing.
Grants to individuals: Bursaries are given in special circumstances to help young people to go sailing. For both organisations and individuals, most bursaries are for part funding only. OYC believes that groups and individuals should see the raising of funds as part of the whole experience. The OYC has a preference for one-off grants.
Grant total: £7,900

Exclusions: Support is only given to those aged between 12 and 24. Funds are very limited, and applications not including proof of an individual's financial position are excluded.

Applications: Applications, in writing, are considered on a regular basis. A strong case must be made when applying, supported by evidence of having sought funding from other sources.

Other information: Non-cash support is given through advice; equipment; and leaflets such as 'Raising Funds for OYC Voyagers'. Other funders include many local and regional charities supporting sail training as a form of personal and social development, and some local authority sports budgets.

RYA Sailability

Contact: Julian Mandiwall, Director, RYA House, Romsey Road, Eastleigh, Hampshire SO50 9YA (01703-627400; Fax: 01703-620545)

Beneficial area: UK

Grants to organisations: None.

Grants to individuals: 'A major development plan is underway throughout the United Kingdom to develop disabled access and facilities within the sport.

'RYA Sailability provides boats, equipment, courses of all kinds, training opportunities, adventure holidays, regattas, racing and cruising … Sailability also supports international racing and our sailors have an impressive record. The UK are World and European Disabled Sailing Champions, and are Paralympic gold medal holders. UK blind and visually impaired sailors are the current world champions.'

The United Kingdom Board Sailing Association

Contact: Louise Roberts, Secretary, PO Box 36, Sarisbury Green, Southampton SO3 6SB (01489-579642)

Beneficial area: United Kingdom.

Membership: Fees are: £17 per year. Benefits include entry into races organised by the UKBSA; magazine; and the issue of sail numbers.

Grants available: None.

Other information: Although largely involved in organising races, the association also publishes 'Raceboards' which gives details on all levels of racing.

Shooting

Clay Pigeon Shooting Association

Contact: Emilio Orduna, Director, Unit O, Earlstrees Court, Earlstrees Road Industrial Estate, Corby, Northants NN17 4AX (01536-443566; Fax: 01536-443438)

The English Shooting Council

Contact: Roger Hanley, Honorary Secretary, c/o London and Middlesex RA, Bisley Camp, Brookwood, Woking, Surrey GU24 0PA (01483-473006; Fax: 01483-472427)

Beneficial area: England.

Grants available: None.

Other information: Non-cash

support is is given through advice.
The English Shooting Council is
the coordinating body, formed by
representatives of the four governing
bodies for shooting in England i.e.
the Clay Pigeon Shooting
Association, the English Pistol
Association, the English Small–Bore
Shooting Union, and the English
Twenty Club (big-bore rifle), who
meet to agree the appointment of
team managers, assistant team
managers, and to agree and oversee
team selection.

**The Great Britain Target
Shooting Federation**
Contact: Keith Murray, Honorary
Secretary, 1 The Cedars, Great
Wakering, Southend-on-Sea
SS3 0AQ (01702-219395)

The National Pistol Association
Contact: Ian McConchie, General
Secretary, 21 The Letchworth Gate
Centre, Protea Way, Pixmore
Avenue, Letchworth, Herts SG6 1JT
(01462-679887)
Beneficial area: England.
Membership: Fees are £44 per
individual; club fees are dependent
on the size of club. Benefits include
advice and organisation of events.
Grants available: None.
Other information: Non–cash
support is given through advice by
phone, fax, or in person at
exhibitions and the like. The
association lobbies on behalf of
shooters and to promote sport
generally.

The National Rifle Association
Contact: Lt Col (Retd) C C
Cheshire, Chief Executive, Bisley
Camp, Brookwood, Woking, Surrey
GU24 0PB (01483-797777;
Fax: 01483-797285)
Beneficial area: England.
Grants to organisations: The
association has supported the
following: loans to affiliated clubs
for range development; grants to
help with touring teams' travel;
support for UK teams' training;
ammunition, accommodation, and
range space. Grants of £10,000
each, have recently been given to
the British Sporting Rifle Club to
refurbish ranges and for ammunition
to British teams training for overseas
tours.
Grants to individuals: None.
Applications: Through the contact.
Other information: Non–cash
support exists in the form of advice
on the administration of firearms
law, insurance policies, the
construction of ranges, and through
training courses for range collecting
offices.

**The National Small–Bore Rifle
Association**
Contact: Jenny Page, Lord Roberts
House, Bisley Camp, Brookwood,
Woking, Surrey GU24 0NP
(01483-476969; Fax: 01483-476392)
Beneficial area: Great Britain.
Membership: Fees vary from £13
for juniors, up to £33.50. Benefits
include competitions, annual
championships, insurance, advice.
There are currently over 7,500
members.
Grants to organisations: Loans of

£500 for capital costs are available to member organisations. The Association covers small-bore rifle, airgun and match cross-bow target shooting.
Grants to individuals: None.
Applications: In writing to the contact. Applications must be from member organisations and are considered as they are received.

Skiing

The British Ski and Snowboard Federation
Contact: Mike Jardine, Chief Executive, 258 Main Street, East Calder, Livingston, West Lothian EH53 0EE (01506-884343; Fax: 01506-882952)
Beneficial area: UK.
Membership: Member groups have a per capita fee for individuals. There are currently eight member groups representing 50,000 individuals.
Grants to organisations: None.
Grants to individuals: Awards are given to selected members of British representative teams only.

The English Schools Ski Association
Contact: Nigel Robinson, Secretary, The Bungalow, Abotts Hill School, Bunker Lane, Hertfordshire HP3 8RP (01442-241183)
Beneficial area: England.
Membership: Fees are £20 per year. Benefits include Sport England and NCSS affiliation and race invites. There are currently 137 member schools.

Grants to organisations: When funds allow one-off grants are given to organisations.
Grants to individuals: One-off payments of race entry fees or towards training costs when funds allow.
Applications: Written applications to the correspondent are considered throughout the year. Applications should state what specifically is needed and how schools' skiing will benefit.
Other information: Advice and various publications are available to members.

The English Ski Council
Contact: Diana King, Chief Executive, Area Library Building, Queensway Mall, The Cornbow, Halesowen, West Midlands B63 4AJ (0121-501 2314; Fax: 0121-585 6448)
Beneficial area: England.
Grants to organisations: In 1994, recurrent grants totalling £3,100 were given to 25 organisations.
Grants to individuals: None.
Grant total: £3,100 (1994)
Other information: Non-cash support is given through advice and information. Members also benefit from the coaching and technical information. In particular the national squad gain from a regular coaching programme.

Uphill Ski Club of Great Britain
Contact: David Whittaker, Development Officer, 12 Park Crescent, London W1N 4EQ

Softball

The National Softball Federation
Contact: Nicola Harper, President, PO Box 10064, London N6 5JN (0181-341 7931; Fax: 0181-348 4522)
Beneficial area: Great Britain.
Membership: £20 per team per year. Benefits include: non-medical insurance cover; newsletters; access to coaches & umpires and relevant courses; and eligibility to participate in the national championships.
Grants available: None.
Other information: Non-cash support is given through publications; rule books, coaching videos, umpire and coaching courses and preferentially priced youth kits.

Speedway

The Speedway Control Board
Contact: A Hughes, ACU Headquarters, Wood Street, Rugby, Warwickshire CV21 2YX (01788-540097; Fax: 01788-552308)
Beneficial area: Great Britain and Eire.
Membership: There is no charge for membership. There are currently 1,200 members.
Grants to organisations: A grant of £1,000 is given to the England under 21 squad.
Grants to individuals: None.
Grant total: £2,000
Exclusions: No grants to individuals.
Applications: Through the contact. Applications are considered regularly.

Squash

The Squash Rackets Association
Contact: Matt Hammond, Chief Executive, Westpoint, 33–34 Warple Way, Acton, London W3 0RQ (0181-746 1616; Fax: 0181-746 0580)

Sub Aqua

British Sub Aqua Club
Contact: David Roberts, Director, Telford's Quay, Ellesmere Port, South Wirral L65 4FY (0151-350 6200; Fax: 0151-350 6215)
Beneficial area: UK.
Membership: Fees are £35 per year. Benefits include: mailings, training system, insurance, organised diving. There are currently 55,000 members.
Grants to organisations: One-off grants for equipment are given through the BSA Jubilee Trust.
Grants to individuals: 'All applications are considered. To be successful, the individual must demonstrate a benefit to scuba diving and the underwater environment.'
Grant total: £25,000 to organisations in 1997.
Applications: Through the contact.

Surfing

The British Surfing Association
Contact: Colin Wilson, Champions Yard, Penzance, Cornwall TR18 2TA (01736-360250; Fax: 01736-331077)
Beneficial area: Great Britain.
Membership: Fees vary from £7.50 to £17. There are currently 2,500 members.

Grants to organisations: None.
Grants to individuals: Small grants are available. Further details on request.
Applications: Written applications are considered throughout the year.

Swimming

The Amateur Swimming Association
Contact: David Sparkes, Chief Executive, Harold Fern House, Derby Square, Loughborough, Leics LE11 5AL (01509-618700; Fax: 01509-618701)

The English Schools' Swimming Association
Contact: Norman Spragg, 2 Waltho Avenue, Maghull, Liverpool L31 6BE (0151-526 2191 – home; 0151-526 1378 – work)
Beneficial area: England.
Membership: By schools' individual affiliation to the division of English Schools' Swimming Association.
Grants available: None.
Other information: Advice and publications are available on good practices in swimming teaching; water safety skills; health & safety measures; dolphin scheme; and the annual ESSA handbook.

The National Coordinating Committee – Swimming for People with Disabilities
Contact: Ms L Butcher, Honorary Secretary, 17 Clews Road, Oakenshaw, Redditch B98 7ST (01527-550909)
Beneficial area: Great Britain and Eire.

Membership: No membership fee is charged as the committee is a charitable organisation whose main purpose is the promotion of swimming for people with any physical disability, learning difficulty or sensory loss, and membership is open to any national organisation with an interest in this aim.
Grants available: None.

Table Tennis

The English Schools' Table Tennis Association
Contact: Geoff Gardiner, 36 Froom Street, Chorley, Lancashire PR6 0AN (01257-264873)
Beneficial area: England.
Membership: Fees are: county schools' TTA £35; local schools' TTA £25; individual schools £18. Benefits include publications and entry for teams and individuals in ESTTA competitions.
Grants to organisations: Loans have occasionally been made to set up a county schools association where none exists.
Grants to individuals: None.
Exclusions: No support for individuals.
Other information: Non-cash support is given through advice and publications.

The English Table Tennis Association
Contact: Robert Sinclair, General Secretary, Queensbury House, Havelock Road, Hastings, E Sussex TN34 1HF (01424-722525; Fax: 01424-422103)
Beneficial area: England.

317

Membership: Affiliation is through team membership. Benefits include eligibility for ETTA events and inclusion on a ranking list.

Grants to organisations: One-off grants are given through the Tom Blun Fund for local league/club administrators to attend seminars.

Grants to individuals: The Ivor Montegue Junior Fund gives one-off awards to young under 17 players who show international potential.

Exclusions: Unaffiliated individuals and clubs are not supported.

Applications: On a form available from the local ETTA Regional Development Officer. Applications are considered periodically throughout the year.

Other information: A wide range of non-cash support is given through equipment and publications and personal advice from regional development officers and national facilities officers.

Tae kwon do

The British Tae kwon do Council
Contact: Mike Dew, 163A Church Road, Redfield, Bristol BS5 9LA (0117-955 1046;
Fax: 0117-955 0589)
Beneficial area: UK.
Membership: Fees vary. There are currently 24,400 members.
Grants available: None.

Tenpin Bowling

British Tenpin Bowling Association
Contact: Pat White, Chairman, 114 Balfour Road, Ilford, Essex IG1 4JD (0181-478 1745;
Fax: 0181-514 3665)

Time Trialing

Road Time Trials Council
Contact: Phil Heaton, National Secretary, 77 Arlington Drive, Pennington, Leigh, Lancs WH7 3QP (01942-603976;
Fax: 01942-262326)
Beneficial area: England, Wales, Isle of Man, Channel Islands.
Membership: Fees are £20 per club per year. Members of affiliated clubs can compete in road time trials. There are currently over 1,000 member clubs.
Grants to organisations: Grants are given for coaching and through a world class performance plan.
Grants to individuals: None.
Applications: Through the contact to be considered at national committee meetings.
Other information: Support is also given through technical help and personnel.

Trampoline

The British Trampoline Federation Ltd
Contact: R C Walker, Secretary, 146 College Road, Harrow, Middx HA1 1BH (0181-863 7278)

Triathlon

The British Triathlon Association
Contact: Elaine Shaw, Chief Executive, PO Box 26, Ashby-de-la-Zouch, Leics LE65 2ZR (01530-414234; Fax: 01530-560279)
Beneficial area: Great Britain.
Membership: Fees are: £22.50 for members of BTA affiliated clubs, £30 for independent members. Benefits include discounted race fees, insurance, race licence, annual handbook and bi-monthly newsletters.
Grants available: None.
Other information: Non-cash support is given through advice on all aspects of triathlon e.g. training, competing, events; equipment for event organisers; and promotional information on training and events.

Tug-of-War

The Tug-of-War Association
Contact: P J Craft, Honorary Secretary, 57 Lynton Road, Chesham, Bucks HP5 2BT (01494-783057; Fax: 01494-792040)

Unihoc

English Unihoc Association
Contact: Lucy Bennett, Secretary, 15 Grovely Cottages, Great Wishford, Salisbury SP2 0NT
Beneficial area: England.

Volleyball

The British Volleyball Federation
Contact: Michael McKeever, Secretary, 27 South Road, West Bridgford, Nottingham NG2 7AG (0115-981 6324; Fax: 0115-945 5429)
Beneficial area: Great Britain.
Other information: Non-cash support given through advice. The BVF is an umbrella organisation of the four home country volleyball associations i.e. England, Northern Ireland, Scotland & Wales, who are primarily responsible for the development of volleyball in their respective countries. For further information contact:
English Volleyball Association: 27 South Road, West Bridgford, Nottingham NG2 7AG (0115-981 6324; Fax: 0115-945 5429)
Northern Ireland Volleyball Association: House of Sport, Upper Malone Road, Belfast BT9 5LA (01232-649250; Fax: 01232-439148)
Scottish Volleyball Association: 48 The Pleasance, Edinburgh EH8 9TJ (0131-556 4633; Fax: 0131-557 4314)
Welsh Volleyball Association: Ms T Barra Shaw, 9 St Denis Road, Heath, Cardiff CF4 4NA (01222-758427)

Water Ski

The British Water Ski Federation
Contact: Gillian Hill, Executive Officer, 390 City Road, London EC1V 2QA (0171-833 2855; Fax: 0171-837 5879)
Beneficial area: Great Britain.
Membership: Benefits include: personal accident insurance and a bi-monthly magazine.
Grants to organisations: Very rarely.
Grants to individuals: Financial support is given to selected British squads and teams, and for training and travel. Only in-house grants are given. In 1993, over 40 individuals received grants from the federation.
Grant total: £20,000 (1993)
Exclusions: Grants limited to selected federation members.
Applications: In writing to the contact.

Weightlifting

The British Amateur Weight Lifters Association
Contact: Jane Gaul, Grosvenor House, 131 Hurst Street, Oxford OX4 1HE (01865-200339; Fax: 01865-790096)
Beneficial area: Great Britain.
Membership: Fees are: Club members £5 (seniors); £3 (juniors); £2 (schoolchildren). Non-club members £10 annually. Life membership is £40 and club registration fee £10 a year. Benefits include: advice and information through an official journal and handbook; certificates for

performance at various weight levels; and training and assessment for leader, teacher, instructor, coach and referee certificates, awards and examinations.
Other information: Additional non-cash support is given through equipment and publications.

Wheelchair Sports

The British Wheelchair Sports Foundation
Contact: Jean Stone, Sports Administrator, Guttmann Sports Centre, Guttmann Road, Stoke Mandeville, Bucks HP21 9PP (01296-395995/484848; Fax: 01296-424171)
Beneficial area: UK.
Membership: Fees are £5. Membership is open to athletes and supporters of wheelchair sports. There are currently 4,000 members.
Grants available: None.
Other information: Non-cash support is through information and advice on wheelchair sport; an annual handbook and regular newsletter; and the use of sports equipment at the Guttmann Sports Centre.

Chapter 16

Tax, VAT and fundraising

■■■

Tax and VAT can seem a daunting subject, especially when all you want to do is play football, train young athletes or just keep your club afloat. Giving general advice on tax and VAT is equally difficult because the situation is so complex. It is complicated because (a) not all income is taxable; (b) there are different types of organisations; (c) there are different types of taxes to consider; and (d) because for every rule there seem to be 10 exceptions.

We have a duty to pay tax, whether we are asked to by the Inland Revenue or Customs and Excise or not. If we get it wrong the penalties can be severe. Not knowing the law is no excuse. You may need to get good quality financial advice and be prepared to spend some time ironing out the financial wrinkles.

> The Inland Revenue are taking an increasingly hard line on tax collection, often going back over past years pursuing interest and penalties. To assist clubs, the Revenue has published a guidance leaflet IR46 which you can obtain from your local tax office. IR46 deals with direct tax responsibilities.

It is important to note that sports organisations enjoy no special tax exemptions or advantages. If you are not careful, unexpected liabilities arise and opportunities to minimise tax are lost. The same rules generally apply if you are a company or an unincorporated association. Registering as a charity can bring savings (for example you should not pay Corporation Tax).

As far as fundraising is concerned, the two main areas to worry about are Corporation Tax and Value Added Tax (VAT). This chapter gives a very quick outline on each, and how they apply to your fundraising. It also has a brief look at PAYE, another major problem area. You may need to take specialist advice. For example, if you are planning a major fundraising campaign, you may go over the VAT threshold for the first time. That will affect not just that appeal but all your other activities as well.

Corporation Tax

If you are an individual, you pay tax on all your income over a certain amount. If you are a company, you only pay tax on your profits through Corporation Tax. However, not all income may be liable to Corporation Tax. For example, if you get your income only from members (e.g. through subscriptions) and you plough any surpluses back for the benefit of those members, this income should not be taxed.

In general, the following sources of income are taxable:

- Investment income including bank, building society and other interest
- Income from properties
- Sponsorship income
- Trading income
- Income from fundraising activities
- Lotteries, raffles and prize draws
- Profits from the sale of capital assets (e.g. land and buildings)

Registered charities should not pay Corporation Tax. It can be one of the single biggest benefits of being a charity. See chapter 17 on Sport and charitable status.

Income from donations is a difficult area. It depends upon the extent of the benefit to the person giving the grant. If the grant is given with no strings attached and there is no benefit to the donor, it is probably not liable to tax. However, if the donor is receiving something in return (e.g. in a sponsorship payment, where the company is paying for a service such as advertising, publicity, free tickets etc.), the payment will be taxable. Grants towards capital spending (e.g. new equipment) may reduce the tax allowances you can claim on that spending. If in doubt, seek professional advice or contact your local tax office sooner rather than later.

When calculating your Corporation Tax liability, you can deduct some of the direct costs incurred in raising the money, plus possibly some of the central costs (e.g. insurance, rent and rates, repairs). Again, you will need to get advice on this. Corporation Tax is due nine months and one day after the year end. Interest runs from that date on any unpaid tax. It is the organisation's duty to pay the due tax at the right time even though the Inland Revenue may not have asked for it, or even be aware of the liability. You should also send a set of income and expenditure accounts each year.

Trading receipts of members' golf clubs

The Inland Revenue gave the following interpretation in August 1994:
'We have been asked whether non-proprietary members' golf clubs are liable to tax on trading income such as visitors' green fees. This article gives our views on when income received by members' clubs for the use of their facilities by non-members is taxable trading income.

Any surplus arising to a members' club from transactions with its members is not normally taxable. Payments by members in respect of their personal guests, even when these are described as 'visitors' fees' are normally regarded as part of that surplus.

But receipts from visitors who, in return for payment on a commercial basis, are allowed to use a club's facilities will be receipts from a taxable trade in the club's hands. This applies to individuals who arrive at a club to use its facilities on a casual basis and to groups who may book in advance.

Such visitors may become 'temporary members' of the club. But this will not prevent receipts from their use of the club's facilities from being taken into account for tax unless their rights as temporary members (such as rights to vote at meetings, participate fully in club activities and generally to exercise control over the running of the club), and the opportunities to exercise them, are similar to those of full members. In computing the taxable income derived from non-members in this way the related expenses will be deductible, including a reasonable proportion of course overheads.'

Value Added Tax (VAT)

VAT is a tax on goods and services (or supplies). These can range from petrol to computers to membership fees. VAT is possibly even more complicated than Corporation Tax and if you get it wrong there are strict penalties. Again, it may well be worth getting professional advice to be sure of the situation. However, here's a general run-down of the situation as far as this book is concerned.

There are four categories of VAT:

- Standard-rated supplies are taxable and attract VAT at the standard rate (currently 17.5%).
- Zero-rated supplies are also taxable and liable to VAT but at 0%. This means that although this income is considered to be taxable, no VAT has to be accounted for.
- Exempt supplies are specifically exempted from VAT and do not attract a VAT charge. Exempt income is not taken into account when deciding whether you have to register for VAT.

- Certain forms of income are entirely outside the scope of VAT, so VAT is not chargeable. Again such income is not taken into account when deciding on registration.

The basic position is that you must register for VAT if the annual value of your VATable supplies (i.e. those which are standard rated or zero rated) exceeds or is likely to exceed the registration threshold (currently £50,000 a year). Please note, this does not include exempt supplies or supplies outside the scope of VAT. Therefore, if your only income is from subscriptions and joining fees (which are exempt from VAT) then you will not have to register for VAT. However, if you land a company sponsorship worth £50,000 a year, then you must register as sponsorship is a full-rated supply. Alternatively, if you have five different areas of full-rated or zero-rated income and they total over £50,000 (even though individually they are less than £50,000), you will have to register. In other words, you need to bear two things in mind:

1. VAT registration is only calculated on your standard-rated and/or zero-rated supplies (ignore exempt supplies and those outside the scope of VAT for this calculation).
2. VAT registration only becomes necessary if VATable supplies total more than £50,000 in one year. Therefore, if they total under £50,000 a year, you don't need to register.

The next question is: 'How do I know which supply falls into which category?' The following is a general list, although do not treat it as fail-safe. There are, unfortunately, lots of exceptions to lots of rules so each case needs to be approached differently.

Standard rated

- Social and non-playing membership subscriptions
- Temporary members' and visitors' fees
- Sponsorship
- Advertising (but see under 'exempt')
- Gate money
- Royalties
- Match fees (but see under 'exempt')
- Hire of equipment and facilities to non-members (but see under 'exempt')
- Catering
- Sales of goods (but see under 'zero rated')
- Vending machine income
- Bar sales
- Telephones
- Gaming machine income
- Profit making competitions (but see under 'exempt')
- Services supplied to non-playing members

- Fundraising events (but see under 'exempt')
- Sales of assets/equipment
- Coaching/course fees (but see under 'exempt')

Zero rated

- Books, magazines and handbooks
- Programmes and fixture cards
- Overseas tours
- Cold take-away food

Exempt
- Subscriptions and joining fees from playing members to non-profit distributing bodies
- Hire of equipment and match, court, pitch and facility fees to members by non-profit distributing bodies
- Fees to members for coaching and refereeing by non-profit distributing bodies
- Perimeter advertising
- Continuous hire of facilities
- Lotteries and raffles
- Other lettings
- Competition fees (where all returned as prizes or when provided by non-profit distributing bodies)
- Interest and insurance commission
- Fundraising events organised by qualifying non-profit distributing bodies

Outside the scope
- Donations
- Grants
- Disciplinary income (e.g. fines by sports governing bodies)
- Insurance settlements
- Compensation payments

In practice, much of your grant income will be outside the scope of VAT. Occasional fundraising should be exempt from VAT. However, if fundraising becomes more regular and starts to contribute a substantial proportion of your revenue, it will probably become VATable.

The consequences of registering
Once you register, you will have to charge VAT on all full-rated supplies at the standard rate (e.g. on catering) and do a quarterly VAT return to Customs & Excise. The good news is that you can 'offset' some VAT you have to pay against the VAT you charge. Either way, you will probably need a VAT specialist to help you, at least in the early stages.

When planning your fundraising, it is worth thinking about the VAT situation. If you are planning major building alterations, is there a way of recovering some or all of the VAT? Will your fundraising mean you go over the VAT threshold anyway? Is there a way around this (e.g. organising payments so that you do receive more than £50,000 VATable income in any one financial year)?

Pay As You Earn (PAYE) and National Insurance

Other taxes sports clubs should bear in mind are Pay As You Earn (PAYE) and National Insurance contributions (NIC). These are taxes on employees' earnings rather than the club's income. However, they can cause problems. The Inland Revenue is tightening up on the rules in these areas and has the power to go back six years if it discovers any problems. You must deal with PAYE and NIC properly.

Pay As You Earn (PAYE) is the system under which the government collects income tax and national insurance by deduction from employees' salaries. Sports organisations act as unpaid collecting agencies for the Inland Revenue and the Contributions Agency paying them the amounts deducted (usually on a monthly basis). Obviously, the big question is what is an 'employee'?

There is no clear legal definition of what is an employee. The historical test is whether there is a 'contract for services' (self-employment) or a 'contract of service' (employment). A key factor is whether the individual is part of the organisation and is required to work specific hours and is entitled to a payment for those hours, rather than on a commission basis. Self-employed people would normally be more flexible in working practices, would not be entitled to holiday or sick pay and would also probably be working for other organisations in a similar capacity. It is the sports organisation's responsibility to establish the correct position (get a ruling from the Inland Revenue or Contributions Agency) since failure to deduct PAYE and NIC where it is due will result in the Inland Revenue looking to the organisation for the tax that is due rather than the individuals concerned. Casual employees (e.g. barmen and event day staff) need careful thought since these are often caught within the PAYE net. Seek clearance from the tax authorities if in doubt.

Take care when reporting to the Inland Revenue, particularly over expenses paid (including travel) and benefits provided to employees. For this purpose employees are split into two categories. Those earning less than £8,500 a year are reported on different forms than directors, officers and employees earning more than £8,500. Usually, forms do not have to be prepared for unpaid directors of sports organisations which are non-profit making.

Difficulties can also arise where expenses payments are made to committee members, players without contracts or agreements, voluntary workers or event day staff. Often such payments are made without any accounting for the actual expenses incurred. The Inland Revenue may agree that such individuals are neither employed nor self-employed if they give their time 'for the love of the game' and do not make a profit. They must be satisfied that the amounts paid are no more than required to reimburse actual expenses. Where more than actual expenses are reimbursed, however, the entire amount will be taxable and the individual will probably be regarded as an employee.

In this area, the main problems are usually with:

- The provision of accommodation to club officers and employees e.g. golf club stewards.
- The payment of expenses which are not accounted for.
- Subsistence expenses which are not accounted for or are paid by a round sum allowance.
- Failure to report car benefits accurately.

Sports organisations would be well advised to ensure that their PAYE and P11D reporting is accurate.

Conclusion

You need to make sure that you get paying taxes right. The Inland Revenue and Customs and Excise will not be swayed by the fact that the committee are volunteers and did not know the law. If tax is due then tax is due and you will have to pay it. This article should have alerted you to the main areas of possible concern. The message is that if you are not sure, get specialist advice and get it early.

Useful Contacts

Inland Revenue (for Corporation Tax and PAYE)
Look under 'Inland Revenue' in your local telephone directory and contact your local office.

Customs and Excise (for VAT)
Look under 'Customs and Excise' in your local telephone directory.

Contributions Agency (for National Insurance)
Look under 'Contributions Agency' in your local telephone directory.

This chapter has been written by Richard Baldwin, Partner, Deloitte & Touche, Chartered Accountants, Hill House, 1 Little New Street, London EC4A 3TR (0171-936 3000).

Chapter 17

Sport and charitable status

■■■

Many sports clubs or organisations involved in sport are eligible for charitable status, as long as their objects, structure and activities meet certain requirements. There are many benefits to being a charity, but it can also bring restrictions. This chapter looks at the pros and cons of being a charity, who can register as a charity and how you do this. When reading the chapter, keep two points in mind:

(a) Can we register as a charity?
(b) Do we want to register as a charity?

> **Please note:**
> All the major sports funders (e.g. Sports Councils, sports governing bodies, the National Lottery and the Foundation for Sport and the Arts) can give grants to sports organisations whether they are or are not registered charities. You do not have to be a charity to gain access to the major funders.

What are the benefits of being a charity?

There are a number of advantages to being a charity. Most of them are financial. Here are some of the main ones:

- Charities are exempted from paying most direct taxes (e.g. Income Tax, Corporation Tax, Capital Gains Tax), although there is no general exemption from VAT.
- Investment income is exempt from tax so bank and building society interest can be paid gross.
- Charities receive a mandatory 80% relief from the Uniform Business Rate. This can be increased to 100% relief at the discretion of the local authority.
- Members of the public are generally sympathetic to charities and people are often more prepared to give time and money to a charity than to a private club.
- Some funders, such as grant-making trusts (see chapter 12), state that they will only give grants to registered charities.
- Other funders (e.g. local authorities) may be reassured by an organisation having charitable status as charities have to spend any grants given for the public benefit rather than in the interests of a privileged few.

- Taxpayers, whether they are members of the public or commercial companies, can make certain payments such as gift aid and covenants to the charity tax-effectively. This adds at least an extra one third to the value of the donation (at 1998/99 tax rates).

What are the disadvantages of being a charity?

The downside to being a charity is largely the extra bureaucracy and more importantly, greater regulation and restrictions on the actions and activities of the organisation. For example:

- Charities have to prepare annual reports, accounts and those with an annual income of £10,000 have to send them to the Charity Commission. They also have to send them to members of the public on request, although you can charge a reasonable administration fee for this. Charities with an annual income of £10,000 must also state the fact that they are a registered charity on most published materials including cheques, receipts and invoices. Charities also have to make an annual return to the Charity Commission although this is not very onerous (particularly for smaller charities).
- If charities are also companies they have to report to Companies House each year and fulfil company law requirements as well as those of charity law.
- Charities are run by trustees (these may also be called management committee members or directors). These people cannot usually receive any benefit from their trusteeship although in some circumstances it is now possible to make provision for some payments to trustees in a new constitution.
- Charity trustees have greater legal responsibilities and potential liabilities.
- Matters such as the disposal of land and buildings are subject to special rules and procedures.
- Charity law imposes restrictions on several types of activity such as political activities and trading.
- Some amendments to the constitution will require Charity Commission consent.
- If a charity is wound up, the assets and funds must all be transferred to another similar charity or for some similar charitable objects.

What is a charity?

A charity is a body which is established exclusively for charitable purposes. This means that all its activities must be charitable in law. It is not enough to be partly charitable. Purely social activities for example are not charitable. If an organisation has exclusively charitable objects then it is automatically a charity. It must register with the Charity Commission if it has a gross annual income of over £1,000.

There is no statutory definition of what is a charity. Sport and charitable status has lots of grey areas. Charity law is based on a Statute of 1601 which has since been clarified by subsequent case law. Charities have to register under one or more of the following 'heads' of charity:

- The relief of poverty;
- The advancement of education;
- The advancement of religion;
- Other purposes beneficial to the community in a way recognised as charitable.

To be a charity, it is not enough simply to be established for worthy or good causes, or to be non-profit making. The objects clause of your constitution must contain exclusively charitable purposes and this must reflect the actual activities of the organisation.

Charities must also exist for public benefit. A squash club limited to 250 selected members is a private members' club and would not pass the benefit test as under current law it is not open enough to members of the public generally to be registered as a charity.

However, just because you have membership fees and subscriptions does not mean you are automatically disallowed from being a charity. It is only if the fees are so high that they exclude many members of the public that this would be a real issue.

Most sports clubs which are charities are registered in one of the following two general categories:

(a) Educational charities
Sport as social and physical training can be seen as an educational activity for charity law purposes. Therefore, an organisation which provides sports facilities for young people (e.g. up to and including those of university age) could register if:

- The facility is clearly non-élitist in its approach. This does not mean that it cannot coach élite individuals and teams; rather, these people cannot be the main focus of the club. It must ensure that all people – whatever their ability – have a chance to participate at a level appropriate to their skills.
- Access to facilities is open to all in the area within the age range. However, membership will clearly be limited to how many the facilities can take and how many the staff can manage.
- There is a clear training and coaching programme for all members, not just the élite.

Educational activity can also be linked to poverty to make it eligible for charitable status. For example, giving grants to socially and economically disadvantaged people to take part in sport would be charitable, as would helping disabled people.

Examples of sports organisations which are registered charities

The following organisations are all registered charities:

Barnet Sports Forum

Crayke & District Sports and
  Leisure Club

Eden Climbing Wall Project

Equestrian Sports Trust

Hockey Association Youth Trust

London Junior Table Tennis

Lytham Community Sports Club

Mablethrope & District Swimming
  Pool Fund

Macclesfield Athletics Track Appeal

Oxford Ice Skating Association Ltd

Portsmouth Junior Rugby Football Club

Royston Eagles Football Club

St Helens Amateur Boxing Club

Waterside Gymnastics Club

(b) Recreational charities

The Recreational Charities Act of 1958 specifically included the provision of facilities for recreation – or other leisure-time occupation in the interest of social welfare – as being charitable. An organisation providing facilities can register as charitable if:

■ It is established for the public at large or for any disadvantaged group (which includes disabled people and young and old people); and
■ The facilities are provided in the interests of social welfare (i.e. improving the conditions of life for those involved).

These clauses can be satisfied if the facilities are used by people with special needs, whether they be young, old or disabled people or those in financial need. Alternatively, the provision of facilities in economically deprived areas, or even where other facilities do not exist locally, could qualify.

The Inland Revenue and Charity Commission have accepted the following wording as being suitable for charity registration:

The object of the Association shall be the provision in the interests of social welfare of facilities for recreation and other leisure-time occupations for the inhabitants of *** being facilities,

(a) of which those persons have need by reason of their youth, age, infirmity or disablement, poverty or social and economic circumstances; and
(b) which will improve the conditions of life for such persons by promoting their physical, mental and spiritual well-being.

(c) Dual status

Some organisations find that they are not exclusively charitable so they cannot register the organisation as a whole. However, they may be able to split off part of their activities and register them. For example, they may run the youth section of the organisation as a legally separate body, and obtain charitable status for this section.

Different legal structures

Charity registration depends on the objects of the organisation, not its legal form. Several legal structures are acceptable. The most common are:

(a) An unincorporated association, society or club (as many sports clubs currently are) which has its own constitution.
(b) A trust, which is governed by a Trust Deed.
(c) A company which has a Memorandum and Articles of Association.

(a) and (b) are less complicated to set up and run than (c). However, they also bring a greater risk of personal liability for their trustees and the property must be held in the names of individuals. The particular circumstances of the organisation will determine the most appropriate legal structure and advice should normally be taken at this point.

How do we register as a charity?

In order to be registered with the Charity Commission they must be satisfied both that your constitution is charitable in law and that you intend to operate within the stated objects. The procedure is as follows:

1. Write to or telephone the Charity Commission for a copy of their charity registration pack (see address below). This includes information on setting up a charity and some of their guidance booklets as well as an application form. Tell them if you intend to use an agreed model constitution as a special application form will be available for these cases.
2. Establish your organisation either by executing and stamping the Trust Deed, adopting the constitution at a members' meeting or incorporating the company.
3. Send a certified copy of the governing document to the Charity Commission, together with completed application forms, a copy of the latest accounts and a declaration by trustees.
4. If all the documentation is acceptable, the charity will be registered and you will receive written confirmation and your charity registration number. If not, the Charity Commission may call for additional information or require amendments to the governing documents. In straightforward cases, particularly those using a model constitution, registration will only take about three weeks. More complex cases may take considerably longer. There may for instance be discussion about whether the facility is only for an élite group (which is not charitable) and how many sports are available (single sport facilities can have problems registering).

Model constitutions

You cannot obtain charitable status without an acceptably written constitution. In particular, the objects clause, which states what the charity intends to do, must comply with charity law. Therefore, it may well be advisable to use a model constitution. Advice and model constitutions are available from:

- The Central Council for Physical Recreation, Francis House, Francis Street, London SW1P 1DE (0171-828 3163; Fax: 0171-630 8820)
- The National Playing Fields Association, 25 Ovington Street, London SW3 1LQ (0171-584 6445; Fax: 0171-581 2402)

The English Sports Council, CCPR and NPFA have combined to produce *Sport and Charitable Status* (£5.00) which includes model trust deeds and a draft constitution.

- For a general charitable trust constitution or Memorandum and Articles of Association contact the Charity Commission (see addresses below). These models do not include objects clauses.

What happens once we are registered?

Once your registration has been accepted, you will receive written confirmation from the Charity Commission and a charity number. If you have an annual income of over £10,000, you should state the fact that you are a registered charity in all correspondence and on all receipts, invoices and cheques. You will need to keep accounts according to Charity Commission requirements (these vary according to the size of your charity). You should also make sure you take advantage of all the financial benefits available.

Sources of advice

The Charity Commission also gives help and advice either by letter, telephone or face-to-face meeting. It is worth mentioning that they can initially be rather sceptical about sport, so be prepared with your arguments before you approach them.
The Charity Commission also produce useful booklets available free of charge. These include:

CC2 Charities and the Charity Commission
CC3 Responsibilities of Charity Trustees
CC11 Remuneration of Charity Trustees
CC20 Fundraising and Charities
CC21 Starting a Charity
CC27 Provision of Alcohol on Charity Premises

The Charity Commission

The Charity Commission has three offices:

London: Harmsworth House, 13–15 Bouverie Street, London EC4Y 8DP (0870-333 0123).

Liverpool: 2nd Floor, 20 Kings Parade, Queens Dock, Liverpool L3 7SB (0151-703 1500; Fax: 0151-703 1555).

Taunton: Woodfield House, Tangier, Taunton, Somerset TA1 4BL (01823-345000; Fax: 01823-345003).

The Charity Commission website is: www.charity–commission.gov.uk

You may need to get legal advice, especially if you are not using one of the model constitutions. If you need legal advice, make sure you find a solicitor who specialises in charity law.

Scotland and Northern Ireland

The Charity Commission only has jurisdiction in England and Wales.

Organisations in Scotland should contact: The Director, The Scottish Charities Office, Crown Office, 25 Chambers Street, Edinburgh EH1 1LA (0131-226 2626).

Organisations in Northern Ireland should contact: The Department of Health and Social Services, Charities Branch, Annexe 2, Castle Buildings, Stormont Estate, Belfast BT4 3RA (01232-522780).

Other addresses

The following can all give advice:

The Central Council for Physical Recreation, Francis House, Francis Street, London SW1P 1DE (0171-828 3163).

The Directory of Social Change also has information on charitable status. They can be contacted at: 24 Stephenson Way, London NW1 2DP (0171-209 5151).

The National Council for Voluntary Organisations (NCVO) has a Legal Advice Team for Charities. They can be contacted at: Regent's Wharf, 8 All Saints Street, London N1 9RL (0171-713 6161).

The National Playing Fields Association, 25 Ovington Street, London SW3 1LQ (0171-584 6445).

Sport England, 16 Upper Woburn Place, London WC1H 0QP (0171-273 1500).

A word of warning

This chapter has looked at the pros and cons of charitable status. There are clearly many benefits to being a charity. However, if there is a danger that it really restricts what you can do, is it worth it? You almost certainly do not want to change your club out of all recognition simply to achieve a few tax breaks.

This chapter has been written by Lindsay Driscoll, Partner, Sinclair Taylor and Martin Solicitors, 9 Thorpe Close, Portobello Road, London W10 5XL (0181-969 3667).

Useful addresses

■■■■■■■■■■■■■■■■■■■■■■■■■■■■■■■■■■■■

The Sports Councils

United Kingdom
United Kingdom Sports Council
10 Melton Street
London NW1 2EB
0171-3808021;
Fax: 0171-380 8025

England
Sport England
16 Upper Woburn Place
London WC1H 0QP
Information: 0171-273 1500;
Fax: 0171-3835740
Publications: 0990-210255;
Fax: 0990-210266

Sport England East Region
Crescent House
The Crescent
Bedford MK40 2QP
01234-345222; Fax: 01234-359046

Sport England East Midlands Region
Grove House
Bridgford Road
West Bridgford
Nottingham NG2 6AP
0115-982 1887; Fax: 0115-945 5236

Sport England Greater London Region
PO Box 480
Crystal Palace National Sport Centre
Ledrington Road
London SE19 2BQ
0181-778 8600; Fax: 0181-676 9812

Sport England North Region
Aykley Heads,
Durham DH1 5UU
0191-384 9595; Fax: 0191-384 5807

Sport England North West Region
Astley House
Quay Street
Manchester M3 4AE
0161-834 0338; Fax: 0161-835 3678

Sport England South Region
51a Church Street
Caversham
Reading RG4 8AX
0118-948 3311; Fax: 0118-947 5935

Sport England South East Region
PO Box 480
Crystal Palace National Sports Centre
Ledrington Road
London SE19 2BQ
0181-778 8600; Fax: 0181-676 9812

Sport England South West Region
Ashlands House
Ashlands
Crewkerne
Somerset TA18 7LQ
01460-73491; Fax: 01460-77263

Sport England West Midlands Region
Metropolitan House
1 Hagley Road
Five Ways
Edgbaston
Birmingham B16 8TT
0121-456 3444; Fax: 0121-456 1583

Sport England Yorkshire Region
Coronet House
Queen Street
Leeds LS1 4PW
0113-243 6443; Fax: 0113-242 2189

Northern Ireland
Sports Council for Northern Ireland
House of Sport
2a Upper Malone Road
Belfast BT9 5LA
01232-381222; Fax: 01232-682757

Scotland
Scottish Sports Council
Caledonia House
South Gyle
Edinburgh EH12 9DG
0131-317 7200; Fax: 0131-317 7202

Wales
Sports Council for Wales
Sophia Gardens
Cardiff CF1 9SW
01222-397571

National Lottery Sports Funds

England
The Lottery Sports Fund
Lottery Unit
English Sports Council
16 Upper Woburn Place
London WC1H 0QP
0345-649649

Northern Ireland
The Lottery Sports Fund
Sports Council for Northern Ireland
House of Sport
Upper Malone Road
Belfast BT9 5LA
01232-382222; Fax: 01232-383822

Scotland
The Lottery Sports Fund Unit
Scottish Sports Council
Caledonia House
South Gyle
Edinburgh EH12 9DQ
0131-339 9000; Fax: 0131-339 5361

Wales
The SPORTLOT Fund
Sports Council for Wales
Sophia Gardens
Cardiff CF1 9SW
01222-300500 ext. 418

Sportsmatch

England
Sportsmatch Scheme Manager
Warwick House
25-27 Buckingham Palace Road
Victoria
London SW1W 0PP
0171-233 7747; Fax: 0171-828 7099

Scotland
Sportsmatch Scheme Manager
Scottish Sports Council
Caledonia House
South Gyle
Edinburgh EH12 9DQ
0131-317 7200; Fax: 0131-317 7202

Wales

Sportsmatch Scheme Manager
Sports Council for Wales
Sophia Gardens
Cardiff CF1 9SW
01222-300500; Fax: 01222-300600

Other Agencies and Organisations

Disability Sport England
Mary Glen Haig Suite
Sole Cast House
13-27 Brunswick Place
London N1 6DX
0171-490 4919; Fax: 0171-490 4914

Central Council of Physical Recreation
Francis House
Francis Street
London SW1P 1DE
0171-828 3163; Fax: 0171-630 8820

The Charity Commission
St Albans House
57/60 Haymarket
London SW1Y 4QX
0171-210 4556

Customs and Excise
Contact your local office. The
address is in the telephone directory.

Directory of Social Change
24 Stephenson Way
London NW1 2DP
Publications: 0171-209 5151;
Fax: 0171-209 5049

Department of Culture, Media & Sport
Sport and Recreation Division
2-4 Cockspur Street
London SW1Y 5DH
0171-211 6096; Fax: 0171-211 6149

Inland Revenue
Contact your local office. The address
is in the telephone directory.
Institute of Leisure and Amenity
Management (ILAM)
ILAM House
Lower Basildon
Reading RG8 9NE
01491-874800; Fax: 01491-874801

Institute of Sport and Recreation
Management (ISRM)
Giffard House
36-38 Sherrard Street
Melton Mowbray
Leics LE13 1XJ
01664-56553; Fax: 01664-501155

Institute of Sports Sponsorship
Warwick House
25-27 Buckingham Palace Road
Victoria
London SW1W 0PP
0171-233 7747

National Coaching Foundation
114 Cardigan Road
Headingley
Leeds LS6 3BJ
0113-274 4802

National Playing Fields Association
25 Ovington Square
London SW3 1LQ
0171-584 6445; Fax: 0171-581 2402

National Sports Medicine Institute
St Bartholomew's Medical College
Charterhouse Square
London EC1M 6BQ
0171-251 0583

The Womens Sport Foundation
305-315 Hither Green Lane
Lewisham
London SE13 6TJ
Tel/Fax: 0181-697 5370

Youth Sport Trust
Rutland Building
Loughborough University
Loughborough LE11 3TU
01509-228296; Fax: 01509-210851

Index of funders